SCHAUM'S OUTLINE OF

THEORY AND PROBLEMS

of

PERSONAL FINANCE

and

CONSUMER ECONOMICS

•

by

R. ROBERT ROSENBERG, Ed.D., C.P.A.
Educational Consultant
Former President of Jersey City Junior College

and

RALPH V. NAPLES, M.A.
St. Johns River Jr. College, Florida

SCHAUM'S OUTLINE SERIES

McGRAW-HILL BOOK COMPANY

New York   St. Louis   San Francisco   Auckland   Bogotá   Düsseldorf   Johannesburg
London   Madrid   Mexico   Montreal   New Delhi   Panama   Paris
São Paulo   Singapore   Sydney   Tokyo   Toronto

0-07-053834-4

1 2 3 4 5 6 7 8 9 10 11 12 13 14 15 16 17 18 19 20   SH SH   7 9 8 7 6

Library of Congress Cataloging in Publication Data

Rosenberg, Reuben Robert, 1900-

   Schaum's outline of theory and problems of
personal finance, and consumer economics.
   (Schaum's outline series)

   1. Finance, Personal. I. Naples, Ralph V.,
joint author. II. Title.

HG179.R68   332′.024   76-41309
ISBN 0-07-053834-4

Preface

In recent years, because inflation and recession have made each of us more aware than before of the cost of goods and how to shop wisely for them, the study of personal finance and consumer economics has received renewed impetus. This same period has witnessed a rise in Federal consumer legislation to safeguard consumers' rights and interests—for example, in such matters as borrowing and lending and unit pricing.

In *Personal Finance and Consumer Economics* the fundamental topics of consumerism—budgeting, buying, saving, insuring, investing, figuring income tax, and so on—are taken up in a simple, easy-to-comprehend manner for use by all undergraduate students and indeed all consumers. The importance of studying the subject cannot be overemphasized. According to a four-year investigation of adult functional competency, released by the Office of Education (Department of Health, Education and Welfare), almost 30% of the adult American population—or nearly 35 million consumers—perform consumer economic tasks with difficulty, and more than that number—39 million adults—are "functional but not proficient" in dealing with such everyday problems of life as money management, comparison shopping, and figuring sales and income taxes. According to the HEW report, as many as 29 million adults can barely perform *any* basic consumer economic problem. Given these facts, this Outline makes it its goal to offer help and assistance to students and all others who want to master the subject.

Each chapter of the Outline begins with a concise presentation of theory, which is supported by many illustrative examples. The theory section is followed by solved problems, in which answers are worked out in considerable detail and which further illustrate and amplify the theory. Following the solved problems are supplementary problems that reinforce the knowledge gained. The learning-by-doing method by its very nature involves the reader more directly in the subject than any classroom textbook possibly can. This book aims at providing students and others with the means of attaining a reasonable degree of self-assurance about the material by acquiring a more thorough understanding of it.

Because of the increasing interest in the metric system and recent proposals for its adoption in the United States, a chapter on its use is included here, along with many student exercises showing how to convert from the U.S. customary to the metric system.

R. ROBERT ROSENBERG
RALPH V. NAPLES

CONTENTS

CONTENTS

CONTENTS

Chapter 1

Calculating and Budgeting
Personal Income

Personal income is derived mainly from wages or salaries.   In the following discussion, these terms will be used interchangeably; however, *wages* generally implies employee earnings calculated at an hourly rate, while *salaries* refer to those established by a weekly, monthly or annual rate.   Other sources of personal income include bonuses, interest, dividends, rental of personal property, etc.

Because the amount of personal income determines how much can be spent, the amount budgeted should be limited to dependable income, i.e., that which can be realistically expected on a steady basis.   Since, for most people, the bulk of such income is take-home pay, a knowledge of the various types of employee compensation plans is useful.

CALCULATING INCOME FROM WAGES AND SALARIES

1.1 PAYROLL RECORDS

Wages are earned (1) at an hourly rate, (2) on a piece-work rate, (3) on a commission or bonus basis, or (4) by a fixed amount per day or week.   The use of a payroll sheet or payroll register is used to record this information.   Records must be accurately maintained: the employer is required by Federal regulations to withhold income and social security taxes.   He must also file reports and deposit funds collected with the appropriate government agency on a periodic basis.   Each employee must receive from his employer an annual report, Government Form W-2, showing his annual income and total amount of income tax and social security tax withholding.

1.2 WEEKLY PAYROLL SHEETS: HOURLY WAGES

For workers paid an hourly rate, the first step is to record in the proper column the number of hours worked each day.   Next, the daily hours are totaled and placed in the total hours column.   This number is multiplied by the worker's hourly rate to arrive at total wages earned. See Table 1.

Generally, workers are paid overtime rates for time worked in excess of 40 hours during a 5-day week.   On a regular 8-hour weekday, all time worked in excess of 8 hours is considered overtime and is generally paid at a rate one and a half times the regular rate.   If the regular rate is $4.00 an hour, a worker would receive $6.00 an hour for each hour of overtime.   See Table 2.

Many companies pay double time for overtime when work is performed on Sundays or holidays, and time and a half for all Saturday work.   Under normal conditions today, few companies work on Saturday.

Table 1.   Weekly Payroll Sheet—Hourly Wages

Name	S	M	T	W	T	F	S	Total Hours	Rate per Hour	Total Wages Earned
Aaron, John	—	8	8	8	8	8	—	40	$8.00	$ 320.00
Brown, William	—	8	8	8	8	6	—	38	7.50	285.00
Doan, Robert	—	6	6	6	6	6	—	30	6.00	180.00
Klink, Jose	—	7	5	8	8	8	—	36	4.50	162.00
Mooney, Mike	—	8	7	7	7	5	—	34	5.00	170.00
Strong, Mary	—	4	8	8	4	6	—	30	6.00	180.00
										$1,297.00

Table 2.   Weekly Payroll Sheet, Including Overtime

Name	M	T	W	T	F	Total Hours	Reg. Time Hours	Over-time Hours	Reg. Rate	Over-time Rate	Regular Pay	Over-time Pay	Total Pay
Adams, John	8	10	8	6	6	38	38	0	$6.00	$9.00	$ 228.00	$ 0	$ 228.00
Bond, Willie	8	8	6	6	6	34	34	0	5.60	8.40	190.40	0	190.40
Clark, James	9	6	10	8	8	41	40	1	5.00	7.50	200.00	7.50	207.50
Dane, Ruth	9	8	8	8	8	41	40	1	5.20	7.80	208.00	7.80	215.80
Smith, John	8	10	10	8	8	44	40	4	4.80	7.20	192.00	28.80	220.80
Tyler, Mary	8	6	8	8	6	36	36	0	4.80	7.20	172.80	0	172.80
											$1,191.20	$44.10	$1,235.30

1.3   PIECE-RATE SYSTEM

Piece work, as it is commonly called, pays the worker a given amount for the completion of a unit of work or for the performance of a specific operation.   This system enables the diligent, ambitious worker to earn more than fellow workers who do not produce as many units.

EXAMPLE 1

In a machine shop the machine operator is paid $1.00 for each unit he completes.   Rom Jones completed 60 units on one day.   He received $60 for that day's work.

Table 3 shows a typical payroll sheet for piece-rate workers.

Under a *differential* piece-work plan, the rate paid per unit varies according to the number of units produced in a given period, generally a day.   One rate applies for units up to a specified number, and a higher rate is paid for units in excess of that number.   In some cases, the higher rate may be paid for all units if the specified production amount is exceeded.

Table 3. Payroll Sheet for Piece-Rate Workers

Name	M	T	W	T	F	Total Pieces	Rate per Piece	Total Wages
Allen, Jane	100	110	107	93	112	522	35¢	$182.70
Blow, Joe	212	215	203	192	229	1,051	18¢	189.18
Carey, Mike	98	86	93	105	102	484	37¢	179.08
Grow, Willie	798	805	748	812	762	3,925	$4\frac{1}{2}$¢	176.63
Pope, Alan	38	42	36	41	40	197	98¢	193.06
								$920.65

1.4 COMMISSION

Many salespersons work on a *commission* basis. They receive a specific percent of the total volume of sales that they make in a week. This rate varies from one business or service to another. Sometimes, there is a variable scale of commissions which generally increases at different levels of net sales produced.

EXAMPLE 2

Using a variable scale, the Schiffrin Furniture Company pays its salespersons 1% for total sales up to $10,000 in one week, 2% for sales between $10,000 and $20,000, and $2\frac{1}{2}$% for all sales above $20,000. Harold Lamb sold $28,000 worth of furniture during a recent week. His commission is computed as follows:

1% × $10,000	$100
2% on sales total between $10,000 and $20,000	200
$2\frac{1}{2}$% on sales total between $20,000 and $28,000	200
Total commission	$500

1.5 SALARY PLUS COMMISSION PLAN

Some salespersons receive a *salary plus a commission* to be paid in one of several ways:

(a) A fixed amount on each article sold.
(b) A fixed amount on articles sold above a quota.
(c) A percent of the total value of goods sold.
(d) A percent on value of goods sold above a quota.

EXAMPLE 3

Ruth Yates, a salesperson at the Merchandise Mart, receives $70 a week plus a 2% commission on all sales. During the week of May 14, Ruth sold $2,200 worth of merchandise. Her pay for the week is $114.

$$2,200 \times 0.02 = \$44 \qquad \$70 + \$44 = \$114 \text{ pay for the week}$$

EXAMPLE 4

Jake Wright, in furniture sales, receives a weekly salary of $115 plus a $1\frac{1}{2}$% commission on all sales above $3,200. During the week of February 9 his sales slips amounted to $4,995. His pay for the week, therefore, was

$$\$4,995 - \$3,200 = \$1,795 \qquad \$1,795 \times 0.015 = \$26.93$$
$$\$115 + \$26.93 = \$141.93 \text{ pay for the week}$$

1.6 SALARY PLUS BONUS PLAN

This plan allows sales personnel to receive a regular *salary plus a bonus* for exceeding a given quota. The bonus may be either a fixed or graduated percent based upon total sales beyond the quota.

EXAMPLE 5

Millie Hanover, a salesperson for the Bon Hosiery Company, receives a $500 monthly salary plus 4% on all sales above $17,500 per month. During April, her sales totaled $29,798. Her gross pay for the month was $991.92.

$$\$29,798 - \$17,500 = \$12,298 \qquad \$12,298 \times 0.04 = \$491.92$$
$$\$500 + \$491.92 = \$991.92 \text{ gross pay}$$

1.7 PROFIT-SHARING PLANS

Companies which have a *profit-sharing plan* set aside a specific percent of net operating profit each year for the benefit of their employees. The amount distributed to each employee is often based on the number of his or her bonus points. Bonus points are determined by length of employment, salary, attendance, and other criteria.

EXAMPLE 6

The Round Tire Company has set aside 5% of its net operating profit in its profit-sharing fund. There are a total of 1,000 bonus points and a net operating profit of $2,000,000. On 15 bonus points, the share of profits will be $1,500.

$$\$2,000,000 \times 0.05 = \$100,000$$
$$\$100,000 \times 15/1,000 = \$1,500 \text{ share of profits}$$

1.8 PAYROLL DEDUCTIONS

Employers are required by law to withhold certain amounts from the salaries or wages of employees to cover various tax obligations. They may also be authorized by employees to withhold from their earnings certain amounts for other items. The principal payroll deductions are described below.

Social Security—F.I.C.A.

Under the Federal Insurance Contributions Act (F.I.C.A.), employers are required to withhold an amount equal to a specified rate from employees *gross earnings* up to a specified level (in 1976, the rate was 5.85% on the first $15,300 of earnings). This amount is withheld each pay period (see Appendix 1 for a Social Security Payroll Withholding Tax Table), and must be matched by the employer. Once an employee's gross earnings reach $15,300, no more withholding tax is deducted during the calendar year.

EXAMPLE 7

Bert Callous earns $300 a week as an administrative assistant in a chemical plant. Until Bert's salary reaches $15,300 in a calendar year, social security taxes must be withheld from his weekly gross pay. To determine how much tax is to be withheld from his weekly pay we refer to Appendix 1, "Social Security Employee Tax Table" and read under the heading: Wages: "At Least $299.92—But Less than $300.09." Then read to the right, under "Tax To Be Withheld" and find the amount $17.55. $300 × 0.0585 = $17.55. This amount must be matched by Bert's employer, and the combined amount of withholding tax is sent to the Director of Internal Revenue every three months.

If an individual works for more than one employer during a year, each must withhold F.I.C.A. tax. If at the end of the year, more than the maximum of $895.05 (or, $15,300 × .0585) is withheld, the excess should be noted on income tax Form 1040 in order to obtain a refund or credit.

Income Tax Withholding Deductions

The Federal Government also requires that in each pay period employers withhold from each employee's earnings an estimated amount of Federal income taxes due. Income tax tables (see Appendix 2) are used for this purpose by payroll departments; the amount withheld is determined from the employee's gross earnings and his W-4 Form (see Fig. 1-1), which indicates the number of exemptions declared. Some states and cities also require local income taxes to be withheld according to specified rates.

<table>
<tr><td colspan="2">Form **W-4**
(Rev. Sept. 1974)
Department of the Treasury
Internal Revenue Service</td><td colspan="2">Employee's Withholding Allowance Certificate
(This certificate is for income tax withholding purposes
only; it will remain in effect until you change it.)</td></tr>
<tr><td colspan="2">Type or print your full name
Jane L. Doe</td><td colspan="2">Your social security number
0XX – XX – 0XX0</td></tr>
<tr><td colspan="2">Home address (Number and street or rural route)
Rte #1   Box # 100</td><td colspan="2" rowspan="2">Marital status
[X] Single   [ ] Married
(If married but legally separated, or spouse is a nonresident alien, check the single block.)</td></tr>
<tr><td colspan="2">City or town, State and ZIP code
Hope, Alaska,   00900</td></tr>
<tr><td colspan="3">1 Total number of allowances you are claiming . . . .</td><td>1</td></tr>
<tr><td colspan="3">2 Additional amount, if any, you want deducted from each pay (if your employer agrees) . . . .</td><td>$</td></tr>
<tr><td colspan="4">I certify that to the best of my knowledge and belief, the number of withholding allowances claimed on this certificate does not exceed the number to which I am entitled.

Signature ▶ *Jane L. Doe*   Date ▶ January 2   , 19 77</td></tr>
</table>

Fig. 1-1

EXAMPLE 8

Mary Haurahan, a secretary, earns a gross salary of $660 a month. Being single, she has declared one exemption on her Form W-4. The company will deduct $103.60 from her monthly pay for income withholding tax. We know this by referring to the Income Tax Withholding Table in Appendix 2: single persons, monthly payroll period. We read across the column indicating the number of exemptions to 1, then read down the column at the left (wages) to "At Least $640—But Less than $680." The withholding amount of $103.60 is indicated under the number 1, which is at the point of intersection of these two columns.

Other Deductions

In addition to the required social security and income tax withholdings, employees may have other payments deducted from their pay. These may include union dues, group insurance premiums, credit union deductions, savings bond purchases, etc.

The payroll department uses a *payroll register* (see Table 4) to record all salary information. All deductions are totaled and subtracted from gross earnings to determine net pay. Employees have the right to see their payroll data if they suspect that an error has been made in the computation of their pay.

Students or other part-time workers who do not expect to earn $2,050 during the year from wages or other income may sign Form W4-E, which exempts their wages from Federal Income Tax Withholding. If wages are exempt from income tax withholding, there would of course be no income tax to refund.

Table 4. Payroll Register
For the week beginning March 3, 19__ and ending March 9, 19__

Employee Data	Marital Status	Exemptions	Earnings			Deductions				Total	New Pay
			Regular	Overtime	Total	Inc. Tax	F.I.C.A.	Insurance	Other		
Andrews, John	M	3	$210.00	$27.50	$237.50	$29.40	$13.89	$3.50	$7.00	$53.79	$183.71
Bolt, Ruth	S	1	198.00	15.00	213.00	37.10	12.46	2.80	6.00	58.36	154.64
Caan, James	M	4	225.00		225.00	24.50	13.16	3.50	8.50	49.66	175.34

BUDGETING PERSONAL INCOME

1.9 BUDGETING INCOME

A *budget* is a plan or schedule of expenses designed to be accommodated by an estimated or fixed amount of periodic income.   As previously discussed, the amount budgeted, for most people, represents their take-home pay (i.e. *disposable income*).   However, there may be additional sources of income such as interest, dividends, income from rental property, etc.   Only dependable income—that which can be expected on a regular basis—should be used for budget purposes.

EXAMPLE 9

Richard Thompson earned $1,000 per month.   After declaring four exemptions on his W-4 form, his income tax withheld amounted to $115.20. (See Income Tax Withholding Table, Appendix 2.)   His Social Security came to $1,000 × 0.0585, or $58.50. (See Social Security Employee Tax Tables for amounts up to $399.06.)   This gave him a net or take-home pay of $1,000 − $173.70, or $826.30 per month.   This take-home pay was the amount used for budget purposes.   If Thompson had to pay union dues, group insurance premiums, and similar expenses, they too would have been deducted before devising his budget.   (See Appendices 1 and 2.)

1.10 HOW MONEY IS SPENT

Several public and private institutions periodically issue reports regarding the spending patterns of various income groups.   Such statistics provide a useful guide for developing a personal budget.   The data in Fig. 1-2 and Table 5 represent typical expenditure amounts; they should be adjusted to meet individual needs.

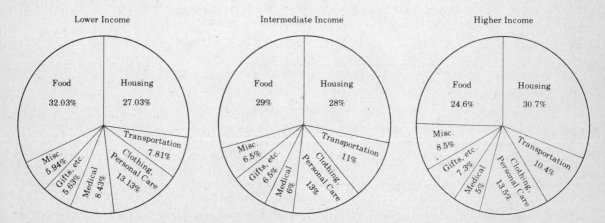

Fig. 1-2   How Money Is Spent: Three Levels of Income for a Family of 4

Table 5. Average Family of 4, Annual Expenses for Three Living Standards

	Lower		Intermediate		Higher	
	Amount	Percent	Amount	Percent	Amount	Percent
Food[1]	$2,050	32.03	$ 2,900	29.0	$ 3,200	24.6
Housing[2]	1,730	27.03	2,800	28.0	4,000	30.7
Transportation[3]	500	7.81	1,100	11.0	1,350	10.4
Clothing and personal care	840	13.13	1,300	13.0	1,750	13.5
Medical[4]	540	8.43	600	6.0	650	5.0
Gifts, contributions	360	5.63	650	6.5	950	7.3
Miscellaneous[5]	380	5.94	650	6.5	1,100	8.5
TOTALS[6]	$6,400	100.00	$10,000	100.0	$13,000	100.0

[1]At home and away from home.
[2]Shelter and household operations.
[3]All modes of transportation.
[4]Medical care and medical insurance.
[5]Savings, babysitters, magazines, etc.
[6]The totals do not include income tax withheld or Social Security tax.

1.11 BUDGET CONSIDERATIONS

When deciding how income should be allocated, the following should be taken into consideration:

Past expenditures.   The amounts spent in the past provide a good indication of future spending patterns.

Future goals.   Beyond basic living requirements, spending is a matter of choices.   It is no more necessary to spend every cent of disposable income on everyday expenses than it is to restrict savings to extra income such as bonuses, interest and other occasional windfalls.

Budget period.   The budget period can be weekly, monthly or annual; however, it generally coincides with the pay period.   It is important to plan for expenses requiring payment at times other than when income is received.

EXAMPLE 10

A family decides to budget 27% of its monthly pay for food, 22% for housing, and 14% for transportation. How much is budgeted for these items, if the monthly take-home pay is $1,400? How much remains for other items? The amounts are computed as follows:

$$
\begin{array}{lll}
\text{Food:} & 0.27 \times \$1,400 & \$378 \\
\text{Housing:} & 0.22 \times \$1,400 & 308 \\
\text{Transportation:} & 0.14 \times \$1,400 & \underline{196} \\
& & \$882
\end{array}
$$

Remaining: $1,400 - $882 = $518

EXAMPLE 11

Jane Jones budgets her income on a monthly basis, which accommodates her rent, food, clothing, car payments and other incidental expenses.   However, she receives a utility bill every two months, and must make a health insurance premium payment quarterly.   From each month's income, therefore, she puts aside an amount equal to one-half of her estimated utility bill (based on past experience) and one-third of the premium amount, so that the amounts of such payments will be available when due.   Essentially, she builds these expenses into her budget on a monthly basis, but disburses them less frequently.

1.12 DEVELOPING A BUDGET

A budget may be as simple or complex as needed.   No matter what the detail of the particular budget, typical expenditures can be grouped according to the following classifications.

Fixed payments.   These are payments due on specified dates—annual, semiannual, quarterly, monthly and, sometimes, weekly.   In some cases, the amount of the payment is fixed (e.g. apartment rental); in others, it may vary considerably from month to month (e.g. telephone bills).   When payment of fixed expenses does not coincide with the budget period, a prorated portion should be accumulated in a savings account each period to cover the expense when it comes due.   Other examples of fixed payments include life insurance, utilities, installment payments, charge accounts, auto license, etc.

One fixed payment especially worth noting is the amount of income taxes (Federal, state, city) due on April 15 for the previous calendar year.   The bulk of these payments will have been withheld from salary by the employer; however, if there are other sources of income, or if exemptions change, withholding may not cover the complete amount due.   An amount should be budgeted each month to cover the estimated tax liability for the year.

Variable payments.   These have no specified payment dates, and generally fluctuate from month to month, even though a uniform amount may be budgeted each period.   Examples of variable items which *may* or *may not* constitute an actual expense during a budget period include house and car repairs, medical bills, home furnishings and improvements, vacations, gifts, etc.

Daily expenses.   These are generally small amounts but their frequency results in considerable sums over the course of the budget period.   In budgeting daily expenses, a review of past expenditures provides a useful guide.   Among the daily expenses for a typical family are groceries, newspapers, cigarettes, bus fare, gas and oil, coffee breaks, etc.

Periodic replacements.   Items such as major appliances (i.e. washing machines, dryers, etc.), televisions and automobiles are normally replaced periodically because their useful lives span only several years.   By estimating the remaining cost of any such item, the replacement can and should be budgeted for on a monthly savings basis.

Savings.   This is what you have left once all expenses are deducted from income.   It may represent deliberate economy of income, "found" money from unmaterialized budgeted expenses, "other" income (from dividends, bonuses, etc.) or any combination of factors.   Use it for long-range goals, for emergency expenses, or retirement spending.

Solved Problems

1.1   Bob Crosby worked $37\frac{1}{2}$ hours last week as a maintenance man at a local plant.   He was paid an hourly rate of \$3.50.   What was his gross pay?

$$\$3.50 \times 37\tfrac{1}{2} = \$131.25 \qquad \text{(See Table 1.)}$$

1.2   Bill Shore was employed as a security guard at the Lamont Foundry during a recent week.   He worked the following number of hours: Monday, 8; Tuesday, 7; Wednesday, $6\frac{1}{2}$; Thursday, 4; Friday, 6.   If his hourly rate of pay is \$4.25, determine his gross pay.

$$8 + 7 + 6\tfrac{1}{2} + 4 + 6 = 31\tfrac{1}{2} \qquad \$4.25 \times 31\tfrac{1}{2} = \$133.88 \text{ gross pay}$$

1.3 Hamilton Cross, a member of the maintenance crew of the Aztec Textile Mill, worked the following number of hours last week: Monday, 8; Tuesday, 10; Wednesday, 8; Thursday, 11; Friday, 8; Saturday, 4.   He receives $4.80 an hour for regular time and time and a half for all hours worked over 40.   How much did his total earnings for the week amount to?

Cross worked 49 hours (8 + 10 + 8 + 11 + 8 + 4).   The overtime rate is computed as follows: $1\frac{1}{2} \times \$4.80 = \$7.20$ per hour.   His total earnings are computed as follows:

Regular (40 hrs @ $4.80)	$192.00
Overtime (9 hrs @ $7.20)	64.80
Total Earnings	$256.80

(See Table 2.)

1.4 Your brother works as an inspector in a factory on a piece-work basis, earning $.48 for each unit of work he inspects.   He completed the following number of units: Monday, 38; Tuesday, 46; Wednesday, 45; Thursday, 51; Friday, 39.   Determine his gross pay for that week.

$$38 + 46 + 45 + 51 + 39 = 219 \qquad 219 \text{ (pieces)} \times \$.48 \text{ (each)} = \$105.12 \text{ gross pay}$$

(See Table 3.)

1.5 You are employed by the Mart Furniture Company as a salesperson at a salary of $95 per week, plus a $1\frac{1}{2}\%$ commission on your total weekly sales.   If you sold $5,200 worth of furniture, determine your pay for the week.

$$\$5,200 \times 0.015 = \$78 \text{ commission} \qquad \$78 + \$95 = \$173 \text{ pay for week}$$

(See Example 1.)

1.6 The Best Used Car Agency pays Sam Palmer a $4\frac{1}{2}\%$ commission on all automobiles he sells.   Sam wanted to buy a new set of golf clubs so he worked diligently and during the month of April sold the following cars at these prices: Auto #1, $1,200; #2, $1,850; #3, $785; #4, $1,975; #5, $895; #6, $3,250; #7, $1,875; #8, $2,950; #9, $3,875; #10, $935.   What was his commission for the month?

Total sales: $19,590 ($1,200 + $1,850 + $785 + $1,975 + $895 + $3,250 + $1,875 + $2,950 + $3,875 + $935).

$$\$19,590 \times 0.045 = \$881.55 \text{ commission}$$

1.7 Joan Hines, an unmarried secretary, earns a gross pay of $195 a week.   She wanted to determine her weekly take-home pay after deductions for Social Security withholding tax and income tax withholding.   Joan, who declares one exemption, worked out her deductions and take-home pay.   What should her results amount to?

Income tax withholding	$32.90
Social Security withholding	11.41
Total withholding taxes	$44.31

$195.00 (gross pay) − $44.31 (withholding taxes) = $150.69 take-home pay.   (See Appendices 1 and 2.)

1.8 Henry Sobel receives a monthly salary of $1,500 as a chemist for the Suez Oil Company. He has declared 4 exemptions on his W-4 form. In addition to income tax and social security withholdings, there is deducted from his pay a group insurance premium of $32.80, union dues of $8.00, and $50 for credit union shares. What is his net pay?

Income tax	$ 225.30
Social Security ($1,500 × 0.0585)	87.75
Group insurance	32.80
Union dues	8.00
Credit union	50.00
Total deductions	$403.85

Monthly salary	$1,500.00
Deductions	403.85
Net pay	$1,096.15

1.9 Determine your take-home pay for the week of May 19 from the following information. Hourly rate of pay, $5.40. You are married and declare two exemptions on your W-4 form. You worked the following hours: Monday, 8; Tuesday, 7; Wednesday, 8; Thursday, $6\frac{1}{2}$; Friday, $9\frac{1}{2}$.

Hours worked: 39. Gross income: 39 × $5.40 = $210.60.

Income tax	$ 28.30
Social Security	12.32
Total withholdings	$ 40.62

Gross pay	$210.60
Total withholdings	40.62
Net pay	$169.98

1.10 John Williams, who is single, works for a construction firm and receives $7.00 an hour for regular time. All time over 40 hours worked per week is paid at time and a half rate. He has declared one exemption on his W-4 form. He also has a weekly deduction of $5.00 for union dues and $8.00 for group insurance premiums. What is his gross pay and take-home pay for the week of June 19, when he worked the following hours? Monday, 10; Tuesday, 10; Wednesday, 8; Thursday, 6; Friday, 10; and, Saturday, 5.

Total hours: 49.

Regular pay (40 × $7.00)	$280.00
Overtime pay (9 × $10.50 [$1\frac{1}{2}$ × 7])	94.50
Gross pay	$374.50

Income tax	$ 83.80
Social Security	21.91
Union dues	5.00
Group insurance	8.00
Total deductions	$118.71

Gross pay	$374.50
Total deductions	− 118.71
Take-home pay	$255.79

1.11 Mr. Young, a married man, who is employed as a salesperson by the Mode Dress Company, is paid $4\frac{1}{2}\%$ commission on all sales. During the month of March, his net sales amounted to $32,500. If he declared 5 exemptions on his W-4 form, what was his take-home pay after the required deductions?

$$\$32,500 \text{ (net sales)} \times 0.045 \text{ (commission)} = \$1,462.50 \text{ gross pay}$$

Income tax	$ 200.70
Social Security ($1,462.50 × 0.0585)	85.56
Total deductions	$ 286.26
Gross pay	$1,462.50
Total deductions	−286.26
Take-home pay	$1,176.24

1.12 John Carlton works on a commission basis based on a graduated scale. He receives 2% commission on all sales; an additional 1% on all sales between $20,000 and $30,000; and $1\frac{1}{2}\%$ on all sales above $30,000. During the month of May he had sales of $36,000. What was his gross pay?

All sales:	$36,000 × 0.02	$720.00
plus	$10,000 × 0.01	100.00
plus	$6,000 × 0.015	90.00
Gross pay		$910.00

1.13 You are single and declare one exemption on your W-4 form. Your friend is married and declares no exemptions. Your gross monthly pay is $820; your friend's gross pay is $780. Which one has more income tax withheld and how much more?

Explanation:

Married persons may, if they so desire, declare fewer exemptions than they actually have, for the following reasons:

1. By having more income tax withheld than is required by law, they receive an income tax refund when they file their annual 1040 tax return.

2. People with other income from which taxes are not withheld, such as from interest, dividends, and the like, build up a reserve which they can use when taxes become due on this income.

3. People with two or more sources of income prefer that their periodic deductions be made from their earnings so that a sufficient amount is built up to pay for taxes on this additional income that places them in a higher income tax bracket. Also, if the withholding tax is less than 80% of the tax due at the end of the year, a penalty is assessed by the Internal Revenue Service.

From your monthly pay of $820, $137.20 income tax is withheld. From your friend's monthly pay of $780, $117.20 tax is withheld. Your income tax withholdings amount to $20 per month more than your friend's.

1.14 Through the end of October, Jan earned $13,800, on which Social Security tax was withheld. If Jan earned $2,300 in November, how much additional social security would be withheld?

You pay only on the first $15,300 of earnings during a calendar year. $15,300 − $13,800 = $1,500 remaining earnings subject to Social Security tax. $1,500 × 0.0585 = $87.75 withheld Social Security tax on November earnings. (See Section 1.8.)

1.15 Harvey Kraft, your neighbor, has a monthly income of $2,400. He has a wife and four children, which entitles him to six exemptions. However, he only declares four exemptions on his W-4 form. How much more income tax withholding is he paying than if he had declared six exemptions?

$2,400 monthly earnings, with 4 exemptions = $495.40 income tax withholdings. $2,400 with 6 exemptions = $452.70 income tax withholding. $495.40 − $452.70 = $42.70. $42.70 more was withheld each month from Kraft's salary because he claimed 4 exemptions instead of the 6 to which he was entitled.

1.16 Your monthly Social Security tax deduction is $58. What is your salary? Prove your answer. (See Social Security Employee Tax Table, Appendix 1.)

$(P = \text{percentage}, B = \text{base}, R = \text{percent})$

$$P = B \times R; P = \$58; B = ?; R = 0.0585$$

$$B = \frac{P}{R} = \frac{\$58}{0.0585} = \$991.45 \text{ monthly salary}$$

Proof: $0.0585 \times \$991.45 = \$58$.

1.17 Mike Swanson, a mechanic at the Auto Shop, has a weekly income tax withholding in the amount of $30.80. Mike is single and has declared one exemption on his W-4 form. What is his approximate gross weekly income?

Between $180 and $190. (See Income Tax Withholding Table, Appendix 2.)

1.18 Your wife has a monthly Social Security tax deduction of $35.10. Her income tax withholding is $74.60. What is her take-home pay? (See Social Security Employee Tax Table, Appendix 1.)

$P = B \times R; P = \$35.10; B = ?; R = 5.85\%$

$$B = P \div R = \$35.10 \div 0.0585 = \$600 \text{ gross pay}$$
$$\$35.10 + \$74.60 = \$109.70 \text{ withholding deductions}$$
$$\$600 - \$109.70 = \$490.30 \text{ take-home pay}$$

1.19 Helen Phillips' gross earnings amount to $750 a month and her husband Harry's to $830 a month. Each of them declare one exemption on their W-4 form. How much is the total combined take-home pay?

Income tax withholding on $750 = $98.60; on $830 = $112.70
Total income tax withholding = $211.30
Social Security withholding tax on $750 = $43.88
Social Security withholding tax on $830 = $48.56
Total Social Security withholding taxes = $92.44 ($43.88 + $48.56)
Total gross pay: $750 + $830 = $1,580
Total withholding = $211.30 (income tax withholding) + $92.44 (Social Security tax withholding) = $303.74

$1,580 (gross pay) − $303.74 (withholding taxes) = $1,276.26 total take-home pay

(See Appendices 1 and 2 for income tax and Social Security tax withholding.)

1.20 Hank Evers, a paper salesperson, receives an annual salary of $10,000 plus a $4\frac{1}{2}\%$ bonus on all sales above his annual quota of $250,000. Last year, his total sales amounted to $398,400. How much did his earnings amount to?

$398,400 - $250,000 = $148,400, $148,400 \times 0.045 = $6,678 bonus.

$10,000 (salary) + $6,678 (bonus) = $16,678 annual earnings.

1.21 The Sharpe Tool Manufacturing Company has a profit-sharing plan for its employees. It sets aside 5% of its net operating profit, which is divided into 400 bonus points. Last year, its net operating profit was $1,600,000. Both you and your wife are employed by the company. If you have been assigned 20 bonus points and your wife 10 points, how much will each of you receive as a bonus?

$1,600,000 \times 0.05 = $80,000; $80,000 \div 400 = $200 per bonus point. You will receive $200 \times 20, or $4,000. Your wife will receive $200 \times 10, or $2,000.

1.22 Mr. and Mrs. Downs, with their two children, plan their expenses by maintaining a strict budget. They live in a rural area, which they consider less expensive than city living. With their annual take-home pay of $13,000, approximately how much should they budget for annual housing costs?

Using Table 5 as a guide, $13,000 \times 30.7\% = $3,991. Therefore, approximately $4,000 per year should be budgeted for annual housing costs.

1.23 You plan to budget approximately 6% of your monthly take-home pay for medical and dental expenses. With a take-home pay of $1,200 per month, approximately how much would be budgeted monthly for these expenses?

$1,200 \times 0.06 = $72 medical and dental expenses

1.24 A young, newly married couple plans to save $100 per month. If their combined monthly take-home pay is $1,600, what percent of their money should be budgeted for savings?

$100 \div $1,600 = 0.0625, or $6\frac{1}{4}\%$

1.25 Burt Hall plans to buy a used car. His wife budgets 12% of their monthly income of $1,000 for transportation. Of this budgetary amount, Burt spends $70 a month for the following automobile expenses: insurance, gas, maintenance, and miscellaneous. How much can Burt afford a month for car payments?

$1,000 \times 0.12 = $120, monthly amount set aside for transportation expenses. $120 - $70 (auto expenses) = $50. His car payments could amount to $50 per month.

1.26 Walter Jackson, a high school athletic director, budgets $120 a month for transportation. Of this amount, $40 a month is set aside for automobile insurance because two of his teenage children drive the family cars. What percent of his transportation budget is spent on insurance?

$40 \div $120 = 0.333, or $33\frac{1}{3}$ of transportation money spent for auto insurance.

1.27   A young married couple with 2 children have a monthly take-home income of $1,160. They wish to buy a house that they estimate will cost them approximately $325 monthly to maintain. Will this amount keep them within 28% of their budget?

        Yes. $1,160 × 0.28 = $324.80.

1.28   Barney Cook earns $18,000 a year. He has declared 5 exemptions on his W-4 form. After income tax withholding and Social Security deductions, approximately how much can his family spend on clothing monthly? They budgeted 11% for this item.

Annual income	$18,000.00
Monthly income ($18,00 ÷ 12)	$ 1,500.00
Monthly income tax withheld*	$ 210.30
Social Security for year ($15,300 × 0.0585)	$ 895.05
Social Security per month ($895.05 ÷ 12)	$ 74.59
Total monthly tax and Social Security ($210.30 + $74.59)	$ 284.89
Monthly income less monthly deductions ($1,500 − $284.89)	$ 1,215.11
Monthly clothing budget ($1,215 × 0.11)	$ 133.66

    *See Appendix 2.

1.29   Ruth Ormond, a high school student, missed the following problem on a recent test. "The Jones family must make installment payments of $50 monthly. What percent of their take-home pay of $750 does this amount represent?" What is the correct amount?

    $50 ÷ $750 = 0.0666, or $6\frac{2}{3}$% of take-home pay.

1.30   The Carlton family of 5 has just relocated to the city. Being unfamiliar with local economic conditions, Mrs. Carlton asked a friend for assistance in developing her budget. The friend advised her to budget 30% for food, 28% for housing, 9% for clothing, and 13% for transportation. The remaining amount should be budgeted at her discretion. With a monthly net income of $1,000, how much remains for Mrs. Carlton to budget for other items?

    30% + 28% + 9% + 13% = 80%.   100% − 80% = 20% remaining. $1,000 × 0.20 = $200 available for other items.

1.31   Ms. Nora Bird, a newly employed secretary, has a monthly income, after deductions, of $640 a month. All expenditures except transportation and savings amount to $560. If she plans to save 5%, how much is left for transportation?

    $640 × 0.05 = $32, savings. $560 + $32 = $592 budgeted for all expenses except transportation.

        $640 − $592 = $48 remaining for transportation

1.32   With a gross income of $15,000, Gerald Hill, claiming 4 exemptions on the W-4 form, budgets 6% annually for education. After deductions, how much is available for education?

Social Security ($15,000 × 0.0585)	$ 877.50
Income tax*	2,012.40
Total deductions	$2,889.90

Take-home pay ($15,000 − $2,889.90)	$12,110.10
Education money ($12,110.10 × 0.06)	$ 726.61

*Computed as follows: Monthly income ($15,000 ÷ 12), $1,250. Income tax withheld on $1,250 (see Appendix 2) is $167.70. Annual withholding tax is $167.70 × 12, or $2,012.40.

1.33 With a monthly take-home pay of $750, Bill Jones, a single man, plans to budget 20% of his pay for his automobile expenses. If auto expenses, except payments on the car loan, amount to $60, approximately how much can he plan a month for car payments?

$750 × 0.20 = $150. $150 − $60 = $90, the approximate amount available for car payments.

1.34 Jackson Burkson, who claims five exemptions on his W-4 form, has a biweekly gross income of $630. After deductions for Social Security tax and income tax withholding, determine how much he can budget for the following items: food, 28%; housing, 24%; clothing, 12%; transportation, 15%.

Gross income (biweekly)	$630.00
Income tax (see "Biweekly Payroll Period" in Appendix 2)	$ 82.10
Social Security ($630 × 0.0585)	
(Note that tables do not include wages above $399.06. For higher amounts, multiply the wages by 5.85%.)	36.86
Total deductions	$118.96
Take-home pay ($630 − $118.96)	$511.04

Food ($511.04 × 0.28)	$143.09
Housing ($511.04 × 0.24)	$122.65
Clothing ($511.04 × 0.12)	$ 61.32
Transportation ($511.04 × 0.15)	$ 76.66

Supplementary Problems

1.35 Mike Rollins, a college football player, works as a lifeguard during the summer vacation. He receives $2.50 an hour for all days worked except Sundays and holidays, for which he receives double pay. During the week of the 4th of July, Mike worked the following hours: Sunday, 6; Monday, 8; Tuesday, 8; Wednesday (holiday), 8; Thursday, 6; Friday, 8. What was his gross pay for this week?   *Ans.* $145.00.

1.36 Mrs. Blount, a secretary at the local air base, is paid biweekly. Her biweekly gross pay is $390; she has declared one exemption on her W-4 form. How much is her take-home pay after required deductions?   *Ans.* $312.88.

1.37   Al Sikes employs three attendants at his service station. His weekly Social Security tax deductions for the three are: John, $7.08; Mike, $8.01; and Bill, $6.67. How much does Al's weekly payroll amount to (rounding to the nearest dollar)?   *Ans*. $372 (rounded).

1.38   Mr. Gibson, the assistant manager of a local hardware store, has a wife and three children. His weekly gross pay is $360. What is Gibson's take-home pay after income tax withholding and Social Security tax deductions? (He declares all allowable exemptions on his W-4 form.)   *Ans*. $285.84.

1.39   Ms. Wanda Kaster, a salesperson for the Beauti-Form Wholesale Cosmetic Company, is paid on a commission basis using the following graduated scale:

>   2% up to $10,000 sales
>   3% from $10,000 through $20,000 sales
> $3\frac{1}{2}$% from $20,000 through $40,000 sales
>   4% on all sales above $40,000

During the month of May, Wanda worked very diligently and compiled a total sales volume of $53,000. What was her gross pay for the month?   *Ans*. $1,720.

1.40   Ms. Linda Murray receives a monthly salary of $1,720. She has a family which she supports and declares 5 exemptions on her W-4 form. After the deductions for the required withholding taxes, what is Linda's take-home pay?   *Ans*. $1,350.48.

1.41   A college student working with a construction crew during the summer, receives $5.40 an hour for regular time and double time for all hours above 40. If he worked the following hours one week: Monday, 10; Tuesday, 12; Wednesday, 2; Thursday, 6; Friday, 10; Saturday, 6, what was his gross pay?   *Ans*. $280.80.

1.42   In your family, members had the following amounts deducted for Social Security taxes for the month of February: father, $48.92; mother, $44.08; brother, $27.35; and you, $33.65. What was the gross income from salaries for your family for that month?   *Ans*. $2,632.48.

1.43   Bill Sanchez and Rudy Gonzalez work in the same department at a paper mill. Bill has a weekly Social Security tax deduction of $12.00; Rudy receives a weekly gross pay of $200. (*a*) Which one has the larger gross pay? (*b*) By approximately how much?   *Ans*.   (*a*) Bill, (*b*) approximately $5.05.

1.44   Bill Young works in a factory which pays him $6.00 an hour, with time and a half for all hours over 40. He is married and has declared 4 exemptions on his W-4 form. He worked the following hours last week: Monday, 9; Tuesday, 9; Wednesday, 10; Thursday, 8; Friday, 12. What will his take-home pay amount to after Social Security and income tax deductions?   *Ans*. $249.25.

1.45   Willie Robinson, a salesperson at Jim Wilson's Sporting Goods Store, receives a salary of $75 a week plus a $3\frac{1}{2}$% commission on all sales. Willie's sales last week amounted to $2,650. What was his gross pay for the week?   *Ans*. $167.75.

1.46   Your husband, who works as a shipping clerk in a local textile factory, has claimed 5 exemptions on his W-4 form. From his biweekly salary, his income tax withholding amount is $55.20. Your brother, who works as a machine operator in the same factory, has claimed 3 exemptions on his W-4 form. From his monthly gross pay, $104.20 is deducted for income tax withholding. (*a*) Which one has the larger monthly gross income? (*b*) By approximately how much?
Ans.   (*a*) Your husband, (*b*) approximately $120 more.

1.47   The piece-work rates at the Acme Furniture Factory are based on the following differential schedule:

> 1–100 pieces, $.80 each
> From 101–150 pieces, $.90 each
> From 151–200 pieces, $.95 each

Harvey Cook completed 174 pieces this week.   Determine his gross pay.   *Ans.* $147.80.

1.48   The Castor Foundry has a profit-sharing plan for its employees.   It sets aside 6% of its gross profit, which is divided into 900 bonus points.   Last year, its gross profit was $1,200,000.   James Burke will receive 8 bonus points and his father who works in the same foundry will receive 20 bonus points.   (*a*) How much is the value of a bonus point?   (*b*) How much will James receive?   (*c*) His father?   *Ans.*   (*a*) $80 each, (*b*) $640 for James, (*c*) $1,600 for his father.

1.49   Alex James would not tell us how much he earned a week, but he stated that his weekly Social Security tax deduction was $10.00.   Bob Slate would not tell us his weekly earnings either, but we found out that he is single, claims one exemption on his W-4 form, and his weekly income tax withholding amounts to $32.90.   (*a*) Which one receives the higher weekly income?   (*b*) By how much?   *Ans.*   (*a*) Bob, (*b*) approximately $20.

1.50   Ruth Wilson, a sales representative for a sporting goods firm, receives a salary of $80 a week plus a 3% commission on all of her sales in excess of $2,200.   Last week Ruth attended a girls' athletic workshop and had total sales in the amount of $5,950.   (*a*) How much did she earn last week?   (*b*) What must her sales total in order to earn $230?   *Ans.*   (*a*) $192.50, (*b*) $7,200.

1.51   Clem Ford, a medical technician in a local hospital, receives a monthly salary of $1,350.   Clem has declared his wife, himself, and his three children as exemptions on his W-4 form.   What is Clem's take-home pay after the required deductions?   *Ans.* $1,099.12.

1.52   Ms. Ruth Jones, a cosmetic salesperson, paid $68 in Social Security taxes last month.   If she receives a 10% commission on her net sales, what were her net sales for the month (rounding to the nearest $10)?   *Ans.* $11,620 net sales for the month.

1.53   Your neighbor held down two jobs in 1976.   One company for whom he worked withheld $698.48 for Social Security taxes and the other withheld $437.12.   How much Social Security tax refund will your neighbor be entitled to for the year?   *Ans.* $240.55.

1.54   Margot Cosindas receives a commission of $3\frac{1}{2}$% on sales of womens' clothing; $2\frac{1}{2}$% commission on young misses' clothing; and $1\frac{1}{2}$% commission on childrens' clothing.   Last month, she was credited with the following net sales:

> Womens' clothing, $14,000
> Young misses' clothing, $6,000
> Childrens' clothing, $8,000

How much did her total commission amount to?   *Ans.* $760.

1.55   Bill and John Billings work at the same factory.   Each had a Social Security tax deduction of $13.98 last week.   Bill is married and has declared 3 exemptions on his W-4 form.   John, who is single, has declared 1 exemption on Form W-4.   What is the approximate take-home pay of each (rounding to the nearest dollar)?   *Ans.*   Bill, $196.00; John, $183.00.

1.56   With a gross income of $1,600 during the month of March, how much would the Kardoviches have as take-home pay for budgeting purposes after income tax and Social Security deductions?   Mr. Kardovich has declared 5 exemptions on his W-4 form.   *Ans.* $1,267.30.

1.57 With take-home pay of $840 monthly, Ms. Kessler budgets 12% for a new automobile. How many months would she have to wait in order to accumulate $1,000 for the down payment? *Ans.* Approximately 10 months.

1.58 Mr. and Mrs. Clem Hewett budget 30% of their annual take-home pay for food. If their monthly food expenditures are approximately $300, what is their annual take-home pay? *Ans.* $12,000.

1.59 Cathy Loomis, a supervisor at the local telephone exchange, plans to set aside $800 this year for her annual vacation for a trip to Spain. If her annual take-home pay is $6,400, what percent must she budget for her vacation? *Ans.* $12\frac{1}{2}$%. (See Problem 1.24.)

1.60 Tania Korman and her boyfriend plan to save $3,000 before they get married. Tania's take-home pay is $720 monthly, of which she plans to save 12%. Her boyfriend receives $850 take-home pay a month, of which he plans to save 15%. Approximately how many months will it take to save the desired amount? *Ans.* Approximately 14 months. (See Problem 1.33.)

1.61 Hank Greenlo, an ardent fisherman, plans to purchase a new fishing boat. Hank has a semimonthly take-home pay of $398. By planning his money carefully, Hank will budget 13% of his pay for the new boat. How long will it take him to save enough money to pay cash for a $1,600 boat? *Ans.* $15\frac{1}{2}$ months.

1.62 Rose Farb, a college student, was given an annual personal allowance of $2,000 by her parents. She plans to budget 35% for clothing, 20% for transportation, 15% for sorority expenses, 18% for food and snacks, and the remainder for cosmetics, etc. How much will be available for each category? *Ans.* Clothing, $700; transportation, $400; food, $360; sorority expenses, $300; cosmetics, etc., $240. (See Problem 1.30.)

1.63 A family of four with $11,000 annual take-home pay would budget approximately how much per year for food, clothing, transportation, and housing? Use the guidance figures for the intermediate level budget in Table 1.   *Ans.*   Food, $3,190; housing, $3,080; transportation, $1,210; clothing, $1,430.

1.64 Sarah and John Saxby have promised to take their family of 5 on a vacation to Europe after saving the necessary money. They plan to save $4,000 for the trip by budgeting 8% of their monthly take-home pay of $1,500. (*a*) Would they have enough money for this trip in 3 years? (*b*) If not, how long will it take?   *Ans.*   (*a*) No. (*b*) It will take 44.4 months.

1.65 Roland Sachs who is employed at the local paper mill as a press operator has a gross salary of $1,150 per month. He has declared 5 exemptions on his W-4 form. After deductions for income tax and Social Security taxes, what percent of his salary is available for budgeting purposes? *Ans.* 83.1%.

1.66 The Hilson family claims that they give 10% of their income to their church. Out of a gross monthly income of $1,500, they contribute $150. What percent of their take-home pay are they contributing? They declare 4 exemptions on their W-4 form and, of course, are subject to Social Security and income tax withholding deductions. *Ans.* Approximately 12.6% of take-home pay.

1.67 John and Michael, brothers, receive weekly personal allowances of $7.50 and $6.50, respectively, from their father. If their father has a take-home pay of $280 a week, what percent of his pay must he budget for the boys' allowances? *Ans.* 5%.

1.68   Mrs. O'Connor wished to buy a new washing machine and dryer on the installment plan, making $30 monthly payments. (*a*) Can she make the payments if she budgets 3% for installment payments on total family take-home pay of $820 a month? (*b*) How much take-home pay would be necessary in order to be able to make $30 a month payments?   *Ans.*   (*a*) No. (*b*) $1,000 per month.

1.69   How much money can Briget Snyder, a single woman, budget for clothing each month if she plans to set aside 12% of her take-home pay for this purpose? She declared one exemption on her semimonthly gross salary of $475. (Social Security and income tax withholding tax deductions must be figured in determining her take-home pay.)   *Ans.* $87.84.

1.70   You budget 12% of your $1,400 monthly take-home pay for transportation. If your car payment installment is 60% of your transportation expense allowance and your insurance costs 15% of this allowance, how much is left for gasoline and maintenance?   *Ans.* $42.

1.71   You have decided to budget 2% of your monthly take-home pay of $940 for gifts, contributions to charity, and books. If you spend $\frac{1}{5}$ of this budget item on books, how much money can you spend on books? How much is left for gifts and contributions to charity?   *Ans.* $3.76 per month on books; $15.04 for gifts and charitable contributions.

1.72   Harriet Frisch budgets 15% of her take-home pay of $180 a week for entertainment and charity. Her sister budgets 13% of her take-home pay of $220 a week for the same purposes. Which one has more money for entertainment and charity? How much more?   *Ans.*   Her sister has $1.60 more per week.

1.73   Your employer has Social Security deductions of $104.80 per month. His Social Security payments will stop for the year in what month?   *Ans.*   September—paying $56.65 in September. (See Problem 1.35.)

1.74   Alan Stein, who manages a local food store, handles all payrolls and payroll deductions. He deducted his own income tax withholding in the amount of $200.70, but failed to deduct his Social Security tax on his gross salary of $13,200. (*a*) How much is his Social Security tax? (*b*) What is his annual net pay?   *Ans.*   (*a*) $772.20. (*b*) $10,019.40.

1.75   Reggie Rollins, a member of our bowling team, remarked that $3,300 had been deducted from his pay last year for income tax and Social Security tax. In a later conversation, he mentioned that 22% of his gross salary was deducted for these taxes. How much is Reggie's gross annual salary?   *Ans.* $15,000.

1.76   Charles Wilson, who declares 6 exemptions on his W-4 form, wishes to budget 27% for food, 24% for housing, 14% for clothing, 12% for transportation, with the remainder going to his wife for her planning. On a take-home salary of $1,650 a month, how much money is put into each category?   *Ans.*   Food, $445.50; housing, $396; clothing, $231; transportation, $198; to wife, $379.50. (See Problem 1.34.)

Chapter 2

Consumer Purchases:
Cash and Credit

Consumers buy typical household staples, appliances, furniture and automobiles for cash or on credit. In either case, prudent purchasing habits can help make living within one's budget a reality and often raises one's standard of living by making money go further.

BUYING CONSUMER GOODS

2.1 BUY FOR CASH

By paying cash for purchases—whether small or large—money in the form of carrying, service or finance charges can be saved (see Sections 2.4 to 2.10). In addition, some merchants allow customers a discount for cash payment of merchandise.

EXAMPLE 1

The Great Western Appliance Center reduces the list price of all major appliances it carries by 10% if the total payment is made in cash at the time the sale is made. Thus, when Jack Smith purchased for cash a new electric range listed at $299, he paid the center only $269.10.

Other merchants sometimes allow a grace period of a specified number of days. If payment is made within the specified time period, the discount may still be obtained.

2.2 DISCOUNT STORES

In many cases, brand-name, first quality items are sold in discount stores for less than full retail price. Discount stores may be part of large chains, or may be small, private operations. Items available in such stores include clothing, appliances, health and beauty aids, and housewares.

EXAMPLE 2

The Big Discount Store is selling a brand name lawn mower for $389. The Fancy Department Store is selling the same lawn mower for $429. What percent of discount are you receiving by buying at the discount store instead of at the department store?

$$\$429 - \$389 = \$40 \text{ saving} \qquad \$40 \div \$429 = 9.32\% \text{ discount}$$

EXAMPLE 3

The Big Man Discount Store sells all electric power tools at $12\frac{1}{2}\%$ below the price quoted at the Super Department Store. How much would you save by purchasing a power saw at the discount store if the saw at the Super Department Store is listed at $289?

$$\$289 \times 12\frac{1}{2} = \$36.13 \text{ savings}$$

2.3 UNIT PRICING

For years the consumer was so badly confused by pricing practices that it was tempting to believe that the confusion was intentionally created. One brand of corn sold 5 cans for 89¢ and its competitor sold 3 cans for 51¢. Which was the more economical buy? To make matters worse, some cereals were packaged in odd sizes and weights, bewildering the shopper further. Which is cheaper, a box of cereal weighing 11 oz at 42¢ or one weighing 18 oz at 59¢? Or is it better to buy a third one weighing $9\frac{1}{2}$ oz at 3 boxes for 79¢?

Unit pricing was introduced to combat this practice. According to *unit pricing*, the price per ounce or pound must be shown on the grocery shelf. That way, no matter what the price of a given box or quantity, the shopper can easily compare one price-per-ounce or -per-pound against another. Thus, spiced peaches would be priced on shelf as follows:

Item Price	Unit Price
34¢	32¢ per lb
Spiced Peaches	
17 oz	

The same grade of peaches in a 29-oz jar:

Item Price	Unit Price
85¢	47¢ per lb
Spiced Peaches	
29 oz	

EXAMPLE 4

Brand X can of peas sells for 27¢ and contains 12 oz. Brand Y can of peas sells for 17¢ and contains 8 oz. Which costs less? Brand Y. Brand X sells at the rate of 36¢ per pound and Brand Y at 34¢. With unit pricing these two basic prices per pound would be clearly displayed for the shopper's convenience.

EXAMPLE 5

A 16-oz bottle of mouthwash sells for $1.29 in one drugstore and the same brand sells for $1.68 in another, but for 18 oz in the second store. Which is the more economical buy? The former: it costs $1.29 for 16 oz, whereas the cost of the other for 16 oz is approximately $1.49.

CREDIT PURCHASES

2.4 THE CONSUMER PROTECTION ACT

A variety of credit arrangements are available to those who do not wish or are unable to pay cash. The need for consumer protection against vague unfair credit agreements prompted enactment of the Consumer Protection Act in 1968. Also known as the "Truth in Lending Act," this requires full disclosure of the terms of credit to the borrower or consumer, with the following items clearly defined in writing:

1. The cash price.
2. Down payment or trade-in.
3. Interest charges expressed in annual percent rate.

4. Administrative charges.
5. Other charges, if any.
6. The amount to be financed.
7. The repayment schedule, including the number of payments and the amount of each payment, as well as total time length or final due date of all payments.

2.5 INSTALLMENT BUYING

Installment buying generally consists of a down payment at the time of purchase and a fixed monthly payment for a prescribed period. The seller must set forth the exact details, amounts, and method of payment in an installment contract, as required by the "Truth in Lending Act." Because of its ease of payment, installment buying costs more than buying for cash.

EXAMPLE 6

A color television set has a cash price of $498. It may be bought on the installment plan with a down payment of $48 and twelve monthly payments of $45 each. That would bring the total to $588, or $90 more than if the set had been bought for cash.

When the installments are always the same amount and the payments are made at regular intervals, you can use the constant ratio formula to determine the interest rate.

$$R = \frac{24 \times C}{P \times (n + 1)}$$

where R = rate of interest, C = interest charge, P = principal or unpaid balance, and n = number of installments.

EXAMPLE 7

A washing machine is listed for cash sale at $239. It may, however, be bought for $39 down and 9 monthly installments of $25. To find the rate of interest you use the constant ratio formula.

First find the interest charge: 9 (installment payments) × 25 = $225. $225 − ($239[cash price] − $39[down payment]) = $225 − $200 = $25 interest charge.

Apply the formula as follows:

$$\text{Rate} = \frac{24 \times \$25}{\$200 \times (9 + 1)} = \frac{\$600}{\$200 \times 10} = \frac{\$600}{\$2,000} = 0.30 \text{ or } 30\%$$

To find the true annual rate of interest, the constant ratio formula is modified as follows:

$$R = \frac{2(WC)}{P \times (n + 1)}$$

where R = effective annual interest rate, W = number of payment periods in a year (12 if monthly, 52 if weekly), C = interest charge, P = principal and n = number of installments.

EXAMPLE 8

Elaine Franco, who is majoring in journalism, felt the need for a typewriter. At a local department store, she purchased a $285 electric typewriter. The manager allowed her to pay on the installment plan on the following terms: $35 down and $11 per week for 24 weeks. To find the rate of interest (*per year*), let W = 52, number of weeks (payment periods in one year); C = $14; P = $250; n = 24. C and P were arrived at as follows. 24 (payments) × $11 = $264, plus $35 down payment = $299. $299 − $285 (cash price) = \$14 carrying charge (*C*). *P* = \$285 (cash) − \$35 (down payment) = \$250. Applying the formula:

$$R = \frac{2(52) \times \$14}{\$250 \times (24 + 1)} = \frac{\$104 \times 14}{\$250 \times 25} = \frac{\$1,456}{\$6,250} = 0.232, \text{ or } 23\%$$

2.6 COMMERCIAL BANK LOANS TO CONSUMERS

Commercial banks charge a simple interest rate for short-term loans. The interest charge is added to the principal. For *simple interest*, use the formula: Interest = principal × rate × time.

$$I = P \times R \times T$$

where *I* = the amount charged in dollars, *P* = principal, or amount of the loan, *R* = rate in percent, and *T* = time (number of days over 360, or number of months over 12).

EXAMPLE 9

You negotiate a \$700 loan from a commercial bank, to be paid back in 6 months at $8\frac{1}{2}\%$ interest. Applying the formula for simple interest, $I = P \times R \times T$, we get:

$$I = \$700 \times 0.085 \times 6/12 \,(\text{or } 180/360) = \$700 \times 0.085 \times \tfrac{1}{2} = \$29.75 \text{ interest}$$

You pay back \$729.75 (\$700.00 + \$29.75) at the end of 6 months.

If the bank *discounts* the loan, the interest charge is deducted by the bank *in advance*. You receive the principal *less* the discount. Then you pay the face amount (principal) at the end of the period of the loan.

EXAMPLE 10

You negotiate a \$700 loan from a commercial bank to be discounted at $8\frac{1}{2}\%$ and to be paid back in 6 months.

$$D \text{ (interest or discount)} = P \times R \times T, \text{ or } \$700 \times 0.085 \times 6/12 = \$29.75$$

Actually, you receive \$700 − \$29.75 = \$670.25. The true annual rate of interest is:

$$D = P \times R \times T$$

$$\$29.75 = \$670.25 \times R \times 6/12 \qquad \$29.75 \div \$335.13 = 0.0887 = 8.9\% = R$$

You actually pay a true annual rate of interest of 8.9%.

2.7 CONSUMER FINANCE COMPANIES

Commonly called small loan companies, a consumer finance company specializes in unsecured small loans. The maximum amount of loan value and interest rates are set by the various states. The loans range from a few hundred dollars to \$5,000 and interest as high as an annual rate of 45%. (Some states permit an even higher rate when the interest is computed on the declining balance of a loan.) Consumers patronize the companies when they are either poor credit risks or have exhausted their credit at other institutions.

The repayment of loans is made weekly or monthly, with a part of each payment including interest and resulting in a reduction of principal. Interest is often charged only on the unpaid balance.

EXAMPLE 11

Honest John's small loan company lends you $500 to be paid back in the amount of $11 a week for 52 weeks.   What is the true annual rate of interest?

$$R = \frac{2 \times W \times C}{P \times (n + 1)}$$

where W = 52 weekly payments, C = $72, $572 − $500 = $72, P = $500, and n = 52.

$$R = \frac{2 \times 52 \times \$72}{\$500 \times (52 + 1)} = \frac{\$7,488}{\$26,500} = 0.28, \text{ or } 28\% \text{ true annual rate of interest}$$

2.8 AUTOMOBILE LOANS: SALES FINANCE COMPANIES

All of the large automobile manufacturers either own or have an agreement with a sales finance company.   While these are convenient sources for automobile loans, the interest rates charged are such that it is generally less expensive to secure financing from a bank.   An example of financing a new car through the manufacturer's facilities follows.

Purchase price		$4,200
Plus: State sales tax, 4%	$168	
Title and license fees	15	
Auto insurance	300	
Credit life insurance	12	495
Total cost		$4,695
Less: Trade-in old car	$695	
Cash down payment	600	$1,295
Balance to finance (24 monthly payments)		$3,400
Finance charge		612
Total amount to be paid		$4,012

24 monthly payments at $167.17 each.   Given the finance charge of $612,

$$\frac{24 \times \$612}{\$3,400 \times (24 + 1)} = 0.173$$

The true annual rate is 17.3%.

EXAMPLE 12

Bill Jones bought a new car for $4,700; terms, $700 down, balance to be paid in equal monthly installments over a 2-year period at 8% interest.   The monthly payments and the actual rate of interest are computed as follows:

Debt:

$$\$4,700 - \$700 = \$4,000 \qquad I = P \times R \times T = \$4,000 \times \frac{8}{100} \times \frac{2}{1} = \$640$$

$$\$4,000 + \$640 = \$4,640$$

Monthly payments:

$$\frac{\$4,640}{24} = \$193.33$$

Actual rate of interest:

$$I = P \times R \times T$$

$$\$640 = \frac{\$4,000}{24} \times R \times \frac{300^*}{12}$$

$$= \frac{\$4,000}{24} \times R \times 25 = \frac{\$100,000R}{24}$$

$$R = \frac{\$640}{\$4,166.67} = 0.1536, \text{ or } 15.4\%$$

*The 24 payments may be considered as 24 separate loans. Thus, the interest for 1 month, plus the interest for 2 months, plus the interest for 3 months, etc. . . . until the interest for 24 months is reached, will give a total of 300.

A short cut to arrive at this figure (300) is simply to multiply (24) by the next higher number (25) and divide by 2.

$$\frac{24 \text{ (monthly payments)} \times 25}{2} = \frac{600}{2} = 300$$

Alternate Method:

$$R = \frac{24 \times C}{P \times (n + 1)} = \frac{24 \times \$640}{\$4,000 \times (24 + 1)} = \frac{24 \times \$640}{\$4,000 \times 25} = \frac{\$15,360}{\$100,000} = 0.1536, \text{ or } 15.4\%$$

2.9   CREDIT UNION LOANS

A credit union is a cooperative association formed by groups of people with a common interest, such as schoolteachers, factory employees, members of a military installation, and the like. Its major purposes are to promote savings and provide loans to its members. These associations may be chartered under state or Federal laws. If Federally chartered, all individual accounts are insured up to $40,000. If state chartered, they *may* be insured but are not necessarily so.

The directors and officers of these associations are elected from the membership and offer their services without compensation. Members' savings are called shares, and interest earned on investments is returned to members as dividends at a prescribed rate.

The monthly payments required and the total amount of interest per amount of loan for specified periods of time are given in Table 1.

EXAMPLE 13

A typical repayment loan schedule for a $4,000 loan at 6% for 24 months is shown in Table 2. (The true annual rate is approximately 12%. The charge is 1% per month on the unpaid balance.) The amount of monthly payment is $188.30.

EXAMPLE 14

Let us assume you borrowed from your credit union $2,000 to be paid back in 12 monthly payments of $177.70 each. To determine the actual interest and true annual rate, multiply the monthly payment of $177.70 by 12 to get the total amount paid: $2,132.40. Subtract from the $2,132.40 the face value of the loan: $2,000. Therefore, the interest is $132.40.

To determine the true annual rate, use the constant ratio formula:

$$R = \frac{24 \times C}{P \times (n + 1)} = \frac{24 \times \$132.40}{\$2,000 \times (12 + 1)} = \frac{\$3,177.60}{\$26,000} = 0.122, \text{ or } 12.2\%$$

Table 1.

6 months			12 months		
Amount of Loan	Payment Monthly	Total Interest	Amount of Loan	Monthly Payment	Total Interest
$ 100	$ 17.26	$ 3.53	$ 100	$ 8.89	$ 6.62
500	86.28	17.65	500	44.43	33.09
1,000	172.55	35.29	1,000	88.85	66.19
1,500	258.83	52.94	1,500	133.28	99.28
2,000	345.10	70.58	2,000	177.70	132.37
2,500	431.38	88.23	2,500	222.13	165.46
3,000	517.65	105.87	3,000	266.55	198.56
3,500	603.92	123.52	3,500	310.98	231.65
4,000	690.20	141.16	4,000	355.40	264.74

18 months			24 months		
$ 100	$ 6.10	$ 9.77	$ 100	$ 4.71	$ 12.98
500	30.50	48.84	500	23.54	64.88
1,000	60.99	97.68	1,000	47.08	129.76
1,500	91.48	146.52	1,500	70.62	194.65
2,000	121.97	195.35	2,000	94.15	259.53
2,500	152.46	244.19	2,500	117.69	324.41
3,000	182.95	293.03	3,000	141.23	389.29
3,500	213.44	341.87	3,500	164.76	454.17
4,000	243.93	390.71	4,000	188.30	519.05

Table 2.

Payment	Unpaid Balance	Interest for Month	Amount Due	Monthly Payment	Balance
1	$4,000.00	$ 40.00	$4,040.00	$188.30	$3,851.70
2	3,851.70	38.52	3,990.22	188.30	3,701.92
3	3,701.92	37.02	3,738.94	188.30	3,550.64
4	3,550.64	35.51	3,586.15	188.30	3,397.85
5	3,397.85	33.98	3,431.83	188.30	3,243.53
6	3,243.53	32.44	3,275.97	188.30	3,087.67
7	3,087.67	30.88	3,118.55	188.30	2,930.25
8	2,930.25	29.30	2,959.55	188.30	2,771.25
9	2,771.25	27.71	2,798.96	188.30	2,610.66
10	2,610.66	26.11	2,636.77	188.30	2,448.47
11	2,448.47	24.48	2,472.95	188.30	2,284.65
12	2,284.65	22.85	2,307.50	188.30	2,119.20
13	2,119.20	21.19	2,140.39	188.30	1,952.09
14	1,952.09	19.52	1,971.61	188.30	1,783.31
15	1,783.31	17.83	1,801.14	188.30	1,612.84
16	1,612.84	16.13	1,628.97	188.30	1,440.67
17	1,440.67	14.41	1,455.08	188.30	1,266.78
18	1,266.78	12.67	1,279.45	188.30	1,091.15
19	1,091.15	10.91	1,102.06	188.30	913.76
20	913.76	9.14	922.90	188.30	734.60
21	734.60	7.35	741.95	188.30	553.65
22	553.65	5.54	559.19	188.30	370.89
23	370.89	3.71	374.60	188.30	186.30
24	186.30	1.86	188.16	188.16*	0
	Total Interest	$519.06			

*Due to rounding off, the last payment is $188.16.

2.10 CREDIT CARDS

Consumers today use over 300 million credit cards of one kind or another. Generally, they fall into one of three categories: (1) the *company-issued* card usable in its specified outlets, such as the Sears, Roebuck credit card or the Exxon gasoline credit card; (2) the *bank-issued* card such as Master Charge or Bank Americard which is honored in innumerable cooperating sales and service businesses; and (3) the *travel-and-entertainment* card issued by private companies such as American Express which are accepted by many businesses here and abroad.

This is about the cheapest means of credit available if managed correctly. No service charge is added if payment is made in full by a specified date, which may be up to sixty days from time of purchase. A service charge is payable on any unpaid balance; this can amount to up to 18% annually.

Solved Problems

Carry answers to 2 decimal places.

2.1 A box of Brand A corn flakes sells for 48¢ and contains 12 oz. Brand B sells for 72¢ and contains 16 oz. What is the unit cost (per pound) of each brand? Which brand is the more economical purchase?

>   *Brand A*: 12 oz for 48¢ = 4¢ per ounce. *Brand B*: 16 oz for 72¢ = $4\frac{1}{2}$¢ per ounce. Brand A is the more economical purchase. (See Example 5.)

2.2 Five pounds of Best brand sugar sells for $2.40 per package. A 1-lb package of Best sugar sells for 53¢. Is it more economical to buy a 5-lb package or a 1-lb package? How much cheaper?

>   First determine the unit (lb) price of the 5-lb package, and then compare it with the price per 1-lb package. 5 lb for $2.40 = 48¢ per pound. Since the 1-lb package costs 53¢, the 5-lb package is 5¢ cheaper per pound.

2.3 Mrs. Solenov purchased a $2\frac{1}{4}$-oz jar of caviar at her favourite grocery store for $1.98. Mrs. Smythe purchased a $3\frac{1}{8}$-oz jar of the same brand of caviar for $2.79 at a delicatessen. (*a*) Determine the unit price of each. (*b*) Which one is cheaper per ounce and by how much?

>   (*a*) Divide $1.98 by $2\frac{1}{4}$ oz: $1.98 ÷ 2.25 = 88¢ per ounce. Next divide $2.79 by $3\frac{1}{8}$ oz: $2.79 ÷ 3.125 = 89.3¢ per ounce.

>   (*b*) The $2\frac{1}{4}$-oz jar is cheaper by 1.3¢ per ounce.

Mrs. Kroll bought an 18-oz jar of peanuts for $.96 at a local convenience store. On the same day, Mr. Kroll bought a 28-oz jar of the same brand at a supermarket for $1.28. (*a*) Determine the unit price per pound of each jar. (*b*) The cheaper jar offers a savings of how much per pound?

>   (*a*) $\dfrac{16}{18} \times \$.96 = \$.85$ per pound (18-oz jar)

> $\dfrac{16}{18} \times \$1.28 = \$.73$ per pound (28-oz jar)

>   (*b*) $.85 − $.73 = $.12.   28-oz jar is $.12 per pound cheaper.

2.5 While shopping in a discount drug store, Mrs. Jacobs and Mrs. Russo noticed three different-sized bottles of the same brand of hair lotion.   A 15-oz bottle was priced at $.89, the 6-oz bottle at $.49, and the 1-lb 4-oz bottle at $1.29.   Mrs. Jacobs figured the unit price per bottle to determine which size was the best buy.   What were her results?

The 15-oz bottle: $.89 ÷ 15 = $.059.   The unit cost is 5.9¢ per ounce.   The 6-oz bottle: $.49 ÷ 6 = $.0816.   The unit cost is 8.2¢ per ounce.   The 1-lb 4-oz bottle: $1.29 ÷ 20 = $.065.   The unit cost is 6.5¢ per ounce.   The 15-oz bottle is the best buy.

2.6 Mrs. Price saw her favorite brand of instant coffee advertised at 27¢ per ounce.

(*a*) How much will an $8\frac{1}{2}$-ounce jar cost?   The special store brand, containing 1 lb 2 oz, sells for $4.68.

(*b*) Which brand would be more economical for Mrs. Price to purchase and by how much?

(*a*) $.27 × $8\frac{1}{2}$ = $2.295, or $2.30 per jar (favorite brand). $4.68 ÷ 1 lb 2 oz = $4.68 ÷ 18 (oz) = $.26 per ounce (store brand).

(*b*) The store brand is 1¢ per ounce cheaper.

2.7 A 3-lb bag of navel oranges containing 8 oranges sells for 69¢.   A half bushel containing 40 oranges and weighing 15 lb sells for $2.50.   What is the price per pound   (*a*) by the bag,   (*b*) by the half bushel?

(*a*) By the bag: 3-lb bag costs $.69. $.69 ÷ 3 = $.23, or 23¢ per pound.

(*b*) By the half bushel: $2.50 ÷ 15 = $.1666, or 17¢ per pound.

2.8 Mrs. Simmons saw a beautiful name brand wristwatch in a discount jewelry store for $78.49.   She saw the same wristwatch in a local department store with a price tag of $102.98.   What percent of savings would Mrs. Simmons realize by purchasing the watch at the discount store?

$$\$102.98 - \$78.49 = \$24.49 \text{ discount in cash}$$
$$\$24.49 \div \$102.98 = 0.2378, \text{ or } 23.8\% \text{ discount in percent of saving}$$

2.9 Mrs. Filmon went shopping for a living room rug.   She found one selling for $249.   Her friend Sheila mentioned that she knew of a discount store that had similar rugs priced at $225 with an $8\frac{1}{3}$% discount.   (*a*) Mrs. Filmon would save how much by buying the rug at the discount store?   (*b*) What percent discount would this amount to?

(*a*) $225 × 0.0833 = $18.749, or $18.75. $225 − $18.75 = $206.25, the selling price, discounted, at the discount store.

$$\$249 - \$206.25 = \$42.75 \text{ savings}$$

(*b*) $$\$42.75 \div \$249 = 0.1716 = 17.2\% \text{ savings}$$

2.10 Mrs. Grove saves redeemable food coupons from packages and advertisements.   She had a coupon worth $.18 on the purchase of an 8-oz jar of peanut butter costing 89¢.   What percent discount does she receive per ounce?

$.18 ÷ $.89 = 0.2022, or 20.2% per 8 oz   20.2% ÷ 8 = 0.025, or 2.5% per ounce

2.11 A building supply company is allowing a 5% discount on all wooden materials and is allowing an $8\frac{1}{2}$% discount on all other materials. You have purchased $175 worth of lumber and $245 worth of asbestos shingles. (*a*) How much dollar discount did you receive? (*b*) What percent of discount did you receive on the total purchase?

(*a*) $175 × 0.05 = $8.75 discount on the lumber. $245 × 0.085 = $20.83 discount on the asbestos shingles.

$$\$8.75 + \$20.83 = \$29.58 \text{ cash discount}$$

(*b*) $$\frac{\text{Total cash discount}}{\text{Total sale value}} = \frac{\$29.58}{\$420} = 0.07, \text{ or a 7\% discount on the total sale value}$$

2.12 A department store is offering a $12\frac{1}{2}$% discount on all cash sales of merchandise. Mrs. Jameson, whose living room furniture had outlived its usefulness, bought for cash a living room suite advertised at $749.50 and a living room chair for $149.99. How much did she save by paying cash?

$$\$749.50 + \$149.99 = \$899.49 \text{ advertised cost}$$
$$\$899.49 × 0.125 = \$112.44 \text{ cash discount}$$

2.13 Joseph DeSanto visited an automobile dealer who is selling all new cars at a discount of $12\frac{1}{2}$% off the suggested price. In addition, the dealer offered to sell DeSanto a car with an additional 6% off the sale price if he ordered a new one today. What will the price be today for an automobile with a list price of $5,295?

$5,295 × 0.125 = $661.88 discount. $5,295 − $661.88 = $4,633.12 sale price. $4,633.12 × 0.06 = $277.99 additional discount.

$$\$4,633.12 − \$277.99 = \$4,355.13, \text{ today's price}$$

2.14 If DeSanto bought the automobile in the previous example, what percent of the suggested price did he actually save?

$$\$5,295 − \$4,355.13 = \$939.87 \text{ discount}$$
$$\$939.87 ÷ \$5,295 = 0.1775, \text{ or 17.8\% discount}$$

2.15 The Kings bought a TV set priced at $585 for $499, at a clearance sale. They bought a power mower, receiving a $16\frac{2}{3}$% discount off the regular price of $747. How much did the two items cost them?

$$\$585 − \$499 = \$86 \text{ discount on TV}$$
$$\$747 × 16\tfrac{2}{3}\% = \$747 × 1/6 = \$124.50 \text{ discount on power mower}$$
$$\$86 + \$124.50 = \$210.50 \text{ total discount}$$
$$\$585 + \$747 = \$1,332. \$1,332 − \$210.50 = \$1,121.50 \text{ net cost}$$

2.16 You bought a 12-volt battery for $29.95 whose retail sales price was $34.88. You also bought 2 steel-belted radial tires for $119.95 whose retail price was $68.75 each. What was your percent discount on this purchase?

$$\$34.88 − \$29.95 = \$4.93 \text{ discount on the battery}$$
$$\$68.75 × 2 = \$137.50. \$137.50 − \$119.95 = \$17.55 \text{ discount on tires}$$
$$\$4.93 + \$17.55 = \$22.48 \text{ total discount received}$$
$$\$137.50 + \$34.88 = \$172.38, \text{ total regular price}$$
$$\$22.48 ÷ \$172.38 = 0.1304, \text{ or 13\% discount}$$

2.17 A local dress shop is selling all dresses at a discount of 15%. Other items will be sold for a discount of $12 off regular price. Jo Rush bought a dress priced at $59.95 and a coat priced at $88.50. What did she pay for these items? What was her percent discount on these purchases?

$59.95 × 0.15 = $8.99 discount on dress
$59.95 − $8.99 = $50.96 cost
$88.50 − $12 = $76.50. $76.50 + $50.96 = $127.46, the total cost of purchases
$59.95 + $88.50 = $148.45, regular price
$148.45 − $127.46 = $20.99 discount
$20.99 ÷ $148.45 = 0.141, or 14.1% discount.

2.18 Manville Department Store is conducting a basement clearance sale at which all merchandise is marked down 40% from the regular price if bought for cash. How much would you have to pay for the following items? How much money would you save? (*a*) A dress listed at $50. (*b*) A pair of shoes listed at $22. (*c*) A sweater listed at $12.48.

(*a*) Dress: $50 × 0.40 = $20 reduction. Cost: $50 − $20 = $30.

(*b*) Shoes: $22 × 0.40 = $8.80 reduction. Cost: $22 − $8.80 = $13.20.

(*c*) Sweater: $12.48 × 0.40 = $4.99 reduction. Cost: $12.48 − $4.99 = $7.49.

$30 + $13.20 + $7.49 = $50.69 total cost

You save $20 + $8.80 + $4.99: $33.79.

2.19 A toy store has on sale girls' doll houses at 35% off the regular cost and boys' wagons at 28% off. The regular price of a girls' doll house is $9.98, and the regular price of a boys' wagon is $9.49. Which item would cost the least and by how much?

Doll house: $9.98 × 0.35 = $3.49 saving.
Sale price: $9.98 − $3.49 = $6.49.
Wagon: $9.49 × 0.28 = $2.66 saving.
Sale price: $9.49 − $2.66 = $6.83.

The doll house costs less by $.34. (See Example 3.)

2.20 Ms. Sacks wishes to buy a new refrigerator priced at $398. The store offers it to her for $379 if she pays cash. What percent discount does she realize by paying cash?

$398 − $379 = $19 discount $19 ÷ $398 = 0.0477, or 4.8% cash discount

2.21 Mrs. Winslow visited Hessey's Department Store, which was holding an annual clearance sale. All boys' clothing was reduced $33\frac{1}{3}$%. Girls' clothing was reduced 28%. Mrs. Winslow bought $99 worth of boys' clothing and $115 worth of girls' clothing. (*a*) How much money did she save? (*b*) What percent of saving did she realize?

(*a*) Boys' clothing: $99 × $\frac{1}{3}$ = $33.00 saving. Girls' clothing: $115 × 0.28 = $32.20 saving.

$33.00 + $32.20 = $65.20 saving

(*b*) Percent saving: $99 + $115 = $214 total regular price.

$65.20 (saving) ÷ $214 (regular price) = 0.3046, or 30.1% savings

2.22 A local furniture store allows a $6\frac{1}{4}\%$ discount on cash purchases. You bought a new dining room set listed at $529.00 for cash and a living room chair listed for $198.50 with your credit card.* What was your percent saving on the total purchase?

> Discount: $529 \times 6\frac{1}{4}\% = \$33.06$.
> Cash price: $529 - \$33.06 = \$495.94$.
> Total purchase price: $495.94 + \$198.50 = \$694.44$.
> Percent saving: $33.06 \div \$694.44 = 4.8\%$.

2.23 Mrs. Price went shopping for childrens' school clothing. In the shopping center, she entered a store that was selling all clothing at list price, less $12\frac{1}{2}\%$ with an additional 5% discount off the net sale price for cash purchases. (a) How much did Mrs. Price save on a total cash purchase of $129.50? (b) What was her percent saving?

(a) $129.50 \times 12\frac{1}{2}\% = \$16.19$ discount. $129.50 - \$16.19 = \$113.31$ net sale price. Therefore $113.31 \times 5\% = \$5.67$ cash discount. Her total savings were:

$$\$16.19 + \$5.67 = \$21.86$$

(b) $$\$21.86 \div \$129.50 = 0.1688, \text{ or } 16.9\% \text{ savings}$$

2.24 Al Burton went shopping around for a used car. He found 2 cars that interested him. The first, with a list price of $2,950, was offered to him for $2,750 if he paid cash. The other, which listed at $3,250, was offered to him for $3,000 cash. (a) Which car would give him the higher percent saving? (b) By how much?

(a) *First Car*:

$$\$2,950 - \$2,750 = \$200 \qquad \$200 \div \$2,950 = 0.0677, \text{ or } 6.8\%$$

Second Car:

$$\$3,250 - \$3,000 = \$250 \qquad \$250 \div \$3,250 = 0.0769 \text{ or } 7.7\%$$

Therefore, the second car would give the higher percent saving.

(b) 0.9% greater saving (7.7% − 6.8% = 0.9%).

2.25 A department store offers a $3\frac{1}{2}\%$ discount on all cash purchases. It also offers a $2\frac{1}{2}\%$ discount off the cash price to the first 25 customers on a certain named date. You are one of the first 25 to enter the store that day and you purchase $218 worth of merchandise. What is your money savings and percent of savings?

$3\frac{1}{2}\%$ *discount*:

$$\$218 \times 0.035 = \$7.63 \text{ cash discount} \qquad \$218 - \$7.63 = \$210.37 \text{ cash price}$$

$2\frac{1}{2}\%$ *discount*:

$$\$210.37 \times 0.025 = \$5.26 \qquad \$7.63 + \$5.26 = \$12.89 \text{ total saving}$$

Percent of Savings:

$$\$12.89 \div \$218 = 0.0591 \text{ or } 5.9\%$$

---

*A credit card purchase is not considered a cash purchase by the store because the store must pay the credit card company a fixed-rate percent of the selling price of the article for the cash that the credit card company is advancing for the card holder.

2.26 Barry Gentry, an accounting major, can purchase a calculator for $69 cash or on the installement plan by paying $19 down and $10 a month for 6 months.   Find the amount by which the installment price exceeds the cash price.

Installment price:

Down payment	$19	
Monthly payments (6 × $10)	60	$79
Cash price		69
Amount greater		$10

The installment price exceeds the cash price by $10.   (See Example 6.)

2.27 Bud Fischer, a boat buff, saw a boat advertised for sale at a cash price of $1,650; or on the installment plan, for $795 down and $100 a month for 12 months.   Bud decided to buy it on the installment plan.   How much was the installment charge?

$$\$100 \times 12 = \$1,200 \qquad \$1,200 + \$795 = \$1,995$$

$$\$1,995 - \$1,650 = \$345 \text{ installment charge}$$

2.28 You can buy a new color TV for $690 cash or on the installment plan by paying 15% additional.   You decide to buy on the installment plan and make a down payment of $133.50, with monthly payments of $30.   How many months will it take to pay for the TV?

$$\$690 \times 0.15 = \$103.50 \qquad \$690 + \$103.50 = \$793.50 \qquad \$793.50 - \$133.50 = \$660$$

$$\$660 \div \$30 = 22 \text{ months}$$

2.29 An electric typewriter may be purchased for $459 cash or on the installment plan by either of two methods: (a) by making a $29 down payment and paying $4.50 a week for 104 weeks, or   (b) by making a $39 down payment and paying $19.50 a month for 24 months.   By which plan would you pay the lesser amount and by how much?

(a)		
	Down payment	$ 29
	Weekly payments (104 × $4.50)	468
	Total cost	$497

(b)		
	Down payment	$ 39
	Monthly payments (24 × $19.50)	468
	Total cost	$507

Plan (a) would cost less by $10.

2.30 A microwave oven may be purchased for $329 cash or on the installment plan by paying $29 down and $15 a month for 24 months.   Find the true rate of interest on this purchase if made on the installment plan.

Installment plan:

Down payment	$ 29
Monthly payments (24 × $15)	360
	$389
Cash price	329
Carrying charge	$ 60

Using the constant ratio formula:

$$R = \frac{24 \times C}{P \times (n+1)} = \frac{24 \times \$60}{\$300 \times (24+1)} = \frac{\$1,440}{\$7,500} = 0.19, \text{ or } 19\%$$

(See Example 7.)

2.31 Arthur and Jane Roundy decided to purchase a stereo for the recreation room. They found exactly what they wanted for $759 cash. Not being able to pay cash, they purchased the stereo on the installment plan by paying $59 down, with a contract to pay $24 a month for 36 months. Determine the installment carrying cost and the true rate of interest.

Installment price:

Down payment	$ 59
Monthly payments (36 × $24)	864
	$923
Cash price	759
Carrying charge	$164

$$R = \frac{24 \times C}{P \times (n+1)} = \frac{24 \times \$164}{\$700 \times (36+1)} = \frac{\$3,936}{\$25,900} = 0.15, \text{ or } 15\%$$

Alternate Method:

$$I = P \times R \times T$$

$$\$164 = \frac{\$700}{36} \times R \times \frac{666}{12} = \$1,078.92R$$

$$R = \$164 \div \$1,078.92 = 0.152 \text{ or } 15\%$$

2.32 Alec Hinton wants to buy a wristwatch for his fiancee. Pastor Jewelers sell watches similar to the one Alec has in mind for $37.50 cash or on the installment plan for $7.50 down and $1.00 a week for 32 weeks. (*a*) How much more than the cash price would Alex have to pay for the watch if he purchases it on the installment plan? (*b*) What is the true rate of interest?

Installment price:

Down payment	$ 7.50
Weekly payments (32 × $1.00)	32.00
	$39.50
Cash price	37.50
Carrying charge	$ 2.00

$$R = \frac{24 \times C}{P \times (n+1)} = \frac{2 \times 52 \times \$2}{\$30 \times (32+1)} = \frac{104 \times \$2}{\$990} = \frac{\$208}{\$990} = 0.21, \text{ or } 21\%$$

Alternate Method:

$$I = P \times R \times T$$

$$\$2 = \frac{\$30}{32} \times R \times \frac{528}{52} = \$9.52R$$

$$R = \$2 \div \$9.52 = 0.21, \text{ or } 21\%$$

(See Example 8.)

2.33 Oscar Landry negotiated a $950 loan from a commercial bank to keep his garage in operation until his business increased. The loan officer arranged for Oscar to pay the amount back in 9 months at an $8\frac{3}{4}\%$ interest rate. How much must Oscar pay back at the end of the term of the loan?

Using the formula $I = P \times R \times T$,

$$I = \$950 \times 0.0875 \times \frac{9}{12} = \$83.125 \times \frac{3}{4} = \frac{\$249.375}{4} = \$62.34$$

$950 + $62.34 = $1,012.34 to be paid back. (See Example 9.)

2.34 Sam Ward needed $1,450 to purchase some new equipment for his poultry farm. The City Savings Bank was willing to lend him this amount on a note for 11 months at a discount rate of $8\frac{1}{2}\%$. (*a*) How much would the discount amount to? (*b*) How much would Sam receive on his loan?

(*a*)

$$D = P \times R \times T$$

$$D = \$1,450 \times 0.085 \times \frac{11}{12} = \$123.25 \times \frac{11}{12} = \frac{\$1,355.75}{12}$$

$$D = \$112.98 \text{ discount}$$

(*b*) $1,450 − $112.98 = $1,337.02 proceeds of loan (See Example 13.)

2.35 Mrs. Keely wanted to borrow money to purchase some new equipment for her beauty shop. She negotiated a 9-month $1,200 loan at her bank. The bank discounted the loan and actually gave her $1,120. What was the discount rate on her loan?

$$D = P \times R \times T$$

$$\$80 = \$1,200 \times R \times \frac{9}{12} = \$900R$$

$R = \$80 \div \$900 = 0.0888$, or 8.8\% discount rate. (See Examples 10 and 14.)

2.36 Harry Seeley needed $500 to complete his school year. The Bolling Commercial Bank approved his loan of $500 at $9\frac{1}{2}\%$ interest for 90 days. How much interest will Harry pay?

$$I = P \times R \times T$$

$$I = \$500 \times 0.095 \times \frac{90}{360} = \$500 \times 0.095 \times \frac{1}{4} = \$125 \times 0.095 = \$11.875, \text{ or } \$11.88 \text{ interest}$$

2.37 Sarah Altman, your sorority sister, borrowed \$900 at the University Bank at an interest rate of 6%. She was required to pay back \$913.50. For how many months did the loan run?

$$I = P \times R \times T$$

$$\$13.50 = \$900 \times 0.06 \times T \qquad \$13.50 = 54T \qquad T = \$13.50 \div 54$$

$$T = 0.25 \text{ (years)} = 0.25 \times 360 = 90 \text{ days, or 3 months}$$

2.38 Mr. Borgson, the proprietor of a feed store, wished to discount a \$750 note at his local bank. The term of the note was for 72 days, and the bank charged him a $9\frac{1}{2}\%$ discount rate. (*a*) How much did Mr. Borgson receive? (*b*) What was the true rate of interest?

(*a*)
$$D = P \times R \times T$$

$$D = \$750 \times 0.095 \times \frac{72}{360} = \$14.25$$

$$\$750 - \$14.25 = \$735.75$$

(*b*)
$$\$14.25 = \$735.75 \times R \times \frac{72}{360} = \$147.15R$$

$$R = \frac{\$14.25}{\$147.15} = 0.0968, \text{ or } 9.7\%$$

2.39 Your friend borrowed \$750 from the bank for 4 months. He has to pay back \$772 when the note becomes due. He forgot what the true rate of interest is and asks you to calculate it for him. How would you do it?

$$I = P \times R \times T$$

$$\$22 = \$750 \times R \times \frac{4}{12} = \$250R. \qquad \$22 \div \$250 = R$$

$$R = 0.088, \text{ or } 8.8\% \text{ interest}$$

2.40 Millie Gilson was unable to negotiate a commercial loan at any local bank for the purchase of merchandise for her boutique. Millie went to the Friendly Finance Company, which discounted her \$500 note. She received \$450 and paid back the \$500 face value of the note at the end of 3 months. What true rate of interest did she pay?

$$D = P \times R \times T$$

$$\$50 = \$450 \times R \times \frac{3}{12} = \$112.50R$$

$$R = \frac{\$50}{\$112.50} = 0.444, \text{ or } 44.4\%$$

Note: You recognize that by discounting (taking the money out in advance), the finance company receives a larger rate of interest.

2.41 Pat Finnegan, who works in the local steel mill, was in desperate need of $72. He negotiated a loan for this amount from a small loan company. He promised to pay back the loan on pay day 10 days hence. If Pat pays the money back on pay day, what rate of interest will he pay?

$$I = P \times R \times T$$

$$\$2 = \$72 \times R \times \frac{10}{360} = \$72 \times R \times \frac{1}{36} = \$2R$$

$$R = 1.00, \text{ or } 100\% \text{ interest}$$

2.42 Mrs. Jones, who had a poor credit rating, needed $625 to prevent her automobile from being repossessed. She was able to negotiate a $625 loan from a small loan company for 72 days at an interest rate of 15%. This loan company computes interest on the basis of a 365-day year. How much interest will she pay?

$$I = P \times R \times T$$

$$I = \$625 \times 0.15 \times \frac{72}{365} = \$93.75 \times \frac{72}{365} = \$6,750 \div 365$$

$$I = \$18.49$$

2.43 John Haney borrowed $550 from a small loan company for 6 months and paid it back in 6 equal monthly installments of $100 each. What was the true rate of interest?

$$R = \frac{24 \times C}{P \times (n + 1)} = \frac{24 \times \$50}{\$550 \times 7} = \frac{\$1,200}{\$3,850} = 0.311, \text{ or } 31\%$$

Alternate Method:

$$I = P \times R \times T$$

$$\$50 = \frac{\$550}{6} \times R \times \frac{21}{12} = \$91.66R \times \frac{7}{4}$$

$$R = 0.311, \text{ or } 31\% \quad \text{(See Example 11.)}$$

2.44 If the loan in Problem 2.43 were discounted, what would be the true rate of interest?

$$R = \frac{24 \times C}{P \times (n + 1)} = \frac{24 \times \$50}{\$500 \times (6 + 1)} = \frac{\$1,200}{\$3,500} = 0.342, \text{ or } 34.2\%$$

Alternate Method:

$$I = P \times R \times T$$

$$\$50 = \frac{\$500}{6} \times R \times \frac{21}{12} = \$83.33R \times \frac{7}{4} = \$145.83R$$

$$R = \frac{\$50}{\$145.83} = 0.342, \text{ or } 34.2\%$$

2.45 Bill Caferi bought a new automobile with a total delivery price of $4,700. He made a down payment of $1,100. The dealer told him he would finance the remaining amount for 3 years at 8% interest, but he would have to pay $600 additional for insurance. What will Caferi's monthly payments be?

List price (delivery)	$4,700
Less down payment	1,100
Balance to be financed	3,600
Plus insurance	600
Balance due plus insurance	$4,200

8% interest for 3 years on $4,200:

$$I = P \times R \times T = \$4,200 \times \frac{8}{100} \times 3 = \$1,008$$

Balance due	$4,200
Plus interest	1,008
Total to be financed	$5,208

Monthly payments:

$$\frac{\$5,208}{36} = \$144.67 \quad \text{(See Example 12.)}$$

2.46 Bill Caferi, in Problem 2.45, decided to pay for the car in two years, thus reducing his interest cost. Also, he discovered that he could purchase his own insurance at a lower rate. When Bill so informed the car dealer, the dealer agreed to charge Bill 7% interest if he would make a $1,500 down payment. After some discussion, Bill and the dealer agreed to these terms. Under this plan, what are Bill's monthly payments?

List price	$4,700
Less down payment	1,500
Balance to be financed	$3,200

7% interest: $I = P \times R \times T$.

$$I = \$3,200 \times \frac{7}{100} \times 2: \qquad 448$$

Total to be financed:	$3,648

Monthly payments:

$$\frac{\$3,648}{24} = \$152$$

2.47 John Rider decided to buy a pick-up truck costing $4,975. The dealer allowed him a trade-in of $975 on his old car. The dealer would finance the truck at $8\frac{1}{2}\%$ interest for 3 years and Rider would be charged $680 for insurance. What are the monthly payments?

List price (delivery)	$4,975
Less trade-in	975
Balance to be financed	4,000
Plus insurance	680
Balance due plus insurance	$4,680

$8\frac{1}{2}$% interest for 3 years on $4,680:

$$I = P \times R \times T = \$4,680 \times 0.085 \times 3 = \$1,193.40$$

Balance due	$4,680.00
Plus interest	1,193.40
Total to be financed	$5,873.40

Monthly payments:

$$\frac{\$5,873.40}{24} = \$244.73$$

2.48 You bought a new car with a $5,200 list price and received $1,600 for your old car. The dealer would finance the new car if you paid for your own insurance and paid him $125 a month for 36 months. What was the true annual rate of interest?

$36 \times \$125 = \$4,500$ installment price $-\ \$3,600$ balance ($5,200 - $1,600) = $900 carrying charge.

$$R = \frac{24 \times C}{P \times (n + 1)} = \frac{\$24 \times \$900}{\$3,600 \times 37} = 0.16, \text{ or } 16\%$$

Alternate Method:

$$I = P \times R \times T$$

$$\$900 = \frac{\$3,600}{36} \times R \times \frac{666}{12}. \qquad \$900 = 100 \times 55.5R$$

$$R = \frac{\$900}{\$5,550} = 0.16, \text{ or } 16\%$$

2.49 A dealer offers you a $2,400 trade-in allowance on your old car if you buy the new $5,800 car you have selected. The terms of the sale on the installment plan are $120 a month for 36 months. (a) How much would you save by paying cash? (b) What is the true interest rate if you use the installment plan?

Balance due ($5,800 list price − $2,400 trade-in)	$3,400
Installment price (36 payments × $120)	4,320

(a) Savings if you paid cash: $4,320 − $3,400 = $920.

(b) True interest rate:

$$R = \frac{24 \times \$920}{\$3,400 \times 37} = \frac{\$22,080}{\$125,800} = 0.175, \text{ or } 17.5\%$$

Alternate Method:

$$I = P \times R \times T$$

$$\$920 = \frac{\$3,400}{36} \times R \times \frac{666}{12} = \$94.44 \times R \times 55.5$$

$$R = \frac{\$920}{\$5,241.42} = 0.175, \text{ or } 17.5\%$$

2.50 Ms. Pomerau, a grammar school teacher, who owned her own home, needed money to pay her real estate taxes. She decided to borrow $500 from the credit union for 6 months. How much will she have to repay the credit union?

(See Table 1.) $86.28 (monthly payments) × 6 = $517.68, the amount to be repaid.

2.51 Michele Langevin, a high school language teacher, decided to visit Europe during her summer vacation. She borrowed $1,000 from the credit union for 12 months and was charged $66.19 interest. What were her monthly payments?

Principal $1,000 + $66.19 (interest) = $1,066.19

$1,066.19 ÷ 12 = $88.85 monthly payments

2.52 Carl Borget, the vice-principal of the local middle school, needed $3,000 with which to purchase a new car. He borrowed $3,000 for 24 months on a signature loan from his credit union. The monthly payments were $141.23. How much interest did he pay on the loan?

24 (payments) × $141.23 = $3,389.52 total amount

$3,389.52 − $3,000 = $389.52 interest charge (rounded on chart to $389.29)

2.53 Stanley Wilkes, a supervisor at the Harden Steel Mill, borrowed $2,500 for 24 months from the company credit union to help pay his son's expenses while away at college. Stanley's payments are $117.69. What is the annual rate of interest on this loan?

24 (payments) × $117.69 = $2,824.56 total amount

$2,824.56 − $2,500 = $324.56 interest charge

$$R = \frac{24 \times C}{P \times (n + 1)} = \frac{24 \times \$324.56}{\$2,500 \times (24 + 1)} = \frac{\$7,789.44}{\$62,500} = 0.1246, \text{ or } 12.5\% \text{ annual rate}$$

Alternate Method:

$$I = P \times R \times T$$

$$\$324.56 = \frac{\$2,500}{24} \times R \times \frac{300}{12} = \$104.16 \times 25 \times R \qquad R = \$324.56 \div \$2,604$$

$$R = 0.1246, \text{ or } 12.5\%$$

(See Example 14.)

2.54 Mr. Jones borrowed $4,200 from his credit union for 30 months. They will charge him 1% per month on the unpaid balance, his monthly payments to be $162.75. How much will he owe after 4 monthly payments?

Table 3.

Payment #	Unpaid Balance	Interest per month	Amount Due	Monthly Payment	Balance
1	$4,200.00	$42.00	$4,242.00	$162.75	$4,079.25
2	4,079.25	40.79	4,120.04	162.75	3,957.29
3	3,957.29	39.57	3,996.86	162.75	3,834.11
4	3,834.11	38.34	3,872.45	162.75	3,709.70

Unpaid balance: $3,709.70. (See Example 13.)

Supplementary Problems

2.55 Patti and Ellen, roommates, went shopping and both bought the same kind of hair dressing. Patti bought a $1\frac{1}{2}$-oz tube for $1.09. Ellen bought a $2\frac{1}{4}$-oz tube for $1.59. What is the cost per ounce of each tube?   *Ans.*   The $1\frac{1}{2}$-oz tube costs 72.7 cents per ounce. The $2\frac{1}{4}$-oz tube costs 70.7 cents per ounce. (See Problem 2.4.)

2.56 Andy Billings went shopping at the Leather Shop, which was advertising a special sale. He purchased a pair of shoes for $18 that were listed at $25.95 and a belt for $3.95 that was listed at $6.95. What percent discount did he receive on this transaction?   *Ans.*   33.3%. (See Problem 2.16.)

2.57 You redeemed coupons on the items listed below at the Variety Store. What percent discount did you receive on the total transaction by redeeming the coupons? (*a*) A $.25 coupon on a $1.98 jar of instant coffee, (*b*) a $.35 coupon on a $2.59 jar of instant tea, (*c*) a $.27 coupon on a $1.19 package of flour.   *Ans.*   15%. (See Problem 2.10.)

2.58 An automobile dealer sold you an automobile for $3,750 which carried a manufacturer's suggested retail price of $4,235. In addition, you paid $745 for optional equipment listed at $1,048. (*a*) The price of the automobile was reduced by what percent? (*b*) The optional equipment was reduced by what percent?   *Ans.*   (*a*) The automobile was reduced by 11.4%. (*b*) The optional equipment was reduced by 28.9%.

2.59 Mrs. Lampson was planning to buy a set of 4 automobile tires from a leading tire store at a cost of $159.98. Her friend told her of an advertisement in the paper where a discount store had a similar set on sale for $137.98. What percent of discount would Mrs. Lampson realize by purchasing them at the discount store?   *Ans.*   13.8%. (See Problem 2.8.)

2.60 Rob and Sally Goss were shopping in a discount drug store where they wanted to buy aspirin at the lowest cost. The following sizes were available: a 250-tablet bottle at $1.19, a 400-tablet bottle at $1.59, and a 24-tablet bottle at $.29. (*a*) What is the cost per tablet in each bottle? (*b*) Which is the best buy?   *Ans.*   (*a*) The 250-count bottle = .476¢, or 5¢ each. The 400-count bottle = .3975¢, or 4¢ each. The 24-count bottle = 1.2¢ each. (*b*) The 400-count bottle is the best buy. (See Problem 2.1.)

2.61   Mrs. Smith bought a portable dishwasher at 22% off the regular price of $198.00. Mrs. Jones bought a built-in dishwasher for 26% off the regular price of $219.00. Which woman paid the least for her dishwasher? How much did each one pay?   *Ans.* Mrs. Smith paid $154.44, saving $43.56. Mrs. Jones paid $162.06, saving $56.94. Mrs. Smith paid the least by $7.62.

2.62   Frank and Nancy Miller went shopping at a local department store that was selling all ladies' clothing at a discount of 22% off list price and all men's clothing at 17% off list price. Nancy's purchases amounted to $198 and Bill's amounted to $127.50. (*a*) How much was their total discount? (*b*) What was their total percent discount?   *Ans.*   (*a*) $65.24, discount, (*b*) 20% discount. (See Problem 2.11.)

2.63   A local electrical applicance store offered the following cash discounts on all purchases: 2% on purchases up to $50, 3% on amounts from $50 to $100, 4% on amounts over $100. In March, you bought merchandise listed at $58, in May at $129, and in September at $98. (*a*) What was your dollar saving, and (*b*) by your percent of saving if you paid cash on the total purchases?   *Ans.*   (*a*) $9.84, (*b*) 3.5%. (See Problem 2.21.)

2.64   Mrs. Young took her daughter shopping to teach her how to learn to be a careful shopper. She pointed out to her the following sized packages of the same cereal. 1-oz packages selling at 8 for 63¢; a 10-oz package selling at 61¢; a 15-oz package selling at 85¢; a 20-oz package selling at $1.07. She asked her daughter to determine the unit price per pound. What were the results?   *Ans.*   8 1-oz packages = $1.26; 10-oz package = $.98; 15-oz package = $.91; 20-oz package = $.86.

2.65   John and Gert Simmons went on a shopping tour seeking the best buys available. After extensive search, they bought the following items at the prices and cash discounts listed: a color TV set listed at $459, with a 15% cash discount; a portable dishwasher listed at $198, with a 10% cash discount; and a clothes dryer listed at $219, with an 11% cash discount. If they paid cash for all items, how much was their discount?   *Ans.* $112.74. (See Problem 2.12.)

2.66   Your brother bought a bicycle, listed at $139.50, for $109.95. Your sister bought a record player, listed at $159.95, for $125. Which one received the higher percent of discount?   *Ans.*   Sister received 21.9%; brother, 21.2%. Sister received 0.7% higher discount.

2.67   Sue, Joan, and Sheila share an apartment and divide the shopping and cooking chores. Yesterday each brought home a loaf of white bread. Sue bought an 18-oz loaf for 45¢; Joan paid 59¢ for a 24-oz loaf; and Sheila paid 55¢ for a 20-oz loaf. (*a*) How much did each loaf cost per pound? (*b*) Which loaf is the best buy?   *Ans.*   (*a*) 18-oz loaf costs 40¢ per pound; the 24-oz loaf costs 39.3¢ per pound; the 20-oz loaf costs 44¢ per pound.   (*b*) The 24-oz loaf is the best buy.

2.68   Bill Gunter collects and redeems all the food coupons he can. Bill's dog food costs are quite high, so when he purchases dog food, he always uses coupons. Today, he purchased a 10-lb bag of dog food, priced at $1.39, for $1.16 because he redeemed a $.23 coupon. What percent of savings did Bill receive?   *Ans.*   16.5%.

2.69   A local hardware store is offering a $12\frac{1}{2}$% discount on all power mowers. You select one that is listed at $798. The one on display has been damaged, so the merchant offers it to you at an additional discount of $16\frac{2}{3}$% of sale price. What would you have to pay for this mower?   *Ans.* $581.87. (See Problem 2.13.)

2.70   You bought the following items at Beta Supply House. A portable sewing machine listed at $309, was reduced by 25%; a color TV set was reduced by $33\frac{1}{3}$% of the $597 list price; and a stereo set was reduced by 23% of the $649 list price. (*a*) How much money did you save? (*b*) What was your percent reduction on the total sale?   *Ans.*   (*a*) $77.75 on the sewing machine; $199.00 on the TV set; $149.27 on the stereo; for a total saving of $426.02. (*b*) 27.4%.

2.71 A local hardware dealer sells all merchandise at a discount of $12\frac{1}{2}\%$ off the list price, plus a $4\frac{1}{2}\%$ discount off the discounted price for paying cash. What percent discount based on list price did your husband receive when he paid cash for merchandise listed at $728?   *Ans.*   16.4%.

2.72 Your home economics instructor brought into class three jars of instant coffee and asked you to determine the unit price per jar. She had the following: a 2-oz jar costing $.87; an 8-oz jar costing $2.79; and a 4-oz jar costing $1.46. What was the unit price per pound?   *Ans.*   2-oz jar, $6.96 unit price per pound; 8-oz jar, $5.58 per pound; 4-oz jar, $5.84 per pound. The 8-oz jar is the best buy.

2.73 Arnie Gold, an avid golfer, was shopping around for a set of golf clubs. He noticed that the Acme Sporting Goods Company had reduced all sets by 27% off the regular price. He went to the Sigma Sporting Goods Store and found that they had reduced all sets by 31% of the regular price. Determine the cost and savings of the following sets of clubs: an Acme set with a price tag of $279; a Sigma set with a price tage of $299.   *Ans.*   The Acme set would cost $203.67; savings, $75.33. The Sigma set would cost $206.31; savings, $92.69. (See Problem 2.20.)

2.74 Your neighbors, the Jettons, were quoted a special price of $8,950 for a swimming pool, including installation. The regular list price of the swimming pool was $9,899. By paying cash, they received an additional $3\frac{1}{2}\%$ discount off the special price. (*a*) What was the cash price of the swimming pool to the Jettons? (*b*) How much less than the regular price was the cash price?   *Ans.*   (*a*) $8,636.75, cash price,   (*b*) $1,262.25 less.

2.75 Mrs. Bonnie Blake works in a department store which allows her a 15% discount on all electrical appliances. She bought a toaster which lists at $13.98; her friend Jane bought a similar one at the list price. How much less did Bonnie pay than Jane?   *Ans.* $2.10. (See Problem 2.9.)

2.76 Mrs. Swan bought an $8\frac{3}{4}$-oz can of apricot halves for $.37. This was a good size for her personal use. She bought a 30-oz can for $.79 to have on hand when she had invited guests. In noticing the different prices, she wanted to figure the unit price per pound of each can. What were her results?   *Ans.*   The unit price per pound of $8\frac{3}{4}$-oz can is 67.7¢; the unit price per pound of the 30-oz can is 42.1¢. (See Problem 2.5.)

2.77 You purchased a new automobile, listed at $5,445, for $4,995 cash. The optional equipment, listed at $785, was sold to you for $675. What percent discount did you receive by paying cash?   *Ans.*   9% cash discount.

2.78 Mrs. Snow saw three different sizes of detergent advertised at her local supermarket. A 9-lb 13-oz box for $3.59; a 20-lb box for $6.49; and a 49-oz box for $1.29. She wanted to purchase the size that had the lowest unit price per ounce. What is the unit price per ounce of each box?   *Ans.*   The 9-lb, 13-oz box costs 2.3¢ per ounce; the 20-lb box costs 2.0¢ per ounce; the 49-oz box costs 2.6¢ per ounce.

2.79 Jake Isaac, your roommate, wants to purchase a good transistor radio for the room. He found one which he likes selling at a cash price of $59.50. On the installment plan it would cost $9.50 down and $11 a month for 5 months. By how much does the installment price exceed the cash price?   *Ans.* $5.00. (See Problem 2.26.)

2.80 Willie Gilson saw a motorcycle for $1,650. His bank said it would lend him $1,750 for 9 months at a discount rate of $7\frac{3}{4}\%$. How much would the discount amount to?   *Ans.* $101.72. (See Problem 2.34.)

2.81 Dania Savings Bank will discount your note for $700 for 6 months at 8%. Pompano Trust Company will lend you $700 on your note for 6 months if you will redeem it for $730 at maturity. Which bank charges the lower interest rate?   *Ans.* Dania Savings Bank charges 8.3%; Pompano Trust Company charges 8.6%. (See Problem 2.39.)

2.82 You borrowed $480 from a small loan company and actually paid back $540. By paying 9 equal monthly payments, what was the amount of each payment and what was the true interest rate?   *Ans.* $60 per monthly payment; interest rate was 30%.

2.83 You borrowed $1,800 for your vacation from the Biscayne Credit Union for 12 months. The equal monthly payments were $159.93. How much interest did you pay? What was the true annual rate?   *Ans.* $119.16 interest; true annual rate = 12.2%. (See Problem 2.53.)

2.84 Mrs. Lenroot negotiated an $1,175 loan from the Florida State Bank for 8 months. The bank discounted the loan and actually gave her $1,105. What was the rate of interest that she was charged on this loan?   *Ans.* 8.93%. (See Problem 2.35.)

2.85 The Best Loan Company offers to make $500 loans, each repayable in 30 equal weekly payments of $18.50. What is the total cost of each loan and the interest rate percent charged?   *Ans.* $55 interest charge; 36.9% interest rate.

2.86 Mrs. Smathers borrowed $5,000 from her company credit union, to be repaid in 36 equal payments of $166.08. Make out a repayment loan schedule for the first three months. Figure 1% interest per month on the unpaid balance. Show the amount of interest paid for each of the first three months.   *Ans.* 1st month, $50; 2nd month, $48.84; 3rd month, $47.67. (See Problem 2.54.)

2.87 Sarah Lee can buy a dining room set for $1,098 cash; or on the installment plan, by paying $16\frac{2}{3}$% additional, with no down payment if she purchases the furniture on the installment plan. If her monthly payments are $42.70, how many months will it take her to pay for it?   *Ans.* 30 months. (See Problem 2.28.)

2.88 Louis Sinatra borrowed $620 from his bank for 3 months. At the end of the three-month period, he paid the bank $631. What was the true rate of interest?   *Ans.* 7%. (See Problem 2.32.)

2.89 The Safe Small Loan Company loaned you $450, which you must pay back in the amount of $480, plus an administrative charge of $6, all payable in 6 equal monthly payments. What was your total carrying charge, and what true rate of interest did you pay?   *Ans.* $36 carrying charge; 27.4% interest rate.

2.90 The Finkels decided to buy an electronic organ for their home. They selected one that could be purchased for $1,495 cash; or if purchased on the installment plans, on either of the following terms: *Plan A*: $495 down and $35 a month for 36 months, or *Plan B*: $295 down and $60 a month for 24 months. (*a*) Which plan would be less costly? (*b*) By how much?   *Ans.* (*a*) Plan A, $1,755; Plan B, $1,735. (*b*) $20 less on Plan B. (See Problem 2.29.)

2.91 Mark Claremont decided to borrow money from his credit union to be used as a down payment on a summer camp. The loan was for $3,900, to be paid back in 36 equal payments of $129.54 each. How much interest did he pay on the loan?   *Ans.* $763.44. (See Problem 2.52.)

2.92 Mr. and Mrs. Bruno purchased a living room suite for their newly married daughter. The suite sold for $2,495 cash, or terms: $495 down and 20 monthly payments of $125. (*a*) How much interest did they pay? (*b*) What was the rate of interest?   *Ans.* (*a*) $500 interest, (*b*) 28.6% rate of interest. (See Problem 2.48.)

2.93 Mary Kessler, a high school art teacher, borrowed $950 from the bank to be used in paying her summer school tuition and other expenses. She will pay back $985 at the end of 6 months. What rate of interest was she charged?   *Ans.*   7.37%.

2.94 A tape recorder and AM-FM radio combination may be purchased for $399 cash; or on the installment plan, by paying $39 down and $33 a month for 10 months. Find the true rate of interest if purchased on the installment plan.   *Ans.*   21.8%. (See Problem 2.30.)

2.95 Mr. Bigelow, a custodian in your office building, went to the bank and borrowed $1,200 at $7\frac{1}{2}$% interest. He was told that he would pay $1,230 back. But he forgot the term of the loan. He wanted you to determine in how many months he would have to repay the loan. What was your response?   *Ans.*   4 months.

2.96 Mrs. Borsky purchased a new car listed at $5,400. The dealer arranged the following terms for her: $900 down, the balance to be paid in 24 months at an interest rate of $8\frac{1}{2}$%. (*a*) How much are Mrs. Borsky's monthly payments? (*b*) What is the true annual rate of interest?   *Ans.*   (*a*) $219.38 per month, (*b*) 16.3% annual rate of interest. (See Problem 2.46.)

2.97 Max Gompers paid the credit union $122.40 a month for 24 months in repayment of a $2,600 loan that he used to purchase a piano. (*a*) How much interest did Max pay? (*b*) What was the true annual rate of interest?   *Ans.*   (*a*) $337.60 interest, (*b*) 12.5% true annual rate of interest.

2.98 A power lawn mower can be purchased for $389 cash. If bought on the installment plan, a $39 down payment and $33 monthly payments must be made for 12 months. How much more than the cash price would the mower cost if purchased on the time payment plan? What is the true interest rate?   *Ans.* $46 more; interest rate is 24.2%.

2.99 The Hampton Automobile Agency was selling all automobiles at list price less 12%. In addition, the agency was giving each purchaser an additional $200 cash bonus on each purchase. You bought a car listed at $4,998. What was the actual cost of this car to you? You paid what percent of the list price?   *Ans.* $4,198.24 cost to you; 84% of list price.

2.100 When you bought your car from the Tropics Auto Company, you received the following invoice:

List price	$5,700
Plus optional equipment	700
Car's price	6,400
Less trade-in on your car	2,200
Amount due	4,200
Plus interest for 30 months at 9%	945
Total unpaid amount	$5,145

30 monthly payments; each, $171.50.

What was the true annual interest rate?   *Ans.*   17.4%, annual rate. (See Problem 2.47.)

2.101 The Adams bought a used motor home for $5,600. He intended to use the motor home on a summer vacation trip to Alaska. They borrowed the money from the Leonia Credit Union, to be paid back in 36 equal monthly payments of $186.01. The rate of interest was 1% per month on the unpaid balance. After 6 payments, the Adams wanted to know their unpaid balance. Make a repayment loan schedule that will show them how much was still due on the loan after the 6 payments.   *Ans.* $4,800.18 unpaid balance.

2.102 Mrs. Trimble was shopping for a refrigerator to replace her old one. She was hoping to obtain one at a bargain price at a clearance sale. She decided on one that sells for $349.50 cash; or on the installment plan, for $49.50 down and $9.50 per week for 35 weeks. (*a*) How much more is the installment price? (*b*) What is the true interest rate?   *Ans.*   (*a*) $32.50 more, (*b*) 31.3%. (See Problem 2.31.)

2.103 Rufus Jacobs borrowed $500 from the Best Loan Agency. The loan was to be repaid in 8 monthly payments of $70 each. His friend Abie Jones borrowed a similar amount from the Smiling Loan Company, to be repaid in 30 weekly payments of $19 each. Each thought they had received the better deal. (*a*) What are the interest charges of each company? (*b*) By how much is one lower than the other?   *Ans.*   (*a*) Rufus' company charges 32% interest; Abie's company charges 47% interest. (*b*) Rufus' company is lower by 15%.

2.104 Walter Monroe needed money quickly to pay his wife's hospital bill. He negotiated a $960 loan with a loan company, agreeing to repay the loan by making $116 monthly payments for 9 months. (*a*) How much interest did Walter pay? (*b*) What was the true interest rate? *Ans.*   (*a*) He paid $84 interest, (*b*) 21% true rate of interest. (See Problem 2.32.)

2.105 The Bosticks wanted to borrow $650 to build a patio in back of their house. They negotiated a loan in that amount at the local savings and loan association. The loan was to be paid back in 8 months at an $8\frac{1}{4}$% interest rate. How much must they pay back?   *Ans.* $685.75. (See Problem 2.33.)

Chapter 3

Banking:
Checking, Borrowing and Saving

The modern commercial bank provides a variety of services to consumers and businesses. For consumers, the most widely used services include checking accounts, savings accounts and loan services. In the latter two, it is important to understand the concept of interest computation, since this represents either additional income or expense.

3.1 CHECKING ACCOUNTS

The most commonly used banking service is the checking account. A check is a written order directing the bank to pay a designated payee a specific amount of money. In writing checks, you use the check itself and a check stub or register, which allows you to maintain a current record of all transactions.

A deposit slip is used when you deposit checks or cash to your account.

You, as a depositor, generally receive a monthly bank statement which shows your transactions and bank balance as of a given date. The statement reflects deposits, canceled checks, collections, charges, and other transactions which affect your account during that period of time.

EXAMPLE 1

You have a balance of $487.50 in your checking account. Fill in the stubs for the following transactions:

(a) 21 June, check #84 to cash, $50.00.

(b) 23 June, check #85 to Dr. Brown, $25.00.

(c) 27 June, check #86 to Jack's Garage, $154.75.

(d) 30 June, deposit of $750.00 and check #87 to Federal Savings & Loan Co., $185.00.

See Fig. 3-1a, b, c and d. Your checkbook balance on 30 June is $822.75.

EXAMPLE 2

You have entered into the following transactions during the month of April.

(a) 9th, check #42 to John Doe, $9.50.

(b) 12th, check #43 to Al's Service Station, $18.98.

(c) 15th, check #44 to Betty's Beauty Salon, $15.00.

(d) 18th, deposit to bank, $498.50.

(e) 20th, check #45 to Electric Utility Co., $87.43.

The check register in Fig. 3-2 shows these transactions and your balance on April 20. Balance brought forward on April 9, $137.96; balance on April 20, $505.55.

(a)

No. 84 $50.00
June 21 19—
to Cash
for Misc.

	DOLLARS	CENTS
BAL. BRO'T FOR'D.	487	50
AM'T DEPOSITED		
,, ,, ,,		
,, ,, ,,		
TOTAL		
AM'T THIS CHECK	50	00
BAL CARD FOR'D	437	50

(b)

No. 85 $25.00
June 23 19—
to Dr. Brown
for visit

	DOLLARS	CENTS
BAL. BRO'T FOR'D.	437	50
AM'T DEPOSITED		
,, ,, ,,		
,, ,, ,,		
TOTAL		
AM'T THIS CHECK	25	00
BAL CARD FOR'D	412	50

(c)

No. 86 $154.75
June 27 19—
to Jack's Garage
for repairs

	DOLLARS	CENTS
BAL. BRO'T FOR'D.	412	50
AM'T DEPOSITED		
,, ,, ,,		
,, ,, ,,		
TOTAL		
AM'T THIS CHECK	154	75
BAL CARD FOR'D	257	75

(d)

No. 87 $185.00
June 30 19—
to Fed. S+L
for mortgage

	DOLLARS	CENTS
BAL. BRO'T FOR'D	257	75
AM'T DEPOSITED	750	00
,, ,, ,,		
,, ,, ,,		
TOTAL	1007	75
AM'T THIS CHECK	185	00
BAL CARD FOR'D	822	75

Fig. 3-1

BE SURE TO DEDUCT ANY PER CHECK CHARGES OR MAINTENANCE CHARGES THAT MAY APPLY

DATE	CHECK NUMBER	CHECKS ISSUED TO OR DEPOSIT RECEIVED FROM	AMOUNT OF DEPOSIT	√	AMOUNT OF CHECK	BALANCE 137 96	
Apr 9	42	John Doe			9 50	128	46
Apr 12	43	Al's Service Station			18 98	109	48
Apr 15	44	Betty's Beauty Salon			15 00	94	98
Apr 18		Deposit	498 50			592	48
Apr 20	45	Electric Utility Co.			87 43	505	55

Fig. 3-2

3.2   RECONCILING YOUR CHECKING ACCOUNT

Each month when the bank sends you a statement showing your bank balance, you should compare it with your checkbook balance. The two should balance, and your checkbook balance should indicate the exact amount of money which you actually have on deposit and which is subject to withdrawal.

To reconcile bank balance:

1. Deduct outstanding checks (checks not returned).
2. Add deposits in transit (not yet received at bank).

Checkbook Balance:

1. Deduct service charge.
2. Deduct other charges.
3. Add collections made by the bank.

Upon receiving the bank statement, review each entry and check off, on the proper stub, each returned check. Add or subtract necessary items as indicated above.

EXAMPLE 3

Your bank statement shows a balance of $348.50 on June 30, 19__. Your checkbook balance as of June 30, 19__, is $275.25. Check #49 for $45.20 and check #51 for $29.30 are not enclosed with your statement. The bank has deducted a service charge (s.c.) of $1.25. Reconcile your statement.

June 30, 19__			June 30, 19__	
Bank balance		$348.50	Checkbook balance	$275.25
Less outstanding checks:			Less service charge:	1.25
#49	$45.20			
#51	29.30	74.50		
Adjusted bank balance		$274.00	Adjusted checkbook balance	$274.00

EXAMPLE 4

Your bank statement shows a balance of $398.35 on October 31, 19__. Your check stub balance as of October 31, 19__ is $453.50. The following checks are not included in your statement:

#114	$ 20.98
#116	48.37
#119	7.25
#122	175.00

1. The statement showed a service charge of $1.75.
2. The bank charged $5.00 for printing of checks.
3. Your check for $500.00 mailed to the bank on October 30 is not shown on the statement.
4. The bank collected a payment of $200 for you.
Statements 1, 2, and 4: These items have not been recorded on check stub.
Statement 3: This item does not appear on bank statement.

	October 31, 19__			October 31, 19__	
Bank balance		$398.35	Check stub balance		$453.50
Less outstanding checks:			Less charges:		
#114	$ 20.98		Service charge,	$1.75	
#116	48.37		Printing checks,	5.00	6.75
#119	7.25				
#122	175.00	251.60			$446.75
		$146.75	Add collection		200.00
Add deposit in transit		500.00			
Adjusted bank balance		$646.75	Adjusted check stub balance		$646.75

INTEREST COMPUTATIONS FOR BORROWING AND SAVING

3.3 FINDING SIMPLE INTEREST—FORMULA: $I = P \times R \times T$

Simple interest is money earned only on the principal over the duration of a loan. Ordinary or banker's interest is calculated on a 360-day year. Exact or accurate interest, used by the Federal Government, is calculated on 365 days, or 366 days in a leap year. $I = P \times R \times T$ where I = interest, P = principal, R = rate, T = time.

EXAMPLE 5

The interest you owe the bank on a loan of $900 for 72 days at 9% (ordinary interest) is computed as follows:

$$I = \$900 \times \frac{9}{100} \times \frac{72}{360} = \$16.20$$

EXAMPLE 6

The interest on a bank loan of $1,200 for 90 days at $7\frac{1}{2}$% is computed as follows:

$$I = \$1,200 \times 0.075 \times \frac{90}{360} = \$22.50$$

($7\frac{1}{2}$% may be changed to 15/200.)

EXAMPLE 7

The exact (accurate) interest you would pay on a $950 loan for 75 days at 8% is computed as follows (using 365 days in a year):

$$I = \$950 \times 0.08 \times \frac{75}{365} = \$950 \times 0.08 \times \frac{15}{73} = \frac{\$1,140}{73} = \$15.616, \text{ or } \$15.62$$

3.4 CALCULATING SIMPLE INTEREST BY THE 6%, 60-DAY METHOD (SHORT METHOD)

To find the interest on any amount for 60 days at 6% interest, move the decimal point in the principal two places to the left. This is demonstrated by multiplying the rate, 6%, by the time, 60 days: 6/100 × 60/360 = 1/100. The resulting fraction will always be 1/100.

Therefore, no matter what the principal of the debt may be, it must be multiplied by 1/100. The quickest way to do this is to move the decimal point in the principal two places to the left. For example, if the principal of a loan amounts to $175.00, the interest at 6% for 60 days is $1.75.

EXAMPLE 8

Using the short method, the interest on a $550 loan for 60 days at 6% is $5.50.

EXAMPLE 9

The interest on a bank loan of $775 for 72 days at 5% is computed as follows:

$$\begin{array}{ll} \$7.75 = & 60 \text{ days' interest at } 6\% \text{ on } \$775 \\ +1.55 = & 12 \text{ days' interest } (1/5 \text{ of } 60) \\ \hline \$9.30 = & 72 \text{ days' interest at } 6\% \\ -1.55 = & 72 \text{ days' interest at } 1\% \ (1/6 \text{ of } 6\%) \\ \hline \$7.75 = & 72 \text{ days' interest at } 5\% \text{ on } \$775 \end{array}$$

EXAMPLE 10

The interest on a loan of $1,650 for 4 days at 9% is computed as follows:

$$\$16.50 = 60 \text{ days' interest at } 6\% \text{ on } \$1,650$$

$$\begin{array}{ll} \$1.10 = & 4 \text{ days' interest } (1/15 \text{ of } 60) \text{ at } 6\% \\ +0.55 = & 4 \text{ days' interest at } 3\% \ (\tfrac{1}{2} \text{ of } 6\%) \\ \hline \$1.65 = & 4 \text{ days' interest at } 9\% \end{array}$$

3.5 FINDING SIMPLE INTEREST—INTEREST TABLES

Table 1 enables us to find simple interest quickly. The base unit is $1.00. Read down the time column for the number of days, then read across to the column under the stated interest rate. Multiply this factor by the amount of money involved. The result is the accrued interest.

EXAMPLE 11

To find the interest on $400 at $6\tfrac{1}{2}$% for 3 months, in the time column of Table 1, read down to 3 months. Then read across to the $6\tfrac{1}{2}$% column: the number, or factor, is 0.016250. Multiply 0.016250 by $400 to obtain the interest, which is $6.500000, or $6.50.

EXAMPLE 12

To find the interest on $750 at 7% for 2 months and 18 days: obtain the factor for 2 months at 7% (0.011667) and the factor for 18 days at 7% (0.003500). Add them together and you have $0.015167. Multiply: 0.015167 × $750 = $11.37525, or $11.38 interest.

EXAMPLE 13

You had $1,000 on deposit in the bank. After 6 months, you received a notice showing that you now had $1,030. The rate of interest is computed as follows: dividing $30 by $1,000 you get 0.030000. This is the amount of interest on $1.00 for 6 months. Read down the time column of Table 1 to 6 months and across to 0.030000 in the % column. You then read up to the column heading. The interest rate is 6%.

Table 1.   Interest Table: Unit $ 1.00, Based on 360 Days

Time	6%	$6\frac{1}{2}$%	7%	Time	6%	$6\frac{1}{2}$%	7%
1 day	0.000167	0.000181	0.000194	21 days	0.003500	0.003792	0.004083
2 days	0.000333	0.000361	0.000389	22 ″	0.003667	0.003972	0.004278
3 ″	0.000500	0.000542	0.000583	23 ″	0.003833	0.004153	0.004472
4 ″	0.000667	0.000722	0.000778	24 ″	0.004000	0.004333	0.004667
5 ″	0.000833	0.000903	0.000972	25 ″	0.004167	0.004514	0.004861
6 ″	0.001000	0.001083	0.001167	26 ″	0.004333	0.004694	0.005056
7 ″	0.001167	0.001083	0.001361	27 ″	0.004500	0.004875	0.005250
8 ″	0.001333	0.001444	0.001556	28 ″	0.004667	0.005056	0.005444
9 ″	0.001500	0.001625	0.001750	29 ″	0.004833	0.005236	0.005639
10 ″	0.001667	0.001806	0.001944	30 ″	0.005000	0.005417	0.005833
11 ″	0.001833	0.001986	0.002139	2 mos.	0.010000	0.010833	0.011667
12 ″	0.002000	0.002167	0.002333	3 ″	0.015000	0.016250	0.017500
13 ″	0.002167	0.002347	0.002520	4 ″	0.020000	0.021667	0.023333
14 ″	0.002333	0.002528	0.002722	5 ″	0.025000	0.027083	0.029160
15 ″	0.002500	0.002708	0.002917	6 ″	0.030000	0.032500	0.035000
16 ″	0.002667	0.002889	0.003111	7 ″	0.035000	0.037917	0.040833
17 ″	0.002833	0.003069	0.003306	8 ″	0.040000	0.043333	0.046667
18 ″	0.003000	0.003250	0.003500	9 ″	0.045000	0.048750	0.052500
19 ″	0.003167	0.003431	0.003694	10 ″	0.050000	0.054167	0.058333
20 ″	0.003333	0.003611	0.003889	11 ″	0.055000	0.059583	0.064167
				12 ″	0.060000	0.065000	0.070000

3.6 COMPOUND INTEREST TABLES

Compound interest is found by adding the interest for one period to the principal and then finding the interest for the next period.   (The principal plus the interest for the first period is now the new principal.)   The interest on various sums of money invested for long periods of time can be easily found by using a compound interest table (see Table 2).

Read down the period column to the desired period, then across to the figure in the desired interest column.   This figure represents the value of $1 at the desired interest rate for a specified period.

EXAMPLE 14

To find the compound amount of $800 at $5\frac{1}{2}$% for 10 periods, find the factor 1.7081 in Table 2 and multiply by $800.

EXAMPLE 15 (See Table 2.)

You deposited $1,000 at $5\frac{1}{2}$% interest several years ago and it has now grown to $1,534.70.   To find out how many periods it has been on deposit read down the $5\frac{1}{2}$% column to the factor 1.5347, then across to the left to find the number of periods: 8.

If your interest is compounded other than annually, multiply the years by the frequency of compounding and divide the interest rate by the frequency.   This gives you the periods and interest rate required to use Table 2.

Table 2. Interest Table: Amount of $1, Compounded Annually

Periods	4%	5%	5½%	6%
1	1.0400	1.0500	1.0550	1.0600
2	1.0810	1.1025	1.1130	1.1230
3	1.1249	1.1576	1.1742	1.1910
4	1.1699	1.2155	1.2388	1.2625
5	1.2167	1.2763	1.3070	1.3382
6	1.2653	1.3401	1.3788	1.4185
7	1.3159	1.4071	1.4547	1.5036
8	1.3686	1.4775	1.5347	1.5938
9	1.4233	1.5513	1.6191	1.6895
10	1.4802	1.6289	1.7081	1.7908
11	1.5395	1.7103	1.8021	1.8983
12	1.6010	1.7959	1.9012	2.0122
13	1.6651	1.8856	2.0058	2.1329
14	1.7317	1.9799	2.1161	2.2609
15	1.8009	2.0789	2.2325	2.3966
16	1.8730	2.1829	2.3553	2.5404
17	1.9479	2.2920	2.4848	2.6928
18	2.0258	2.4066	2.6215	2.8543
19	2.1068	2.5270	2.7656	3.0256
20	2.1911	2.6533	2.9178	3.2071
21	2.2788	2.7860	3.0782	3.3996
22	2.3699	2.9253	3.2475	3.6035
23	2.4647	3.0715	3.4262	3.8197
24	2.5633	3.2251	3.6146	4.0489
25	2.6658	3.3864	3.8134	4.2919

EXAMPLE 16 (See Table 2.)

You deposited $800 at 8% interest, compounded semiannually, 5 years ago. To find out the amount of interest compounded multiply 5 years by 2 = 10 periods. 8% ÷ 2 = 4%. 10 periods @ 4% = 1.4802. 1.4802 × $800 = $1,184.16 compounded amount.

$$\$1,184.16 - \$800 = \$384.16 \text{ compounded interest}$$

Bankers and other lenders often use time tables in conjunction with interest tables when interest due is based on the number of days a loan will be outstanding. To determine the number of days between any two dates, find the numbers corresponding to the dates shown in Table 3 and subtract.

Each full year is figured on the basis of 365 days. If, however, the period includes the 29th of February of a leap year, add 1 to the total number of days.

EXAMPLE 17 (See Table 3.)

To find the exact number of days from May 3, 1977, to August 29, 1977, compute as follows. May 3 is the 123d day. August 29 is the 241st day.

$$241 - 123 = 118 \text{ days}$$

Table 3.   Time Table

Day of Month	Jan	Feb	Mar	Apr	May	Jun	Jul	Aug	Sep	Oct	Nov	Dec
1	1	32	60	91	121	152	182	213	244	274	305	335
2	2	33	61	92	122	153	183	214	245	275	306	336
3	3	34	62	93	123	154	184	215	246	276	307	337
4	4	35	63	94	124	155	185	216	247	277	308	338
5	5	36	64	95	125	156	186	217	248	278	309	339
6	6	37	65	96	126	157	187	218	249	279	310	340
7	7	38	66	97	127	158	188	219	250	280	311	341
8	8	39	67	98	128	159	189	220	251	281	312	342
9	9	40	68	99	129	160	190	221	252	282	313	343
10	10	41	69	100	130	161	191	222	253	283	314	344
11	11	42	70	101	131	162	192	223	254	284	315	345
12	12	43	71	102	132	163	193	224	255	285	316	346
13	13	44	72	103	133	164	194	225	256	286	317	347
14	14	45	73	104	134	165	195	226	257	287	318	348
15	15	46	74	105	135	166	196	227	258	288	319	349
16	16	47	75	106	136	167	197	228	259	289	320	350
17	17	48	76	107	137	168	198	229	260	290	321	351
18	18	49	77	108	138	169	199	230	261	291	322	352
19	19	50	78	109	139	170	200	231	262	292	323	353
20	20	51	79	110	140	171	201	232	263	293	324	354
21	21	52	80	111	141	172	202	233	264	294	325	355
22	22	53	81	112	142	173	203	234	265	295	326	356
23	23	54	82	113	143	174	204	235	266	296	327	357
24	24	55	83	114	144	175	205	236	267	297	328	358
25	25	56	84	115	145	176	206	237	268	298	329	359
26	26	57	85	116	146	177	207	238	269	299	330	360
27	27	58	86	117	147	178	208	239	270	300	331	361
28	28	59	87	118	148	179	209	240	271	301	332	362
29	29		88	.119	149	180	210	241	272	302	333	363
30	30		89	120	150	181	211	242	273	303	334	364
31	31		90		151		212	243		304		365

EXAMPLE 18 (See Table 3.)

To find the exact number of days from November 27, 1977, to February 9, 1978, compute as follows. November 27th is the 331st day. $365 - 331 = 34$, the number of days remaining in year. February 9th is the 40th day.

$$34 + 40 = 74 \text{ days}$$

BORROWING WITH NOTES

3.7 PROMISSORY NOTES

A promissory note (see Fig. 3-3) is a written promise to pay a given amount of money at a designated time in the future. Noninterest-bearing notes require no interest. Interest-bearing notes state a specific rate of interest.

```
$ 750 00/100              Groveton, Miss.        June 25    19 77

     Sixty days                    after date  I  promise to pay to

the order of    Mary Macon

     Seven Hundred Fifty and 00/100 xxxxxxxxxxxxxxxxxxxxxxxxx Dollars

at   Merchants Bank

Value received

No.   84   Due  August 24, 1977        John J. Doe
AO 41
```

Fig. 3-3

EXAMPLE 19 (See Table 3.)

I, John J. Doe, promise to pay Mary Macon $750, 60 days after June 25, 1977. The date the full amount is due on is August 25, 1977. (June 25th is the 176th day; 176 + 60 = 236; the 236th day is August 24, 1977.)

3.8 DISCOUNTING A NOTE

People frequently "sell" or discount a note at a bank prior to its maturity date. This allows them to receive and use the money due, less the discounted amount, before the note is due.

EXAMPLE 20 (See Table 3.)

Refer to the promissory note in Fig. 3-4.

(a) To find the due date and figure the amount of interest, using a 360-day year, compute as follows. March 5th is the 64th day. 64 + 80 = 144. May 24th is the 144th day (due date).

$$I = P \times R \times T$$

$$I = \$400 \times 0.065 \times \frac{80}{360} = \$5.777, \text{ or } \$5.78 \text{ interest}$$

```
$ 400 00/100            Rodeo, Wyoming       March 5    19 77

   Eighty days                   after date  I  promise to pay to

the order of    Allen Johns

   Four Hundred and 00/100 xxxxxxxxxxxxxxxxxxxxxxxxxxxxxxxx Dollars

at   Cattleman's Bank

Value received  with 6½% interest

No.  112   Due  May 24, 1977        William Grow
AO 41
```

Fig. 3-4

(b) To figure the amount of interest, using a 365-day year, compute as follows.

$$I = P \times R \times T$$

$$I - \$400 \times 0.065 \times \frac{80}{365} = \frac{\$2,080}{365} = \$5.698, \text{ or } \$5.70$$

(c) The difference between (a) and (b) is $.08, using 365 days.

EXAMPLE 21 (See Table 3.)

Nancy Brown gave you her note promising to pay you $200, 60 days after June 20, 1978, without interest. On July 5, 1978, you asked the bank to discount the note. They agreed to do so at a discount rate of 8%. Let us say you want to determine   (a) the due date of note,   (b) the term of discount (number of days), and   (c) how much you would receive on July 5th.

(a) June 20th is the 171st day.   171 + 60 = 231.   Therefore, August 19 is the due date.

(b) July 5th is the 186th day.   231 − 186 = 45 days in the discount period.

(c) $D = P \times R \times T$: $D = \$200 \times 0.08 \times 45/360 = \$2.00$.   You receive $198.

EXAMPLE 22

Al Jelinski promised to pay you $1,200, 90 days after June 28, 1978, without interest.   On August 7, 1978, you asked the bank to discount the note at their rate of $8\frac{1}{2}\%$.   Let us say you want to determine the exact interest by using a 365-day year and want to find   (a) the due date of note,   (b) the term of discount, and   (c) how much you would receive on August 7.

(a) June 28th is the 179th day.   179 + 90 = 269.   September 26 is the due date.

(b) August 7th is the 219th day.   269 − 219 = 50 days in discount period.

(c) $D = P \times R \times T$: $D = \$1,200 \times 0.085 \times 50/365 = \$5,100/365 = \$13.97$ discount.

$$\$1,200 - \$13.97 = \$1,186.03 \text{ (proceeds) amount received}$$

EXAMPLE 23 (See Table 3.)

You received a promissory note from Hilda Cohane for merchandise sold to her.   The note, for $750 and bearing interest at $7\frac{1}{2}\%$, was due 90 days after August 15, 1978.   On September 29, 1978, you asked the bank to discount this note.   Their discount rate is $8\frac{1}{2}\%$.   Let us say you want to determine   (a) the due date,   (b) the maturity value,   (c) the term (days) of discount,   (d) the amount of discount based on a 360-day year,   (e) the amount (proceeds) you received on September 29, and   (f) the amount of discount based on a 365-day year and the proceeds of the note.

(a) August 15th is the 227th day.   227 + 90 = 317.   The due date is November 13.

(b) $I = P \times R \times T$: $I = \$750 \times 0.075 \times 90/360 = \$14.06$.

$$\$750 + \$14.06 = \$764.06 \text{ maturity value}$$

(c) September 29th is the 272d day.

$$317 - 272 = 45 \text{ days, the term of discount}$$

(d) $D = P \times R \times T$:

$$D = \$764.06 \times 0.085 \times \frac{45}{360} = \$8.12 \text{ discount}$$

(e) $764.06 − $8.12 = $755.94 amount received (proceeds).

(f) $D = P \times R \times T$: $D = \$764.06 \times 0.085 \times 45/365 = \$2,922.53/365 = \$8.006$, or $8.01 discount.

$$\$764.06 - \$8.01 = \$756.05 \text{ amount received (proceeds)}$$

$$\$756.05 - \$755.94 = \$.11 \text{ increased amount received by using a 365-day year}$$

Solved Problems

3.1   Your check stub balance on March 31 was $582.50.   Fill in your check stubs for the following transactions.

(*a*) April 3, check #38 to cash, $75.

(*b*) April 7, check #39 to telephone company, $27.98.

(*c*) April 12, check #40 to Best Oil Company, $74.29.

(*d*) April 14, check #41 to Don's Market, $89.49.

(*e*) April 16, deposit of $475.

(*f*) April 19, check #42 to mortgage company, $225.00.

What is your check stub balance on April 20?

    Balance: $565.74.   (See Fig. 3-5.)

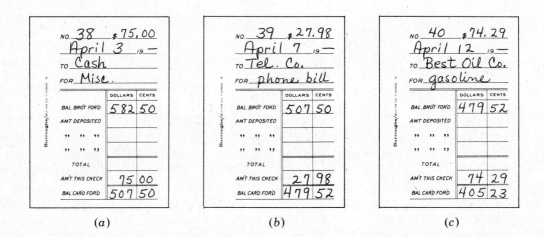

(a)   (b)   (c)

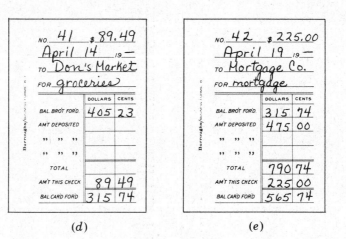

(d)   (e)

Fig. 3-5

3.2   Marcia LaRue entered into the following transactions during the month of November (see Fig. 3-6).

(a) 12th, check #86 to beauty shop, $18.00.

(b) 14th, check #87 to Electric Company, $69.98.

(c) 17th, deposit of $495.

(d) 19th, check #88 to Bill's Garage, $98.50.

(e) 26th, check #89 to supermarket, $116.47.

Complete the check register for these transactions and show your balance on November 26.   Balance brought forward November 10, $118.63.

BE SURE TO DEDUCT ANY PER CHECK CHARGES OR MAINTENANCE CHARGES THAT MAY APPLY

DATE	CHECK NUMBER	CHECKS ISSUED TO OR DEPOSIT RECEIVED FROM	AMOUNT OF DEPOSIT	✓	AMOUNT OF CHECK	BALANCE 118 63
Nov 12	86	Beauty Shop			18 00	100 63
Nov 14	87	Electric Co.			69 98	30 65
Nov 17		Deposit	495 00			525 65
Nov 19	88	Bill's Garage			98 50	427 15
Nov 26	89	Supermarket			116 47	310 68

Fig. 3-6

(See Example 2.)

3.3   Your bank statement shows a balance of $238.79 on July 31.   Your check stub balance is $94.18 on July 31.   Checks #83 for $86.49 and #85 for $59.72 are not enclosed with your statement.   The bank has deducted a service charge of $1.60.   Reconcile your bank statement.

Bank Balance, July 31		$238.79	Checkbook balance		$94.18
Less outstanding checks:			Less service charge:		1.60
#83	$86.49				
#85	59.72	146.21			
Adjusted bank balance		$ 92.58	Adjusted checkbook balance		$92.58

(See Example 3.)

3.4   Your brother asked you to reconcile his bank statement.   The bank statement shows a balance of $219.88 on March 31.   His check register shows a balance of $618.55 on March 31.   The following checks are not included in his statement: #32, $19.75; #35, $87.49; and #37, $51.84.   The statement showed a service charge of $1.75.   The bank charged $6.00 for the printing of checks.   Your brother mailed a check for $800 to the bank on March 30 to be deposited to his account but the deposit was not shown on the statement.   The bank collected a note for $250 for your brother and credited his bank account with it.

Bank Balance, March 31	$219.88	Check register balance, March 31	$618.55

Less outstanding checks		Less service charge $1.75
#32 $19.75		Printing of checks 6.00
#35 $87.49		
#37 $51.84	159.08	

Bank Balance, March 31 $219.88   Check register balance, March 31 $618.55

Less outstanding checks   Less service charge $1.75
    #32 $19.75   Printing of checks   6.00   7.75
    #35 $87.49   610.80
    #37 $51.84   159.08

                                    60.80
Add deposit in transit   800.00   Add collection of note   250.00

Adjusted bank balance $860.80   Adjusted total $860.80

(See Example 4.)

3.5 Ms. Hattie Cook borrowed $450 on her note from the bank for 60 days. If the rate of interest on the loan was $8\frac{1}{2}\%$, how much interest did Cook owe the bank on the maturity date of the note?

$$I = P \times R \times T$$

$$I = \$450 \times 0.085 \times \frac{60}{360} = \$6.375, \text{ or } \$6.38 \text{ interest}$$

(See Example 5.)

3.6 Cy Whitmore needed a short-term loan to buy feed for his chickens.   He expected to be able to repay the loan in 70 days.   If Cy borrowed $475 at $7\frac{3}{4}\%$ interest, how much would he have to repay the bank?

$$I = P \times R \times T$$

$$I = \$475 \times 0.0775 \times \frac{70}{360} = \$7.157, \text{ or } \$7.16 \text{ interest}$$

$$\$475 + \$7.16 = \$482.16 \text{ payment}$$

(See Example 6.)

3.7 Chester Fortuna, who operates a local appliance repair shop, borrowed $625 on his note to purchase some new electronic test equipment.   How much was the interest charge if a 365-day year was used in computing the interest on Chester's $625 loan for 45 days at $8\frac{1}{2}\%$?

$$I = P \times R \times T$$

$$I = \$625 \times 0.085 \times \frac{45}{365} = \$6.549, \text{ or } \$6.55 \text{ interest}$$

(See Example 7.)

3.8 Patti Lansdale needed $500 to get through the current semester at school. Her parents would not send her any more money for 45 days. Patti borrowed $500 on her note from the university bank. She repaid the bank 45 days later by redeeming her note for $505. What rate of interest did she pay?

$$I = P \times R \times T$$

$$\$5 = \$500 \times R \times \frac{45}{360} = \$62.50R$$

$$R = \$5 \div \$62.50 = 0.08, \text{ or } 8\%$$

3.9 Andrew Berne paid $12 interest on a $7\frac{1}{2}\%$ 48-day loan, which he needed to purchase some special tools for his plumbing shop. How much was the loan?

$$I = P \times R \times T$$

$$\$12 = P \times 0.075 \times \frac{48}{360} = 0.01P$$

$$P = \$12 \div 0.01 = \$1,200, \text{ amount of loan}$$

3.10 Wilson McGuire, a fellow employee at the local paint factory, asked you to determine how much interest he would be charged on a $488 loan for 90 days at 6%. (Use the short method.)

$$\$4.88 = 60 \text{ days' interest at } 6\% \text{ on } \$488$$
$$\underline{2.44} = 30 \text{ days' interest } (\tfrac{1}{2} \text{ of } 60 \text{ days, or } \tfrac{1}{2} \text{ of } \$4.88)$$
$$\$7.32 = 90 \text{ days' interest at } 6\% \text{ on } \$488$$

3.11 Marilyn Hoople borrowed a sum of money from her bank for 72 days at 5%. Due to recent illness, Marilyn had forgotten the amount of the loan, remembering only that the interest charge was $3.50. What was the amount of the loan?

$$I = P \times R \times T$$

$$\$3.50 = P \times 0.05 \times \frac{72}{360} = 0.01P$$

$$P = \$3.50 \div 0.01 = \$350 \text{ amount of loan}$$

3.12 Phyliss Randall was being interviewed for a position at a local bank. While discussing simple interest, the interviewer gave Phyliss a simple interest table and asked her to find the amount of simple interest on $800 for 2 months at $6\frac{1}{2}\%$. What was the amount? (Use Table 1.)

$$0.010833 \times \$800 = \$8.66640, \text{ or } \$8.67 \text{ interest}$$

(See Example 11.)

3.13 Ike Grakow, a teenager, worked during the summer at various odd jobs and earned $595. He put all his earnings in the bank at 6% interest. After 3 months and 16 days, he withdrew it all for Christmas gifts. How much interest did Ike receive?

Factor for 3 months = 0.015000; factor for 16 days = 0.002667.

0.015000 + 0.002667 = 0.017667   0.017667 × $595 = $10.511, or $10.51 interest

(See Example 12.)

3.14 You had $2,000 on deposit in the bank. At the end of one year, your savings account amounted to $2,130. What rate of interest did you receive?

$2,130 − $2,000 = $130 interest on $2,000 for one year. 1% of $2,000 for 1 year = $20 interest. $130 ÷ $20 = $6\frac{1}{2}$% rate of interest received on $2,000 in one year. (See Example 13.)

3.15 Your daughter deposited $300 in the bank at $5\frac{1}{2}$% interest compounded annually. If she made neither withdrawals nor deposits to the account for 6 years, (a) how much did her deposit grow to, and (b) how much did her initial deposit earn?

(a) $300 × 1.3788 = $413.64 amount on deposit after 6 years.

(b) $413.64 − $300 = $113.64 compounded interest earnings. (See Example 14 and Table 2.)

3.16 You made a deposit of $2,000 in a savings account. At 6% interest compounded annually, the account has now grown to $3,581.60. For how many years has it been invested?

$3,581.60 ÷ $2,000 = 1.7908. Read down 6% column to this factor, then across to period column. Answer is 10 years. (See Example 15.)

3.17 Millie Fletcher made a deposit in her home town bank at 5% interest compounded annually. She moved away and forgot about the account. Millie was notified by the bank that her initial deposit made 23 years ago has now grown to $6,143.00. How much was her original deposit?

$1 deposited 23 years ago at 5% interest, compounded annually, now amounts to $3.0715. $6,143.00 ÷ $3.0715 = $2,000 original deposit.

3.18 Jack Sanders bought a $1,500 certificate of deposit 6 years ago. The certificate paid 8% interest compounded semiannually. (a) If Jack had not drawn any of the interest earnings, how much is the compounded amount today? (b) Compound interest?

(a) $1,500 × 1.6010 = $2,401.50 compounded amount.

(b) $2,401.50 − $1,500 = $901.50 compound interest. (See Example 16.)

3.19 Joseph Calkin invested $1,000 six years ago, which has now grown to $1,601. The interest was compounded semiannually. What was the annual rate of return?

$1,601 ÷ $1,000 = 1.6010, answer 8%. Read down Periods column to 12, across to 1.6010, under 4%. 6 (years) × 2 = 12 (periods), because the interest was compounded twice a year. If interest is compounded semiannually at 4%, the annual rate is 8%. Conversely, an annual rate must be divided by 2, to obtain the semiannual rate, which is the number of times compounded during the year.

3.20 The Hassad Furniture Company received two notes from customers in payment of furniture purchased. One note was dated April 17, 1977 and due July 19, 1977; the other was dated October 14, 1977 and due February 14, 1978. What was the exact number of days to the maturity date of each note?

First note: April 7th is the 97th day; July 19th is the 200th day. 200 − 97 = 103 days to maturity. *Second note*: October 14th is the 287th day. 365 − 287 = 78 days. February 14th is the 45th day. 78 + 45 = 123 days to maturity. (See Example 18.)

3.21 On what day was the full amount due on the note shown in Fig. 3-7?

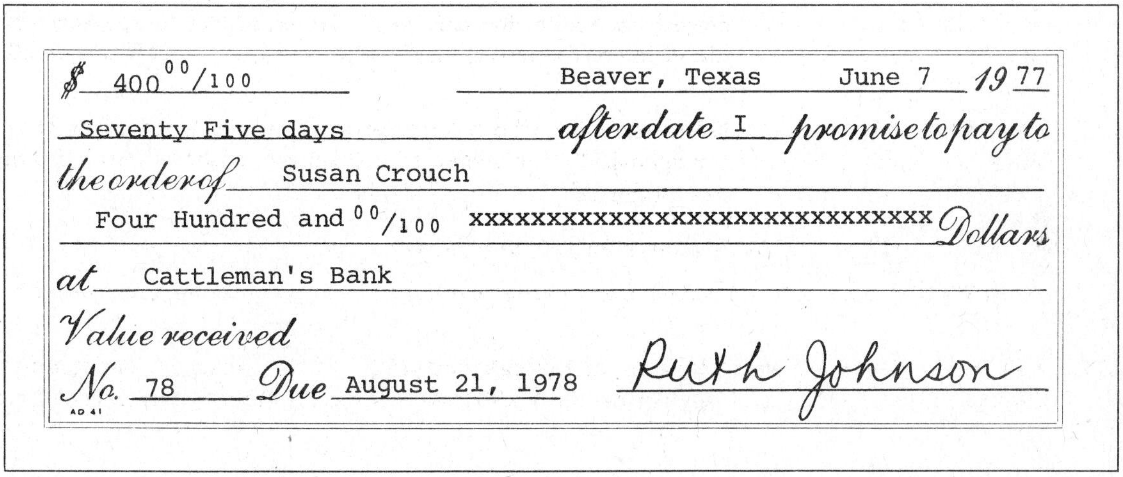

$ 400 ^{00}/100 _____   _____ Beaver, Texas   June 7 *19* 77

Seventy Five days _____   *after date* I *promise to pay to*

the order of ___ Susan Crouch _____

Four Hundred and ^{00}/100 xxxxxxxxxxxxxxxxxxxxxxxxxxxxxx *Dollars*

at ___ Cattleman's Bank _____

Value received

No. 78 _____ *Due* August 21, 1978   *Ruth Johnson*

AD 41

Fig. 3-7

June 7th is the 158th day. 158 + 75 = 233. The 233rd day is August 21. The full amount was due on August 21. (See Example 19.)

3.22 From the information in the note shown in Fig. 3-8, compute the maturity value of the note.

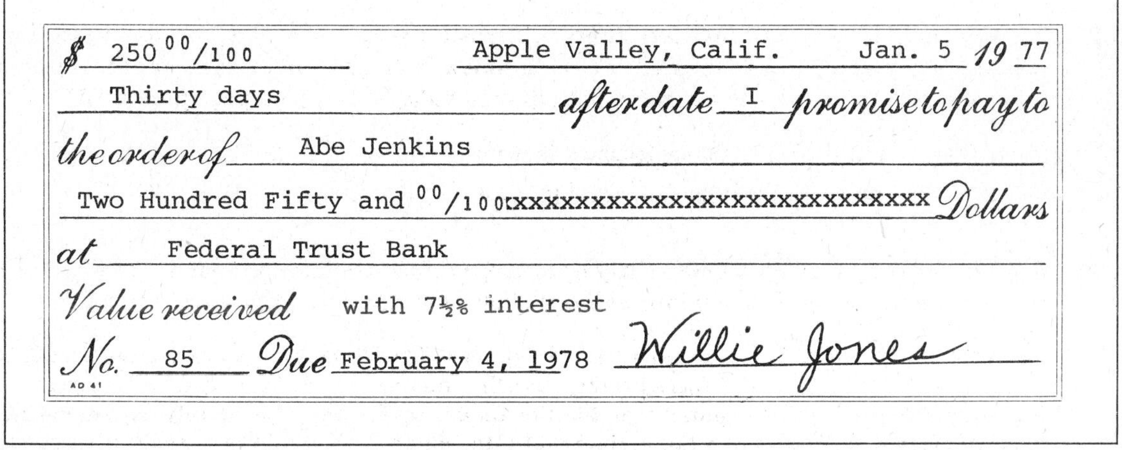

$ 250 ^{00}/100 _____   Apple Valley, Calif.   Jan. 5 *19* 77

Thirty days _____   *after date* I *promise to pay to*

the order of ___ Abe Jenkins _____

Two Hundred Fifty and ^{00}/100 xxxxxxxxxxxxxxxxxxxxxxxxxxxxxx *Dollars*

at ___ Federal Trust Bank _____

Value received   with $7\frac{1}{2}$% interest

No. 85 _____ *Due* February 4, 1978   *Willie Jones*

AD 41

Fig. 3-8

(a) What is the due date? (b) How much must he pay?

(a) January 5th is the 5th day. 5 + 30 days (term of note) = 35th day from beginning of year. 35th day falls on the 4th day of February, which is the due date.

(b)
$$I = P \times R \times T$$

$$I = \$250 \times 0.075 \times \frac{30}{360} = \$1.562, \text{ or } \$1.56. \qquad \$250 + \$1.56 = \$251.56$$

(See Example 20 and Table 3.)

3.23 Interest was received by Ike Kline on the note shown in Fig. 3-9. (a) What was the rate of interest if the amount of interest received was $10.20? (b) On what day was the money due?

$ 680 ^{00}/100 _____ _____ Salem, Oregon _____ April 20 _19 78_

Seventy Two days _____ *after date* I *promise to pay to*

the order of _Ike Kline_ _____

_____ Six Hundred Eighty and ^{00}/100 xxxxxxxxxxxxxxxxxxxxxxxxx *Dollars*

at _____ Mercantile Trust Bank _____

Value received with interest

No. _105_ *Due* July 1, 1978 _____ *William Billings*

Fig. 3-9

(a)
$$I = P \times R \times T$$

$$\$10.20 = \$680 \times R \times \frac{72}{360} = \$136R \qquad R = \$10.20 \div \$136 = 0.075, \text{ or } 7.5\%$$

(b) April 20th is the 110th day. 110 + 72 = 182. 182d day is July 1st.

3.24 Sarah Porter gave her sister, Nancy Corrigan, her $450 note, due 60 days after May 13, 1977 without interest. Nancy took the note to her bank on June 18 and discounted it at $8\frac{1}{2}\%$ interest. Determine (a) the due date of note, (b) the term of discount, and (c) how much Nancy would receive on June 18.

(a) May 13th is the 133d day. 133 + 60 = 193: July 12 due date.

(b) June 18th is the 169th day. 193 − 169 = 24 days, term of discount.

(c) $D = P \times R \times T$: $D = \$450 \times 0.085 \times 24/360 = \$2.55$.

$$\$450 - \$2.55 = \$447.45, \text{ the amount received on June 18}$$

(See Example 21.)

3.25   John Wadley sold his used car for $1,200 to a neighbor, accepting in payment a note due 90 days after May 12, 1977 with interest at $8\frac{1}{2}\%$.   On June 22, Wadley asked the bank to discount the note.   The bank discounted the note at 9%.   Determine   (*a*) the due date,   (*b*) the maturity value,   (*c*) the term of discount (days),   (*d*) the amount of discount, and   (*e*) the amount Wadley received on June 22 (proceeds).

(*a*)   May 12th is the 132d day.   132 + 90 = 222.   The 222d day is August 10, due date.

(*b*) $I = P \times R \times T$: $I = \$1,200 \times 0.0825 \times 90/360 = \$24.75$.

$$\$1,200 + \$24.75 = \$1,224.75$$

(*c*)   June 22d is the 173d day.

$$222 - 173 = 49 \text{ days}$$

(*d*) $D = P \times R \times T$:

$$D = \$1,224.75 \times 0.09 \times \frac{49}{360} = \$15.00$$

(*e*) $\$1,224.75 - \$15.00 = \$1,209.75$ proceeds; amount received on June 22

(See Example 23.)

3.26   Tony Pastor repaired Rose Stone's roof, for which he received a promissory note in the amount of $500 at $6\frac{1}{2}\%$ interest, due 60 days after September 10, 1977.   Tony needed some cash to pay his helper, so he discounted the note at his bank on October 1.   The discount rate was 8%.   Determine   (*a*) the due date,   (*b*) the maturity value,   (*c*) the term of discount,   (*d*) the amount of discount, and   (*e*) the proceeds of discounted note.

(*a*)   September 10th is the 253d day.   253 + 60 = 313.   November 9 is the due date.

(*b*) $I = P \times R \times T$

$$I = \$500 \times 0.065 \times \frac{60}{360} = \$5.416, \text{ or } \$5.42$$

$$\$500 + \$5.42 = \$505.42 \text{ maturity value}$$

(*c*)   October 1st is the 274th day.

$$313 \text{ (due date)} - 274 \text{ (discount date)} = 39, \text{ the term of the discount}$$

(*d*) $D = P \times R \times T$:

$$D = \$505.42 \times 0.08 \times \frac{39}{360} = \$4.38, \text{ amount of discount}$$

(*e*) $\$505.42 - \$4.38 = \$501.04$ proceeds; amount Tony received on October 1

Supplementary Problems

3.27 Sylvia Porter, a student at the state university, maintains her own checking account. Her parents deposit money in her account at a bank located in their home town. Sylvia's checkbook balance on March 14 is $98.17. She made the following transactions during the month of March:

  (a) March 15, check #12 to college book store, $12.95.
  (b) March 21, check #13 to cash, $10.00.
  (c) March 23, check #14 to the Steak House, $5.75.
  (d) March 28, deposit of $50.00.
  (e) March 31, check #15 to sorority, $15.00.

What is Sylvia's checkbook balance on April 1?   *Ans.* $104.47.   (See Problem 3.1.)

3.28 Abe Gold had to borrow $1,800 for 4 days and was charged 9% interest. Use the short method to determine the amount of interest Abe had to pay.   *Ans.* $1.80.   (See Problem 3.10.)

3.29 Oscar Boley's uncle deposited a sum of money in a bank at $5\frac{1}{2}$% interest compounded annually to provide for Oscar's college education. Now, 18 years later, Oscar has on deposit $13,107.50. How much was the original deposit?   *Ans.* $5,000.   (See Problem 3.17.)

3.30 Jack Kise received the following note: "I, Rose Noyes, promise to pay Jack Kise or order $380 with interest at $9\frac{1}{4}$%, 72 days after June 19." (a) What is the due date of the note? (b) How much must she pay?   *Ans.*   (a) August 30, (b) $387.03.   (See Problem 3.22.)

3.31 Eric and Martha Sundstrom, a newly married couple, saved $835 toward the purchase of some furniture. They put it in the bank at $6\frac{1}{2}$% simple interest until they decided what to buy. After 2 months and 21 days, they withdrew their money in order to purchase their furniture. How much more than their original amount did they receive?   *Ans.* $12.21.   (See Problem 3.13.)

3.32 Henry Bancord received a promissory note for $580 in evidence of money due him by a friend. The note was due 48 days after September 26, 1977, with interest of $6\frac{1}{2}$%. On October 16, Bancord discounted the note at the bank at $8\frac{1}{2}$%. Determine: (a) the due date, (b) the maturity value, (c) the term of discount, (d) the amount of discount, and (e) the amount Bancord received.   *Ans.*   (a) November 13, (b) $585.03, (c) 28 days, (d) $3.87, (e) $581.16.   (See Problem 3.25.)

3.33 Debbie Rosen received a check from her parents in the amount of $530 to pay her tuition, which was due in 45 days. She put the check in her checking account rather than lending it to a student who offered her 8% interest for the 45-day period. How much did she lose by not lending it? (Use the 365-day method.)   *Ans.* $5.23.   (See Problem 3.7.)

3.34 Your son deposited $800 in the bank on which he was paid $5\frac{1}{2}$% interest, compounded annually. (a) How much will his deposit amount to after 4 years, if he permitted the interest to accumulate? (b) How much compound interest will be due him?   *Ans.*   (a) $991.04, (b) $191.04.

3.35 Walter Ansley, a supervisor at the Jackson Chemical Company, received a bonus in the amount of $880. He invested it at 8% interest, compounded semiannually, and decided to leave it untouched until he needed it. This year, which is eleven years later, he wanted to find out: (a) how much his investment amounts to, and (b) the amount of compound interest.   *Ans.*   (a) $2,085.51, (b) $1,205.51.   (See Problem 3.18.)

3.36 On a recent television program, the host gave the contestants 15 seconds to answer the following question. "If your spouse paid $8.50 interest on a 45-day loan at 8%, how much was the amount of the loan?"   *Ans.* $850.   (See Problem 3.11.)

3.37 Your daughter asked you to complete her check register after she had issued the following checks during the month of January and had made a $200 deposit to her checking account on January 16.

  (a) 3d, check #64 to the Dress Shop, $98.98.
  (b) 8th, check #65 to the Shoe Mart, $86.50.
  (c) 15th, check #66 to the Wig Fashions, $58.99.
  (d) 16th, deposit of $200.
  (e) 23d, check #67 to the Vogue Shop, $78.98.

The check register had a balance brought forward of $243.17 on January 3. What was the balance on January 23?   *Ans*. $119.72. (See Problem 3.2.)

3.38 Henry Blake borrowed $1,500 from Hank Snow, a fellow truck driver. He paid Hank $1,516.50 at the end of 99 days. What rate of interest did he pay?   *Ans*.   4%. (See Problem 3.8.)

3.39 On April 30, Ms. Judy Robbins received her bank statement, which showed a balance of $202.95. Her check register showed a balance of $703.60 on that day. In checking her account, Judy noted that the following checks were outstanding:

  Check #57, $83.29.
  Check #59, $17.91.
  Check #60, $79.50.

The statement showed a service charge of $1.35. The bank charged $5.00 for the collection of a note. Her deposit of $950 on April 30 was not recorded on the statement. The bank collected a note of $275 for her. Reconcile Judy's statement.   *Ans*. $972.25. (See Problem 3.4.)

3.40 Wally Jacques needed $397.50 cash to have his truck engine rebuilt. He borrowed this amount from the bank for 60 days at $8\frac{3}{4}\%$ interest. How much interest did he pay? *Ans*. $5.80. (See Problem 3.5.)

3.41 Olin Graham received an annual statement from the bank that showed he had $4,280 in his savings account. He recalled that he had opened his account with a $4,000 deposit a year ago. If this bank computes the interest annually, what rate of simple interest did Olin receive? *Ans*.   7%. (See Problem 3.14.)

3.42 Dick Trombley gave a promissory note to his roommate, Bert South, who loaned him $375 without interest, payable 70 days after his college graduation on June 12. Bert, in need of money, discounted the note at his bank on July 2 at $7\frac{3}{4}\%$. Determine: (a) the due date, (b) the term of discount (days), and (c) the amount Bert received.   *Ans*.   (a) August 21, (b) 50 days, (c) $370.96. (See Problem 3.24.)

3.43 The loan officer at the local bank offered to lend Frank Wilkes $750 if he pays back $757.50 in 48 days. As this conversation was by telephone, Frank didn't clearly understand the rate of interest that was quoted. What was the interest rate?   *Ans*. $7\frac{1}{2}\%$.

3.44 Ms. Molly Pickens deposited $4,000 in the bank at $5\frac{1}{2}\%$ interest, compounded annually. This amount has now grown to $8,023.20. For how many years has the $4,000 been on deposit? *Ans*.   13 years. (See Problem 3.16.)

3.45 Joe Small gave Sally Goss the following note: "I, Joe Small, promise to pay Sally Goss $630, with interest, 75 days after February 22, 1977." If Joe paid Sally $640.50, what was the rate of interest that he paid her?   *Ans*.   8%.

3.46 Phil Bankstrom, who operates the local feed and grain store, accepted a promissory note from Ollie Swanson, a local farmer, dated November 24, 1976. The note was payable on March 28, 1977. For how many days must Phil wait for his money?   *Ans*.   124 days. (See Problem 3.20.)

3.47 Bolic Braun has $989.95 in a special investment account. The amount originally deposited in this account 7 years ago was $500. If the interest was compounded semiannually, what was the annual rate of interest?   *Ans.*   10%. (See Problem 3.19.)

3.48 Beth Norbert, a secretary at your office, received her bank statement on March 31. The statement showed a balance of $389.47. Her checkstub balance on March 31 was $38.76. She asked you to reconcile the bank statement for her. You noticed that the following checks were outstanding:

Check #73 for $86.57.
Check #74 for $40.49.
Check #75 for $225.00.

The bank had deducted a service charge of $1.35. What was her correct balance?
Ans. $37.41. (See Problem 3.3.)

3.49 The bank sent Paul Adams a notice of credit for interest in the amount of $19.50 on his $600 account, which he opened 6 months ago. What rate of interest did he receive?   *Ans.* $6\frac{1}{2}$%.

3.50 Ben Jolson received a promissory note from Charles Long, a friend, to whom he had loaned $480 at 5% interest. The note was due 72 days after April 1, 1978. The bank discounted the note for Jolson on May 9, 1978, at $7\frac{1}{2}$%. Determine: (*a*) the due date, (*b*) the maturity value, (*c*) the term of discount, (*d*) the amount of discount, and (*e*) the amount Jolson received.   *Ans.*   (*a*) June 12, (*b*) $484.80, (*c*) 34 days, (*d*) $3.43, (*e*) $481.37.

Chapter 4

Automobile Ownership

One of the largest expenditures an individual may make is the purchase of an automobile. Before doing so, it is important to know how much it will actually cost to purchase and operate. The most significant expenses include depreciation (which affects an auto's trade-in value), operating and maintenance, taxes, and insurance.

4.1 PURCHASING A NEW AUTOMOBILE

Let us consider buying a car on a time-payment basis. A down payment is required which may be made in cash or by trading-in another automobile or both. You may obtain a loan from the automobile agency, from your bank, or from other sources, and then make monthly payments as stipulated in your contract.

Table 1.   Monthly Loan Payment Chart

Interest Rate	Amount of Loan	1 yr Monthly Payments	2 yrs Monthly Payments	3 yrs Monthly Payments	4 yrs Monthly Payments
$7\frac{1}{2}\%$	$1000	$ 86.76	$ 45.00	$ 31.11	$ 24.18
	1500	130.14	67.50	46.66	36.27
	2000	173.51	90.00	62.21	48.36
	2500	216.89	112.50	77.77	60.45
	3000	260.27	135.00	93.32	72.54
	3500	303.65	157.50	108.87	84.63
	4000	347.03	180.00	124.42	96.72
	4500	390.41	202.50	139.98	108.81
	5000	433.79	225.00	155.53	120.89
	5500	477.17	247.50	171.08	132.98
	6000	520.54	270.00	186.64	145.07
$8\frac{1}{2}\%$	1000	87.22	45.46	31.57	24.65
	1500	130.83	68.18	47.35	36.97
	2000	174.44	90.91	63.14	49.30
	2500	218.05	113.64	78.92	61.62
	3000	261.66	136.37	94.70	73.94
	3500	305.27	159.09	110.49	86.27
	4000	348.88	181.82	126.27	98.59
	4500	392.49	204.55	142.05	110.92
	5000	436.10	227.28	157.84	123.24
	5500	479.71	250.01	173.62	135.57
	6000	523.32	272.73	189.41	147.89

EXAMPLE 1

Fred Carter purchased a new car on the installment plan.   The list price was $5,495.   Other charges amounted to $200.   Fred received a trade-in allowance of $1,695 on his old car.   Let us suppose he wants to know how much his monthly payments would amount to for a 2-year period at $7\frac{1}{2}\%$ interest; for a 3-year period at $7\frac{1}{2}\%$ interest.

First he determines his total charges, which are $5,495 (list price) + $200 (other charges): $5,695.   From this total charge of $5,695 he subtracts the trade-in price of $1,695, giving $4,000, the amount to be repaid.

Referring to Table 7-1, interest rate $7\frac{1}{2}\%$, for a loan of $4,000 payable in 2 years, he sees that the monthly payment is $180.00.   To find the amount of monthly payments for a three-year term, he uses the same procedure but reads under the column heading "3 years."   Monthly payments will be $124.42.

EXAMPLE 2

Bill Snow bought a new car and after all charges and the trade-in allowance on his used car were figured, he had an unpaid balance of $3,500.   He arranged a loan for $3,500 at $8\frac{1}{2}\%$ interest to be paid back in 2 years.   He wants to determine the following: (a) how much his monthly payments would be; (b) how much he would pay back; and   (c) what his rate of interest would actually be.

Using the $8\frac{1}{2}\%$ interest rate on Table 7-1 ($3,500, 2 years)

(a) The monthly payments amount to $159.09.

(b) The amount to be paid back is $159.09 (monthly payment) × 24 (number of payments): $3,818.16.

(c) The amount of interest to be paid is $3,818.16 (amount to be paid back) − $3,500 (principal): $318.16.

Formula for figuring rate:

$$R = \frac{24 \times C}{P \times (n + 1)}, \text{where } C = \$318.16, P = \$3,500, n = 24$$

Therefore,

$$R = \frac{24 \times \$318.16}{\$3,500 \times (24 + 1)} = \frac{\$7,635.84}{\$87,500} = 0.0872, \text{ or } 8.7\% \text{ interest}$$

Alternate Method:

$$I = P \times R \times T$$

$$I = \$318.16, P = \$3,500, T = \frac{300}{12}$$

You actually pay interest for each month.   Add the months $(1 + 2 + 3 + \cdots + 24) = 300$.   Use the shortcut method, by multiplying the number of months (24) by the next consecutive number (25), which equals 600, and divide this product by 2. $600 \div 2 = 300$, thus receiving the same answer.

$$\$318.16 = \frac{\$3,500}{24} \times R \times \frac{\overset{25}{\cancel{300}}}{\underset{1}{\cancel{12}}} = \frac{\$3,500 \times 25 \times R}{24} = \frac{\$87,500R}{24} = \$3,645.83R$$

$$R = \frac{\$318.16}{\$3,645.83} = 0.0872, \text{ or } 8.7\% \text{ interest}$$

EXAMPLE 3

Rufus Jackson bought a used car for $2,500. Terms: $500 down and $100 a month for 24 months.   To determine the actual rate of interest that Rufus paid, compute as follows:

$$R = \frac{24 \times C}{P \times (n + 1)}$$

where $C = \$400$. 24 payments $\times$ \$100 = \$2,400 total payments. \$2,400 (total payments) $-$ \$2,000 (principal) = \$400 interest. $P = \$2,000$ unpaid balance. $n = 24$.

$$R = \frac{24 \times \$400}{\$2,000 \times (24 + 1)} = \frac{\$9,600}{\$50,000} = 0.192, \text{ or } 19.2\% \text{ interest}$$

4.2 DEPRECIATION COSTS

In car ownership, depreciation is usually the largest expense for the average consumer. There is no set rule for figuring the depreciation of automobiles. Dealers use a so-called Blue Book value, depending on the make, year, and type of automobile. The greatest depreciation on an automobile is during the first year of use. Each succeeding year, the percent and amount of depreciation decreases. Thus on a \$4,000 car, the depreciation on the car during its first year might be computed at a rate as high as 25% of the cost of the car; the second year, a 20% rate might be used; the third year, 15%; and the fourth and succeeding years, 5% to 10% annually. Also, the depreciation might be figured on the original cost or on the declining value of the car. For consumer purposes, owners usually use the straight-line method to determine the average annual depreciation cost over a period of years.

EXAMPLE 4

Ike Smith paid \$5,000 for a car which he traded in 4 years later. He received a trade-in allowance of \$1,800. His average annual depreciation was \$800, computed as follows: the car decreased in value during the 4 years from \$5,000 to \$1,800, which equals \$3,200 depreciation. Therefore,

$$\$3,200 \div 4 \text{ (years)} = \$800$$

EXAMPLE 5

Had Ike Smith kept his \$5,200 car for 8 years and received a \$400 trade-in allowance, his average annual depreciation would have amounted to \$600.

$$\$5,200 \text{ (purchase price)} - \$400 \text{ (trade-in allowance)} = \$4,800, \text{ the amount of depreciation}$$

$$\$4,800 \text{ (depreciation)} \div 8 \text{ (years)} = \$600$$

One method of obtaining an accelerated depreciation is the "sum-of-the-years'-digits" method. This method allows for greater depreciation of an asset in the first year than in the second, greater in the second year than in the third, etc. First, one must estimate the number of useful years of the automobile, truck, or piece of equipment. After determining the number of useful years, obtain the sum of all of the years. As an example, a truck will be used for 6 years. Thus: $6 + 5 + 4 + 3 + 2 + 1 = 21$. The first year's depreciation is computed by obtaining 6/21 of the total depreciation. The second year's depreciation is 5/21 of the total depreciation. The third year's is 4/21 of the total depreciation, etc.

Thus, the Oban Trucking Company bought a truck for \$16,000 which they estimated would have a useful life of 5 years, with a trade-in value of \$1,000 at the end of this period. Using the sum-of-the-years'-digits method, the depreciation on the truck for each of the first two years would be determined as follows:

\$16,000 (cost) $-$ \$1,000 (trade-in value) = \$15,000, allowable depreciation. Sum-of-the-years'-digits: $5 + 4 + 3 + 2 + 1 = 15$.

First year:

$$\frac{5}{15} \times \$15,000 = \$5,000 \text{ depreciation}$$

Second year:

$$\frac{4}{15} \times \$15,000 = \$4,000 \text{ depreciation}$$

4.3 OPERATING COSTS

The cost of operating a car includes such items as gasoline, oil, repairs, and replacement items like tires and batteries.

EXAMPLE 6

You travel approximately 1,000 miles a month in your car. You get 18 miles per gallon of gasoline at a cost of 56.9¢ per gallon. You consume one quart of oil per month at a cost of $1.00 per quart. (*a*) What is your monthly cost for these items? (*b*) What is the average cost per mile for gas and oil?

(*a*) To obtain the cost of gasoline, divide the number of miles driven by the miles per gallon. Multiply the product by the cost of 1 gallon of gasoline. 1,000 (miles driven) ÷ 18 (miles per gallon) = 55.6 gallons. 55.6 (gallons) × $.569 (cost per gallon) = $31.64 (monthly cost for gas). Adding $1 (cost for oil) gives $32.64, the monthly cost of gas and oil.

(*b*) Divide the monthly cost of gasoline and oil by the number of miles driven to find the cost per mile. $32.64 (monthly cost) ÷ 1,000 (miles) = 0.0326, or 3.3¢ per mile cost of gas and oil.

EXAMPLE 7

During the year, you spent the following amounts on the maintenance and repair of your 3-year-old car. One new set of tires, $159; two tune-ups at $34.50 each; four oil and lubrication changes, $11.95 each; and a new muffler at $18.95. You drove 12,000 miles during the year. You want to know the following. (*a*) What was your average monthly cost for the maintenance and repair? (*b*) What was the average cost per mile for these expenses?

(*a*) Figure all costs and divide by 12 to get the average monthly cost. Tires, $159. 2 (tune-ups) × $34.50 (cost) = $69. 4 (oil changes) × $11.95 (cost) = $47.80. Muffler, $18.95. Add these for the total cost: $159 + $69 + $47.80 + $18.95 = $294.75.

$$\$294.75 \text{ (total cost)} \div 12 \text{ (months)} = \$24.56 \text{ average monthly cost}$$

(*b*) Divide the annual cost by the number of miles driven to find the average cost per mile:

$$\$294.75 \text{ (annual cost)} \div 12,000 \text{ miles} = 0.0245, \text{ or } 2.5¢ \text{ average cost per mile}$$

EXAMPLE 8

Alan Rose and his family drive their automobile an average of 18,000 miles a year. The license and insurance cost $310 per year. The average annual depreciation is $800. Other nonoperating costs amount to $40 per year. (*a*) What is the average nonoperating cost per mile? (*b*) What was Alan's nonoperating cost of this vehicle for the last 3 years?

(*a*) Total all nonoperating costs for the year, and divide this total cost by the number of miles driven:

$$\$310 \text{ (insurance)} + \$800 \text{ (depreciation)} + \$40 \text{ (miscellaneous)} = \$1,150$$

$$\$1,150 \text{ (total nonoperating cost)} \div 18,000 \text{ (miles)} = \$.0638, \text{ or } 6.4¢ \text{ per mile}$$

(*b*) Multiply the total nonoperating cost per year by the number of years:

$$\$1,150 \text{ (total nonoperating costs per year)} \times 3 \text{ (years)} = \$3,450, \text{ the total for 3 years}$$

EXAMPLE 9

Al Green kept very accurate records of his car expenses, so he could figure his annual costs and his cost per mile of operation. Al bought a car for $4,295, which he traded in 5 years later. The trade-in value was $595. He drove 72,000 miles and averaged 16 miles per gallon at an average cost of 53.9¢ per gallon. The other expenses for the five-year period were: insurance, $1,448; oil and lubrication, $212.50; maintenance, $798; new replacement items, such as tires, battery, etc., $753; and miscellaneous expenses, $109. (*a*) What was his total expense for the five-year period? (*b*) What was the average cost per mile?

(*a*) Figure all expenses. Depreciation: $4,295 (original cost) − $595 (trade-in value) = $3,700. Gas: Divide the number of miles driven by the average number of miles per gallon. Multiply this result by the cost of gas per gallon. 72,000 (miles) ÷ 16 (miles per gallon) = 4,500 gallons consumed.

$$4,500 \text{ (gallons)} \times \$.539 \text{ (cost per gallon)} = \$2,425.50, \text{ cost of gas}$$

Add all costs to obtain total cost: $3,700 (depreciation) + $2,425.50 (gas cost) + $1,448 (insurance) + $212.50 (oil and lubrication) + $798 (maintenance) + $753 (replacement items) + $109 (miscellaneous) = $9,446, the total expenses for 5 years.

(*b*) Divide total expenses by the number of miles driven to obtain the average cost per mile

$$\$9,446 \text{ (total expenses)} \div 72,000 \text{ (miles)} = 0.1311, \text{ or } 13.1¢ \text{ per mile}$$

4.4 AUTOMOBILE TAXES

Taxes account for a sizable portion of your automobile expense. Consumers pay state and Federal taxes on the purchase and operation of cars, such as on gasoline, oil, maintenance, parts, tires, and so on.

EXAMPLE 10

Bill Johnson purchased 85 gallons of gasoline last month at an average cost of 65.9¢ per gallon. The Federal tax is 4¢ per gallon and the state tax is 8¢ per gallon. How can he determine (*a*) how much Federal tax he paid? (*b*) state tax? (*c*) what percent of his cost was for taxes?

(*a*) Multiply the number of gallons by 4¢ to obtain the Federal tax.

$$85 \times \$.04 = \$3.40 \text{ Federal tax}$$

(*b*) Multiply the number of gallons by $.08 to obtain the state tax.

$$85 \times \$.08 = \$6.80 \text{ state tax}$$

(*c*) Multiply the number of gallons by the cost per gallon to obtain total cost. Add the Federal and state tax to obtain the total tax cost. To obtain the percent of cost, divide the total tax cost by the total gasoline cost. 85 × $.659 = $56.02 cost of gasoline. $3.40 + $6.80 = $10.20 total tax.

$$\$10.20 \text{ (total tax)} \div \$56.02 \text{ (total cost)} = 0.182, \text{ or } 18.2\%$$

4.5 TYPES OF AUTOMOBILE INSURANCE

The five major types of automobile insurance which owners should consider are:

(1) Bodily injury liability.
(2) Property damage liability.
(3) Medical payments.
(4) Comprehensive coverage.
(5) Collision.

The costs of these various insurance types are discussed in Section 6.6.

Bodily Injury Liability

This type protects the driver of an automobile from financial loss in the event he inflicts injury on anyone during an automobile accident in which he may be at fault. The basic amount of coverage for this type of insurance is commonly "10 and 20." This indicates that in case of an accident, the insured is protected up to a maximum amount of $10,000 for one person and a maximum of $20,000 for an accident involving more than one person. Should the court award more than $10,000 to one person, or more than $20,000 to several persons in the same accident, the insured must pay the remaining amounts above the $10,000 or $20,000 limits.

Property Damage Liability

Most companies require the purchase of property damage liability along with the bodily injury liability. This type of insurance covers the insured for damages caused to another's property, such as: automobile, house, store front, or other object. The amount of coverage may be for $5,000, $10,000, or more; the most common policy is written for $10,000. A typical automobile insurance policy would be expressed as "25 and 50 and 10." This would indicate bodily injury liability insurance in case of an accident in the amount of $25,000 maximum for one person, with a $50,000 maximum for several persons, plus property damage liability with a $10,000 maximum.

Medical Payments

Under this type of policy, the insuring company agrees to pay all medical expenses resulting from an accident up to the maximum amount for which you are insured. This coverage applies to you and members of your family, if insured while walking or in an automobile.

Comprehensive Coverage

The insured is protected against financial loss resulting from peril, such as fire, wind, riot, falling objects, theft, and the like. This type is usually written with a $50 or $100 deductible amount. In case of loss, the insured pays the deductible amount and the insurance company pays the remainder.

Collision

A collision policy covers damage done only to your car as a result of hitting an object, or overturning. It does not cover injuries or damage to the other car. This coverage is usually written with a $50 or $100 deductible clause. The insured pays the deductible portion as a result of damage; the insurance company pays the remainder.

EXAMPLE 11

John Axe had liability insurance in the amount of "10 and 20 and 5." He was involved in an accident that resulted in a pending lawsuit. How much is the maximum that the insurance company will pay in the case of court-ordered settlement awards? According to the "10 and 20 and 5" formula, the company will pay for bodily injury liability for one person up to $10,000 maximum, for more than one person up to $20,000 maximum, for property damage up to $5,000 maximum.

4.6   COST OF AUTOMOBILE INSURANCE

Automobile insurance premiums (the cost of insurance to the consumer) are calculated from a variety of rate tables. They vary according to the kinds of coverage desired by the consumer.

Base Premiums. States are divided into territories in which the base premiums are established according to accident rate experience factors. Your base premium is established by the territory in which your automobile is garaged. See Table 2.

Table 2. Base Premiums for Private Automobiles

Bodily Injury	Territory					
	05	07	08	11	12	16
10–20	$62	$100	$72	$ 76	$64	$69
15–30	67	108	78	82	69	75
25–50	72	116	84	88	74	80
50–100	78	125	90	95	80	86
100–300	83	134	96	102	86	92
Property Damage						
$ 5,000	$38	$50	$47	$48	$52	$45
10,000	40	53	49	50	55	47
25,000	41	54	51	52	56	49

Factor Tables. After obtaining the base premium, it is multiplied by factors (numbers) that depend upon age, driver training, marital status, use of car, number of accidents, and so on. See Tables 3, 4, and 5.

Table 3. Factors for No Youthful Operators

Age and Sex	Pleasure Use	Work, less than 10 Miles	Work, 10 Miles or More	Business Use	Farm Use
Principal, 65 or over	1.00	1.10	1.40	1.50	0.75
One, female, 30–64	0.90	1.00	1.30	1.40	0.65
All other	1.00	1.10	1.40	1.50	0.75

EXAMPLE 12

Your daughter, Sue, is the only youthful operator of your car that is garaged in Territory 05. She is 19 years old, unmarried, and has had driver training. The car is used for pleasure only, and you have had no accidents. You would like to know what the cost will be for a 100–300 bodily injury liability policy.

See Table 2 "Base premiums for Private Automobiles." Read down to 100–300, then right under "Territory 05"; read $83. In Table 4, obtain the factors for an unmarried female age 19 with driver training, under "Pleasure or Farm Use." Find factor 1.15. (*Note*: Table 3 does not apply.) Next, on Table 5, under "Number of Accidents," find factor + 0.00. Therefore, multiply the base premium by the combined factors only.

$$\$83 \text{ (base)} \times 1.15 \text{ (factor)} = \$95.45 \text{ cost}$$

Table 4. Youthful Operator

	Age	Unmarried Female		Unmarried Male (not Owner)		Married Male	
		Pleasure or Farm Use	Driven to Work	Pleasure or Farm Use	Driven to Work	Pleasure or Farm Use	Driven to Work
Without Driver Training	17 or less	1.60	1.85	2.55	2.80	2.20	2.45
	18	1.55	1.80	2.30	2.55	1.90	2.15
	19	1.50	1.75	2.30	2.30	1.65	1.90
	20	1.45	1.70	1.80	2.05	1.45	1.70
With Driver Training	17 or less	1.20	1.45	1.85	2.10	1.50	1.75
	18	1.20	1.45	1.80	2.05	1.45	1.70
	19	1.15	1.40	1.75	2.00	1.40	1.65
	20	1.15	1.40	1.70	1.95	1.35	1.60
With or Without Driver Training	21	1.10	1.35	1.60	1.85	1.30	1.55
	22	1.10	1.35	1.45	1.70	1.25	1.50
	23	1.05	1.30	1.30	1.55	1.20	1.45
	24	1.05	1.30	1.15	1.40	1.15	1.40

Table 5. Safe Driver Factors

Number of Accidents	0	1	2	3	4
Factor	+ 0.00	+ 0.30	+ 0.70	+ 1.20	+ 1.80

EXAMPLE 13

Your son Bill is now 16 years old and you allow him to drive your car. He has had no driver training. You drive 25 miles to work and have had one accident during the previous year. If your automobile is garaged in Territory 12, how much will you pay for a $10,000 property damage insurance policy?

Table 2. Find the base premium for $10,000 property damage. Under "Property Damage $10,000," read to the right under Territory 12: find $55 base premium. Table 4. Read down to "Without Driver Training, 17 or Less," then to the right under "Unmarried Male, Driven to Work," and find factor 2.80. Table 5. Read under "1" accident, factor + 0.30. Total factor: 2.80 + 0.30 = 3.10. Multiply the base premium by the total factor.

$$\$55 \text{ (base premium)} \times 3.10 = \$170.50 \text{ cost}$$

EXAMPLE 14

Mr. and Mrs. Young are both in their thirties and own an automobile which is used in their business. No one else drives the car, which is garaged in Territory 16. They had two accidents last year. How much will a 100 and 300 bodily injury policy, with a $25,000 property damage policy, cost them?

See Table 2. "Territory 16": bodily injury base premium on 100 and 300 = $92. Property damage base premium on $25,000 = $49. Table 3. Operator factor, read down to "All Other," then across to "Business Use." Read 1.50. Table 5. Accident factor: read under "2" accidents. Find factor + 0.70. Total factor: 1.50 + 0.70 = 2.20. *Bodily injury premium*: $92 × 2.20 = $202.40. *Property damage premium*: $49 × 2.20 = $107.80.

$$\$202.40 + \$107.80 = \$310.20 \text{ total premium}$$

Other Insurance Rates. Typical rates for medical payments, comprehensive coverage and collision policies are shown in Tables 6, 7 and 8 respectively.

Table 6.   **Medical Payments**

Amount	Territory					
	05	07	08	11	12	16
$ 500	$ 6	$10	$ 7	$ 8	$ 6	$ 7
750	7	11	8	9	7	8
1,000	8	12	9	10	8	9
2,000	10	14	11	12	10	11
5,000	13	17	14	15	13	14

EXAMPLE 15

Ruth Smith, single, aged 22, drives the family car. The car, which is used for pleasure only and is garaged in Territory 08, has not been involved in any accidents. How much will her father's insurance premium be for 50 and 100 bodily injury liability, $25,000 property damage, and $5,000 medical payment insurance?

See Table 2. "Territory 08," base premium bodily injury 50 and 100 = $90. Property damage: $25,000 = $51. Table 6, medical payments, $5,000 = $14.

$$\$90 + \$51 + \$14 = \$155 \text{ total base premium}$$

Operator factor, Table 4, under "With or Without Driver Training," aged 22, read to the right under "Unmarried Female, Pleasure," find factor 1.10. No other factors are required. Multiply the base premium by the factor:

$$\$155 × 1.10 = \$170.50 \text{ total premium}$$

EXAMPLE 16

You decided to buy a $50 deductible comprehensive policy on your 2-year-old pleasure car classified as Symbol 3. The car is garaged in Territory 08. How much less would this cost than full coverage comprehensive? You are 65 years old and have been involved in one accident.

See Table 7. Read down to "Territory 08, Age 2–3 years," then to the right under "Full Coverage, Symbol 3," find $15. Under $50 deductible, find $13. Table 3, factor is 1.00. Table 5, 1 accident, factor + 0.30. Total factor: 1.00 + 0.30 = 1.30. Multiply the base premium by the factor. *Full coverage*: $15 (base) × 1.30 (factor) = $19.50. *$50 deductible*: $13 (base) × 1.30 (factor) = $16.90.

$$\$19.50 - \$16.90 = \$2.60 \text{ cheaper for } \$50 \text{ deductible}$$

Table 7. Comprehensive Coverage

Territory	Age Group	Full Coverage					$50 Deductible				
		Symbol Group					Symbol Group				
		1,2	3	4	5	6	1,2	3	4	5	6
05	0–1	$31	$42	$52	$70	$91	$26	$34	$43	$58	$75
	2–3	21	31	39	53	68	19	26	32	43	56
	4–5	17	23	29	38	50	14	19	24	32	41
	6	14	19	23	32	41	12	15	19	26	34
08	0–1	15	20	25	34	44	13	17	21	28	37
	2–3	11	15	19	25	33	9	13	16	21	28
	4–5	8	11	14	19	24	7	9	12	16	20
	6	7	9	11	15	20	6	8	9	13	17
16	0–1	11	15	19	26	33	10	14	17	23	30
	2–3	9	11	14	19	25	8	10	13	17	22
	4–5	6	8	10	14	18	6	7	9	13	17
	6	5	7	9	12	15	5	6	8	10	13

EXAMPLE 17

You are a married male, aged 22, and drive a 3-year-old car, classified as Symbol 4, to work. The car is garaged in Territory 16. You have had one accident in the previous year. How much will a $100 deductible collision policy cost you?

See Table 8. Base premium, collision: "$100 Deductible." Read down to "Territory 16, Age Group 2,3." Then to the right under "$100 Deductible," read $55 base premium, under "Symbol Group 4." Table 4. Youthful operator factor: find opposite Age 22, under "Married Male, Driven to Work," factor 1.50. Table 5: read under "Number of Accidents," 1, and find factor + 0.30.

$$1.5 + 0.30 = 1.80 \text{ total factor}$$

Multiply the base premium by the factor.

$$\$55 \times 1.80 = \$99, \text{ the total cost of \$100 deductible}$$

EXAMPLE 18

Your client, Ms. Young, is a single, 44-year-old secretary. She owns a 2-year-old automobile, Symbol 4, and lives in Territory 08. Compute the total cost of her insurance policy for the following coverage: bodily injury liability, 50 and 100; property damage, $10,000; medical payments, $5,000; $50 deductible comprehensive; and $100 deductible collision. She drives 13 miles to work; had no accidents during the past year.

Table 8. Collision Coverage

Territory	Age Group	$50 Deductible					$100 Deductible				
		Symbol Group					Symbol Group				
		1, 2	3	4	5	6	1, 2	3	4	5	6
05	1	$101	$114	$134	$161	$188	$84	$95	$112	$134	$157
	2, 3	75	86	101	121	141	63	72	84	101	118
	4, 5	66	74	87	105	122	55	62	73	87	102
	6	55	63	74	88	103	46	53	62	74	86
08	1	57	65	76	91	106	45	51	60	72	84
	2, 3	43	49	57	68	80	34	38	45	54	63
	4, 5	37	42	49	59	69	29	33	39	47	55
	6	31	36	42	50	59	25	28	33	40	46
16	1	67	76	89	107	125	55	62	73	88	102
	2, 3	50	57	67	80	93	41	47	55	66	77
	4, 5	44	49	58	69	81	36	40	47	57	66
	6	36	42	49	59	69	30	34	40	48	56

Obtain the base premiums: Territory 08.

Table 2, bodily liability 50 and 100	$ 90
Table 2, property damage, $10,000	49
Table 6, medical payments, $5,000	14
Table 7, $50 deductible comprehensive, Territory 08; Age 2 years; Symbol 4	16
Table 8, $100 deductible collision, Territory 08; Age 2 years; Symbol 4	45
Total base premium =	$214

Obtain the factors: Table 3. No youthful operators, one female operator, 30–64 years old; drives to work more than 10 miles; factor 1.30. Multiply the base premium by the factor.

$214 (base premium) × 1.30 (factor) = $278.20 cost

EXAMPLE 19

Your family car is driven by your daughter, who is 19 years old and who has taken a driver training course. The car is driven only for pleasure. It is 4 years old, Symbol 2, and garaged in Territory 05. What will the amount of the premium be for the following coverage: bodily injury liability, 50 and 100; property damage, $10,000; medical payments, $5,000; $50 deductible comprehensive; and $50 deductible collision? You had one accident last year.

Use procedures explained above to read tables: obtain the base premium.

Table 2, bodily injury liability, 50 and 100	$ 78
Property damage, $10,000	40
Table 6, medical payments $5,000	13
Table 7, $50 deductible comprehensive	14
Table 8, $50 deductible collision	66
Total base premium =	$211

Obtain the multiplying factor: Table 4, age 19, with driver training; pleasure driving, factor 1.15. Table 5: 1 accident, factor + 0.30. Total factor 1.15 + 0.30 = 1.45. Multiply the base premium by the factor.

$$\$211 \times 1.45 = \$305.95$$

Solved Problems

4.1 Jan Rollins purchased a new car on the installment plan. The total purchase price amounted to $5,785; she received $1,285 for her old car. She decided to pay off the debt in three years. (a) How much are the monthly payments at $8\frac{1}{2}\%$ interest? (b) How much at $7\frac{1}{2}\%$ interest?

(a) See Table 1. $5,785 − $1,285 = $4,500 unpaid balance. Interest rate $8\frac{1}{2}\%$. Read down under "Amount of Loan" to $4,500; then across under "3 Years" and find $142.05, monthly payments.

(b) Interest rate, $7\frac{1}{2}\%$. Use same procedure as above. Find $139.98, monthly payment. (See Example 1.)

4.2 Fred Wills purchased a new car and after all charges and trade-in allowance, he had an unpaid balance of $4,000. He arranged a loan at $8\frac{1}{2}\%$ interest for the $4,000 to be paid back in 4 years. (a) How much are his monthly payments? (b) How much will he pay back? (c) What rate of interest is Fred actually paying?

(a) See Table 1. Use interest rate $8\frac{1}{2}\%$. Read down to $4,000; then across under "4 Years." Find $98.59, monthly payments.

(b) $98.59 (monthly payments) × 48 = $4,732.32, total amount.

(c) $4,732.32 (total amount due) − $4,000 = $732.32, total charge.

$$R = \frac{24 \times C}{P \times (n + 1)} = \frac{24 \times \$732.32}{\$4,000 \times (48 + 1)} = \frac{\$17,575.68}{\$196,000} = 0.0896, \text{ or } 9\% \text{ interest}$$

where C = $732.32; P = $4,000; n = 48.

Alternate Method:

$$I = P \times R \times T$$

$$I = \$732.32; P = \$4,000 \qquad T = \frac{1176}{12} \left(T = \frac{48 \text{ months} \times 49}{2} \right) = \frac{2352}{2} = 1,176$$

$$\$732.32 = \frac{\$4,000}{48} \times R \times \frac{1176}{12} = \$83.33 \times R \times 98 \qquad \$732.32 = \$8,166.34R$$

$$R = \frac{\$732.32}{\$8,166.34} = 0.08967, \text{ or } 9\% \text{ interest}$$

(See Example 2.)

4.3 Your son Bill purchased a used car from a used car lot for $2,798. Bill agreed to make a down payment of $598 and to make 24 payments of $110 each. (*a*) What amount was the carrying charge? (*b*) What actual interest rate did he pay?

(*a*) $2,798 (selling price) − $598 (down payment) = $2,200 unpaid balance. 24 payments × $110 monthly − $2,640 total amount to be paid.

$$\$2,640 \text{ (amount to be paid)} - \$2,200 \text{ (unpaid balance)} = \$440 \text{ carrying charge}$$

(*b*)

$$R = \frac{24 \times C}{P \times (n+1)} = \frac{24 \times \$440}{\$2,200 \times (24+1)} = \frac{\$10,560}{\$55,000} = 0.192, \text{ or } 19.2\% \text{ interest}$$

where $C = \$440$; $P = \$2,200$; $n = 24$ payments.

Alternate Method:

$$I = P \times R \times T$$

$$\$440 = \frac{\$2,200}{24} \times R \times \frac{300}{12} = \$91.666 \times R \times 25 = \$2,291.65R$$

$$R = \frac{\$440}{\$2,291.65} = 0.192, \text{ or } 19.2\% \text{ interest}$$

(See Example 3.)

4.4 Mary Wilson was offered a trade-in allowance of $2,000 on her car. She had purchased the car for $4,700 3 years ago. How much was the average annual depreciation on the car?

$$\$4,700 \text{ (cost)} - \$2,000 \text{ (trade-in value)} = \$2,700 \text{ depreciation}$$

$$\$2,700 \text{ (depreciation)} \div 3 \text{ (years)} = \$900 \text{ average annual depreciation}$$

(See Example 4.)

4.5 Mary Wilson, who owned a 2-year-old car, decided to keep the car for 3 more years. At the end of this time, she traded the car in and received a trade-in allowance of $1,200. The original cost was $4,700. What was the average annual depreciation?

$$\$4,700 \text{ (cost)} - \$1,200 \text{ (trade-in value)} = \$3,500 \text{ depreciation}$$

$$\$3,500 \text{ (depreciation)} \div 5 \text{ (years)} = \$700 \text{ average annual depreciation}$$

(See Example 5.)

4.6 Your family car is driven approximately 1,500 miles a month. The car gets 14 miles on a gallon of gasoline. The gasoline is purchased at a cost of 64.9¢ per gallon. It consumes one quart of oil for each 750 miles driven at a cost of 95¢ per quart. (*a*) What is the monthly cost for gasoline and oil? (*b*) What is the average cost per mile for gas and oil?

(*a*) Divide the miles driven by miles per gallon of gasoline. This gives us the number of gallons of gasoline consumed. Multiply the gallons consumed by the cost per gallon. 1,500 (miles driven) ÷ 14 (miles per gallon) = 107.1 gallons of gasoline. 107.1 (gallons consumed) × $.649 = $69.51, the cost of gasoline. 1,500 (miles driven) ÷ 750 (miles per quart) = 2 quarts of oil. 2 (quarts of oil) × $.95 = $1.90, the cost of oil.

$$\$69.51 \text{ (cost of gas)} + \$1.90 \text{ (cost of oil)} = \$71.41, \text{ the cost per month for gas and oil}$$

(b) To find cost per mile for gas and oil, divide the cost by the number of miles driven.

$71.41 (cost) ÷ 1,500 = 0.0476, or 4.8¢, cost per mile for gas and oil

(See Example 6.)

4.7 The maintenance and repair costs on your 4-year-old car for the past year were: one set of tires, $149.50; four oil and lubrication changes, $10.90 each; one battery, $29.95; two tune-ups at $24.95 each; and one muffler at $17.95. The car was driven 14,000 miles. (a) What was your average monthly cost for maintenance and repair? (b) What was the average cost per mile for these expenses?

(a) Total all costs and divide by 12. Tires, $149.50; oil and lubrication, 4 × $10.90 or, $43.60; battery, $29.95; tune-ups, 2 × $24.95 or, $49.90; muffler, $17.95. $149.50 + $43.60 + $29.95 + $49.90 + $17.95 = $290.90 total annual cost.

$290.90 (total cost) ÷ 12 (months) = $24.24 average monthly cost

(b) Divide total annual cost by total miles driven.

$290.90 (total cost) ÷ 14,000 (miles driven) = $.0207, or 2.1¢ per mile

(See Example 7.)

4.8 In planning his annual budget, Joe Adams wanted to figure out how much to budget for transportation. His 3-year-old car is paid for. Last year, he drove 18,000 miles, getting 16 miles on a gallon of gasoline. Gasoline costs 65.9¢ per gallon. Other expenses were: insurance, $350; maintenance and repairs, $295. (a) How much should he budget per month for transportation? (b) How much does it cost per mile to operate his car?

(a) Figure all costs and divide by 12 to determine monthly costs. Gasoline: divide miles driven by miles per gallon; multiply this figure by the cost per gallon of gasoline. 18,000 (miles) ÷ 16 (miles per gallon) = 1,125 gallons. 1,125 (gallons) × $659 (cost per gallon) = $741.38 gasoline cost. $741.38 (gasoline) + $350 (insurance) + $295 (maintenance) = $1,386.38, the total cost per year.

$1,386.38 (total cost) ÷ 12 (months) = $115.53, the monthly budgeting cost

(b) Divide total cost by miles driven to obtain average cost per mile.

$1,386.38 (total cost) ÷ 18,000 (miles) = $.077, or 7.7¢ per mile

(See Example 8.)

4.9 Ms. Billings, an accountant, kept a record of all her car expenses. All told, she paid $4,295 for her 6-year-old car. When she traded it in for a new car, she received a trade-in allowance of $295. She had driven the car 68,000 miles. She averaged 14 miles on a gallon of gasoline that cost 54.9¢ per gallon. Other expenses for the 6-year period were: insurance, $1,588; oil and lubrication, $287.95; maintenance, $868; replacement items, $735; and miscellaneous expenses, $94.50. (a) How much did the car cost her for the six years? (b) What was the average cost per mile?

(a) Figure all expenses. Gasoline: divide the number of miles driven by the average miles per gallon; multiply the result by the cost of gasoline per gallon. 68,000 (miles) ÷ 14 (miles per gallon) = 4,857, gallons (rounded). 4,857 (gallons) × $.549 (cost per gallon) = $2,666.49 cost of gasoline. Depreciation: $4,295 (original cost) − $295 (trade-in) = $4,000 depreciation. Total all expenses:

$2,666.49 (gasoline) + $4,000 (depreciation) + $1,588 (insurance)

+ $287.95 (oil and lubrication)

+ $868 (maintenance) + $735 (replacement items) + $94.50 (miscellaneous expenses)

= $10,239.94, total cost for 6 years

(b) Divide the total cost by the number of miles driven to obtain average cost per mile.

$10,239.94 ÷ 68,000 = $.15 (15¢) per mile

(See Example 9.)

4.10 You purchased 112 gallons of gasoline last month at an average cost of 67.9¢ per gallon. The Federal tax is 4¢ per gallon and the state tax is 8.5¢ per gallon. (a) How much did you pay for Federal tax? (b) For state tax? (c) What percent of your cost was for taxes?

(a) Multiply the number of gallons consumed by the Federal tax.

112 (gallons) × $.04 (federal tax) = $4.48 Federal tax

(b) Multiply the number of gallons consumed by the state tax.

112 (gallons) × $.085 (state tax) = $9.52 state tax

(c) Divide total tax by the total gasoline cost. 112 (gallons) × $.679 (cost per gallon) = $76.05 total gasoline cost. $4.48 (Federal tax) + $9.52 (state tax) = $14 total gas tax.

$14 (total gas tax) ÷ $76.05 (total gas cost) = 0.184, or 18.4% percent of gas cost for taxes

(See Example 10.)

4.11 Ruth drove 14,000 miles last year, getting an average of 21 miles on a gallon of gasoline. The average cost of 65.9¢ per gallon of gasoline included 4¢ per gallon for Federal tax and 8¢ per gallon for state tax. (a) How much Federal gas tax did she pay? (b) State tax? (c) Her gas tax was what percent of the total cost?

(a) Determine the number of gallons of gasoline consumed by dividing the total miles driven by the average mileage per gallon; multiply the result by the amount of tax per gallon. 14,000 (miles driven) ÷ 21 (miles per gallon) = 666.7 gallons.

666.7 (gallons) × $.04 (federal tax) = $26.67 total federal tax

(b) 666.7 (gallons) × $.08 (state tax) = $53.34 total state tax. (c) Obtain the total of all taxes and divide by total cost of gas. 666.7 (gallons) × $.659 (cost per gallon) = $439.36 total gas cost. $26.67 (federal tax) + $53.34 (state tax) = $80.01 total tax.

$80.01 (total tax) ÷ $439.36 (total gas cost) = 0.182, or 18.2% of cost.

(See Example 11.)

4.12 Frank Brill had bodily injury liability insurance in the amount of 10 and 20. He injured two persons when his car got out of control and jumped the sidewalk. The injured people sued and were awarded $12,000 and $8,000 respectively. (a) How much did Frank have to pay? (b) How much did the insurance company pay?

(a) The maximum coverage for the first person on a 10 and 20 policy is $10,000.

$12,000 − $10,000 = $2,000, the amount Frank had to pay

(b) The insurance company paid $10,000 for the first person and $8,000 for the second person.

$10,000 + $8,000 = $18,000 total paid by insurance company

(See Example 11.)

4.13 Your son Frank, who is 18 years old, is allowed to drive your car that is garaged in Territory 08. The car is used for pleasure only and Frank has had driver training. With one accident last year, how much will you pay for 50 and 100 bodily injury liability insurance?

See Table 2, base premium. Read down to 50 and 100, then across under "Territory 08." Read $90 base premium. Table 4, youthful operator. Read down to "With Driver Training, Age 18," then across under "Unmarried Male, Pleasure Only"—find 1.80 factor. Table 5, safe driver, read under "1" accident, find factor +0.30. Total factor: 1.80 + 0.30 = 2.10. Multiply the base premium by the total factor 2.10.

$$\$90 \times 2.10 = \$189 \text{ total cost}$$

(See Example 12.)

4.14 Your unmarried daughter, Sarah, is 18 years old and has had driver training. You drive your car to work 14 miles and have had two accidents in the previous year. The automobile is garaged in Territory 07. How much will you pay for a $5,000 property damage policy?

See Table 2, property damage, base premium. Read down to $5,000, then across under "Territory 07," find $50. Table 4, youthful operator. Read down to "With Driver Training, Age 18," then under "Unmarried Female, Driven to Work," find factor 1.45. Table 5, safe driver factors, read under "2" accidents, factor +0.70. Total factor: 1.45 + 0.70 = 2.15. Multiply the base premium by the total factor.

$$\$50 \times 2.15 = \$107.50 \text{ total cost}$$

(See Example 13.)

4.15 As a 40-year-old unmarried schoolteacher, Ms. Wimple drives her car to school, which is 15 miles one way. She has had no accidents during the previous year. If the car is garaged in Territory 12, how much will she pay for bodily injury liability 50/100 and property damage insurance of $10,000?

Table 2, base premium, Territory 12. Bodily injury 50 and 100; $80, base premium. Property damage, $10,000; $55, base premium. $80 + $55 = $135 total base premium. Table 3, no youthful operators; at "One, Female, 30–64," read across to "Work, 10 Miles or More," and find factor 1.30. Multiply the base premium by the factor.

$$\$135 \text{ (base premium)} \times 1.30 \text{ (factor)} = \$175.50 \text{ total cost}$$

(See Example 14.)

4.16 Lynn Fergy, single, aged 19, drives her family car, which is used for pleasure only. The car is garaged in Territory 12, and the family had one accident last year. How much will the premium amount to for the following coverage? Bodily injury liability, 100 and 300; property damage, $25,000; and medical payments, $2,000. Lynn has not had driver training.

(Read the tables as explained previously.) Table 2, Territory 12, base premium

Bodily injury liability, 100 and 300	$ 86
Property damage, $25,000	56
Table 6, medical payments, $2,000	10
Total base premium =	$152

Table 4, youthful operator; "Without Driver Training, Unmarried Female"; pleasure only, age 19;

factor 1.50. Table 5, number of accidents, 1, factor + 0.30. Total factor: 1.50 + 0.30 = 1.80. Multiply the total base premium by the total factor.

$$\$152 \times 1.80 = \$273.60 \text{ total cost of insurance}$$

(See Example 15.)

4.17   You decided to buy full coverage comprehensive insurance on your 1-year-old car. It is classified Symbol 3 and is garaged in Territory 05. Your twin brother bought a $50 deductible comprehensive policy on his 1-year-old car, classified Symbol 1, also garaged in Territory 05. You are both married, have had no accidents last year, and are 24 years old. You both drive to work. (*a*) Which one pays the least? (*b*) By how much?

(*a*) See Table 7, comprehensive coverage. Your coverage: Territory 05, Symbol 3, Age Group 1; $42, base premium, full coverage. Table 4, youthful operator, age 24, "Married Male," "With or Without Driver Training," "Drive" to Work: 1.40 total factor. Multiply the base premium by the total factor.

$$\$42 \times 1.40 = \$58.80 \text{ for full coverage}$$

Your brother's coverage: Table 7, $50 deductible, Territory 05, Symbol 1, Age Group 1, base premium, $26. Table 4, same as above, total factor, 1.40. $26 × 1.40 = $36.40 for $50 deductible. Your twin brother pays the least.

(*b*) Your brother pays $36.40; you pay $58.80. Your brother's insurance cost is less by $22.40.

(See Example 16.)

4.18   Your family pleasure car is driven by your 18-year-old daughter, who has not had driver training. The car is 2 years old, classified as Symbol 5, and garaged in Territory 05. If you had two accidents last year, how much will a $50 deductible collision policy cost?

See Table 8. Base premium collision, $50 deductible, Territory 05, Symbol 5, Age Group 2; base premium, $121. Table 4; youthful operator, "Without Driver Training," age 18, pleasure car, factor 1.55. Table 5; number of accidents 2, factor + 0.70. 1.55 + 0.70 = 2.25 total factor. Multiply the base premium by the total factor.

$$\$121 \text{ (base premium)} \times 2.25 = \$272.25 \text{ total cost}$$

(See Example 17.)

4.19   Mrs. Ball, a 66-year-old widow, had a 3-year-old car, classified as Symbol 3, and garaged in Territory 05. She uses her car for pleasure only and had one accident last year. Compute the cost of her premium for the following coverage: bodily injury liability, 25 and 50; property damage, $5,000; medical payments, $5,000; $50 deductible comprehensive and $50 deductible collision.

Obtain the base premiums for Territory 05.

Table 2, bodily injury liability 25 and 50	$ 72
Table 2, property damage, $5,000	38
Table 6, medical payments, $5,000	13
Table 7, $50 deductible comprehensive	26
Table 8, $50 deductible collision	86
Total base premium =	$235

Obtain the factor. Table 3, no youthful drivers, principal 65 or over, pleasure, factor 1.00. Table 5, 1 accident, factor + 0.30. 1.00 + 0.30 = 1.30 total factor. Multiply base premium by total factor.

$$\$235 \times 1.30 = \$305.50 \text{ total cost}$$

(See Example 18.)

4.20 Mr. and Mrs. Thomas Amajian, a middle-aged couple, are the only drivers of a 3-year-old car, classified Symbol 5, and garaged in Territory 08. They drive the car to work 18 miles and have had no accidents in the previous year. How much money will they save on automobile insurance this year if they drop their $50 deductible comprehensive and their $50 collision policies?

Territory 08, Age 2–3, Symbol 5.

Table 7: $50 deductible comprehensive	$21 base
Table 8: $50 deductible collision	68 base
Total base =	$89

Table 3, all other, work more than 10 miles, factor 1.40. Multiply the total base premium by the factor.

$$\$89 \times 1.40 = \$124.60 \text{ savings}$$

(See Example 19.)

Supplementary Problems

4.21 Your dad bought a compact car for $2,500, 8 years ago. He received a $100 trade-in allowance when he purchased a new car. What was his average annual depreciation?   *Ans*. $300. (See Problem 4.5.)

4.22 You received a $1,295 trade-in on your car which cost you $3,695 four years ago. You had driven it 48,000 miles and averaged 16 miles on a gallon of gasoline. Average cost per gallon of gasoline was 58.9 cents. Your expenses on the car during the four years were: maintenance and repairs, $635; oil and lubrication, $179; replacement parts, $585; insurance and tags, $1,145; and miscellaneous expenses, $59. (*a*) What was the average cost per year? (*b*) Per month? (*c*) Per mile driven? *Ans*.   (*a*) $1,692.50, (*b*) $141.04, (*c*) 14.1 cents. (See Problem 4.9.)

4.23 Your family pleasure car is garaged in Territory 11; and is driven by your son, Tom, who is 17 years old and has not had driver training. (*a*) If there were no accidents last year, how much will the premium be for 50 and 100 bodily injury liability insurance? (*b*) How much would it be if you had one accident?   *Ans*.   (*a*) $242.25, (*b*) $270.75. (See Problem 4.13.)

4.24 You bought full coverage comprehensive insurance on your new car; it is classified Symbol 4 and garaged in Territory 16. As a 23-year-old married male who drives the car to work: (*a*) how much will the premium amount to? (*b*) How much less would a $50 deductible comprehensive policy cost? You had no accidents last year.   *Ans*.   (*a*) $27.55, (*b*) $2.90 less. (See Problem 4.17.)

4.25 Ruth and Jim Franks purchased a new automobile; the unpaid balance after miscellaneous charges and trade-in allowance on their old car amounted to $3,500. The Franks could afford payments of approximately $110 per month. (*a*) For how many years should they take out a loan at $7\frac{1}{2}$% interest? (*b*) At $8\frac{1}{2}$% interest?   *Ans*.   (*a*) Monthly payments for 3 years at $7\frac{1}{2}$% amount to $108.87. (*b*) Monthly payments for 3 years at $8\frac{1}{2}$% amount to $110.49. (See Problem 4.1.)

4.26 You travel 2,000 miles a month in your car and average 23 miles on a gallon of gasoline costing 65.9¢ per gallon. You add 1 quart of oil per month at a cost of $1.10 per quart. (*a*) What is your cost per month for gas and oil? (*b*) What is the average cost per mile for gas and oil? *Ans*.   (*a*) $58.41, (*b*) 2.29¢. (See Problem 4.6.)

4.27   How much gasoline tax did you pay last year if you drove 18,000 miles and averaged 21 miles on a gallon of gasoline that cost 64.9¢ per gallon?   Federal gas tax is 4¢ per gallon; state tax is 9¢ per gallon.   (*a*) How much was the tax?   (*b*) What percent of gasoline cost was the tax?   *Ans*.   (*a*) $111.42,   (*b*) 20% of cost.   (See Problem 4.10.)

4.28   Nancy, an unmarried student 20 years old, drives her father's car, which he also uses for business.   The car is 2 years old and is garaged in Territory 08.   Nancy has had driver training and the family had one accident the previous year.   How much will the premium amount to for $25,000 property damage coverage?   *Ans*. $86.70.   (See Problem 4.14.)

4.29   Your family business car had two accidents last year.   It is driven by your 19-year-old son, who has not had driver training.   The 2-year-old car is garaged in Territory 05 and is classified Symbol 5.   How much would a $50 deductible collision policy cost?   *Ans*. $363.   (See Problem 4.18.)

4.30   There is an unpaid balance of $4,500 on your new car.   You arranged a loan at $8\frac{1}{2}\%$ interest, with monthly payments over a 3-year period.   (*a*) How much are your monthly payments?   (*b*) How much will you pay back?   (*c*) What is the actual interest rate on the loan?   *Ans*.   (*a*) $142.05, (*b*) $5,113.80,   (*c*) 8.8%.   (See Problem 4.2.)

4.31   The maintenance costs last year on your car were: new tires, $139.50; oil and lubrication, $47.95; tune-ups, $58.95; new battery, $32.95; and minor repairs, $27.95.   You drove 17,000 miles during the year.   (*a*) What was your average monthly expense for maintenance?   (*b*) What was the average cost per mile for maintenance?   *Ans*.   (*a*) $25.61, (*b*) 1.8 cents per mile.   (See Problem 4.7.)

4.32   The Allen family drove 2,700 miles while on vacation.   They get 17.5 miles on a gallon of gasoline that costs 68.9¢ per gallon.   The Federal gas tax is 4¢ per gallon and the state tax is 8.5¢ per gallon.   Their toll fees amounted to $23.50.   (*a*) How much Federal gas tax did they pay?   (*b*) State tax?   (*c*) What percent of the total operating costs were the gas taxes and toll fees?   *Ans*.   (*a*) $6.19,   (*b*) $13.12,   (*c*) 33%.   (See Problem 4.11.)

4.33   Bill Swing, a 44-year-old bachelor, uses his car for business and has had no previous accidents.   The car is garaged in Territory 11.   (*a*) How much will he pay for bodily injury liability 100 and 300 and $25,000 property damage coverage?   (*b*) What would he pay if he had been involved in three accidents?   *Ans*.   (*a*) $231,   (*b*) $415.80.   (See Problem 4.15.)

4.34   Jim Lynch, a 68-year-old widower, owns a 4-year-old car, Symbol 5, garaged in Territory 16.   He uses it only for pleasure and has had no accidents during the previous year.   (*a*) Compute the cost of his premium for the following coverage: bodily injury liability 100 and 300; property damage $25,000;   medical payments $5,000; $50 deductible comprehensive;   and $50 deductible collision.   (*b*) How much would he pay if he had two accidents last year?   *Ans*.   (*a*) $237,   (*b*) $402.90.   (See Problem 4.19.)

4.35   Patricia bought a used car while at college.   The selling price was $2,650.   The salesman offered to finance it, if Patricia made a $650 down payment and agreed to pay $98 a month for 2 years.   (*a*) What was the amount of carrying charge?   (*b*) What was the actual interest rate?   *Ans*.   (*a*) $352,   (*b*) 16.9%.

4.36   Your car expenses last year for 16,000 miles of driving were: gasoline, 64.9¢ per gallon (you averaged 19 miles on a gallon); license, tag, and insurance, $398; maintenance, repairs, $269; and average annual depreciation, $950.   (*a*) What did it cost you to drive your car last year?   (*b*) What was the average cost per mile?   *Ans*.   (*a*) $2,163.46,   (*b*) 13.5¢.   (See Problem 4.8.)

4.37   Ruth Gaines was insured for 25 and 50 bodily injury liability.   She injured three persons in an accident, who sued her and who were awarded the following amounts: $35,000, $6,000, and $4,000.   (*a*) How much must she pay in claims?   (*b*) How much will the company pay? *Ans.*   (*a*) $10,000,   (*b*) $35,000.   (See Problem 4.12.)

4.38   Fred Gruber, a single, 18-year-old male, has had driver training.   He drives the family car, which is also used for business.   The car is garaged in Territory 08.   The Grubers had no accidents during the previous year.   How much will the premium amount to for the following coverage: bodily injury liability 50 and 100; property damage, $10,000; and medical payments, $5,000?   *Ans*. $313.65. (See Problem 4.16.)

4.39   Mr. and Mrs. Frank McMackin, a retired couple in their sixties, drive their 2-year-old car for pleasure only.   They have not been involved in any car accidents at any time.   They decided to drop their $50 deductible comprehensive and $50 deductible collision policies.   The car is classified Symbol 5 and is garaged in Territory 16.   By how much will this reduce their premium? *Ans*. $97.   (See Problem 4.20.)

4.40   Jack Brown purchased a car for $3,800 four years ago.   He now decides to buy a new car and is offered a trade-in allowance of $900 on his old car.   What was his average annual depreciation? *Ans*. $725.   (See Problem 4.4.)

Examination I

1. John Kislak, a maintenance handyman at the Atlas Paper Mill, receives $4.60 an hour regular pay plus time and a half for all hours worked over 40 hours a week. Due to the illness of one of his crew members, John worked the following number of hours last week. Monday, 10; Tuesday, 9; Wednesday, 7; Thursday, 10; and Friday, $10\frac{1}{2}$. Determine John's gross pay for the week.

2. Margie Lenhart who is single, receives a gross monthly pay of $690. She declares one exemption on her W-4 form. She asked you to figure her take-home pay after income tax and social security withholding. (See Appendixes 1 and 2, Income Tax and Social Security Withholding tables.)

3. Ken Brooks works in the furniture department of a local department store. Ken works on a commission basis. A graduated scale of pay provides for 1% commission on all sales, an additional $1\frac{1}{2}\%$ on all sales between $30,000 and $40,000, and 2% on all sales over $40,000. During the month of May, Ken's sales totaled $49,000. (a) What was his gross pay? (b) Referring to the tables used in 2 above, compute his take-home pay.

4. Ms. Ruth Williams, the head bookkeeper at Jason's Department Store, has a monthly social security tax deduction of $46.80, plus an income tax withholding amount of $137.20 a month. (a) What is Ruth's gross pay? (b) Her take-home pay? (See Appendices 1 and 2.)

5. Stewart Granger, a regional sales supervisor for an electronics firm, who earns $24,000 a year, declared 5 exemptions on his W-4 form. After income tax withholding and Social Security deductions, Stewart budgeted 12% of his monthly take home pay for clothing expenses. To how much does this amount?

6. Jack Fram, who drives a truck for the Interstate Van Line, is single and has a monthly take-home pay of $785. Jack's personal automobile expenses amount to $65 a month, not including car loan payments. If he budgets 18% of his monthly take-home pay for automobile expenses, how much can he plan per month for car payments?

7. Jake Lonnett stopped by the grocery store on his way home from work and bought a $1\frac{1}{2}$-pound package of ground beef for $1.49. Sandra, his wife, also brought home a package of ground beef weighing $2\frac{1}{2}$ pounds, for which she paid $2.35. Which size package was the more economical?

8. An automobile dealer is selling all new cars at a discount of 12% off the suggested price. In addition, he will sell you a car with an additional 5% off the discount price if you order a new one today. What will the price be if you order a new automobile today with a suggested price of $5,895?

9. At a special sale, you bought a set of shock absorbers, installed, for $49.98. The shock absorbers retail at $64.95. You also bought 4 steel-belted radial tires for $199.98, which had a retail price of $65.90 each. What percent discount did you receive on each purchase?

10. Ms. Irene Cassell, who operates her own florist shop, decided to purchase a microwave oven to save time in the preparation of her meals. Upon shopping around, she found one which sold for $349 cash, or on the installment plan by paying $49 down and $12 a month for 30 months. Find the installment carrying costs and the actual rate of interest.

11. Joe Small, who owned a small paint contracting business, needed money to purchase some new ladders, scaffolding, and miscellaneous equipment. He negotiated a $950 loan, to be discounted at $8\frac{3}{4}\%$, for 75 days from his bank. (a) How much money did he receive? (b) What true rate of interest is Joe paying?

12. You decided to buy a car with a delivery price of $4,688. The dealer allowed you $688 on your old car. If the dealer financed the car for you and charged you $8\frac{1}{2}\%$ interest payable in equal monthly installments over a 3-year period, to how much would your monthly payments amount?

13. Henry Mann borrowed $2,800 from his company credit union for 24 months, with monthly installment payments of $131.81. (*a*) How much interest did he pay? (*b*) To how much did the annual rate of interest amount?

14. Your bank statement shows a balance of $482.79 on April 30; your checkstub balance on that date was $174.84. Checks #58 for $78.92, #59 for $185.50, and #61 for $49.98 are not enclosed with your statement. The bank has deducted a service charge of $1.45 and a charge of $5.00 for printing checks. Reconcile your bank statement.

15. Andy Taylor left for the armed services 18 years ago and never returned to his hometown. At the time he left for army service, he had an account in the City Savings and Loan Association that he forgot about. His local bank finally located him and forwarded a bank statement, which indicated that his original deposit had been compounded anually at $5\frac{1}{2}\%$ interest and had now grown to $3,932.25. How much was Andy's original deposit? (See Compound Interest table on page 52.)

16. Zeke Atkins, a local boat dealer, received a promissory note from Oscar Varnes, the chairman of a local social organization, for $1,500 at $8\frac{1}{2}\%$ interest, due 72 days after April 20, 1977; for payment of a fishing boat which the social club is going to award as a raffle prize. On May 19, Zeke discounted the note at his bank at a discount rate of 9%. Determine: (*a*) the due date, (*b*) the maturity value, (*c*) the term of discount (days), (*d*) the amount of discount, and (*e*) the amount Zeke received on May 19.

17. Ms. Jackson purchased a car from a used car dealer. The selling price was $2,495; she made a down payment of $695 and agreed to make 24 monthly payments of $92 each. (*a*) What amount was the carrying charge? (*b*) What was the actual rate of interest?

18. Joseph Grubb drives his car approximately 1,800 miles a month. The car averages 16.5 miles to the gallon of gasoline. Gasoline cost is 69.9 cents per gallon. The car consumes one quart of oil for each 900 miles traveled, at a cost of $1.05 per quart. (*a*) What is Grubbs' monthly cost for gasoline and oil? (*b*) What is his average cost per mile for gas and oil?

19. Your family pleasure car is 2 years old, classified Symbol 4, garaged in Territory 16. It is also driven by your 18-year-old, unmarried daughter, who has had driver training. You have had one accident during the previous year. Using the table in Chapter 7, compute your premium for the following insurance coverage; bodily injury liability 50 and 100; property damage $10,000; medical payments $5,000, $50 deductible comprehensive; and $50 deductible collision.

20. Ms. Henery is a 65-year-old unmarried lady, who owns a 4-year-old car, classified as Symbol 3, garaged in Territory 8. She only drives for pleasure and was involved in one accident in the previous year. How much less will her premium be if she does not renew her full comprehensive coverage and her $50 deductible collision coverage?

Solutions to Examination I

1. $10 + 9 + 7 + 10 + 10\frac{1}{2} = 46\frac{1}{2}$ hours; 40 hours at \$4.60 = \$184 regular pay.
   $6\frac{1}{2}$ hours at \$6.90 = \$44.85 overtime pay.
   \$184 (regular pay) + \$44.85 (overtime pay) = \$228.85 gross pay.

2. \$690 gross income tax withholding, one exemption, \$112.00. Social Security tax; \$690 × 0.0585 = \$40.37.
   \$112 (income tax withholding) + \$40.37 (Social Security) = \$152.37;
   \$690 − \$152.37 = \$537.63 take-home pay.

3. (a) \$49,000 × 0.01 = \$490 on all sales;
   \$30,000 − \$40,000 = \$10,000 × 0.015 = \$150;
   \$40,000 − \$49,000 = \$9,000 × 0.02 = \$180.
   \$490 + \$150 + \$180 = \$820 gross pay.

   (b) \$137.20 (income tax withholding) + \$47.97 (Social Security) = \$185.17.
   \$820 − \$185.17 = \$634.83 take-home pay.

4. \$46.80 (Social Security withholding) ÷ 0.0585 = \$800 gross pay.
   \$46.80 (Social Security) + \$137.20 (income tax withholding) = \$184 withholding deductions.
   \$800 (gross pay) − \$184 (withholding) = \$616 take-home pay.

5. \$24,000 ÷ 12 = \$2,000 monthly gross pay.
   Income tax withholding with exemptions = \$347.30.
   Social Security: \$15,300 × 0.0585 = \$895.05, the maximum annual amount.
   \$895.05 ÷ 12 = \$74.59, the average monthly Social Security deduction.
   \$2,000 − \$421.89 (\$347.30 + \$74.59) = \$1,578.11, the average monthly take-home pay.
   \$1,578.11 × 0.12 = \$189.37, the approximate monthly clothing budget.

6. \$785 × 0.18 = \$141.30 budget allowance.
   \$141.30 − \$65 = \$76.30 available for car payment.

7. \$1.49 ÷ 1.5 = \$.993 = \$1.00 per pound (rounded figure).
   \$2.35 ÷ 2.5 = \$.94 per pound. (More economical.)

8. \$5,895 × 0.12 = \$707.40 discount.
   \$5,895 − \$707.40 = \$5,187.60 sale price.
   \$5.187.60 = 0.05 = \$259.38 additional discount.
   \$5,187.60 − \$259.38 = \$4,929.22, today's price.

9. \$64.95 − \$49.98 = \$14.97 discount on shock absorbers.
   \$65.90 × 4 = \$263.60, regular price of tires.
   \$263.60 − \$199.98 = \$63.62, the discount on tires.
   \$14.97 + \$63.62 = \$88.59, the discount.
   \$64.95 + \$263.60 = \$328.55, the regular price.
   \$88.59 ÷ \$328.55 = 0.269, or 26.9% discount.

10. (a) Down payment, \$49; monthly payments, 30 × 12, or \$360; installment price = \$409, − \$349 (cash price) = \$60 carrying costs.

    (b) $R = \dfrac{24 \times C}{P \times (n+1)} = \dfrac{24 \times \$60}{\$300 \times (30+1)} = \dfrac{\$1,440}{\$9,300} = 0.1548$, or 15.5%.

11. (a) $D = P \times R \times T$: $D = \$950 \times 0.0875 \times \dfrac{75}{360} = \dfrac{\$6,234.375}{360} = \$17.32$ discount.

$\$950 - \$17.32 = \$932.68$, the amount received.

(b) $D = P \times R \times T$: $\$17.32 = \$932.68 \times R \times \dfrac{75}{360}$; $\$17.32 = \dfrac{\$69,951R}{360}$; $\$17.32 = \$194.31R$; $R = 0.089$, or 8.9%, interest.

12. $\$4,688$ (list price) $- \$688$ (trade in) $= \$4,000, + \$790$ (insurance) $= \$4,790$, to be financed at $8\frac{1}{2}\%$ for 3 years.

$I = P \times R \times T$: $I = \$4,790 \times 0.085 \times 3$; $I = \$1,221.45$;

$\$4,790 + \$1,221.45 = \$6,011.45$, the total to be financed.

$\$6,011.45 \div 36 = \$166.98$ monthly payments.

13. $\$131.81 \times 24 = \$3,163.44$, the total amount to be repaid.

$\$3,163.44 - \$2,800 = \$363.44$ interest charge.

$R = \dfrac{24 \times C}{P \times (n + 1)} = \dfrac{24 \times \$363.44}{\$2,800 \times 25} = \dfrac{\$8,722.56}{\$70,000} = 0.1246$, or 12.5%.

14.

Bank balance, April 31,		$482.79	Checkstub balance,		$174.84
Less outstanding checks			Less:		
#58	$ 78.92		Service charge	$1.45	
#59	185.50		Printing checks	5.00	6.45
#61	49.98	314.40			
Adjusted bank balance		$168.39	Checkstub balance		$168.39

15. $\$3,932.25$ (compounded amount) $\div 2.6215$ (value of \$1 at $5\frac{1}{2}\%$ interest, compounded annually) $= \$1,500$, the original amount.

16. (a) April 20th is the 110th day; $110 + 72 = 182$; 182nd day is July 1.

(b) $I = P \times R \times T$: $I = \$1,500 \times 0.085 \times \dfrac{72}{360} = \$25.50$.

$\$1,500 + \$25.50 = \$1,525.50$, the maturity value.

(c) May 19th is the 139th day; $182 - 139 = 43$ days.

(d) $D = P \times R \times T$: $D = \$1,525.50 \times 0.09 \times \dfrac{43}{360} = \dfrac{\$5,903.69}{360} = \$16.40$ discount.

(e) $\$1,525.50 - \$16.40 = \$1,509.10$, the amount received on May 19.

17. (a) $\$2,495$ (selling price) $- \$695$ (down payment) $= \$1,800$, the unpaid balance. 24 (payments) $\times \$92 = \$2,208$, the amount to be paid. $\$2,208$ (amount to be paid) $- \$1,800$ (unpaid balance) $= \$408$, the carrying charge.

(b) $R = \dfrac{24 \times C}{P \times (n + 1)} = \dfrac{24 \times \$408}{\$1,800 \times (24 + 1)} = \dfrac{\$9,792}{\$45,000} = 0.2175$, or 21.8%.

(c) $I = P \times R \times T$: $\$408 = \dfrac{\$1,800}{24} \times R \times \dfrac{300}{12}$; $\$408 = \dfrac{\$540,000R}{288}$; $\$408 = \$1,875R$; $R = \$408 \div \$1,875$; $R = 0.2175$, or 21.8%.

18.   (a) 1,800 miles ÷ 16.5 mpg = 109.09 gallons, rounded to 109.   109 (gallons) × $.699 (per gallon) = $76.19, the gasoline cost. 1,800 ÷ 900 = 2 quarts of oil; $1.05 × 2 = $2.10, the oil cost. $76.19 + $2.10 = $78.29, the cost for gas and oil.

      (b) $78.29 (total cost) ÷ 1,800 (miles) = $.0434, or 4.34¢, per mile.

19.
Table 2: 50 and 100	$86 base
Table 2: $25,000	49 "
Table 6: $5,000	14 "
Table 7: $50 deductible	13 "
Table 8: $50 deductible	67 "

        Total base premium = $229

    Table 4: 18-year-old, unmarried female, driver training, pleasure driving, factor, 1.20.
    Table 5: one accident, factor, 0.30.
    Total factor: 1.20 + 0.30 = 1.50.
    $229 (base premium) × 1.50 (factor) = $343.50, the total premium.

20.
Table 7: full comprehensive	$11 base
Table 8: $50 deductible collision	42 "

        Total base = $53

    Table 5: 1 accident, factor, + 0.30.
    Table 3: principal, 65 or over; factor, 1.00.
    Total factor: 1.00 + 0.30 = 1.30.
    $53 (base premium) × 1.30 = $68.90 less.

Chapter 5

Housing Costs

Consumers have the option of buying or renting their living quarters. Their choice depends on their lifestyle and financial capability. *Renting* property means paying a monthly rental fee. *Buying* property usually means making a monthly *mortgage* payment. The essential difference between the two is *equity*. When you rent a house or apartment, the landlord owns the property. When you make payments on a mortgage, you slowly acquire equity in the house, which means you end up owning the property.

Property owners are investors who expect a profit on their capital investment. They rent or lease property in anticipation of a profit that is in excess of current interest rates on other investments which entail less risk. The renters must pay for all expenses related to the property plus an additional amount to allow for a profit. See Section 7.1.

5.1 BUYING A HOUSE

The costs associated with buying a new house are numerous, and require careful consideration—particularly for those who are going from a rental to an ownership situation. It is important to relate the cost of home ownership to rental cost and personal income.

For some, the amount of the monthly payment may be the deciding factor in determining whether to buy or rent. These payments are based on the amount of the loan, the interest rate, and the term of the loan (see Sections 5.2 and 5.3).

EXAMPLE 1

Mr. and Mrs. South, who have two children and live in a rented apartment that they feel has become too small for their needs, decided to move to the suburbs. They thought they would rent a three-bedroom house until they were sure that the suburbs was where they wanted to live. But after studying the matter, they found that a 20-year mortgage on a similar house would actually come to a few dollars less than renting a house. After carefully weighing all options and by reworking their budget, the Souths decided that in the long run it would be decidedly to their advantage to buy a house on mortgage. The annual total rental expenses for the South family last year were: rent, $1,800; electricity, $840; water, sewage disposal, and garbage collection, $350; telephone, $198; heating oil, $210; installment purchases of appliances, $600; maintenance and repair, $150; and landscaping and yard care, $180. (*a*) What were their average monthly housing costs? (*b*) If the monthly housing costs are 30% of Mr. South's annual income, what is his annual income?

The Souths purchased a $37,500 house with a 20% down payment. The mortgage loan was for 25 years at an interest rate of $8\frac{1}{2}\%$. Monthly payments amount to $241.57. (*c*) The annual mortgage payments represent what percent of Mr. South's annual income? Other housing costs amount to $110 a month. (*d*) The monthly costs of home ownership are what percent lower than the monthly rental costs?

(*a*) Add all housing expenses and divide the total by 12 (months). $1,800 (rent) + $840 (electricity) + $350 (water, etc.) + $198 (telephone) + $210 (heating oil) + $600 (appliances) + $150 (maintenance) + $180 (yard care) = $4,328 annual cost.

$$4,328 \div 12 = \$360.67 \text{ average monthly cost}$$

(b) Divide the total annual cost by the percent of income to obtain approximate annual income.

$$P = B \times R \qquad \$4,328 = B \times 0.30 \qquad B = \$4,328 \div 0.30 = \$14,426.67$$

(c) The annual mortgage payment divided by the annual income equals the percent of annual income. $241.57 (monthly payment) × 12 = $2,898.84 annual mortgage payment.

$$\$2,898.84 \text{ (annual payment)} \div \$14,426.67 \text{ (annual income)} = 0.2009, \text{ or } 20.1\%$$

(d) The monthly rental costs = $360.67. The monthly ownership costs are $241.57 + $110, or $351.59. $360.67 − $351.57 = $9.10 less than monthly rental cost as a result of home ownership. Divide the amount of difference between monthly rental costs and monthly ownership costs by the monthly rental costs to obtain the percent.

$$\$9.10 \text{ (difference)} \div \$360.67 \text{ (rental cost)} = 0.0252, \text{ or } 2.5\% \text{ lower}$$

When planning a home purchase, the following rules of thumb provide useful guidelines:
(1) The purchase price of a house should not exceed $2\frac{1}{2}$ times the annual take-home earnings of the consumer.

EXAMPLE 2

Mr. and Mrs. Jackson plan to purchase a larger house for their growing family. With annual take-home earnings of $14,000, approximately how much can they afford to pay for a house?

Use the $2\frac{1}{2}$ times earnings rule.

$$\$14,000 \text{ (annual take-home pay)} \times 2\frac{1}{2} = \$35,000 \text{ approximate amount they could pay}$$

(2) It is advisable to budget not more than one week's take-home pay for monthly housing costs. Studies indicate that monthly housing costs (including mortgage payment, taxes, insurance and maintenance) generally approximate 1% of the purchase price of the house.

EXAMPLE 3

The Merritt family has an annual take-home pay of $18,000. In anticipation of moving, Mr. and Mrs. Merritt wish to know how much money they should budget for monthly housing costs.

Obtain the monthly take-home pay by dividing the annual pay by 12. Multiply this amount by 25% to obtain the approximate amount for housing costs.

$$\$18,000 \div 12 = \$1,500 \text{ take-home earnings per month}$$

$$\$1,500 \times 0.25 = \$375, \text{ the approximate amount for monthly housing costs}$$

See Problem 5.2.

EXAMPLE 4

Mr. Belk is an articulate man who maintains his property in an excellent manner. As a retired accountant, his hobby is working on his house and grounds. He paints his house every three years at a cost of $450; his yard and landscaping expenses are $100 a year; other maintenance expenses are $80 a year. In addition, he also places $75 a year in a special account for a new roof. He would like to determine (a) how much money should be set aside each month for these expenses, and (b) what percent of his total housing costs of $350 these expenses are.

(a) Total the average annual cost of all items and divide by 12 to obtain the average monthly cost. $450 (paint) ÷ 3 (years) = $150 per year. $150 (paint) + $100 (landscaping) + $80 (miscellaneous) + $75 (roof) = $405 total annual cost.

$$\$405 \text{ (annual cost)} \div 12 = \$33.75 \text{ average monthly amount for maintenance}$$

(b) Divide the maintenance expenses by total housing costs to obtain the percent of total cost.

$$\$33.75 \text{ (maintenance cost)} \div \$350 \text{ (total monthly housing cost)}$$
$$= 0.096, \text{ or } 9.6\% \text{ of total monthly housing costs}$$

Perhaps the most significant expense is the down payment required by the loan source. The amount of down payment to be accumulated varies with the type of loan obtained (see Section 5.2). In addition, the buyer must allow for specific closing costs, which are also payable at the time of purchase. Typically, closing costs include: legal fees, recording fees, property survey, appraisal, title insurance, state mortgage taxes and prorations of insurance or other expenditures paid in advance by the seller.

EXAMPLE 5

Your parents purchased a new house at an appraised value of $43,500. Mr. Solomon, the real estate agent, prepared the following statement, which included those costs which your father must pay at the time of closing. Legal fees, $200; recording fees, $12; survey, $75; appraisal, $60; title insurance, $190; state mortgage tax, $55; and a proration of prepaid insurance, $110. (a) What is the total amount of closing costs? (b) This amount is what percent of the appraised value?

(a) Add all costs to obtain total closing costs.

$$\$200 + \$12 + \$75 + \$60 + \$190 + \$55 + \$110 = \$702 \text{ total closing costs}$$

(b) Divide the total closing costs by the appraised value to obtain the percent.

$$\$702 \div \$43,500 = 0.016, \text{ or } 1.6\% \text{ of appraised value}$$

5.2 HOME LOANS AND DOWN PAYMENTS

The three basic types of home loans available today are conventional, Federal Housing Authority insured and Veterans Administration loans. All are available from the same sources: banks, savings and loan associations, insurance companies and mortgage bankers.

The conventional loan. Under this type of loan, the lender is protected only by the value of the property. The agreement to repay the loan is strictly between the lender and borrower. If the borrower defaults, the lender gets the property. It follows, then, that the down payment under such terms generally runs from 20% to 30% of the property's appraised value. In a conventional loan, the borrower promises to repay a specified sum each month over the life of the loan, which generally runs from 5 to 30 years. Most mortgage loans are conventional loans.

EXAMPLE 6

Mr. Bates, a sales representative, was transferred to Preston. Bates's new sales manager recommended an excellent house which was appraised at $41,500. The local savings and loan association approved a conventional mortgage loan for him if he could arrange for a 25% down payment. After careful deliberation, Mr. and Mrs. Bates decided to purchase the property. (a) How much was the required down payment? (b) To how much will the mortgage loan amount? (c) What percent of the appraised value did the loan represent?

(a) Multiply the appraised value by the percent of down payment provided to find the amount of the down payment.

$$\$41,500 \text{ (appraised value)} \times 0.25 \text{ (percent of down payment)} = \$10,375 \text{ required down payment}$$

(b) Subtract the amount of down payment from the appraised value to obtain the amount of the mortgage loan.

$$\$41,500 \text{ (appraised value)} - \$10,375 \text{ (down payment)} = \$31,125 \text{ amount of the mortgage loan}$$

(c) Divide the amount of the loan by the appraised value to find the percent.

$$\$31,125 \div \$41,500 = 0.75, \text{ or } 75\%$$

The F.H.A. insured loan. This type of loan is backed by the Federal Housing Administration, which insures the lending source against loss in the event of borrower default. The borrower pays a premium (e.g., .05%) on the unpaid balance of the loan for such insurance. This generally enables the borrower to finance a home at lower down payment rates based on the appraised value of the property (see Table 1), possible lower interest rates, and perhaps a longer repayment schedule than would otherwise be available. The limit on an F.H.A. insured mortgage is $45,000.

Table 1

Appraised Value	Percent of Down Payment	Amount of Down Payment
Up to $25,000	3%	Up to $750
$25,000–$35,000	10%	$1,000
$35,000–$45,000	20%	$2,000

EXAMPLE 7

Mr. and Mrs. Singleton decided to buy a new house in the suburbs at the time when their children were reaching the teenage growing-up period. After a thorough search, they found a house well suited to their needs. The F.H.A. appraisal was in the amount of $39,850. (a) What is the required down payment? (b) How much will the loan amount to?

(a) The required down payment is shown in Table 1. Appraised value, $39,850. 3% of first $25,000 = $750. 10% of ($35,000–$25,000) $10,000 = $1,000. 20% of ($39,850 – $35,000) $4,850 = $970.

$$\$750 + \$1,000 + \$970 = \$2,720 \text{ required down payment}$$

(b) Subtract the down payment from the appraised value to obtain the amount of the loan.

$$\$39,850 \text{ (appraised value)} - \$2,720 \text{ (down payment)} = \$37,130 \text{ amount of loan}$$

The VA loan. The Veterans Administration requires no down payment for its loan guarantee, which has a maximum of $12,500 at no charge to the veteran. VA loans are obtained through standard mortgage sources who may require some down payment. However, the VA endorsement based on careful appraisal generally enables the borrower to conclude favorable financing arrangements.

5.3 THE AMORTIZED MORTGAGE LOAN

The terms of an amortized mortgage loan require a fixed monthly payment for the duration of the loan. Each payment includes interest and reduction of principal. The loan is completely paid off after the required number of payments. To figure the monthly payments required to liquidate the amortized mortgage loan at a fixed interest rate for a specified number of years, the following table is presented.

Table 2. Monthly Payments Required To Pay Principal and Interest on a
Loan of $1,000

Term of Loan	6%	7%	$7\frac{1}{2}$%	8%	$8\frac{1}{2}$%	9%
5 years	$19.34	$19.81	$20.04	$20.28	$20.52	$20.76
10 years	11.11	11.62	11.87	12.14	12.40	12.67
15 years	8.44	8.99	9.27	9.56	9.85	10.15
20 years	7.17	7.76	8.06	8.37	8.68	9.00
25 years	6.45	7.07	7.39	7.72	8.06	8.40
30 years	6.00	6.66	7.00	7.34	7.69	8.05

EXAMPLE 8

After searching for a house, the Jacksons found a suitable one that had a sale price of $38,500, with a required down payment of $8,500. They contacted a mortgage broker who would arrange a mortgage loan for the balance at 8% interest for 30 years. How much will the Jacksons pay per month on this loan?

Obtain the amount of loan by subtracting the down payment from the cost price.

$38,500 − $8,500 = $30,000, the amount of the mortgage loan

See Table 2. Read down the left-hand column under term of loan, then to the right under the 8% interest rate column. Where the two intersect, read $7.34. This is the monthly payment required to pay principal and interest on $1,000. Multiply this figure, $7.34, by the amount of the loan.

$7.34 × 30 (number of thousands) = $220.20, the monthly payment required

After determining the amount of the monthly payment, a loan payment schedule is generally made by the lending agency.

EXAMPLE 9

Table 3 was computed from the following information. Al Johns received a mortgage loan of $33,000 with interest at 9% for 25 years. He wants to (a) determine the amount of the monthly payment and (b) construct a mortgage loan payment schedule showing the first five payments.

(a) From Table 2, determine the monthly payment. Read down to 25 years, then to the right under the 9% column and find $8.40. The amount to pay off is $33,000. Multiply $8.40 × 33 (number of thousands): $277.20 is the amount of the monthly payment.

(b) To find the monthly interest charge, multiply the amount of the loan by the annual interest rate. Divide the result by 12 to obtain the monthly interest payment. $33,000 × 0.09 = $2,970, the annual amount. $2,970 ÷ 12 = $247.50 interest for the first month. Monthly payment − interest payment = amount applied to principal. $277.20 − $247.50 = $29.70, applied to principal. The

Table 3. (Mortgage loan payment schedule: loan of $33,000, interest
9%, term 25 years, monthly payment, $277.20.)

Payment Number	Monthly Payment	Applied to Interest	Principal	Unpaid Balance
1	$277.20	$247.50	$29.70	$32,970.30
2	277.20	247.28	29.92	32,940.38
3	277.20	247.05	30.15	32,910.23
4	277.20	246.83	30.37	32,879.86
5	277.20	246.60	30.70	32,849.26

amount applied to principal is now subtracted from the amount of the loan. The difference is the unpaid balance:

$$\$33,000 \text{ (original loan)} - \$29.70 = \$32,970.30 \text{ unpaid balance}$$

To figure Payment #2: interest is paid only on the unpaid balance. Multiply the amount of unpaid balance by the annual interest rate.

$$\$32,970.30 \times 0.09 = \$2,967.33$$

Divide that by 12: $247.28, amount of interest on second payment. Next: subtract this amount of interest from the monthly payment to obtain the amount to be applied to principal.

$$\$277.20 - \$247.28 = \$29.92$$

applied to principal. Subtract the amount applied to the principal from the unpaid balance to arrive at the new unpaid balance after the second payment. The same procedure is continued for the total number of payments, at which time the unpaid balance will reach zero and the total loan will be repaid.

Payment #3:

$$\$32,940.38 \text{ (unpaid balance)} \times 0.09 = \$2,964.63$$

Divide that by 12: $247.05.

$$\$277.20 \text{ (monthly payment)} - \$247.05 \text{ (interest)} = \$30.15 \text{ (amount applied to principal)}$$

$$\$32,940.38 \text{ (unpaid balance)} - \$30.15 \text{ (principal payment)}$$
$$= \$32,910.23, \text{ unpaid balance, end of third payment}$$

Note: The annual interest rate may be divided by 12 to obtain the monthly interest rate. By multiplying the monthly interest rate by the unpaid balance, the amount of interest is obtained immediately.

Payment #4:
$$9\% \text{ (annual interest rate)} \div 12 = 0.09 \div 12 = 0.0075, \text{ monthly interest rate}$$

$$\$32,910.23 \text{ (unpaid balance)} \times 0.0075 \text{ (monthly interest rate)} = \$246.83, \text{ amount of interest}$$

$$\$277.20 - \$246.83 = \$30.37, \text{ principal reduction}$$

$$\$32,910.23 - \$30.37 = \$32,879.86, \text{ unpaid balance after fourth payment}$$

Payment #5:

$$\$32,879.86 \times 0.0075 = \$246.60$$

$$\$277.20 - \$246.60 = \$30.60, \text{ principal reduction}$$

$$\$32,879.86 - \$30.60 = \$32,849.26, \text{ unpaid balance at end of fifth payment}$$

EXAMPLE 10

Al and Mary Frank made their last monthly payment on their home. They had repaid an $8\frac{1}{2}\%$, 30-year mortgage loan of $37,500. They decide to figure out how much interest they paid over the thirty years. From Table 2, they obtain the monthly payment on $1,000 at $8\frac{1}{2}\%$ for 30 years. Payment amounts to $7.69. They multiply this amount by 37.5 (number of thousands) to obtain the monthly payment.

$$\$7.69 \text{ (payment for \$1,000)} \times 37.5 \text{ (number of thousands)} = \$288.38 \text{ monthly payment}$$

They multiply the amount of monthly payment by the total number of months to obtain the total amount paid in 30 years.

$$\$288.38 \text{ (monthly payment)} \times 12 \text{ (months)} \times 30 \text{ (years)}$$
$$= \$288.38 \times 360 \text{ (payments)} = \$103,816.80, \text{ total amount paid}$$

They subtract the original loan amount from the total amount paid to obtain the amount of interest paid on the loan.

$$\$103,816.80 \text{ (30 year total)} - \$37,500 \text{ (loan amount)} = \$66,316.80, \text{ total 30 year interest}$$

Lending agencies may require consumers to pay for insurance and taxes in advance. Normally 1/12 of the annual cost of each is added to the monthly mortgage payment. This money is placed in an escrow account to be available when these payments are due.

EXAMPLE 11

Mrs. Wilson received a letter from the mortgage banking institution servicing her mortgage loan. She was informed that in addition to paying her monthly mortgage payment of $219.50, she must remit payment for her annual taxes of $720 and her annual insurance premium in the amount of $180. These obligations will be prepaid monthly and placed in an escrow account. What is her new monthly payment?

The insurance and taxes are paid in advance by monthly payments. Figure the monthly payment for these and add them to the monthly mortgage loan payments.

Thus, $720 (taxes) ÷ 12 = $60. $180 (insurance) ÷ 12 = $15

$219.50 (mortgage loan) + $60 (taxes) + $15 (insurance) = $294.50, total monthly payment

5.4 INCOME TAX DEDUCTIONS

The Internal Revenue statutes allow private property owners to itemize mortgage interest costs and real estate taxes as deductible items on their income tax returns.

EXAMPLE 12

The Johnson family, which owns their single-family residence, paid $1,250 interest on their mortgage loan and $898 real estate taxes last year. In addition they paid $130 for homeowner's insurance and had maintenance expenses of $260. Mr. Johnson asked you to determine how much of these expenditures could be applied as itemized deductions on his income tax return.

Only mortgage interest and real estate taxes are allowable deductions on private property.

$1,250 (mortgage interest) + $898 (real estate taxes) = $2,148, the deductible amount

If part of the property is rented, the owner may deduct a prorated amount of expenses for income tax purposes. Deductions would apply to maintenance and repair, taxes, mortgage interest, and depreciation. The proprietor would declare rental payments as income.

Depreciation for a house is figured on the straight-line basis. A fixed amount per year for depreciation is allowable for the estimated life of the house.

EXAMPLE 13

Ms. Blake, a schoolteacher, purchased a duplex for $40,000. She lives in one half of the duplex and rents the other half to a tenant. The income from the rental assists her in defraying the housing costs. After consulting a tax accountant, who estimated the usable life of the house to be 40 years, she used this figure in calculating her annual depreciation allowance. What amount of annual depreciation did she deduct on her income tax return?

Divide the cost by the estimated number of years the house will be used to determine the annual amount of depreciation.

$40,000 (cost) ÷ 40 (years) = $1,000 annual depreciation.

Ms. Blake lives in one half of the house and rents the other half.   Therefore, only one half of the annual depreciation is allowed.

$1,000 (annual depreciation) ÷ 2 = $500 annual allowable deduction for depreciation

EXAMPLE 14

Ms. Young purchased a $32,000 house with a use expectancy of 40 years.   She rents one half of it to an elderly couple.   Her housing costs last year were: property taxes, $748; mortgage interest, $980; insurance, $140; maintenance and repair, $280; and landscaping, $120.   To how much will her itemized deductions amount for income tax purposes?

Determine the annual depreciation of the house.

$32,000 (cost) ÷ 40 (years) = $800 annual depreciation allowance

Total all housing costs and divide by two.   (*Note*: She occupies one half of the house and rents the other half.) $800   (depreciation) + $748   (taxes) + $980   (mortgage   interest) + $140   (insurance) + $280 (maintenance) + $120 (landscaping) = $3,068 total costs.

$3,068 ÷ 2 = $1,534 total itemized deductions

EXAMPLE 15

Mr. and Mrs. Robinson, who have owned their home for 10 years, decide to sell it.   They believe that residence in a trailer park would be more convenient for them.   They want to know what the actual monthly costs are for their house.   They present the following information to an accountant.   The average monthly housing costs are $375; they can make a net profit of $7,500 on the sale of the house.   The itemized deductions, over the 10 years, for taxes and interest provided them with an income tax savings of $4,000.   What was the actual monthly housing cost arrived at by the accountant?

Add their net profit and income tax savings to obtain their total amount of return.

$7,500 (profit) + $4,000 (tax savings) = $11,500 total return

Divide this amount by 120 (10 [years] × 12 [months]) to obtain their monthly return.

$11,500 (total return) ÷ 120 (10 [years] × 12 [months]) = $95.83 (monthly return)

Subtract the monthly return from monthly costs to obtain their actual monthly cost.

$375 (monthly costs) − $95.83 (monthly return) = $279.17 actual monthly costs

5.5   CUSTOM BUILDING

There are many expenses involved in having a house built to specifications.   Unlike buying a resale for a negotiated price, the costs of building include purchasing the lot, engaging an architect and/or contractors plus construction labor.

EXAMPLE 16

Mr. Brock contracted with a local builder to construct a house on a cost plus 12% basis.   He had purchased a lot for $4,000 several years ago.   The contractor presented the following bill upon completion.   Excavation, $750; plumbing, $3,200; foundation and masonry, $2,800; carpentry and lumber, $16,990; painting, $1,995; heating and air conditioning, $3,300; electrical work, $2,250; landscaping, $1,000; and miscellaneous expenses, $400.   How much did this house cost Mr. Brock, including the land?

Total all housing costs.   Obtain 12% of this for the builder's fee.   Add the builder's fee and the cost of the land to the total housing costs. $750 (excavation) + $3,200 (plumbing) + $2,800 (masonry) + $16,990 (carpentry and lumber) + $1,995 (painting) + $3,300 (heating and air conditioning) + $2,250 (electrical work) + $1,000 (landscaping) + $400 (miscellaneous) = $32,685, builder's costs.   Builder's fee is $32,685 (builder's costs) × 0.12 (builder's fee) = $3,922.20.

$$\$32,685 \text{ (building costs)} + \$3,922.20 \text{ (12\% fee)} + \$4,000 \text{ (cost of land)}$$
$$= \$40,607.20, \text{ the total cost of house and land}$$

EXAMPLE 17

A contractor will build your home for a total cost of $43,500, which includes everything except the cost of the land. You decide to build most of it yourself but will subcontract the plumbing, electrical wiring, and heating and air conditioning. Upon completion, your bills are: plumbing, $1,990; electrical work, $2,100; heating and air conditioning, $3,000. Your total bill for all materials, tools, landscaping, and part-time helpers amounted to $24,550. In addition, you had to pay monthly rent of $225 for three additional months due to the extra length of time it took you to complete the project. (*a*) How much money did you save by doing it yourself? (*b*) What percent of saving, based on the contractor's cost, did you realize?

(*a*) Add all expenses to determine the total cost. $1,990 (plumbing) + $2,100 (electrical) + $3,000 (heating and air conditioning) + $24,550 (your total bill) + ($225 × 3) $675 (additional rent) = $32,315, the total cost of the house. Subtract your total cost from the contractor's cost to obtain your amount of saving.

$$\$43,500 \text{ (contractor's cost)} - \$32,315 \text{ (your cost)} = \$11,185 \text{ saving}$$

(*b*) To determine percent of saving, divide the amount of saving by the contractor's cost.

$$\$11,185 \text{ (saving)} \div \$43,500 \text{ (contractor's cost)} = 0.257, \text{ or } 25.7\% \text{ saving}$$

5.6 MOBILE HOMES

Some consumers prefer to purchase mobile homes rather than conventional homes. Generally the monthly payments are smaller and the term of loan is for a shorter duration. However, mobile home owners must purchase a home site or rent park space with the necessary utility hook-ups. This style of living is proving to be very attractive to young married couples as well as older couples.

EXAMPLE 18

Mr. and Mrs. Gott, a retired couple, decided to move out of the city. After due consideration, they purchased a mobile home priced at $4,995 in a very pleasant mobile home park. Mr. South, the mobile home agent, arranged a mortgage loan for them at $8\frac{1}{2}\%$ interest for 8 years, after a down payment of $1,995. The Gotts had monthly loan payments of $86.36 and a monthly park rental fee of $65. At the end of 8 years, they sold the mobile home for $2,500. (*a*) What was their total mobile home cost for the 8 years? (*b*) What was their average monthly cost?

(*a*) Multiply the monthly payments plus the park rental fee by the total period of time. Add the down payment to this amount to obtain total amount spent. From total amount spent subtract the amount for which it was sold to obtain total cost.

$$\$86.36 \text{ (monthly payment)} + \$65 \text{ (rental fee)} = \$151.36 \text{ monthly costs}$$

$$\$151.36 \text{ (monthly costs)} \times 96 \text{ (8 [years]} \times 12 \text{ [months])} = \$14,530.56 \text{ total payments}$$

$$\$14,530.56 + \$1,995 \text{ (down payment)} = \$16,525.56 \text{ total amount spent}$$

$$\$16,525.56 - \$2,500 \text{ (sale price)} = \$14,025.56 \text{ total cost for 8 years}$$

(*b*) To obtain monthly costs, divide total cost by the number of months.

$$\$14,025.56 \div 96 \text{ (8} \times 12) = \$146.10 \text{ average monthly cost}$$

INSURANCE

5.7 THE HOMEOWNER'S POLICY

Today's homeowner needs protection against a variety of hazards: fire, theft, numerous kinds of damages, liability, etc. While separate policies are available to cover these hazards individually, the *homeowner's policy* will provide comprehensive coverage against a host of perils at a premium cost which is considerably less than for comparable coverage in separate policies. Comprehensive policies differ in the number of hazards covered.

5.8 AMOUNTS OF COVERAGE

The amount of the other property coverage is based upon a percentage of the amount of coverage on the main dwelling. See Table 4 for examples of such percentage breakdowns.

Table 4.

Property Coverage	Insured Value
Dwelling, 100%	$40,000 (full value)
Appurtenant private structure	$4,000 (10% of dwelling)
Personal property	$20,000 (50% of dwelling)
Additional living expenses	$8,000 (20% of dwelling)

EXAMPLE 19

Glenn and Barbara Fell live in a Cape Cod house with a market value of $36,000. They purchased a homeowner's policy for the full value of the house, $36,000. How much coverage did they have for each type of risk? If the garage is not affixed to their dwelling, what is the maximum amount they would receive if it were destroyed? To arrive at the answers you compute as follows:

Dwelling, 100%	$36,000
Appurtenant private structures (10% of $36,000)	3,600
Personal property (50% of $36,000)	18,000
Additional living expenses (20% of $36,000)	7,200
Total amount of coverage =	$64,800

The garage would be covered for a maximum amount of $3,600.

In addition, the various homeowner's policies generally provide the same amounts of liability protection. Typically, this includes personal liability (up to $25,000), medical payments ($500 to one person), and damage to another's property (up to $250).

5.9 PREMIUM RATES AND DEDUCTIBLES

Rates are based on many significant factors, such as: type of dwelling, material the house is constructed of, adequacy and efficiency of fire protection, state and local regulations, and the like. In most policies there is a deductible amount, usually $50, which the insured must pay. Policies with $100 deductibles are also available; these generally result in lower premiums because the insurance company's risk is less.

The premiums are generally based on a three-year period; payments may be prepaid annually. See Table 5.

Table 5.   Homeowner's Policy (Form HO-2)
3-Year Prepaid Premiums

Amount of Coverage	Group 1		Group 3		Group 7	
	All Perils Deductible	Full Cover	All Perils Deductible	Full Cover	All Perils Deductible	Full Cover
$ 8,000	$117	$132	$133	$150	$141	$157
12,000	128	144	147	165	154	172
15,000	143	161	163	183	171	192
20,000	177	199	202	228	212	237
25,000	221	249	253	285	265	297
30,000	271	305	311	348	325	363
35,000	328	370	376	422	393	439
40,000	386	433	440	496	462	516
45,000	443	498	506	569	530	592
50,000	500	562	571	642	598	669

Policy amounts are recorded to the nearest $1,000.   *Example*: $24,750 is rounded to $25,000.

EXAMPLE 20

Your house has a market value of $29,850.   You are in Group 1 and wish to purchase a homeowner's policy HO-2 with a face value of $30,000 for full coverage.   To find out how much a 3-year premium would amount to read down to $30,000, then right to "Full Cover" in Group 1.   Find $305, the 3-year premium on the policy.   (*Note*: $29,850 rounds up to $30,000.)

5.10   COINSURANCE

Most homeowner's policies contain an 80% coinsurance clause.   Under a policy containing this clause, the dwelling is insured for 80% of its replacement value.   If insured for less than 80% of value, the owner must share part of the loss or damage caused by fire.

The coinsurance clause in a policy does not mean that only the minimum amount of insurance required is the maximum amount collectible.   If the property is insured for its full replaceable value, the full amount would be collected in case of total loss.   Here, as in the ordinary fire insurance policy, no more than the actual loss nor more than the actual amount of insurance carried, whichever is smaller, can be collected.

EXAMPLE 21

Herbert Fredericks owned a house valued at $30,000, which he insured for $18,000.   A recent fire damaged the house in the amount of $8,000.   (*a*) How much of the loss must the insurance company pay under a policy containing an 80% coinsurance clause?   (*b*) For how much of the loss is Fredericks responsible?

(*a*)   80% $\times$ 30,000 = $24,000 maximum amount of indemnity due from insurance company in case of loss of $24,000 or more. $18,000 (amount of coverage) $\div$ $24,000 (minimum amount of insurance required to be carried) = $\frac{3}{4}$.   The insurance company must indemnify the insured for $\frac{3}{4} \times$ $8,000, or, $6,000.

$$\text{Amount paid out} = \frac{\text{Amount of coverage}}{80\% \text{ of property value}} \times \text{loss}$$

(b) \$8,000 (loss) − \$6,000 (paid by company) = \$2,000, Fredericks' share of loss.   Using the formula:

$$\text{Amount paid out} = \frac{\$18,000}{80\% \times \$30,000} \times \$8,000 = \frac{\$18,000}{\$24,000} \times \$8,000 = \$6,000$$

5.11 SHORT RATE CANCELLATION

The insured may wish to cancel a policy that has not matured.   The amount of refund due is based on a short rate cancellation table.   See Table 6.

Table 6. Short Rate Cancellation Table

Policy in Force	Percent of Premium Earned by Policy		Policy in Force		Percent of Premium Earned by Policy
	Term				Term
Days	1 year	3 years	Years	Days	3 years
1	5	1.9	1	0	37.0
2	6	2.2	1	31–35	40.1
3–4	7	2.6	1	61–65	42.6
5–6	8	3.0	1	91–95	45.2
7–8	9	3.3	1	121–125	47.8
9–10	10	3.7	1	181–185	53.0
19–20	15	5.6	1	271–275	60.8
30–32	19	7.0	2	0	68.5
44–47	23	8.5	2	31–35	71.5
59–62	27	10.0	2	121–125	79.3
74–76	31	11.5	2	151–155	81.9
88–91	35	13.0	2	181–185	84.5
121–124	44	16.3	2	271–275	92.2
179–182	60	22.2	2	331–335	97.4

EXAMPLE 22

A property owner paid \$109 for a homeowner's policy, 1-year term, and decided to cancel it after 6 months.   How much would his refund amount to?   On Table 6, read down the left-hand column to 179–182 days, then, across under 1-year term.   Find 60.   60% of premium is earned by insurance company.   Multiply the premium by the percent earned.   Subtract the result from the premium, to obtain the insured's refund.   \$109 (premium) × 60% = \$65.40 earned by company.   \$109 (premium) − \$65.40 = \$43.60 insured's refund.

EXAMPLE 23

Agnes and Paul Sproule bought a house in the suburbs for which they paid \$44,000.   The savings and loan association which gave them their mortgage loan required an adequate amount of insurance coverage.   The Sproules bought a homeowner's policy containing an 80% coinsurance clause.   They bought a full coverage HO-2 policy, in group 3, and paid the 3-year premium on December 1, 1974.   On November 30, 1976, they cancelled the policy.   How much refund will they receive?

Value of dwelling = \$44,000.   80% of \$44,000 = \$35,000 minimum coverage required under 80% clause policy if full loss up to 80% of replacement value of property is to be recovered from insurance company in case of loss.

$$\$44,000 \times 80\% = \$35,200 \text{ (round to } \$35,000 \text{ value)}$$

Table 5, Group 3, full coverage, HO-2.   Read down to \$35,000, then across to Group 3 full coverage, find \$422, premium.

Table 6. The policy has been in force 2 years. Read down policy-in-force column to 2 years, then across under "3-year Term" to find 68.5 percent premium earned by policy. Multiply the premium amount by the percent premium earned.

$$\$422 \text{ (premium)} \times 68.5\% = \$289.07, \text{ the premium earned by insurance company}$$

Subtract the amount of premium earned from the total premium paid to obtain Sproule's amount of refund.

$$\$422 \text{ (premium)} - \$289.07 \text{ (earned)} = \$132.93, \text{ the amount of refund due insured}$$

EXAMPLE 24

Ms. Blake owns a house that has a replacement value of $25,000. She bought a homeowner's policy containing an 80% coinsurance clause, under Group 7, with an "all perils deductible" provision. She decided to insure the house for $15,000. (a) How much was the premium? (b) She had a fire damage in the amount of $4,000 to her living area. What is the maximum amount which she can collect, with the $100 deductible provision?

(a) Dwelling, $25,000 × 80% = $20,000, the full coverage required under maximum recovery provision of policy. She insures for $15,000. Table 5, HO-2, Group 7, all perils deductible. Read down to $15,000, across to Group 7 under "all perils deductible," find $171, premium. Fire damage of $4,000 is prorated.

(b)
$$\text{Amount paid out} = \frac{\text{Amount of coverage}}{80\% \text{ of property value}} \times \text{loss} = \frac{\$15,000}{80\% \times \$25,000} \times \$4,000 = \$3,000$$

Subtract the deductible amount from the amount to be paid out as maximum amount she can collect.

$$\$3,000 - \$100 \text{ (deductible)} = \$2,900$$

Solved Problems

5.1 Ms. Cook, the coroner for Johnson County, decides to buy a house in the country. She realizes that she should not pay more than $2\frac{1}{2}$ times her annual income which is $14,000. Up to what amount should she pay for a house?

$$\$14,000 \times 2\frac{1}{2} = \$35,000 \quad \text{(See Example 2.)}$$

5.2 Ms. Blackwell and her friends were discussing household costs. Most of the women apply the 1% rule of thumb, according to which all monthly housing costs, including mortgage payments, taxes, insurance, and maintenance, should amount to no more than approximately 1% of the purchase price of the house. If Ms. Blackwell purchases a house costing $32,500, approximately how much will she spend on her monthly maintenance?

$$\$32,500 \times 0.01 = \$325 \text{ maintenance}$$

5.3 Peg and Tom Franks have been house-hunting in their spare time. They found a dream place at $42,000. How much should their annual income amount to in order for them to afford this house?

Using the $2\frac{1}{2}$ times annual income rule of thumb, $42,000 ÷ $2\frac{1}{2}$ = $16,800, the approximate income required.

5.4   Mr. and Mrs. Billings live with their three children in the city in a rented three-bedroom house.   In contemplating a move to the suburbs, they wished to figure their present monthly housing costs which they could compare with friends living in a nearby suburban area.   Their itemized housing expenses for last year were: rent, $1,500; electricity, $612; water, sewage, and garbage disposal, $240; telephone, $68; heating oil, $165; installment payments for appliances, $348; maintenance and repairs, $75; and, yard care, $60.   (a) What was their average monthly housing cost?   (b) If this amount is 28% of the families annual income, what is their annual income?

(a) Total all annual housing expenses and divide by 12 months to obtain monthly cost. $1,500 (rent) + $612 (electricity) + $240 (sewage, etc.) + $68 (telephone) + $165 (heating oil) + $348 (installment purchases) + $75 (maintenance) + $60 (yard care) = $3,068 total annual housing costs.

$$\$3,068 \text{ (annual costs)} \div 12 = \$255.67 \text{ monthly housing costs}$$

(b) To find annual income, divide the total annual housing costs by the percent of total which it represents. $P = B \times R$. $P = \$3,068$, $B = ?$ (income), $R = 28\%$.

$$\$3,068 = B \times 0.28 \qquad B = \$3,068 \div 0.28 = \$10,957.14 \text{ annual income}$$

(See Example 1.)

5.5   The Greens have sufficient monthly income to spend $255 a month for housing costs.   Mr. Green has been offered an opportunity to purchase a house appraised at $32,500.   With a down payment of 20%, a local bank will arrange a mortgage loan for the remaining amount with an interest rate of $7\frac{1}{2}\%$.   Additional costs of ownership will be $70 a month.   Mr. Green would like to know if he can afford   (a) a 25-year loan,   (b) a 30-year loan, or   (c) whether he should rent a house at $250 per month.

(a) Obtain the amount of mortgage loan by multiplying the appraised value by 20% to obtain the down payment.   Subtract the down payment from appraised value to obtain the amount of mortgage loan.

$$\$32,500 \times 0.20 = \$6,500 \text{ down payment}$$
$$\$32,500 - \$6,500 = \$26,000 \text{ amount of loan}$$

From Table 2 determine the monthly payments for a $7\frac{1}{2}\%$ loan for 25 years and one for 30 years.

$7\frac{1}{2}\%$ in 25 years = $7.39 for $1,000 $7.39 × 26 (thousands) = $192.14 monthly payments

(b) $7\frac{1}{2}\%$ in 30 years = $7.00 per $1,000 $7.00 × 26 (thousands) = $182 monthly payments

(c) $182.00 ($7\frac{1}{2}\%$ for 30 years) + $70 = $252

Therefore, the Greens can afford to buy the house with a 30-year mortgage.

5.6   The Lakeland Realty Company has a seven-room house for sale which has an appraised value of $43,800.   They will arrange for an FHA approved loan, if the purchaser has an approved credit rating.   The Blounts, potential purchasers, requested the following information.   (a) How much is the required down payment?   (b) To how much will the mortgage loan amount?

(a) FHA required down payment.   See Table 1.   3% of the first $25,000 = $750.   10% of $10,000 ($25,000 up to $35,000) = $1,000.   20% of $8,800 ($35,000 up to $43,800) = $1,760.   Total required down payment:
$$\$750 + \$1,000 + \$1,760 = \$3,510$$

(b) $43,800 (appraised value) − $3,510 (down payment) = $40,290 total amount of loan

5.7   Fran and John Young found in the suburbs an attractive house with an appraised value of $37,990. After searching for a mortgage loan, they found a bank that would arrange for a conventional loan in the amount of 75% of the appraised value. (*a*) How much will the bank lend the Youngs?   (*b*) To how much will their down payment amount?

(*a*) Multiply the appraised value by the percent of value the bank will lend.

$37,990 (appraised value) × 0.75 (percent of value) = $28,492.50, the amount of loan

(*b*) Subtract the amount of loan from the appraised value to obtain down payment.

$37,990 (appraised value) − $28,492.50 (amount of loan)
= $9,497.50, the amount of down payment

5.8   A local bank arranged a mortgage loan of $32,500 on a house appraised at $40,625, for Harold Grant, who purchased the house in a new development in the suburbs. (*a*) How much was the required down payment?   (*b*) What percent of the appraised value was the mortgage loan?

(*a*) Subtract the amount of loan from the appraised value to obtain the down payment.

$40,625 (appraised value) − $32,500 (amount of loan) = $8,125 down payment

(*b*) Divide the amount of the loan by the appraised value to find the percent.

$32,500 (amount of loan) ÷ $40,625 (appraised value) = 0.80, or 80% of the appraised value

5.9   The Owens family contracted to purchase a new three-bedroom house appraised at $33,995. They were notified that their closing costs would consist of the following expenses: legal fees, $150; title insurance, $275; state mortgage tax, $35; proration of prepaid insurance, $40; recording fees, $9.50; survey, $60; and appraisal, $50. (*a*) What is the total amount of closing costs?   (*b*) This amount is what percent of the appraised value?

(*a*) Add all costs to obtain total closing costs. $150 (legal fees) + $9.50 (recording fees) + $60 (survey) + $50 (appraisal) + $275 (title insurance) − $35 (state mortgage tax) + $40 (insurance proration) = $619.50.

(*b*) $619.50 ÷ $33,995 = 0.018, or 1.8%

5.10 Sarah and Bob Gibson wish to purchase a home. Their combined take-home pay is $16,800. They could afford to purchase a house of what appraised value?

Use the $2\frac{1}{2}$ times annual earnings rule. $16,800 (take-home pay) × 2.5 = $42,000, the approximate amount they could afford to pay.

5.11 The Sloans, a newly married couple have an annual income of $21,000. They wish to move into a single-residence house but do not know how much they can afford for monthly housing costs. How much can they afford?

Find the monthly take-home pay by dividing the annual pay by 12. Take 25% of this amount to obtain the approximate amount available for housing costs.

$21,000 (annual income) ÷ 12 = $1,750 monthly income

The approximate amount available for housing costs is

$1,750 × 0.25 = $437.50

5.12   Mr. and Mrs. Anderson have decided that they can budget $395 a month for housing costs if they purchase a new house. They plan to purchase a house and asked you to figure approximately how much they can afford for one. (*a*) What amount did you arrive at? (*b*) Approximately how much should their annual take-home pay amount to?

(*a*) Use 1% guidance rule. Monthly housing costs amount to approximately 1% of the cost of the house. If 1% = $395, 100% = $39,500, the approximate amount they can pay for a house.

(*b*) Use the rule of thumb that a house should not cost more than $2\frac{1}{2}$ times one's annual take-home pay. Divide the cost of the house by $2\frac{1}{2}$ to obtain the minimum annual desirable take-home pay.

$$\$39,500 \text{ (approximate cost)} \div 2.5 = \$15,800 \text{ annual take-home pay}$$

5.13   Silas Grim, the chief accountant in your office, made a down payment of $10,000 on the house he purchased for $42,900. He obtained a mortgage loan at a local bank for the balance at $8\frac{1}{2}\%$ interest for a 30-year term. What is the amount of his monthly payments?

Obtain the amount of the loan by subtracting the down payment from the purchase price.

$$\$42,900 - \$10,000 = \$32,900, \text{ the amount of the loan}$$

See Table 2. Read down under "Term of Loan" to 30 years, then to the right under $8\frac{1}{2}\%$, find $7.69, the monthly payment required to pay principal and interest on $1,000. Multiply: $7.69 × 32.9 (amount of loan in thousands) = $253, the monthly payment required.

5.14   Bill Yates received a mortgage loan of $37,500, with interest at 8% for 20 years. (*a*) Figure the amount of his monthly payments. (*b*) Construct a mortgage loan payment schedule showing the first four payments.

(*a*) From Table 2, determine the monthly payment. Read down to 20 years. Then to the right under the 8% column, find $8.37, the amount to pay off $1,000. Multiply: $8.37 × 37.5 (amount of loan in thousands) = $313.88, the amount of the monthly payment.

(*b*) To construct a loan payment schedule, find the monthly interest charge, multiply the amount of the loan by the annual interest rate, and divide the result to obtain the monthly interest payment.

$$\$37,500 \times 0.08 = \$3,000, \text{ annual amount}$$
$$\$3,000 \div 12 = \$250, \text{ monthly amount (for first payment)}$$

Monthly payment − interest payment = amount applied to reduction of principal.

$$\$313.88 - \$250 = \$63.88$$

Subtract the amount applied to principal from the original loan to obtain the unpaid balance.

$$\$37,500 \text{ (original loan)} - \$63.88 \text{ (reduction of principal)} = \$37,436.12$$

unpaid balance after first payment.

Second payment: Multiply the amount of unpaid balance by the annual interest rate and divide by 12.

$$\$37,436.12 \times 0.08 = \$2,994.89, \text{ annual interest}$$

$$\$2,994.89 \div 12 = \$249.57, \text{ monthly interest}$$

Interest is paid only on the unpaid balance. Subtract the monthly interest from the monthly payment to obtain the amount applied to the principal.

$$\$313.88 - \$249.57 = \$64.31, \text{ amount applied to principal}$$

Subtract this amount from the unpaid balance.

$$\$37,436.12 - \$64.31 = \$37,371.81, \text{ new unpaid balance}$$

Third payment: Proceed as above.

Note: The annual interest rate may be divided by 12 to obtain the monthly interest rate. $0.08 \div 12 = 0.0066666$, monthly interest rate. You may now multiply this factor by the unpaid balance and obtain the monthly interest payment directly.

$$\$37,371.81 \text{ (unpaid balance)} \times 0.0066667 \text{ (monthly interest rate)}$$
$$= \$249.14, \text{ amount of monthly interest}$$

$$\$313.88 - \$249.14 = \$64.74, \text{ reduction of principal}$$

$$\$37,371.81 - \$64.74 = \$37,307.07, \text{ unpaid balance after the third payment}$$

Fourth payment:

$$\$37,307.07 \text{ (unpaid balance)} \times 0.0066667 \text{ (monthly interest rate)} = \$248.72, \text{ amount of interest}$$

$$\$313.88 - \$248.72 = \$65.16, \text{ reduction of principal}$$

$$\$37,307.07 - \$65.16 = \$37,241.91, \text{ unpaid balance after fourth payment}$$

Mortgage loan payment schedule, loan of $37,500, interest 8%, term 20 years, monthly payment: $313.88.

Payment Number	Monthly Payment	Applied to Interest	Principal	Unpaid Balance
1	$313.88	$250.00	$63.88	$37,436.12
2	313.88	249.57	64.31	37,371.81
3	313.88	249.14	64.74	37,307.07
4	313.88	248.72	65.16	37,241.91

5.15 Bill Long just finished paying off his mortgage loan of $27,800 on which he had been paying 6% interest for 25 years. (*a*) How much did he actually pay? (*b*) How much interest did he pay over the period of the loan?

(*a*) Obtain the monthly payment for $1,000 at 6% for 25 years. Table 2: the monthly payment is $6.45. Multiply: $6.45 (monthly payment) × 27.8 (amount in thousands) = $179.31, monthly payment. Obtain the full amount paid by multiplying the monthly payment by the number of payments. $179.31 (monthly payment) × 300 (25 × 12, number of payments).

$$\$179.31 \times 300 = \$53,793, \text{ total amount paid}$$

(*b*) Subtract the original loan value from the total paid in to obtain the amount of interest paid over the term of the loan.

$$\$53,793 \text{ (total paid)} - \$27,800 \text{ (mortgage loan)} = \$25,993, \text{ total interest paid}$$

5.16 The Smythes arranged a mortgage loan with monthly payments of $208.90 on the new house they had recently purchased. Two weeks after they moved in, the lending institution informed them that they must also pay a monthly pro rata share of the annual insurance premium, which is $148, and of the real estate taxes, which are $660 annually.   Calculate their total monthly payment.

  Obtain the monthly pro rata share for insurance and taxes. Divide the annual rate by 12.   Add all payments to arrive at total monthly payment.

$$\$148 \text{ (insurance)} \div 12 = \$12.33$$

$$\$660 \text{ (taxes)} \div 12 = \$55$$

$$\$208.90 \text{ (loan payment)} + \$12.33 \text{ (insurance)} + \$55 \text{ (taxes)} = \$276.23, \text{ the total payment}$$

5.17 The Cohens have a $23,500 mortgage loan on their house at 7% for 25 years.   They have paid on this mortgage loan for 12 years, and it is approximately 28% paid off.   (*a*) How much interest have they paid during the 12 years?   (*b*) How much interest will they pay for the full 25 years?

(*a*) Obtain the monthly payment.   Table 2: $23,500 at 7% for 25 years is $7.07 (for $1,000) $\times$ 23.5 (number of thousands) = $166.15 per month.   Multiply the monthly payment by the number of months to obtain the amount paid.

$$\$166.15 \text{ (monthly payment)} \times 12 \text{ (years)} \times 12 \text{ (months)}$$
$$= \$23,925.60, \text{ amount paid during 12 years}$$

To obtain the approximate amount of the loan paid off, multiply the amount of the loan by the percent paid off.

$$\$23,500 \text{ (amount of loan)} \times 0.28 \text{ (percent paid off)}$$
$$= \$6.580, \text{ amount of loan paid off (reduction of principal)}$$

Subtract the amount paid off from the amount paid to date to obtain the amount of interest paid.

$$\$23,925.60 \text{ (paid to date)} - \$6,580 \text{ (amount paid off)} = \$17,345.60, \text{ interest paid to date}$$

(*b*) To obtain total amount of interest payable in 25 years, multiply the monthly payment amount by the total number of payments.   Subtract the original loan value from this amount to obtain the total amount of interest.

$$\$166.15 \times 25 \times 12 = \$49,845, \text{ total amount paid}$$

$$\$49,845 \text{ (total paid)} - \$23,500 \text{ (loan value)} = \$26,345, \text{ the total amount of interest payable}$$

5.18 The Andrews wish to set aside each month an amount of money sufficient to pay for the maintenance and repair costs of their house.   From previous receipts, they have calculated the following maintenance expenses: painting of house every 3 years, $525; yard and landscaping, $100 per year; general repairs and maintenance, $120 per year; miscellaneous costs, $75 per year.   They plan to set aside $80 a year for a new roof to replace the present roof when it becomes necessary.   (*a*) How much should they set aside each month to meet these expenses?   (*b*) What percent of their total monthly housing costs of $380 is this maintenance expense?

(*a*) Total all annual expenses and divide by 12 to obtain monthly costs.

$$\$525 \text{ (painting)} \div 3 \text{ (years)} = \$175, \text{ annual painting expense}$$

$$\$175 \text{ (paint)} + \$100 \text{ (lawn)} + \$120 \text{ (general maintenance)} + \$75 \text{ (miscellaneous)} + \$80 \text{ (roof)}$$
$$= \$550 \text{ annual costs}$$

$$\$550 \div 12 = \$45.83, \text{ the monthly amount to be set aside for expenses}$$

(*b*) To find the percent of monthly housing costs, divide maintenance expenses by total housing costs.

$45.83 (maintenance expenses) ÷ $380 (total housing costs)
= 0.1206, or 12.1% of total housing costs

5.19 Bob and Sandra Lake, local schoolteachers, wish to purchase a home. In reviewing their budget, they find that they can afford to pay $380 a month for housing costs, of which $120 would be for taxes, insurance, and maintenance. They plan to purchase a house priced at $48,500, with a 30% down payment and interest at $8\frac{1}{2}$% on the mortgage loan. For how many years should the term be? (*a*) 20 years? (*b*) 30 years?

(*a*) Obtain the amount of the mortgage loan. On Table 2, calculate the monthly payments for 20 years. $48,500 (cost) × 0.70 (100% − 30%) = $33,950, amount of mortgage loan

The monthly payment on $1,000 at $8\frac{1}{2}$% for 20 years is $8.68. Read down Table 2 to 20 years, then across under the $8\frac{1}{2}$% column to $8.68 per thousand (rate of payment).

$8.68 (payment per $1,000) × 33.95 (number of thousands) = $294.69

The monthly payments for 20 years.

(*b*) Calculate the monthly payments for 30 years in Table 2. Find the amount of $7.69 for $1,000.

$7.69 × 33.95 = $261.08, monthly payment for 30 years

Term 30 years is most suitable.

$380 (planned amount) − $120 (other expenses) = $260 available for monthly payments

5.20 The Sloans pay $180 a month rent for a house they can buy for $17,800, with a down payment of $3,800. Total housing costs per year would be $2,100. (*a*) How much would they save per month by buying the house? (*b*) To what percent of savings would this amount?

(*a*) Obtain the monthly cost of ownership. Subtract this amount from the monthly rental payment to obtain the savings.

$2,100 (annual costs) ÷ 12 = $175 monthly cost of ownership

$180 (monthly rental) − $175 (ownership cost) = $5 savings

(*b*) Divide the monthly savings by monthly rental cost to obtain percent of saving.

$5 (saving) ÷ $180 (monthly rental cost) = 0.0277, or 2.8% saving

5.21 Mr. and Mrs. Barren retired and moved to a small quiet city. After their first year, they calculated their housing expenses in order to prepare their income tax return. They computed the following amounts: mortgage interest, $1,188; real estate tax, $695; insurance, $128; maintenance costs, $350; landscaping, $120. If this is a private dwelling, what amount can apply to itemized deductions on their tax return?

Only mortgage interest and real estate taxes are deductible on a private dwelling. $1,188 (mortgage interest) + $695 (real estate tax) = $1,883 deductible amount.

5.22 Ms. Aragon purchased a duplex that cost her $44,000. She lives in one half and rents the other. For income tax purposes she estimated the expected useful life of the house to be 40 years. What is her annual depreciation allowance?

Use the straight-line method. Divide the cost of the property by the number of years of life to obtain the annual depreciation allowable. $44,000 (cost) ÷ 40 (years) = $1,100 per year. Since she lives in one half and rents the other half, only one half of the annual amount of depreciation may be deducted. $1,100 (annual amount) ÷ 2 = $550 allowable annual depreciation.

5.23 Mrs. Johns rents one half of her home to an elderly couple. The house cost $30,000 and has a life expectancy of 50 years. Her housing costs last year were: taxes, $780; mortgage interest, $220; insurance, $160; maintenance and repairs, $412; and yard care, $212. To how much will her itemized deductions amount for income tax purposes?

Determine her depreciation allowance. Total all deductible items, then divide by two. $30,000 (cost) ÷ 50 = $600 annual depreciation. She lives in half of the house and rents the other half. $600 (depreciation) + $780 (taxes) + $220 (interest) + $160 (insurance) + $412 (maintenance) + $212 (yard care) = $2,384 total expenses. $2,384 (total expenses) ÷ 2 = $1,192 allowable for income tax deductions.

5.24 Jake and Millie Short owned a house for eight years. Their monthly housing costs amounted to $360. They sold the house at a price which netted them a profit of $5,800. Their itemized deductions over the eight years for taxes and interest resulted in an income tax saving of $3,400. What were their actual monthly housing costs?

Add their profit on the sale plus the income tax saving to obtain their total amount of return. $5,800 (profit) + $3,400 (tax savings) = $9,200 total return. Divide total return by the number of months to obtain the average monthly return. $9,200 ÷ 96 (8 × 12) = $95.83 monthly return. Subtract this monthly return from the monthly cost to obtain the actual cost. $360 (monthly cost) − $95.83 (monthly return) = $264.17 actual monthly cost.

5.25 Ms. Olson contracted with a local builder to construct a house for her. He estimated the costs to be: lot, $3,800; materials, $7,200; plumbing, heating, and electrical work, $3,950; labor, $7,900; landscaping, $490; plus his fee of 12% based on the construction cost. How much will this house cost her?

Total all housing costs, take 12% of the total for his fee, total them, and then add in the cost of the land. $7,200 (materials) + $3,950 (plumbing, etc.) + $7,900 (labor) + $490 (landscaping) = $19,540, total costs. $19,540 (total costs) × 0.12 (fee) = $2,344.80 builder's fee. $19,540 (costs) + $2,344.80 (fee) + $3,800 (lot) = $25,684.80 total cost to her.

5.26 A contractor will build a home for Chester Carpenter for $47,500, which includes everything except the cost of the land. Carpenter decided to build most of the house himself, subcontracting the excavating, plumbing, heating and air conditioning, and electrical wiring. Upon completion, his expenses were: $500, excavation and base; $1,850, plumbing; $2,000, electrical work; $3,500, heating and air conditioning; $17,895, lumber, materials, and tools; $1,800, landscaping and driveway; $3,600, part-time labor. Also, he paid $900 additional rent for the time delay. (a) How much did he save by doing it himself? (b) What percent of saving did he realize based on the contractor's price?

(a) Add all expenses to determine total cost. $500 (excavation) + $1,850 (plumbing) + $2,000 (electrical work) + $3,500 (heating and air conditioning) + $17,895 (materials) + $1,800 (landscaping) + $3,600 (labor) + $900 (additional rent) = $32,045 total cost. To obtain saving, subtract total cost from contractor's price. $47,500 − $32,045 = $15,455 total savings.

(b) To determine percent savings, divide savings by contractor's price. $15,455 ÷ $47,500 = 0.3253, or 32.5% saving.

5.27 The Applebys bought a mobile home priced at $8,990 on which they made a down payment of $1,490. They borrowed the balance at 9% interest for 10 years. The monthly loan payments on this loan are $95.01, the monthly park rental fee is $60. At the end of the 10 years, they sold the home for $1,990. (a) How much did their home cost them for the 10 years? (b) What was the average monthly cost?

(a) Obtain total costs by adding the total monthly payments and the total monthly park rental. To this amount add the down payment, then subtract the selling price. $95.01 (monthly payments) + $60 (rental fee) = $155.01 monthly costs. $155.01 (monthly costs) × 10 years × 12 months = $18,601.20 total monthly costs. $18,601.20 (costs) + $1,490 (down payment) = $20,091.20. $20,091.20 (amount spent) − $1,990 (sale price) × $18,101.20 total cost to them.

(b) Divide the total cost to them by the number of months occupied, to find the average monthly cost. $18,101.20 (total cost) ÷ 120 (10 [years] × 12 [months]) = $150.84 average monthly cost.

5.28 Frank and Amy Gardner located a beautiful home in the country appraised at $41,900. Their application for an FHA insured mortgage loan was approved. They requested that the real estate broker calculate the following: (a) The amount of down payment. (b) The amount of their monthly mortgage payment on the loan at the rate of $8\frac{1}{2}$% interest for 25 years. (c) The additional monthly amount required to be put in escrow for annual real estate taxes of $900 and the insurance premium of $150.

(a) FHA down payment

3% on first $25,000 ($25,000)	$ 750
10% on $25,000 to $35,000 ($10,000)	1,000
20% on $35,000 to $41,900 ($6,900)	1,380
Total down payment =	$3,130

(b) $41,900 (appraised value) − $3,130 (down payment) = $38,770 amount of mortgage loan. Table 2: $8\frac{1}{2}$%, 25 years, read down "Term of Loan" column to 25 years, then across to $8.06 under $8\frac{1}{2}$% column. This is the amount of monthly mortgage payment on each $1,000. $8.06 × 38.77 = $312.49 monthly payment.

(c) Find additional monthly amount to be put in escrow. Divide annual amounts by 12 to obtain monthly amounts. $900 (annual taxes) ÷ 12 = $75 per month. $150 (insurance) ÷ 12 = $12.50 per month. $75 (taxes) + $12.50 (insurance) = $87.50, additional monthly amount for taxes and insurance.

5.29 Howard Baker's house was valued at $45,000 in the current market. His homeowner's policy was issued for the market value, $45,000. (a) How much coverage does the policy provide for each type of risk? (b) If the house is destroyed by fire, what is the maximum amount payable for additional living expenses?

(a)

Dwelling, 100%	$45,000
Appurtenant private structures (10% of $45,000)	4,500
Personal property (50% of $45,000)	22,500
Additional living expenses (20% of $45,000)	9,000
Total amount of coverage =	$81,000

(b) Additional living expenses maximum = $9,000. (See Example 19.)

5.30 The Olson family bought a 3-bedroom house on the edge of town for $39,900. The Olsons decide to buy a homeowner's policy (HO-2) with all perils deductible because of their proximity to fire and police protection. They come under Group 3 and wish to insure for total actual value. To how much will their 3-year premium amount?

Table 5: Read down to $40,000 ($39,900 rounds to $40,000), then across under Group 3, all perils deductible, and find $440. (See Example 20.)

5.31 Hymie Schmidt, who owns a house valued at $35,000, decided to insure it for only $24,000, because they have no children living at home. Schmidt has a homeowner's policy, which includes an 80% coinsurance clause. A recent fire in his living area caused by a burning cigar resulted in a $9,000 damage. (a) How much of the loss is covered by insurance? (b) How much must Schmidt pay?

(a) Full coverage with an 80% coinsurance clause (80% × $35,000) = $28,000. The loss will be prorated according to the following formula: Schmidt carries $24,000 worth of insurance coverage. Amount paid out by insurance company:

$$\frac{\text{amount of coverage}}{80\% \text{ of property value}} \times \text{loss} = \text{indemnity paid}$$

$$\frac{\$24,000}{80\% \times \$35,000} \times \$9,000 = \frac{\$24,000}{\$28,000} \times \$9,000 = \frac{6}{7} \times \$9,000 = \$7,714.29$$

The loss covered by insurance, paid by company.

(b) $9,000 − $7,714.29 = $1,285.71, the amount paid by Schmidt

(See Example 21.)

5.32 Ms. Rose Jewel paid $118 for a 1-year term homeowner's policy. Due to a disagreement with her insurance agent over a deductible clause in the contract, Rose decided to cancel the policy after 4 months. To how much would her refund amount?

Table 6: short-rate cancellation table. Read down the left-hand column to 121–124 (4 months), then right, under 1-year term. Find 44. 44% of premium is earned. Multiply the premium by the amount earned. Subtract the result from the premium to obtain her refund. $118 (premium) × 44% = $51.92, the premium earned.

$118 (premium) − $51.92 = $66.08, her refund

(See Example 22.)

5.33 Mr. and Mrs. Clyde Bunker own a house that has a market value of $37,500. Their insurance counsellor recommended that they buy a $30,000 homeowner's policy with an 80% coinsurance clause.* The Bunkers purchased a form (HO-2) with full coverage, in Group 7. They paid for the 3-year premium on April 1, 1976, and cancelled it on September 30, 1977. How much refund did the Bunkers receive?

Value of dwelling, $37,500; coinsurance 80%; 80% × $37,500 = $30,000 (basis for premium). Table 5: Group 7, full coverage, HO-2. Read down to $30,000, then across under full cover, find $363 for a 3-year prepaid premium. Table 6: short-term cancellation table; read down the column "Policy in Force," to 1 year, 181–185 days, then to the right, find 53, which indicates that 53% of the premium has been earned. Multiply the premium by the percent of premium earned. Subtract the result from the premium amount to obtain the amount of refund. $363 (premium) × 53% = $192.39 earned.

$363 (premium) − $192.39 (earned) = $170.61, the amount of refund

(See Example 23.)

---

*80% clause doesn't mean you can only collect 80% of value of property. You collect less if property is insured for less than 80% of value; you collect full loss up to 80%, if insured for 80% of value. If insured for 100% of value of property, you can collect full market value of property, if a total loss is suffered.

5.34   Chester Smart owns a house valued at $24,900 which he insured for $12,000. He bought a homeowner's policy (HO-2) containing an 80% coinsurance clause, under Group 3, with an all perils deductible. The deductible amount is $100 for all perils. (*a*) How much was his 3-year premium? (*b*) If fire caused $5,000 damage to the house, how much indemnity did he receive from the insurance company?

   (*a*) Dwelling: $24,900 × 80% = $20,000. ($24,900 × 0.80) = $19,920 (round to $20,000). Table 5: HO-2, Group 3, all perils deductible. Read down to $12,000 and across to Group 3. Under "All Perils Deductible," find $147 premium.

   (*b*) Fire damage of $5,000 is prorated. Amount paid out:

$$\frac{\text{amount of coverage}}{80\% \text{ of property value}} \times \$5,000 = \frac{\$12,000}{80\% \times \$24,900} \times \$5,000 = \frac{\$12,000}{\$20,000} \times \$5,000$$

$$\text{amount paid out} = \frac{3}{5} \times \$5,000 = \$3,000$$

   From the $3,000, subtract the $100 deductible to get the receipts:

$$\$3,000 - \$100 = \$2,900$$

(See Example 24.)

Supplementary Problems

5.35   The Simons wish to purchase a new house. With an annual take-home pay of $18,000, how much can they afford for monthly housing costs?   *Ans.* $375.

5.36   The Waltons completed paying off their mortgage loan of $25,500 at 6% in 30 years. (*a*) How much money did they pay over the 30 years? (*b*) How much of this was interest?   *Ans.*   (*a*) $55,080, (*b*) $29,580.

5.37   Bill Young, your associate, pays $225 a month rent for a house he can purchase for $19,500, with a down payment of $2,500. Bill estimates that the total housing costs per year would be $2,550, if he were the owner. (*a*) How much money per month would he save by purchasing the house? (*b*) This would amount to what percent of savings?   *Ans.*   (*a*) $12.50, (*b*) 5.6%.

5.38   The Adams have an opportunity to purchase a house appraised at $39,850 if they have the required FHA down payment available. (*a*) To how much will the FHA down payment amount? (*b*) The mortgage loan will amount to how much?   *Ans.*   (*a*) $2,720, (*b*) $37,130.

5.39   Dorothy Johns, your hair stylist, told you that her monthly mortgage loan payment is $198.48 and that she also pays a monthly pro rate share of her taxes and insurance. Her annual real estate taxes are $480; the insurance premium is $126. Calculate her total monthly payment.   *Ans.* $248.98.

5.40   Oscar Gant, who works with you, owns his home and decided to itemize his deductions on his income tax return this year. He asked you to figure the itemized deductions and the total amount for him. His housing expenses last year were: insurance, $132; real estate taxes, $588; maintenance and repair, $110; house painting, $550; mortgage interest, $506; and landscaping, $98. What will his total itemized deductions amount to on his income tax return?   *Ans.* $1,094.

5.41   Mr. Barnes, a local contractor, quoted the following costs to build a new house for Jan Conway: lot, $4,750; material, $8,500; plumbing, $1,950; heating and electrical work, $3,700; labor, $9,800; landscaping and driveway, $3,200; plus his fee of 15% based on all construction costs. How much will this house cost Jan?   *Ans.* $35,972.50.

5.42   In a rented house, last year the Arnolds spent the following amounts for housing costs: rent, $1,800; electricity, $740; water and garbage disposal, $270; telephone, $128; heating oil, $225; installment payments for appliances, $360; maintenance and repairs, $90; and yard care, $88. (*a*) What was their average monthly housing cost? (*b*) If this amount is 28% of the family's annual income, what is their annual income?   *Ans.*   (*a*) $308.42, (*b*) $13,217.86.

5.43   A lending agency will lend a purchaser, on a conventional loan, 75% of the $48,500 appraised value on a house. (*a*) How much will they lend? (*b*) How much is the down payment? *Ans.*   (*a*) $36,375, (*b*) $12,125.

5.44   The Williams family can budget $350 a month for housing costs. (*a*) Approximately how much can they pay for a new house? (*b*) Approximately how much should their annual income be? *Ans.*   (*a*) $35,000, (*b*) $14,000.

5.45   Al and Ruth Lake have a $28,500 mortgage loan at 8% for 30 years. They have made payments for 15 years and the loan is 23% paid off. (*a*) How much interest have they paid during the 15 years? (*b*) How much interest will they pay over the entire 30 years?   *Ans.*   (*a*) $31,099.20, (*b*) $46,808.40.

5.46   The Bronsons purchased a duplex house for $36,000. The house has a useful life expectancy of 30 years. If they rent the other half, to how much would their depreciation allowance per year amount? Use the straight-line method of depreciation. (*a*) What is their annual depreciation allowance? (*b*) How much depreciation allowance will they have written off after 12 years? *Ans.*   (*a*) $600, (*b*) $7,200.

5.47   Mr. Frisbee could have had a house constructed by a local builder for $35,900. This price included everything except the lot. He decided to build most of it himself but subcontract the excavating, plumbing, heating and electrical work. Upon completion his total expenses were: excavation, $450; plumbing, $1,700; heating and electrical work, $2,800. He paid out: lumber, materials and tools, $13,650; landscaping and driveway, $1,350; part-time labor, $1,990. In addition, it cost him $720 for additional rent due to the time delay resulting from doing it himself. (*a*) How much did he save by doing it himself? (*b*) What percent of savings did he realize based on the builder's price?   *Ans.*   (*a*) $13,240, (*b*) 36.9%.

5.48   A financial institution granted Ms. Willis a mortgage loan of $28,500 on a house appraised at $39,900. (*a*) How much was her down payment? (*b*) What percent of the appraised value was the loan?   *Ans.*   (*a*) $11,400, (*b*) 71.4%.

5.49   After a lengthy search, Maude and Ted Masten decided to purchase a house for $41,500 with an $8,000 down payment. They obtained a mortgage for the balance at 9% interest for 30 years. What was the amount of their monthly payments?   *Ans.* $269.68.

5.50   The Guests wish to set aside each month an amount of money sufficient to pay for their maintenance and repair costs. From previous experience, they have calculated the following expenses: house painting every 4 years, $600; landscaping and yard care, $88 per year; general repair and maintenance, $185 per year; plumbing and electrical work, $80 per year; miscellaneous expenses, $100 per year. (*a*) How much should they set aside each month to meet these expenses? (*b*) What percent of their total monthly housing costs of $340 is this maintenance expense?   *Ans.*   (*a*) $50.25, (*b*) 14.8%.

5.51   Ms. Baker owns a house which cost her $28,000. She rents one third of it. For straight-line depreciation purposes, it has a useful life expectancy of 40 years. Her house expenses last year were: mortgage interest, $480; taxes, $588; maintenance and repair, $390; insurance, $150; and yard maintenance, $120. To how much will her income tax deductions amount? *Ans.* $809.33.

5.52   Ms. Crouch bought a mobile home priced at $7,990 and made a down payment of $1,490. She borrowed the balance at $8\frac{1}{2}$% interest for 10 years. The monthly loan payments on this loan are $80.59; the monthly park rental fee is $55. At the end of the 10 years, she sold the mobile home for $1,800. (a) How much did this home cost her for the 10 years? (b) What was her average monthly cost?   Ans.   (a) $15,960.80,   (b) $133.01.

5.53   On a new house appraised at $36,500, the purchaser must pay the following closing costs: legal fees, $175; recording fees, $14; survey, $75; appraisal, $60; title insurance, $250; state tax, $48; and a proration of prepaid insurance of $60. (a) What is total amount of closing costs? (b) This is what percent of the appraised value?   Ans.   (a) $682,   (b) 1.9%.

5.54   After finding a very pleasant house which they decided to buy, the Jacobs went to several financial institutions shopping for a mortgage loan. They decided to obtain the loan from a bank which would lend them $34,800 at $8\frac{1}{2}$% interest for 25 years. (a) How much are their monthly payments? (b) Construct a mortgage loan schedule showing the first three payments.   Ans.   (a) $280.49.
(b)

Payment Number	Monthly Payment	Applied to Interest	Principal	Unpaid Balance
1	$280.49	$246.50	$33.99	$34,766.01
2	280.49	246.26	34.23	34,731.78
3	280.49	246.02	34.47	34,687.31

5.55   Jane Miller can afford to pay approximately $350 a month for housing costs, of which $95 is for taxes, insurance, and maintenance. If she bought a house costing $39,900 with a 20% down payment and interest at 9%, should the term be 20 years, 25 years, or 30 years?   Ans.   For 30 years. $256.96 monthly payments + $95 other costs = $351.96.

5.56   The Martins owned their home for 9 years at a monthly house cost of $415. Upon being transferred to another city, they sold it at a profit of $7,800. They decided to calculate their actual monthly housing costs after the sale of the property. Their itemized deductions for taxes and interest over the 9 years allowed them an income tax saving of $4,300. What were their actual housing costs?   Ans. $302.96.

5.57   The Atkins decided to buy a house appraised at $43,500 with an FHA approved mortgage loan. Their loan is at $8\frac{1}{2}$% interest annually for 30 years. (a) How much is their down payment? (b) To what will their monthly mortgage loan payment amount? (c) They will also pay monthly a pro rata amount sufficient to meet annual taxes of $1,320 and an annual insurance premium of $192. To how much additional will this amount?   Ans.   (a) $3,450. (b) $307.98,   (c) $126.

5.58   Jack Stonewall and Gloria Steiner, who plan to get married in the near future, decided to purchase a home immediately. Their combined annual incomes amount to $22,500 take-home pay. How much can they afford to pay for a house?   Ans. $56,250.

5.59   Carlton Evans owned a house valued at $50,000, which he insured for $32,000. He did not consider it necessary to have full coverage because the fire station was a half mile from his house and a fire hydrant was only 75 feet from the house. Carlton's homeowner's policy has an 80% coinsurance clause. How much will the insurance company's indemnity amount to if Carlton has fire damage in the amount of: (a) $12,000, (b) $9,000.   Ans.   (a) $9,600, (b) $7,200. (See Problem 5.31.)

5.60 Walter Bigelow paid $124 for a 1-year term homeowner's insurance policy. Two months later, Walter was transferred by the electronics firm for which he worked. He sold his house and cancelled his policy. How much refund did he receive?   *Ans.* $90.52.   (See Problem 5.32.)

5.61 Helen and Mike Carey own a house with an actual market value of $43,800. They purchased a homeowner's policy form (HO-2), Group 1, with full coverage. Their policy has an 80% coinsurance clause. They paid for a 3-year premium on September 1, 1975, and cancelled it on June 1, 1977, because one of their friends has gone into the insurance business and they wanted their friend to insure their house. (*a*) How much of the premium was used? (*b*) What is the amount of refund?   *Ans.*   (*a*) $224.96, (*b*) $145.04.   (See Problem 5.33.)

5.62 Ms. Sloan owns a house valued at $18,750, which she insured for $12,000 with a homeowner's (HO-2) policy under Group 7, with an all perils deductible clause. This policy carries an 80% coinsurance clause. The deductible amount is $50 for all perils. (*a*) How much premium did she pay for a 3-year policy? (*b*) How much did the insurance company reimburse her for a fire loss of $5,000?   *Ans.*   (*a*) $154, (*b*) $3,950.   (See Problem 5.34.)

5.63 The Sokol family own a house with a market value of $60,000. They carry a homeowner's policy for the face amount of $60,000. (*a*) Under this policy, how much protection do they have for each type of coverage? (*b*) If the property is destroyed by fire, what is the maximum amount payable for personal property?   *Ans.*   (*a*) Dwelling, $60,000; appurtenant private structure, $6,000; personal property, $30,000; additional living expenses, $12,000; total, $108,000. (*b*) $30,000.

5.64 James Regal, a local school principal, owns a house that has a market value of $44,800. Mr. Regal has a homeowner's policy (HO-2), Group 7, with full coverage. If the house is insured for total actual value, to how much did Regal's 3-year premium amount?   *Ans.* $592.   (See Problem 5.30.)

Chapter 6

Personal Insurance

The purpose of insurance is to protect individuals from large, unexpected and/or uncontrollable losses. The principle is that people pool their money for mutual protection; each contributes a small share (the premium) so that when one member of the group suffers a large loss, the individual is reimbursed from the group's contributions. Insurance companies administer these funds and determine premium rates based on past experience and statistical data.

In Chapters 4 and 5, the impact of insurance on automobile and home ownership was described. This chapter deals with the basic forms of personal insurance: life insurance, Social Security, and medical insurance plans.

LIFE INSURANCE

Life insurance provides financial protection to the insured's beneficiaries in the event of his death. However, it may also be used as a form of savings for one's older years if death has not intervened. There are several major types of life insurance, each of which has varying advantages and disadvantages. The final criteria in the selection of life insurance narrows down to how much a person can afford to carry and the purposes for which the insurance is purchased. The major types are:

(1) Term insurance.
(2) Whole life insurance.
(3) Limited-payment life insurance.
(4) Endowment insurance.

In addition, there are combination policies designed to meet the varying needs of people.

6.1 TERM INSURANCE

At an early age, this type of insurance provides the greatest amount of coverage for the least amount of money. It is not a permanent type as it has no cash, loan, or extended-term value. Term insurance is strictly for protection only. The premiums charged are quoted in annual rates of $1,000 of face value. A typical rate table charged by life insurance companies is shown below. Note the age difference for male and female insureds. Premiums are based on mortality rates computed by insurance company actuaries.

(*Note*: Some insurance companies use a different age differential between male and female insurance premium rates.)

118

Table 1.   Five-Year Term Life
Annual Premium for Each $1,000 of Face Value

Age			Age		
Male	Female	Premium	Male	Female	Premium
15	18	$3.30	30	33	$3.52
16	19	3.31	31	34	3.61
17	20	3.32	32	35	3.72
18	21	3.33	33	36	3.86
19	22	3.34	34	37	4.02
20	23	3.35	35	38	4.20
21	24	3.36	36	39	4.40
22	25	3.37	37	40	4.62
23	26	3.38	38	41	4.86
24	27	3.39	39	42	5.14
25	28	3.40	40	43	5.46

EXAMPLE 1

Willie Jordan, a 25-year-old married man, has a wife and two children.   Willie, a security guard at a local manufacturing plant, who is frequently ill, wants life insurance protection for his family.   To obtain maximum coverage possible with a low premium rate, Willie purchased a $25,000 face value 5-year term life insurance policy.   Determine his annual premium.

Table 1: read down under "Male" to age 25, then across under "Premium," to $3.40. $3.40 is the annual premium for each $1,000 of face value term insurance.   Multiply the face value of $1,000 by the face value of the policy.

$3.40 (per thousand) × 25 (thousands) = $85.00 annual premium

EXAMPLE 2

Bill and Sue Boyle, a newly married couple, decided to purchase a 5-year term insurance policy with a face value of $15,000 on the life of each.   They are both 22 years old.   (a) How much will Bill's annual premium amount to?   (b) To how much will Sue's premium amount?

(a) Table 1: for Bill, age 22, read down "Male" column to 22, then across to "Premium." Find $3.37 for $1,000.   Multiply $3.37 (per $1,000) × 15 (thousands): $50.55 annual premium.

(b) For Sue, age 22, read down "Female" column to 22, then across under "Premium."   Find $3.34 per $1,000.   Multiply $3.34 (per $1,000) × 15 (thousands): $50.10 annual premium.   (Note: At the same age, a female pays a lesser rate.)

6.2 WHOLE LIFE INSURANCE

Whole life insurance, also known as "ordinary" or "straight life," provides protection during the lifetime of the insured.   It is the least costly form of permanent life insurance.   Permanent types of life insurance have a cash, loan, paid-up, and extended-term value.

6.3 LIMITED PAYMENT LIFE INSURANCE

Limited payment life insurance provides permanent protection. Premium payments are completed in a fixed period of time—generally after 20 or 30 years or at a specified age. Upon completion of payments, the insured is protected for life. His/her policy has cash, loan, paid-up, and extended term value.

6.4 ENDOWMENT INSURANCE

This type of insurance is an insured savings plan. It is purchased for a given number of years, usually 20 or 30. Upon completion of the payments, the insured receives the face value of the policy either in a lump sum or in a series of monthly payments. In the event the insured dies before completing payments, the beneficiary receives the face value of the policy. Typical premium rates for whole life, limited payment life, and endowment insurance are shown below.

Table 2. Annual Life Insurance Rates Per $1,000

Male Age	Whole Life		20-Payment Life		20-Year Endowment	
	$5,000–9,999	$10,000–19,999	$5,000–9,999	$10,000–19,999	$5,000–9,999	$10,000–19,999
20	15.41	15.04	19.44	19.06	47.80	46.98
25	17.55	17.18	22.01	21.64	48.05	47.22
30	20.26	19.89	25.01	24.64	48.53	47.71
35	23.71	23.34	28.55	28.18	49.39	48.57
40	28.17	27.80	32.76	32.39	50.88	50.96
45	33.91	33.54	37.76	37.38	52.49	51.57
50	41.42	41.05	43.89	43.52	56.29	55.39
55	51.33	50.96	51.91	51.54	62.18	61.24
60	64.58	64.21	61.44	61.07	71.02	70.98

(*Note*: Females may subtract 3 years from the male age and apply that rate. A 23-year-old female would pay the same rate as a 20-year-old male.)

EXAMPLE 3

Albie Galento, aged 40, supports a family of five. Upon receiving a recent promotion to a supervisory position at the local fish cannery, Albie decided to increase his life insurance protection. To supplement his group life insurance policy, Albie purchased a $15,000 whole life policy. What are Albie's annual payments for this policy?

On Table 2, read down to age 40, then across under "Whole Life" ($10,000–$19,999). Find $27.80, which is the premium-rate for $1,000 insurance coverage. Multiply the face value by the premium rate per $1,000.

$$\$27.80 \times 15 \text{ (thousands)} = \$417 \text{ annual premium}$$

EXAMPLE 4

Marge Sokol, a hair stylist at The Style Shoppe, was discussing with a customer the importance and reasons for having life insurance protection. The customer convinced Marge that she should have sufficient protection to defray funeral and related expenses. Marge, age 23, decided to purchase a 20-payment life insurance policy with a face value of $8,000. How much are her annual payments?

Female, aged 23, would use the male rate at age 20. Table 2: read across from age 20, and under 20-Payment Life ($5,000–$9,999), find $19.44, rate per $1,000 of insurance. Multiply the rate per $1,000 by the face value of the policy.

$$\$19.44 \text{ (per } \$1,000) \times 8 \text{ (thousands)} = \$155.52 \text{ annual premium}$$

EXAMPLE 5

Jim Talbot, a newly married man, age 25, wanted to purchase $18,000 worth of insurance, which he could pay off in 20 years. Jim didn't know whether to purchase an endowment policy or a 20-payment life policy. Explain to Jim: (a) how much more he would pay annually for a 20-year endowment than for a 20-payment life policy, and (b) how much more he would have paid over the 20 years.

(a) Table 2: 20-Payment Life, age 25. Read to the right, under 20-Payment Life ($10,000–$19,999), and $21.64, rate per $1,000.

$$\$21.64 \text{ (per } \$1,000) \times 18 \text{ (thousands)} = \$389.52 \text{ annual premium}$$

To find the total of the premiums paid in 20 years, multiply the annual premium by 20.

$$\$389.52 \text{ (annual premium)} \times 20 \text{ (years)} = \$7,790.40$$

20-Year endowment: age 25. Read to the right, under 20-Year Endowment ($10,000–$19,999), and find $47.22, per $1,000. $47.22 (per $1,000) × 18 (thousands) = $849.96 annual premium. $849.96 (annual premium) × 20 (years) = $16,999.20. The amount more annually for 20-year endowment policy:

$$\$849.96 - \$389.52 = \$460.44$$

(b) The amount more for 20-year endowment over 20-year period:

$$\$16,999.20 \text{ (total 20-year endowment)} - \$7,790.40 \text{ (total 20-payment life)} = \$9,208.80$$

SOCIAL SECURITY

Social Security benefits are payable under three conditions.

(1) Retirement.
(2) Disability.
(3) Survivorship.

We should have an understanding of Social Security and its benefits, because we might at any time be entitled to some of them.

6.5 RETIREMENT

Earnings credits are based upon the number of quarters of coverage earned while under covered employment. Each three-month period of the calendar year is a quarter: January–March, April–June, July–September, and October–December. By earning $50 or more during a period, one receives a quarter of coverage. To be "fully insured," you must have the required number of quarters, depending upon your age. See Table 3. (*Note*: Part of the money withheld for Social Security benefits is invested in a hospital insurance fund which pays hospital bills for workers and their dependents once they reach age 65. See Section 6.)

Table 3.

Year in Which You Were Born	Year You Are 65	Quarters of Coverage Needed for Retirement Benefits		Quarters of Coverage Needed for Hospital Insurance	
		Men	Women	Men	Women
1892 or earlier	1957 or earlier	6	6	0	0
1893	1958	7	6	0	0
1894	1959	8	6	0	0
1895	1960	9	6	0	0
1896	1961	10	7	0	0
1897	1962	11	8	0	0
1898	1963	12	9	0	0
1899	1964	13	10	0	0
1900	1965	14	11	0	0
1901	1966	15	12	0	0
1902	1967	16	13	0	0
1903	1968	17	14	3	3
1904	1969	18	15	6	6
1905	1970	19	16	9	9
1906	1971	20	17	12	12
1907	1972	21	18	15	15
1908	1973	22	19	18	18
1909	1974	23	20	21	20
1910	1975	24	21	24	21
1911	1976	25	22	25	22
1912	1977	26	23	26	23
1913	1978	27	24	27	24
1917	1982	31	28	31	28
1921	1986	35	32	35	32
1925	1990	39	36	39	36
1929 or later	1994 or later	40	40	40	40

EXAMPLE 6

Mr. Alan Jones, born in 1911, is planning to retire when he becomes 65. Therefore, in addition to a small company pension, Alan is planning on Social Security benefits so that he may enjoy his golden years. How many quarters of coverage must Alan have in order to receive retirement benefits in 1976? Alan's twin sister, Ms. Edna Jones, also plans to retire when he does. How many quarters of coverage does Edna need?

Mr. Jones: On Table 3 read down under "Year of Birth," then across to "Year You Are 65," continue across to quarters of coverage under men. Find 25.

Ms. Jones: Using the same procedure, read under the column "Women," and find 22. *Note*: With enough quarters of coverage, one may retire as early as age 62, but with reduced benefits.

6.6 DISABILITY

Disability benefits depend upon the number of credits acquired at the age you become disabled.

(1) Under age 21—you need 6 quarters of coverage in the three years before disability.
(2) Age 24–31—you need credit for half the time between your 21st birthday and the time you become disabled.
(3) Age 31 or later—5 years of your work (20 quarters) must be in the 10-year period just before you become disabled.

EXAMPLE 7

Walter Gross, a 29-year-old construction worker, sustained a disabling injury when he fell from the roof on which he was working. In order to receive disability benefits under Social Security, how many quarters of coverage must Walter have earned?

Between age 24–31, he must have earned credits for half the time between his 21st birthday and disability at age 29.   29 − 21 = 9 (years).   8 (years) × 4 (quarters) = 32 quarters.

$$32 \text{ (quarters)} \div 2 \text{ (half the time)} = 16 \text{ quarters required}$$

6.7 SURVIVORSHIP

If the insured worker dies, benefits can be payable to survivors as follows:

(1) Unmarried children under 18 (or 22, if full-time students).
(2) Unmarried children 18 or over who were severely disabled before age 22 and who continue to be disabled.
(3) Widow or dependent widower, 60 or over.
(4) Widow under 60 caring for a worker's child who is eligible for benefits.
(5) Lump sum at worker's death, $255.

EXAMPLE 8

Rose Fagin's father died at the age of 59 with full coverage for Social Security benefits.   Rose has a mother, 58; herself, a 16-year-old student; and a working brother, aged 21.   Who in the family is eligible for Social Security benefits?   Rose and her mother: Rose's mother, a widow under 60, caring for a worker's dependent child, and Rose, an unmarried dependent, under 18.

6.8 BENEFITS

Benefits are based upon the worker's average yearly earnings. Table 4 shows typical monthly benefits. (*Note*: This table of rates is subject to change.)

EXAMPLE 9

Mr. and Mrs. Oscar Latour have eagerly awaited the day that Oscar would retire at age 65. At that time Mrs. Latour will become 62 years old. This will allow them to draw full benefits under Social Security. Oscar's average annual earning upon which Social Security benefits are figured amount to $5,000. (*a*) How much will he receive a month? (*b*) How much will Mrs. Latour receive?

(*a*) Mr. Latour: retired at 65, read across under average yearly earnings, $5,000.   Find $286.10.

(*b*) Mrs. Latour: read down to wife, age 62, no child, then across under $5,000.   Find $107.40.

Table 4. Examples of Monthly Social Security Payments
(Effective June 1975)

	Average yearly earnings after 1950*						
	$923 or less	$3,000	$4,000	$5,000	$6,000	$8,000	$10,000
You, the worker Retired at 65	101.40	209.70	246.80	286.10	323.40	402.00	445.40
Under 65 and disabled	101.40	209.70	246.80	286.10	323.40	402.00	445.40
Retired at 62	81.20	167.80	197.50	228.90	258.80	321.60	356.40
Your wife At 65	50.70	104.90	123.40	143.10	161.70	201.00	222.70
At 62, with no child	38.10	78.70	92.60	107.40	121.30	150.80	167.10
Under 65 and one child in her care	50.80	111.00	175.00	242.00	270.00	301.60	334.20
Your widow At 65 (if worker never received reduced retirement benefits)	101.40	209.70	246.80	286.10	323.40	402.00	445.40
At 60 (if sole survivor)	74.90	150.00	176.50	204.60	231.30	287.50	318.50
At 50 and disabled (if sole survivor)	56.80	105.00	123.50	143.10	161.80	201.10	222.80
Widowed mother (or father) caring for one child	152.20	314.60	370.20	429.20	485.20	603.00	668.20
Maximum family payment	152.20	320.60	421.80	528.10	593.30	703.60	779.60

*Generally, average earnings covered by Social Security are figured from 1951 until the worker reaches retirement age, becomes disabled, or dies. The maximum benefit for a retired worker in 1975 (June or later) is $341.70, based on average yearly earnings of $6,504. The higher benefits shown in the chart, based on average earnings shown in the columns on the right, generally will not be payable until later years.

EXAMPLE 10

When Cindy's father died, she was a full-time student, aged 19. Her brother was 14 years old and her mother 55. What is the maximum family payment they may receive if her father's average annual earnings were (a) $4,000? (b) If they were $5,000?

(a) See Table 4. Read down the column to maximum family payment, then across under $4,000. Find $421.80.

(b) Read under $5,000. Find $528.10.

(Note: A widowed mother with 2 or more dependents is entitled to maximum family payments.)

EXAMPLE 11

Your Aunt Jean, 60 years old, is the sole survivor of her family. Your uncle, fully covered by Social Security, died at the age of 63. His average annual earnings were $3,000. What benefits will your aunt receive?

A lump sum death payment of $255. Plus $150 per month (Table 4: read down to Age 60 (sole survivor), across under "Average Annual Earnings, $3,000," and find $150 monthly benefits).

MEDICAL INSURANCE PLANS

6.9　MEDICAL AND HEALTH INSURANCE

Prepaid medical insurance is generally sold to persons through a group coverage program. It contains benefits for hospital care, doctor's services, and major medical benefits. Plans are tailored for specific groups, which makes it necessary for persons covered under a plan to refer to the master contracts issued to their employer or group. A typical policy includes the following benefits with premium rates for $15.70 per month for a single person and $43.54 per month for families.

Hospital Care

Number of hospital days	70 days per confinement
Daily board and room allowance (Semiprivate room)	Paid in full
Emergency room service (For accidents)	Paid in full
Hospital services (Outpatient minor surgery)	Paid in full
Paid-in-full hospital services (Most services necessary to recovery, such as: drugs, laboratory, and X-rays)	

Physician's Care

Surgery: Up to $417 (maximum for any one procedure)

In-hospital medical visits: Up to $15.00 first day, up to $5.00 beginning on the second day of confinement, up to a maximum of $360

Combinations of care: Up to $1,000 maximum per confinement

Special in-hospital medical care: Up to $63 during first 48 hours of confinement for intensive care

Anasthesia (in-patient): Up to $250 per confinement

X-ray services: Up to $71 maximum for any one procedure

Pathology: Up to $25

Pediatric care (in-patient)
　Well baby: $13, first week
　Premature baby: $8, first day

Exchange transfusions: $104

Major Medical Benefits

Maximum available during lifetime of the contract: $10,000
Deductible: $100
Coinsurance: 80%–20%
Room allowance: Semiprivate rate

After hospital and physician coverages have paid $3,000 in benefits, this major medical portion will pay expenses up to the lifetime maximum ($10,000) for the remainder of the calendar year.

EXAMPLE 12

The Brown family was insured under a group medical plan which included hospital care, physician's care, and major medical benefits. Last year, Tommy, age 18, was injured in a fall from his motorcycle. He was hospitalized for 15 days in a semiprivate room. His surgeon submitted a bill for $800 for surgery. The X-ray charges were $150. (a) How much was Tommy Brown's total bill for this injury? (b) How much did the insurance company pay?

(a) Hospital care: semiprivate room paid for by the insurance. Surgery insurance pays up to $417 for any one procedure. $800 (charge) − $417 (coverage) = $383 paid by Brown. X-ray services: up to $71 for any one procedure. $150 (charge) − $71 (coverage) = $79 paid by Brown.

$$\$383 + \$79 = \$462 \text{ total paid by Brown}$$

(b) The insurance paid for the cost of a semiprivate room. Insurance coverage: $417 for surgery; $71 for X-rays. Total bill payable by the insurance: $417 + $71 = $488, plus the hospital's rate for a semiprivate room for 15 days.

6.10 MEDICARE

Medicare is a health insurance program administered as part of Social Security. It is for people age 65 and older, as well as disabled persons under 65, who receive other Social Security benefits.

There are two basic parts to Medicare: Part A—hospital insurance and Part B—medical insurance.

Hospital insurance. All persons enrolled in the Social Security program are entitled to Part A coverage once they reach age 65. Medicare helps pay for necessary in-patient hospital care according to the following schedule, on a benefit period basis:

(1) Deductible amount in each benefit period, $104. The patient pays the first $104 of the hospital bill.
(2) The insurance will pay for all other covered services up to 60 days.
(3) From the 61st through the 90th day, it will pay for all covered services, over $26 a day.
(4) For in-patient hospital care of more than 90 days, the patient pays a maximum of $52 a day for each reserve day, up to 60 days. Each person covered under Medicare has 60 reserve days in his or her lifetime.*

A benefit period is a way of measuring your use of services. The first benefit period starts upon entry to a hospital after the hospital insurance begins. Upon being out of a hospital for

---

*These reserve days may be used in the event a person stays in the hospital more than 90 days in a benefit period. Once a reserve day is used, it is never gotten back. They are not renewable.

60 consecutive days, a new benefit period starts upon reentry to a hospital. There is no limit to the number of benefit periods one can have.

EXAMPLE 13

Mrs. Jones, who is covered by hospitalization benefits under Medicare, was hospitalized for 18 days. (*a*) How much did she have to pay for hospital expenses during this stay? (*b*) How much would she pay for a 75-day period?

(*a*) The deductible amount for each benefit period is $104. Medicare will pay for all other covered services up to 60 days.

(*b*) Deductible amount, $104. From the 61st through the 90th day, Mrs. Jones would pay $26 a day. 75 − 60 = 15 days; 15 days × $26 (per day) = $390.

$$\$104 \text{ (deductible)} + \$390 = \$494 \text{ total payment due}$$

Medical Insurance. Part B under Medicare helps pay for doctor's services, out-patient services, and other services not covered by the hospital insurance part of Medicare. People who have hospital insurance can sign up for medical insurance; the basic premium is $7.20 a month. This insurance has a $60 deductible charged to the patient once each calendar year. After the first $60 of covered expenses in a calendar year has been paid by the patient, the medical insurance will pay 80% of the reasonable charges for any additional covered services during the rest of the year.

EXAMPLE 14

Mr. Billings, age 68, was insured under Medicare for hospitalization and medical expenses. Last year, Medicare allowed $680 of his medical expenses. (*a*) How much did he actually pay? (*b*) How much did the medical insurance part of Medicare (Part B) pay?

(*a*) There is a $60 deductible from allowable medical expenses each calendar year. Medicare under Part B pays 80% of all reasonable charges beyond the $60 deductible. $680 − $60 = $620. 80% × $620 = $496 paid by Medicare. $620 − $496 = $124 charged to Mr. Billings.

$$\$124 + \$60 = \$184, \text{ the amount paid by Billings}$$

(*b*) $496 paid by Medicare under Part B.

Solved Problems

6.1 Ron and Elsie Jacobson, a newly married couple, decided that each should buy some life insurance to protect one another financially in the case of the untimely death of either. Until they were more secure in their jobs, they each elected to purchase a $12,000 face value 5-year term life insurance policy. If both are 25 years of age, (*a*) how much is the annual premium for Elsie? (*b*) For Ron?

(*a*) Table 1: read down under "Female," age 25, then across to $3.37, premium for $1,000. Multiply the annual premium for $1,000 by the face value of the policy.

$$\$3.37 \text{ (per } \$1,000) \times 12 \text{ (thousands)} = \$40.44 \text{ annual premium}$$

(*b*) Table 1: for male 25, find $3.40 per $1,000.

$$\$3.40 \text{ (per } \$1,000) \times 12 \text{ (thousands)} = \$40.80 \text{ annual premium}$$

(See Example 1.)

6.2   Mike, age 23, without much material assets but with a wife and 2 children decided to buy a $12,000 face value 5-year term insurance policy to provide financial protection for his family if he died. Mike's brother, age 33, decided to buy a similar policy with a $10,000 face value to provide additional financial security for his wife and children. (*a*) Which one will pay a larger annual premium? (*b*) By how much?

(*a*) Table 1: read down under "Male," age 23, then across under premium. Find $3.38 per $1,000 annual premium. Multiply the annual premium for each $1,000 by the face value of the policy.

$$\$3.38 \text{ (per thousand)} \times 12 \text{ (thousand)} = \$40.56 \text{ annual premium}$$

(*b*) Use the same procedure as above for age 33. Find $3.86, annual premium per $1,000.

$$\$3.86 \text{ (per thousand)} \times 10 \text{ (thousand)} = \$38.60 \text{ annual premium}$$

Mike pays $1.96 per year more. (See Example 2.)

6.3   John Flagstaff, age 40, with a wife and three teenage children, decided to purchase additional life insurance to provide his family with more financial protection in the event of his death. John purchased a 20-payment life insurance policy with a face value of $18,000. How much less would he pay annually for a whole life policy?

Table 2: read down under "Male," age to 40, then across under 20-payment life ($10,000–$19,999). Find $32.39, annual premium per $1,000. Multiply the annual premium per $1,000 by the face value of the policy. $32.39 (per $1,000) × 18 (thousands) = $583.02 annual premium for a 20-payment life insurance policy.

Use the same procedure as above for whole life, age 40. Read $27.80 per $1,000 under ($10,000–$19,000). $27.80 × 18 = $500.40 annual premium for a whole life policy.

$$\$583.02 - \$500.40 = \$82.62 \text{ less per year for a whole life policy}$$

(See Example 3.)

6.4   Ms. Beth Parks, age 33, bought a $16,000 face value 20-year endowment policy. She wanted to provide for her widowed sister and also use this type of policy as a means of saving. (*a*) How much are her annual payments? (*b*) How much would she pay annually for a whole life and a 20-payment life policy for the same face value?

(*a*) Table 2: read down to "Male," age 30 (females may subtract three years from their age and use the male rate), then across to 20-year endowment under $10,000–$19,999. Find $47.71, annual premium per $1,000. Multiply the annual premium per thousand by the face value of the policy to obtain the annual premium.

$$\$47.71 \text{ (per } \$1,000) \times 16 \text{ (thousands)} = \$763.36 \text{ annual premium}$$

(*b*) Use same procedure as above. Whole life: age 30, annual premium per $1,000 = $19.89. $19.89 × 16 = $318.24 annual premium. 20-payment life: age 30, $24.64, annual premium per $1,000.

$$\$24.64 \times 16 = \$392.24 \text{ annual premium}$$

Total amount of annual premiums for whole life and 20-payment life policies:

$$\$318.24 + \$392.24 = \$710.48$$

(See Example 4.)

6.5   Alec Young, age 35, who planned to retire at an early age, decided to purchase insurance protection for his wife and two children, which could be paid up prior to his retirement.   His insurance agent suggested that he purchase a $8,000 face value, 20-year endowment policy, which would include both the savings and insurance features.   He suggested that he also purchase a $14,000 face value 20-payment life policy at the same time.   (*a*) What will Alec pay annually for each policy?   (*b*) Which one is less costly and by how much?

(*a*) Table 2: read down to age 35, then across to 20-year endowment under $5,000–$9,999.   Find $49.39, annual premium per $1,000.   Multiply the annual premium per $1,000 by the face value to obtain the annual premium.

$$\$49.39 \times 8 \text{ (thousands)} = \$395.12$$

20-payment life policy, $14,000, face value.   Use same procedure as above.   Read under 20-payment life ($10,000–$19,999).   Find $28.18 per $1,000 annual premium.

$$\$28.18 \times 14 \text{ (thousands)} = \$394.52$$

the annual premium for a 20-payment life policy.

(*b*) The 20-payment life policy is less costly by $.60 per year.

$$\$395.12 - \$394.52 = \$.60$$

(See Example 5.)

6.6   To receive Social Security benefits upon retirement at age 65,   (*a*) how many quarters of coverage would your father need if he were born in 1921?   (*b*) How many would he need if born in 1925?

(*a*) See Table 3.   Read down under year in which born, then across to quarters of coverage, under "Men."   Year 1921: read across to 35 quarters.

(*b*) Year 1925: read across to 39 quarters.   (See Example 6.)

6.7   Nathan Cushman became disabled at the age of 25.   (*a*) How many quarters of coverage must he have earned in order to receive disability benefits?   (*b*) How many quarters would he need if he became disabled at age 33?

(*a*) Between age 24–31, he must have earned credits for half the time between his 21st birthday and his disability age, 25.   25 − 21 = 4 (years),   4 (years) × 4 (quarters) = 16 quarters.

$$16 \text{ (quarters)} \div 2 = 8 \text{ quarters required}$$

(*b*) Age 33: age 31 or later, 5 years of his work, 20 quarters, must be credited in the 10-year period before he became disabled.   Years of age: 33 − 10 = 23.   He must have earned 20 quarters of coverage since his 23rd birthday.   (See Example 7.)

6.8   Your uncle John died at the age of 52 with full coverage for Social Security benefits.   He left his wife, age 50; a son, age 16; and a daughter, age 18 and unmarried, who works full time.   (*a*) Who in their family is eligible to receive benefits?   (*b*) At what age will the benefits stop?

(*a*) Son, age 16; wife, age 50.

(*b*) Benefits will stop when his son marries or reaches age 18.   However, they will continue until his son reaches age 22, if he is a full-time student.   (See Example 8.)

6.9   Jose Lopez is retiring at age 62.   His wife is also 62 years of age.   (a) If they have no
dependent children, to how much will their monthly benefits under Social Security
amount if his average annual earnings amount to $4,000?   (b) With average annual
earnings of $6,000?

   (a) See Table 4: read down the column "The Worker," to retired at 62, then across under average
       annual earnings of $4,000.   Find $197.50.   Read down to "Your Wife, Age 62, with No
       Child."   Read to the right under $4,000, find $92.60.   Add the two together to obtain total
       monthly benefits.

$$\$197.50 + \$92.60 = \$290.10$$

   (b) If his average annual earnings amounted to $6,000, the worker, under column $6,000, will
       receive $258.80 a month.   Wife, age 62, with no child, will receive $121.30.   The total
       monthly benefits:

$$\$258.80 + \$121.30 = \$380.10$$

(See Example 9.)

6.10   When Alex Dupont died, he left a 20-year-old daughter who was a full-time student; his
wife aged 52; and three working sons above the age of 18.   (a) How much will the
family receive per month if the father's average annual earnings were $900?   (b) If
they were $3,000 per year?

   (a) See Table 4.   Read down to "Widowed Mother, Caring for One Child," then to the right under
       $923 or less.   Find $152.20 per month.

   (b) Read down to "Widowed Mother, Caring for One Child," then to the right under $3,000, and
       find $314.60.   (See Example 10.)

6.11   Andy Bithlo, a lathe operator in a local machine shop, died, leaving his wife Angela as
his sole survivor.   Andy had full Social Security coverage with average annual earnings
of $5,000.   What Social Security benefits did Angela receive?

   A lump sum payment of $225 at death.   Plus $286.10 per month.   (Table 4: read down to "Your
Widow at 65," then across to $5,000.   Find $286.10 monthly benefits.)   (See Example 11.)

6.12   Ms. Blunt is covered under Medicare for hospital insurance.   Last year, she had an
illness which hospitalized her for 24 days.   Five months later she was hospitalized for
73 days.   How much did she have to pay for normal hospital expenses during the year?

   First illness of 24 days duration; Ms. Blunt pays the deductible amount of $104.   Second ill-
ness of 73 days duration; Ms. Blunt pays the $104 deductible amount required during the first 60
days.   For the remaining 13 days (73 − 60), Ms. Blunt must pay $26 a day. $26 × 13 =
$338. $338 + $104 = $442, total amount for the second illness.

   $104 (first illness) + $442 (second illness) = $546, total amount

(See Example 13.)

6.13   Your grandfather, Zeke Tolles, a retired accountant, has Medicare medical insurance.
Due to illness last year, his allowable medical charges amounted to $550.   (a) How much of
this amount did your grandfather have to pay?   (b) How much did the insurance coverage
pay?

(a) There is a $60 deductible amount per calendar year. The insurance pays 80% of all reasonable charges beyond the $60 deductible. $550 − $60 = $490. 80% × $490 = $392 paid by the insurance. $490 − $392 = $98 due.

$$\$60 \text{ (deductible)} + \$98 \text{ (due)} = \$158 \text{ paid by your grandfather}$$

(b) $392 paid by the medical insurance under Medicare. (See Example 14.)

6.14 The Stone family was insured under a group medical plan which included hospital care, physician's care, and major medical benefits. Last year, Mrs. Stone entered a hospital for surgery. She was in a semiprivate room for 35 days at a rate of $75 per day. Her other charges were: surgery, $1,400; anesthesia, $350; X-rays, $195. (a) Of the total charges, how much did Mrs. Stone pay? (b) How much did the insurance company pay?

(a) *Hospital care*: paid for by the insurance company.
　Semiprivate room: 35 days × $75 (per day) = $2,625.
　Surgery: insurance pays $417 maximum for any one procedure. $1,400 (surgery charge) − $417 = $983 charge to Mrs. Stone.
　Anesthesia: up to $250 per confinement; $350 (charge) − $250 = $100 charge to Mrs. Stone.
　X-ray: up to $71 maximum for any one procedure. $195 (charge) − $71 = $124 charge to Mrs. Stone.
　Total charges to Mrs. Stone:

$$\$983 + \$100 + \$124 = \$1,107$$

(b) Total insurance coverage payment:

$$\$2,625 + \$417 + \$250 + \$71 = \$3,363$$

(See Example 12.)

Supplementary Problems

6.15 Wally Stone, age 20, who recently obtained steady employment at the local paper mill, bought an $18,000 5-year term life insurance policy to provide financial protection for his bride-to-be. This prompted Wally's father, age 40, to purchase a similar policy having a $12,000 face value, to provide protection for his wife and children. (a) Which one will pay the higher annual premium? (b) By how much? *Ans.* (a) Father, (b) by $5.22. (See Problem 6.2.)

6.16 Steve Young, age 20, was in an automobile accident which paralyzed his legs, rendering him completely disabled. Steve had worked steadily for the past two years. He had paid his Social Security tax regularly. (a) How many quarters of coverage must Steve have earned to receive disability benefits? (b) How many quarters would he need had he been age 30? (c) Age 37? *Ans.* (a) 6, (b) 18, (c) 20. (See Problem 6.7.)

6.17 Your Aunt Martha has Medicare hospitalization insurance. She was ill three times last year. The first time she was in the hospital for 18 days. Three months later, she was in the hospital for 78 days. After being home for 10 weeks, she reentered the hospital for 15 days. How much did she pay for normal hospital expenses last year? *Ans.* $780. (See Problem 6.12.)

6.18 Bob Stanton, age 35, decided to purchase $15,000 worth of life insurance to provide additional financial security for his wife and family. Bob could afford $750 a year for additional insurance. (a) Could Bob purchase both a whole life and a 20-payment life policy? (b) Could he purchase a 20-year endowment policy? *Ans.* (a) No, (b) yes. (See Problem 6.3.)

6.19 Roscoe Turner, a sales clerk at a local hardware store, died at the age of 64, with full Social Security coverage earned. Roscoe left his wife and a dependent granddaughter, aged 15. (*a*) Who in the family is entitled to receive benefits? (*b*) At what age will the benefits stop?   *Ans*. (*a*) His wife and granddaughter. (*b*) The granddaughter's benefits will stop when she reaches age 18—or at 22, if she continues to be a full-time student. (See Problem 6.8.)

6.20 Mrs. Julia Poulin, your neighbor, has Medicare medical insurance (Part B). Due to injuries sustained in a fall last year, her total allowable medical expenses amounted to $790. (*a*) Of this amount, how much did Julia pay? (*b*) How much did the insurance pay?   *Ans*.   (*a*) $206, (*b*) $584. (See Problem 6.13.)

6.21 Ms. Clark, age 28, a high school home economics teacher, plans to retire early so she can travel and enjoy her leisure. She purchased a $12,000 face value 20-year endowment policy as a part of her investment plan. (*a*) How much are her annual payments? (*b*) How much would she pay for a whole life and a 20-payment life policy of the same face value?   *Ans*. (*a*) $566.64, (*b*) $465.84.

6.22 Olie Munson, the maintenance supervisor at your apartment building, has decided to retire at age 62. Olie has a wife who is 59 and a 17-year-old daughter who attends high school. Olie's average annual earnings under Social Security are $5,000. (*a*) How much will the family receive in monthly Social Security benefits? (*b*) How much more would they receive if he were retiring at age 65?   *Ans*.   (*a*) $470.90, (*b*) $57.20. (See Problem 6.9.)

6.23 Frank Welch has a prepaid family group medical plan which includes hospital care, physician's care, and major medical benefits. As a result of a kidney stone operation last year, Mrs. Welch was hospitalized in a semiprivate room for 18 days at the rate of $65 per day. Other charges were: surgical, $1,200; intensive care during the first day of confinement, $100; anesthesia, $300; and X-ray, $180. (*a*) How much did Frank have to pay for this confinement? (*b*) How much did the insurance company pay?   *Ans*.   (*a*) $979, (*b*) $1,971. (See Problem 6.14.)

6.24 Roger Beaumont, age 40, had wanted to purchase more life insurance to provide his wife and two children with additional protection. Upon receiving a promotion to service manager at the garage where he was employed, Roger purchased a $13,000 face value 20-payment life policy and a $16,000 face value whole life policy. (*a*) Which policy has the lower annual premium? (*b*) By how much?   *Ans*.   (*a*) 20-payment life, (*b*) $23.73. (See Problem 6.5.)

6.25 Your next-door neighbor, Roscoe Bateman, a construction worker, was killed in an automobile accident leaving his wife, age 48, a 17-year-old daughter, and three younger sons. What are the maximum family monthly Social Security benefits if Roscoe had average annual earnings of (*a*) $900, (*b*) $4,000, (*c*) $6,000?   *Ans*.   (*a*) $152.20, (*b*) $421.80, (*c*) $593.30. (See Problem 6.10.)

6.26 Grace Bilko, 28, and her brother Aaron, 38, support their invalid mother. They wanted to provide her with financial support in the event of their deaths. They wanted protection only, so they each decided to buy an $18,000 face value 5-year term insurance policy. (*a*) What is the amount of annual premium for Grace? (*b*) For Aaron?   *Ans*.   (*a*) $61.20, (*b*) $87.48. (See Problem 6.1.)

6.27 To receive Social Security benefits upon retirement at age 65, how many quarters of coverage does anyone need if he were born, (*a*) in 1917, (*b*) in 1911, (*c*) in 1939?   *Ans*. (*a*) 31, (*b*) 25, (*c*) 40. (See Problem 6.6.)

6.28 George McAlister, aged 63, died as a result of a heart attack, leaving his widow, Beatrice, age 60. George was fully covered under Social Security and had average annual earnings of $4,000. What benefits will Mrs. McAlister receive?   *Ans*.   Lump sum death payment of $255; $176.50 monthly benefits. (See Problem 6.11.)

Chapter 7

Investments

Individuals who accumulate money may wish to invest it to make a profit. Investments in savings accounts and home ownership have been discussed in previous chapters. Other investment opportunities include real estate, stocks, bonds, and mutual funds.

A universal measure of profitability is the *annual rate of return*. Expressed as a percentage, this compares annual profit with the total amount of money invested.

7.1 REAL ESTATE: RATE OF RETURN FROM RENTS

Investors often purchase real property, buildings, and land for the purpose of making a profit. The return on the investment must be sufficient to pay for all such expenses as taxes, insurance, maintenance, and allowance for depreciation, and at the same time yield a profit.

EXAMPLE 1

Mr. Brown, owner of the Towers apartment complex, charges a rental fee which allows him to realize a 10% profit on all rental units. Ms. Sarah Upton leases an apartment which costs Mr. Brown $270 a month to maintain. (*a*) How much rent must she pay in order that he realize his 10% profit on her monthly payments? (*b*) If he owns 16 apartments, how much is his annual profit?

(*a*) Divide the monthly apartment cost by 90% (100% − 10%). Ninety percent represents that portion of the total rent required. $P = B \times \$$; where $P = \$270$, $B = ?$ (required rent), $R = 100\% - 10\% = 90\%$.

$$\$270 = B \times 0.90. \qquad B = \$270 \div 0.90 = \$300 \text{ required rental payment}$$

(*b*) Determine the annual profit per apartment. Obtain monthly profit and multiply by 12. Then multiply annual profit for an apartment by the number owned. $300 (rent) − $270 (cost) = $30 per month. $30 × 12 = $360 per year per apartment.

$$\$360 \text{ (per apartment)} \times 16 \text{ (number owned)} = \$5,760 \text{ annual profit}$$

EXAMPLE 2

You buy a duplex house for $42,400 as an investment. The terms are a down payment of $9,400 and a $7\frac{1}{2}\%$ mortgage on the balance. Your annual expenses are mortgage interest, $2,475; insurance, $240; maintenance, $450; and taxes, $1,298. You rent out the property for $500 a month. Find (*a*) the net return, and (*b*) the percent return on your investment.

First obtain the total income. Then determine the total expenses. From total income, subtract total expenses for the net return. Next, from the cost of the property, subtract the amount of the mortgage outstanding to obtain your investment (equity). And finally, divide the net return by the amount invested to obtain the percent of return on your investment. These steps are shown in tabular form as follows:

Annual rent (12 × $500)		$6,000
Total expenses:		
Mortgage interest	$2,475	
Insurance	240	
Maintenance	450	
Real estate taxes	1,298	4,463
Net return		$1,537

Cost of property	$42,400
Mortgage outstanding	33,000
Investment	$ 9,400

To obtain percent of return use the formula $P = B \times R$, where P = percentage (part), B = base, R = rate. $1,537 = \$9,400 \times R$: $R = \$1,537 \div \$9,400 = 0.1635$, or 16.4% return. Therefore:

(a) $1,537 net return.

(b) 16.4% rate of return on investment.

EXAMPLE 3

Max Goldman had invested some of his earnings in rental property because of its high rate of return. This investment allowed him to diversify his investments and also to receive current income which he could invest in other ventures. Last year, Max received a net return of $3,600 in this property investment, which yielded him a 12% return. What was the amount of his investment?

Formula: $P = B \times R$; where $P = \$3,600$ (net return), B = investment, $R = 12\%$.

$$B = \$3,600 \div 0.12 = \$30,000 \text{ investment}$$

7.2 INVESTING IN STOCK

People invest in stocks with the hope of realizing capital growth as well as dividends. Stockbrokers buy and sell stock for other people for a fee called a commission. It is desirable and advantageous to be familiar with the stock quotations published in the financial sections of leading newspapers and know how to interpret them.

Stockmarket Quotations

Figure 7-1 contains a sample lising of stock quotations as published in a newspaper. Let us use AmT&T as our example on how to read the quotations.

New York Stock Exchange prices

	PE	Sales hds	High	Low	Close	Chg
A Hess .30b	4	247	$20\frac{5}{8}$	$19\frac{5}{8}$	$19\frac{7}{8}$	$-\frac{3}{8}$
AmAirlin	..	105	$8\frac{1}{4}$	$7\frac{7}{8}$	$8\frac{1}{4}$	...
A Brnds 2.68	7	104	$39\frac{1}{4}$	$37\frac{7}{8}$	$38\frac{1}{4}$	$-1\frac{1}{4}$
A Home .88	24	640	$35\frac{3}{4}$	$34\frac{1}{4}$	$35\frac{3}{8}$	$-\frac{5}{8}$
AmHosp .30	23	227	$31\frac{3}{8}$	30	30	$-1\frac{1}{8}$
AmMotors	..	300	$6\frac{1}{2}$	$6\frac{1}{4}$	$6\frac{1}{4}$	$-\frac{1}{8}$
ANatG 2.54b	7	93	$34\frac{1}{2}$	$33\frac{3}{4}$	$34\frac{1}{8}$	$-\frac{1}{4}$
AmStand .80	6	169	$14\frac{5}{8}$	$13\frac{5}{8}$	$14\frac{1}{2}$	$+\frac{3}{8}$
AmT&T 3.40	10	1020	$49\frac{5}{8}$	$48\frac{1}{2}$	$49\frac{1}{8}$	$+\frac{3}{8}$
AMF In 1.24	13	139	20	$19\frac{5}{8}$	$19\frac{3}{4}$	$-\frac{1}{4}$
Block HR .80	9	98	$14\frac{1}{2}$	14	$14\frac{1}{3}$	$-\frac{1}{8}$
Boeing .80	8	288	$28\frac{5}{8}$	$27\frac{7}{8}$	$28\frac{3}{8}$	...

	PE	Sales hds	High	Low	Close	Chg
Interlake 2a	3	26	$31\frac{1}{8}$	$31\frac{1}{8}$	$31\frac{1}{4}$	$-\frac{5}{8}$
IBM 7	15	452	$192\frac{1}{4}$	$190\frac{1}{4}$	$190\frac{5}{8}$	$+\frac{1}{8}$
IntHarv 1.70	4	324	$24\frac{3}{8}$	$23\frac{3}{8}$	24	$-\frac{1}{4}$
Jostens 1	10	11	$23\frac{5}{8}$	$23\frac{3}{8}$	$23\frac{5}{8}$	$+\frac{3}{8}$
JoyMfg 1.60	12	139	$79\frac{3}{4}$	$74\frac{1}{4}$	$76\frac{3}{8}$	$-3\frac{1}{2}$
KaisrAl 1.20	5	172	$31\frac{3}{8}$	$30\frac{1}{4}$	$30\frac{7}{8}$	$-\frac{3}{4}$
KayserR .60	34	7	$12\frac{7}{8}$	$12\frac{5}{8}$	$12\frac{7}{8}$	$+\frac{1}{4}$
Kellogg .70	18	28	$19\frac{1}{2}$	19	19	$-\frac{1}{4}$
Kennecott 2	12	561	$35\frac{5}{8}$	$34\frac{5}{8}$	$35\frac{3}{8}$	$+\frac{7}{8}$
Lehmn .72e	..	100	$11\frac{3}{8}$	$11\frac{1}{8}$	$11\frac{3}{4}$	...
LevitzFurn	110	435	$5\frac{5}{8}$	$5\frac{5}{8}$	$5\frac{1}{2}$	$-\frac{1}{8}$

	PE	Sales hds	High	Low	Close	Chg
Maytg 1.30a	19	46	$29\frac{3}{4}$	$29\frac{1}{4}$	$29\frac{1}{2}$	$+\frac{1}{4}$
McDonalds	28	416	51	50	$50\frac{3}{8}$	$+\frac{1}{8}$
Pennzol 1.20	6	554	$20\frac{3}{8}$	20	$20\frac{1}{4}$	...
PepsiCo 1.60	16	65	$63\frac{1}{2}$	$62\frac{1}{4}$	$62\frac{5}{8}$	...
Pfizer .76a	15	590	$28\frac{1}{2}$	$27\frac{7}{8}$	28	$-\frac{3}{8}$
PitneyB .60	9	377	$17\frac{5}{8}$	$16\frac{3}{4}$	$17\frac{1}{4}$	$-\frac{1}{2}$
Polaroid .32	33	2169	$38\frac{5}{8}$	$37\frac{7}{8}$	$38\frac{3}{8}$	$-\frac{1}{2}$
Raytheon 1	11	145	$50\frac{1}{2}$	$49\frac{1}{2}$	$49\frac{7}{8}$	$-\frac{1}{8}$
RCA 1	17	611	$18\frac{3}{4}$	$18\frac{1}{8}$	$18\frac{1}{2}$	$+\frac{1}{4}$
Safewy 1.80	13	119	49	$47\frac{1}{2}$	$47\frac{3}{4}$	$-1\frac{1}{4}$
StJoMin 1.20	6	167	$32\frac{1}{4}$	$31\frac{1}{2}$	$31\frac{1}{2}$	$-\frac{1}{2}$

Fig. 7-1

(1) The abbreviated name is in the left-hand column reading down.

(2) The number 3.40 that appears to the right of the name is the current annual amount of dividend per share ($3.40).

(3) Under the heading PE we find the number that indicates that the price per share is currently 10 times the annual earnings per share (price/earnings ratio).

(4) Under the sales in the hds (hundreds) column, 1,020 indicates that 102,000 shares were sold that day (1,020 × 100).

(5) Under High, $49\frac{1}{8}$ indicates that the highest price paid for a share that day was $49.125. Stock prices are indicated in eighths, fourths, and halves. ($\frac{1}{8}$ = $.125, $\frac{1}{4}$ = $.25, $\frac{3}{8}$ = $.375, etc.)

(6) Under Low, $48\frac{1}{2}$ indicates that the lowest price paid for a share was $48.50.

(7) Under Close, $49\frac{1}{8}$ indicates that this was the price of the last purchase of the day: $49.125.

(8) Under Change, $+\frac{3}{8}$ indicates that the last purchase of the day was $.375 higher than the closing price of the previous day. A minus (−) sign, would indicate that the last purchase of the day was that much lower than closing price of the previous day.

The following examples offer an exercise in reading stock prices in newspaper quotations. The calculation of commission and fees will be presented later in this chapter.

EXAMPLE 4

Walter Slezak, a local pharmacist, wanted to diversify his portfolio. He was interested in purchasing some airplane manufacturing stock, which he believed would go up in the near future. Upon looking over the stock quotations in the morning paper, Walter noted the price that Boeing common stock was quoted at the high for the day. Disregarding commission and fees, what would Walter have paid for 100 shares at the quoted price?

See Fig. 7-1. Read down to Boeing, then to the right under High: $28\frac{5}{8}$, or $28.625. For 100 shares of Boeing stock:

$$100 \times \$28.625 = \$2,862.50$$

EXAMPLE 5

Ruth Mason, a medical secretary, had been carefully watching the price of American Motors (Am Motors) common stock, in anticipation of investing in this stock. Ruth wants to invest some of her savings in automobile stock which she feels will rise soon. If Ruth buys shares of American Motors at their closing price today, would they have cost more or less than at the close of the previous day? By how much?

See Fig. 7-1. Am Motors closed at $6\frac{1}{4}$, or $6.25. They had a change of $-\frac{1}{8}$ from the previous day. They cost $\frac{1}{8}$, or $.125, a share less at today's closing price than at yesterday's closing price. They closed at $6\frac{3}{8}$, or $6.375, the day before.

EXAMPLE 6

Alan Napier, the proprietor of a local office supplies store, has been investing in IBM stock for the past several years. Yesterday, Alan bought 100 shares of IBM at their low. His sister Rose bought 100 shares at their high the same day. Disregarding commission and fees, how much more did Rose pay than Alan?

See Fig. 7-1. IBM: Low, $190\frac{1}{4}$ = $190.25. 100 × $190.25 = $19,025. IBM: High, $192\frac{1}{4}$ = $192.25. 100 × $192.25 = $19,225. The amount more that Rose paid:

$$\$19,225 - \$19,025 = \$200$$

EXAMPLE 7

Jim Asbury needed some money to purchase a new pick-up truck for his dry cleaning business. Jim already had two outstanding notes payable, so he decided to sell 150 shares of McDonald's common, which he had purchased several months ago at $60\frac{3}{4}$. If Jim sold his stock yesterday, how much did he gain or lose on this transaction? (Disregard commission and fees.)

See Fig. 7-1. McDonalds: close $50\frac{3}{8} = \$50.375$. $150 \times \$50.375 = \$7,556.25$ selling price. $150 \times \$60.75 = \$9,112.50$ purchase price. Loss on sale:

$$\$9,112.50 - \$7,556.25 = \$1,556.25$$

Dividends

The board of directors of a corporation sets aside a specified amount of money from earnings for distribution among stockholders. This sharing of profits with stockholders is called dividends. Generally, the annual declared dividend is divided by four, as most corporations pay them on a quarterly basis. An annual dividend of $2.00 per share is declared by the Samco Corporation. Each share will entitle a stockholder to $.50 a share quarterly.

EXAMPLE 8

Hal Bright owns 500 shares of stock of the Investo Corporation, which has declared an annual dividend of $1.50 per share on common stock. To find out how much will Hal receive each quarter on his stock divide the annual declared dividend by 4. Then, to obtain the quarterly return, multiply this amount by the number of shares owned: $1.50 ÷ 4 = $.375 per quarter. Return per quarter:

$$500 \times \$.375 = \$187.50$$

7.3 THE RATE OF RETURN ON STOCK INVESTMENTS

This is a percent value representing the return or profit on your investment. It is obtained by dividing the dollar amount of return by your amount of investment.

EXAMPLE 9

Joseph Jonathan received a quarterly dividend of 20 cents per share on stock which he bought at $16.50 per share. He received a quarterly dividend of 30 cents a share on another stock which he bought at $22.25 per share. A third stock paid him a quarterly dividend of 25 cents per share plus an extra dividend of 25 cents at the end of the year, for which he paid $17.75 a share. What is his annual rate of return on each stock?

Obtain the annual rate of yield by dividing the annual dividend by the cost per share. *First stock*: $.20 × 4 = $.80 annual dividend. $.80 (annual dividend) ÷ $16.50 (cost per share) = 0.0484, or 4.84% rate of yield. *Second stock*: $.30 × 4 = $1.20 annual dividend. $1.20 (annual dividend) ÷ $22.25 (cost per share) = 0.0539, or 5.39% rate of yield. *Third stock*: $.25 × 4 = $1.00 annual dividend. $1.00 (annual dividend) + $.25 (extra dividend) = $1.25 total dividends for the year.

$$\$1.25 \text{ (total dividend)} ÷ \$17.75 \text{ (per share)} = 0.0704, \text{ or } 7.04\% \text{ rate of yield}$$

EXAMPLE 10

Rollie Henley inherited 500 shares of mining stock from his grandfather. The selling price per share, including commission, at the time of inheritance was $8.00. The present price per share is $20.50. This stock is paying a quarterly dividend of 25 cents per share. (a) What was the rate of yield on the price of the stock when he received it? (b) On the current selling price?

(a) Obtain the annual dividend and divide it by the value of stock at time of inheritance. $.25 (quarterly dividend) × 4 = $1.00 annual dividend.

$1.00 (annual dividend) ÷ $8.00 = 0.125, or 12.5% rate of yield on value at time he received stock

(b) Divide the annual dividend by the current costs to get rate of yield.

$1.00 (annual dividend) ÷ $20.50 (current cost) = 0.0487, or 4.9%

7.4 COMPUTING BROKERAGE FEES

Stockbrokers charge a fee, called a commission, for services rendered in buying and selling stock.   Most stocks traded on exchanges are in multiples of 100, which are called round lots.   Shares traded in other amounts are called *odd lots*.   For example, 48 shares are an odd lot.   For commission rates, see Table 1.

EXAMPLE 11

James Williams bought 500 shares of Eastern Railroad through his broker at $20\frac{3}{8}$ a share.   To find the amount of commission on the transaction see Table 1.   Obtain the cost of the purchase. $20\frac{3}{8}$, or $20.375 (price per share) × 500 (shares) = $10,187.50 total cost.   From Table 1, read under multiple round lot orders: on $5,000 to $19,999 the commission is 1.1178% + $28.324. $10,187.50 (cost) × 0.011178 = $113.87587. $113.87587 + $28.324 = $142.19987, or $142.20.   Read under "*Plus*;" for Orders $5,000 or More, First through Tenth Round Lot: $7.452 per lot.   500 shares = 5 round lots.   5 × $7.452 = $37.26.   Commission fee:

$$\$142.20 + \$37.26 = \$179.46$$

EXAMPLE 12

Willie Radcliff, a mechanic in a local garage who is also a car racer, bought 200 shares of Race Car Corporation common stock with his recent winnings.   The broker quoted the stock at $20 per share.   How much commission did Willie pay?

See Table 1.   Under representative charges, read down under column "Price of Shares" to 20, then across under column heading "200 Shares."   Find $84.16 commission fee.

Other Taxes and Fees

The seller of stock through the New York Stock Exchange must also pay a tax to the state of New York.   In addition, the Securities and Exchange Commission charges a fee to the seller.   Because of the relatively small amount involved, these items, though worthy of mention, are not to be computed in the problems that follow.

EXAMPLE 13

Charles Schapp needed some cash to pay for his wife's medical bills due to her recent illness.   Charles sold 200 shares of Energy Inc., a growth common stock, through his broker at $21\frac{3}{8}$.   The N.Y. State tax and the S.E.C. fee amounted to $10.48.   How much did Charles receive on this transaction?

See Table 1.   Determine the total selling price and figure the commission, using Table 1.   Add the commission and other charges.   Subtract the amount from the selling price to obtain his proceeds.

Selling price: 200 × $21.375 = $4,275.   *Commission*: read under multiple round lot orders: $2,500 to $4,999—commission: 1.0692% + $27.136. $4,275 × 0.010692 = $45.7083, + $27.136 = $72.844.   *Plus*: for Orders Less than $5,000, First through Tenth Round Lot, $7.128 per lot.   200 shares; 2 (round lots) × $7.128   (per   lot) = $14.256. $72.844 + $14.256 = $87.10   commission. $87.10   (commission) + $10.48 (other) = $97.58 commission and other charges.   Amount received:

$$\$4,275 \text{ (selling price)} - \$97.58 = \$4,177.42$$

Table 1. Retail Stock Commissions

<table>
<tr><td colspan="10" align="center">BASIS OF CALCULATIONS</td></tr>
</table>

100 Share Orders and Odd Lot Orders	Multiple Round Lot Orders
$ 100 to $ 799 2.376 % + $ 8.6032	$ 100 to $ 2,499 1.5444% + $ 15.256
800 to 2,499 1.5444 + 15.256	2,500 to 4,999 1.0692 + 27.136
2,500 to 4,999 1.0692 + 27.136	5,000 to 19,999 1.1178 + 28.324
5,000 to 300,000 1.1178 + 28.324	20,000 to 29,999 0.7452 + 102.844
	30,000 to 300,000 0.4968 + 177.364

<table>
<tr><td colspan="2" align="center">PLUS</td></tr>
</table>

For Orders Less Than $5,000	For Orders $5,000 or More
1st through 10th Round Lot $7.128 per lot	1st through 10th Round Lot $7.452 per lot
11th Round Lot and Over 4.752 per lot	11th Round Lot and Over 4.968 per lot

The Commission on Any 100 Share Order Will Not Exceed
For Orders Involving Less Than $5,000 $78.22
For Orders Involving $5,000 or More   81.73

The Commission on Any Multiple Round Lot Order Will Not Exceed
For Orders Involving Less Than $5,000 $78.22 per round lot
For Orders Involving $5,000 or More   81.73 per round lot

For orders where principal is less than $100.00, the
commission will be 9.072% of the money involved plus $1.00.

REPRESENTATIVE CHARGES

Price of Shares	100 Shares	200 Shares	300 Shares	400 Shares	500 Shares	600 Shares	700 Shares	800 Shares	900 Shares
2	13.36	25.71	38.07	50.42	62.78	75.13	86.77	96.99	107.21
4	18.11	35.21	52.32	68.48	81.78	95.09	106.97	118.37	129.78
6	22.86	44.72	64.44	80.83	94.85	107.40	121.94	135.48	155.75
8	27.61	54.22	73.71	89.86	105.54	121.23	143.08	158.48	175.87
10	30.70	60.40	80.60	98.42	116.24	140.10	158.73	177.36	195.99
12	33.79	66.58	87.01	106.97	132.65	153.52	174.38	195.25	216.11
15	38.42	73.47	96.63	124.20	149.42	173.64	197.86	222.08	246.30
20	46.14	84.16	117.75	147.56	177.36	207.17	236.98	266.79	296.60
25	53.87	94.85	134.52	169.91	205.31	240.71	276.11	311.50	337.58
30	59.21	110.30	151.28	192.27	233.25	274.24	311.50	341.31	371.12
35	64.56	121.47	168.05	214.62	261.20	304.05	337.58	371.12	400.92
40	69.90	132.65	184.82	236.98	289.14	326.40	363.66	395.96	423.28
45	75.25	143.83	201.59	259.34	307.77	348.76	386.02	415.83	445.64
50	78.22	155.01	218.35	281.69	326.40	371.12	403.41	435.70	467.99
60	81.73	162.46	243.19	311.50	363.66	400.92	438.18	475.44	512.70
70	81.73	162.46	243.19	323.92	388.50	430.73	472.96	515.19	557.42
80	81.73	162.46	243.19	323.92	404.65	460.54	507.74	554.93	602.13
90	81.73	162.46	243.19	323.92	404.65	485.38	542.51	594.68	646.85
100	81.73	162.46	243.19	323.92	404.65	485.38	566.11	634.42	691.55
150	81.73	162.46	243.19	323.92	404.65	485.38	566.11	646.84	717.57
200	81.73	162.46	243.19	323.92	404.65	485.38	566.11	646.84	727.57

7.5 PREFERRED STOCK

This type of stock pays a dividend in a fixed dollar amount or expressed as a percent of its par value. Of course, the dividend is paid only if the company makes a profit and declares the dividend. For example, the Delta Corporation pays 6% on its \$100 par value preferred stock. The dividend can be stated as a \$6 dividend on its \$100 par value stock. You actually may pay more or less than \$100 per share for the stock, depending upon its market value, but the dividend in this case is figured only on the par value.

EXAMPLE 14

Martha Greeley, a retired bookkeeper, purchased 250 shares of $6\frac{1}{2}$% preferred stock, par value \$100, of the Off-Shore Oil Company at $94\frac{7}{8}$ a share, at the recommendation of her broker. Martha wants income-producing investments to help supplement her Social Security retirement benefits. (*a*) How much will Martha receive in quarterly dividends? (*b*) What rate of return will she receive on this investment?

(*a*) Multiply the dividend rate by the par value to obtain the annual dividend. Divide the annual dividend by four to obtain the quarterly dividend per share. Multiply the result by the number of shares owned to find the quarterly amount. $0.065 \times \$100 = \$6.50$ annual dividend per share. $\$6.50 \div 4 = \$1.625$ quarterly dividend per share. Total quarterly dividends are:

$$\$1.625 \text{ (quarterly dividend)} \times 250 \text{ (shares)} = \$406.25$$

(*b*) Divide the annual dividend per share by the cost per share to obtain the rate of yield on the investment.

$$\$6.50 \div \$94.875 = 0.0685, \text{ or } 6.85\%$$

7.6 INVESTING IN BONDS

Investments in bonds are made in order that a fixed amount of income may be received and as much risk as possible avoided. A bond is a promissory note wherein the issuer promises to pay a fixed annual rate of return for the life of the bond, and at maturity to pay back the par value of the bond. Bonds are issued by corporations, by municipalities, and by the Federal government.

A bondholder receives interest for the use of his money and is not a part owner of the issuing company, as is a stockholder. Interest is based on the par value of the bond, not on the purchase price. Bonds quoted on the New York Stock Exchange have a par value of \$1,000

Prices on the New York Stock Exchange
Bond Market

		Yld	High	Low	Last	Net Chg
AllSup	$5\frac{3}{4}$s87	13.2	$43\frac{3}{4}$	$43\frac{1}{4}$	$43\frac{1}{2}$	$-\frac{1}{8}$
Alcoa	9.45s20	9.2	$103\frac{1}{4}$	$102\frac{1}{2}$	$103\frac{1}{4}$	+1
Alcoa	9s95	9.0	100	99	100	+1
Alcoa	6s92	7.6	80	$78\frac{7}{8}$	79	−1
Alcoa	$5\frac{1}{4}$s91	5.5	$97\frac{1}{2}$	$94\frac{1}{2}$	$95\frac{1}{2}$	$+\frac{1}{2}$
Alcoa	$4\frac{1}{4}$s82	5.1	83	$82\frac{5}{8}$	$82\frac{5}{8}$	$+\frac{1}{8}$
Alcoa	3s79	3.6	$83\frac{1}{2}$	$83\frac{1}{2}$	$83\frac{1}{2}$	...
AlumC	$9\frac{1}{2}$s95	9.9	$95\frac{1}{2}$	$95\frac{1}{2}$	$95\frac{1}{2}$	$-2\frac{1}{2}$
AlumC	$4\frac{1}{2}$s80	5.0	$89\frac{1}{4}$	$87\frac{1}{2}$	$89\frac{1}{4}$	$+2\frac{3}{4}$
AMAX	$9\frac{3}{8}$s20	9.6	$99\frac{1}{2}$	95	$97\frac{1}{2}$	$-2\frac{1}{2}$
AMAX	$8\frac{1}{2}$s96	9.3	$91\frac{5}{8}$	$91\frac{5}{8}$	$91\frac{5}{8}$	$+\frac{5}{8}$
AMAX	$8\frac{1}{2}$s84	8.5	$100\frac{1}{2}$	$100\frac{1}{2}$	$100\frac{1}{2}$	$+\frac{1}{4}$
AMAX	8s86	8.8	$91\frac{5}{8}$	90	91	$+\frac{1}{4}$
AMAX	$7\frac{1}{2}$s78	7.7	99	98	98	$-\frac{5}{8}$
Amerac	5s92	7.7	$64\frac{5}{8}$	64	$64\frac{5}{8}$	$+\frac{1}{8}$

		Yld	High	Low	Last	Net Chg
AT&T	$8\frac{3}{4}$s20	8.7	$101\frac{7}{8}$	100	$100\frac{1}{2}$	$-\frac{7}{8}$
AT&T	8.70s02	8.7	101	$99\frac{1}{2}$	$99\frac{1}{2}$	$-\frac{1}{4}$
AT&T	8.80s05	8.8	$101\frac{1}{2}$	100	$100\frac{1}{4}$	$-\frac{3}{8}$
AT&T	$8\frac{5}{8}$s07	8.7	$99\frac{3}{4}$	$98\frac{1}{8}$	$98\frac{5}{8}$	$-\frac{1}{8}$
AT&T	$7\frac{3}{4}$s82	7.9	$98\frac{5}{8}$	$98\frac{1}{4}$	$98\frac{1}{4}$	$-\frac{1}{8}$
AT&T	$7\frac{3}{4}$s77	7.7	$101\frac{3}{4}$	$100\frac{1}{2}$	101	$-\frac{1}{2}$
AT&T	$7\frac{1}{8}$s03	8.4	$86\frac{3}{8}$	$84\frac{1}{2}$	$84\frac{1}{2}$	−1
AT&T	7s2001	8.4	$85\frac{5}{8}$	$83\frac{1}{8}$	$83\frac{1}{2}$	$-1\frac{1}{2}$
AT&T	$6\frac{1}{2}$s79	6.9	$95\frac{3}{8}$	$94\frac{1}{2}$	$94\frac{1}{2}$	$-\frac{1}{4}$
AT&T	$4\frac{3}{8}$s85	5.8	$76\frac{1}{2}$	75	$75\frac{3}{4}$	$-\frac{1}{4}$
AT&T	$3\frac{7}{8}$s90	6.2	$63\frac{3}{4}$	$62\frac{1}{2}$	$62\frac{1}{2}$	$-\frac{1}{2}$
AT&T	$3\frac{1}{4}$s84	4.7	$69\frac{1}{2}$	69	$69\frac{1}{2}$	$+\frac{1}{2}$
AT&T	$2\frac{7}{8}$s87	4.7	$61\frac{1}{8}$	61	$61\frac{1}{8}$	$+1\frac{1}{8}$
AT&T	$2\frac{3}{4}$s75	2.8	99	$98\frac{7}{8}$	99	$+\frac{1}{8}$
AT&T	$2\frac{3}{4}$s80	3.4	$81\frac{7}{8}$	$80\frac{1}{2}$	$80\frac{1}{2}$	$-\frac{3}{4}$
AT&T	$2\frac{3}{4}$s82	3.8	$74\frac{3}{4}$	73	73	−1
AT&T	$2\frac{5}{8}$s86	4.3	62	61	$61\frac{1}{2}$	$+\frac{1}{2}$

		Yld	High	Low	Last	Net Chg
BudgInd	6s88	13.0	48	46	46	+1
Bulova	6s90	10.3	60	$57\frac{1}{2}$	$58\frac{1}{2}$	$-\frac{1}{2}$
Burl Ind	9s95	9.6	$94\frac{1}{8}$	$94\frac{1}{8}$	$94\frac{1}{8}$	$+1\frac{1}{8}$
Chris Cr	6s89	12.5	48	$47\frac{1}{4}$	48	...
Chrysler	9s76	9.0	104	97 19-32	100	...
ChryF	$8\frac{7}{8}$s95	12.0	$74\frac{1}{4}$	$73\frac{1}{2}$	$74\frac{1}{4}$	...
City In	$7\frac{1}{2}$s90	10.1	$75\frac{1}{4}$	73	74	+1
Clark	$10\frac{1}{4}$s79	9.7	$105\frac{1}{2}$	$105\frac{1}{2}$	$105\frac{1}{2}$	$+\frac{1}{2}$
Clark	8.80s76	8.7	$101\frac{3}{4}$	101	$101\frac{1}{4}$	$-\frac{1}{2}$
CraneCo	7s93	9.2	$78\frac{1}{8}$	76	$76\frac{1}{2}$	$-2\frac{1}{4}$
CraneCo	7s94	9.3	76	$75\frac{1}{4}$	$75\frac{1}{2}$	$-\frac{1}{4}$
Crane	$6\frac{1}{2}$s92	8.1	80	76	80	

Fig. 7-2

but are quoted in terms of 100% of par value. A typical quote would be: XYZ Corp 6s 92 at 98. This would indicate that the XYZ Corporation is paying 6% (6s) interest on this issue which matures in 1992 (92). The selling price is $980 (98% of $1,000 par value). Figure 7-2 shows a typical listing of bond quotations as published in a newspaper.

Bond quotations are similar to stock quotations, with a few differences. Let us examine the line for Chrysler.

		Yld	High	Low	Last	Net Chg
Chrysler	9s 76	9.0	104	97 19–32	100	...

1. The "9s" following the name of the corporation indicates the rate of interest that the company is paying on the bond. ("s" replaces the % sign). 9s indicates 9%.

2. The "76" following the 9s indicates the year of maturity, 1976. During this year, the owners will redeem the bonds at par value.

3. Under "Yld," the 9.0 indicates 9%, the current rate of yield, based on its selling price.

4. Under "High," the 104 shows that this was the highest selling price during this day, at $1,040.

5. Under "Low," the 97 19–32 shows the lowest selling price for the day. (*Note*: Bonds may be quoted in values of 32 nds. [19–32 amounts to $.59375.] The bond sold for $975.9375. Bonds are quoted in terms of 100%.

6. Under "Last" the 100 indicates that the bond sold for 100% of par value, $1,000.

7. The net change column is blank, meaning that there was no change from yesterday's last sale, which was also $1,000.

Commission

The commission charge for buying or selling bonds is usually set by the brokerage firm. The New York Stock Exchange sets a minimum charge, but individual firms differ in charges. Commission charges range from $5.00 per $1,000 bond to $15 per $1,000 bond.

EXAMPLE 15

Clyde Allen, the cashier at a local bank, is a conservative investor who prefers fixed income rather than taking a risk on growth investment. Yesterday, Clyde bought 5 Amax 8s 86 bonds at their low price for the day. How much did he pay for this transaction if the commission fee was $5.00 per bond?

Use Fig. 7-2. (Note that Amax, like many corporations, has other issues of bonds outstanding.) Read down the column to Amax 8s 86 and find the low of 90. This means the price of the bond is 90% of the par value of $1,000, or (90 × $1,000) = $900, the low price for the day. Multiply the number of bonds, 5, by the cost per bond. 5 × $900 = $4,500. $5.00 × 5 = $25.00 commission. Total cost:

$$\$4,500 + \$25.00 = \$4,525$$

EXAMPLE 16

Lewis Everett, a bond salesman, checks the bond market quotations every day in order to make recommendations to his clients. A client called Lewis and wanted yesterday's quotations on Clark $10\frac{1}{4}$s 79. What was the price of this bond?

See Fig. 7-2. Notice that the high, low, and last were all $105\frac{1}{2}$. Multiply 1.055 (105.5%) × $1,000 to get $1,055, the market price of the bond.

Note that if a bond sells for more than its par value, it is sold at a premium. $1,055 − $1,000 = $55 bond premium. Bonds sold at less than par value are sold at a discount.

Bond Interest

The interest payments on bonds are made periodically—annually, semiannually, or quarterly. If the payments are due on April 1 and September 1, the holder on those dates receives the accumulated interest. However, if the bond is bought before the interest payment date, the buyer pays the seller the amount of accrued interest to date plus the market value of the bond.

EXAMPLE 17

You bought 5 ABC 6s 92 bonds for $97\frac{1}{2}$, on May 31. The interest dates are April 1 and October 1. (*a*) How much accrued interest will you pay? (*b*) How much will this transaction cost you? (Disregard commission and taxes.)

(*a*) Determine the amount of accrued interest on one bond from April 1 to May 31. The annual amount of interest is 6s (6%) multiplied by $1,000, or $60. $60 ÷ 2 = $30 semiannually. Determine the number of days from April 1 to May 31. 60 days. Use the formula: $I = P \times R \times T$ to find the accrued interest.

$$I = \$1,000 \times 6\% \times 60 \text{ days} = \$1,000 \times 0.06 \times \frac{\overset{1}{\cancel{60}}}{\underset{6}{\cancel{360}}} = \$10$$

$10 × 5 = $50 total accrued interest.

(*b*) Determine the cost of the five bonds. $97\frac{1}{2}$ quoted price is $975 per bond. $975 × 5 = $4,875 market value for five bonds. Total cost:

$$\$4,875 + \$50 \text{ (accrued interest)} = \$4,925$$

7.7   COMPUTING THE RATE OF RETURN ON BOND INVESTMENTS

The *rate of interest* is a fixed amount based on the par value of the bond. The *rate of return* is the actual rate the buyer receives on his investment.

A 6% $1,000 bond purchased at 100%, or par value, will yield 6%. However, if this same bond is purchased for less than par value, the yield will be higher. Rate of yield is determined by dividing the amount of interest by the cost of the bond. Rate = $60/$1,000 = 6%, if bought at par value. A 6% $1,000 bond is purchased at 90. Bond interest is $60 per year. Purchase price is $900.

$$R = \frac{\$60 \text{ (interest)}}{\$900 \text{ (cost)}} = 0.0666, \text{ or } 6.67\% \text{ yield}$$

If the purchase price is more than the par value, the yield will be lower. If a 6% $1,000 bond is purchased at 102, the interest is $60 and the cost is $1,020. Yield:

$$R = \frac{\$60 \text{ (interest)}}{\$1,020 \text{ (cost)}} = 0.0588, \text{ or } 5.88\%$$

EXAMPLE 18

Gus and Gert Stromberg are building a retirement fund by investing their money in bonds. Last year they bought 10 United Gas Corporation $5\frac{1}{2}$% bonds at $88\frac{1}{2}$ and paid a brokerage charge of $6.00 per bond. What is their rate of yield?

Find the interest on one bond. $I = P \times R \times T$. $I = \$1,000 \times 5\frac{1}{2}\% \times 1$ year. $I = \$1,000 \times 0.055 \times 1$, or $55 annual interest.

Rate = interest ÷ cost. Cost = $88\frac{1}{2}$, or 0.885 × \$1,000 = \$885, market value. \$885 (market value) + \$6.00 (brokerage cost) = \$891 (total cost). Yield:

$$R = \$55 \div \$891 = 0.0617, \text{or} \ 6.17\%$$

7.8   U.S. GOVERNMENT SAVINGS BONDS

The Federal government issues savings bonds in various denominations and terms. The Series E bonds feature appreciation: they are purchased at 75% of the maturity or par value. At maturity, the par value of the bond will be paid to the holder. See Table 2.

Table 2.   Series E Bond Prices

Denomination	Purchase Price
$ 25	$ 18.75
50	37.50
75	56.25
100	75.00
200	150.00
500	375.00
1,000	750.00

Series E Bonds may be redeemed at any time after two months of the purchase date. Table 3 shows a sampling of values at time of redemption.

EXAMPLE 19

Berth Jennings bought one Series E \$100 bond in December of 1970. When she redeemed it in July of 1975: (a) how much money did she receive? (b) How much interest did she receive?

(a) Series E, \$100; cost, \$75. (See Table 2.) Table 3, "Redemption Values," in December 1970 find under "\$100" the amount \$93.32.

(b) She paid \$75 and received \$93.32. Interest received:

$$\$93.32 - \$75 = \$18.32$$

Series H Bonds are current income bonds bought at par value with interest paid semiannually, beginning six months after purchase. The yield averages close to 6%. The denominations are in the amounts of \$500, \$1,000, and \$5,000.

EXAMPLE 20

Joel Clark inherited a sum of money which he invested in 4 Series H \$1,000 bonds and in 2 \$5,000 Series H bonds. If the interest rate is $5\frac{3}{4}\%$, how much will Joel receive semiannually?

The interest could be figured separately for each denomination or for the total amount of money. They all pay the same interest. It would be simpler to figure the interest on the total value. $I = P \times R \times T$. P = total of all bonds. 4 \$1,000 bonds and 2 \$5,000 bonds = \$4,000 + \$10,000 = \$14,000. $R = 5\frac{3}{4}\%$ or 0.0575. $I = 6$ months or $\frac{1}{2}$ year = \$14,000 × 0.0575 × $\frac{1}{2}$ = \$402.50 semiannual interest.

7.9   MUTUAL FUNDS: INVESTING COMPANIES

This type of investment is for people who prefer to have an investment company handle their money. The management company has basic investment policies which are explained in a

Table 3.   U.S. Savings Bonds, Series E: Redemption Values by Denomination—July 1975

Issue Year	Issue Months	$25	$50	$75	$100	$200	$500	$1,000	$10,000
1975	June thru July				[Not eligible for payment]				
	Feb. thru May	18.75	37.50	56.25	75.00	150.00	375.00	750.00	7,500.00
	Jan.	19.10	38.20	57.30	76.40	152.80	382.00	764.00	7,640.00
1974	Aug. thru Dec.	19.10	38.20	57.30	76.40	152.80	382.00	764.00	7,640.00
	Feb. thru July	19.61	39.22	58.83	78.44	156.88	382.20	784.40	7,844.00
	Jan.	20.10	40.20	60.30	80.40	160.80	402.00	804.00	8,040.00
1973	Dec.	20.10	40.20	60.30	80.40	160.80	402.00	804.00	8,040.00
	Aug. thru Nov.	20.05	40.10	60.15	80.20	160.40	401.00	802.00	8,020.00
	June thru July	20.55	41.10	61.65	82.20	164.40	411.00	822.00	8,220.00
	Feb. thru May	20.50	41.00	61.50	82.00	164.00	410.00	820.00	8,200.00
	Jan.	21.03	42.06	63.09	84.12	163.24	420.60	841.20	8,412.00
1972	Dec.	21.03	42.06	63.09	84.12	168.24	420.60	841.20	8,412.00
	Aug. thru Nov.	20.98	41.96	62.94	83.92	167.84	419.60	839.20	8,392.00
	June thru July	21.55	43.10	64.65	88.20	172.40	431.00	862.00	8,620.00
	Feb. thru May	21.49	42.98	64.47	85.96	171.92	429.80	859.60	8,596.00
	Jan.	22.09	44.18	68.27	88.36	176.72	441.80	883.60	8,836.00
1971	Dec.	22.09	44.18	66.27	88.36	176.72	441.80	883.60	8,836.00
	Aug. thru Nov.	22.04	44.08	66.12	88.16	176.32	440.80	881.60	8,816.00
	June thru July	22.70	45.40	68.10	90.80	181.60	454.00	908.00	9,080.00
	Feb. thru May	22.64	45.28	67.92	90.56	181.12	452.80	905.60	9,056.00
	Jan.	23.33	46.66	69.99	93.32	186.64	466.60	933.20	9,332.00
1970	Dec.	23.33	46.66	69.99	93.32	186.64	466.60	933.20	9,332.00
	Aug. thru Nov.	23.27	46.54	69.81	93.08	186.16	465.40	930.80	9,308.00
	June thru July	23.99	47.98	71.97	95.96	191.92	479.80	959.60	9,596.00
	Feb. thru May	23.94	47.88	71.82	95.76	191.52	478.80	957.60	9,576.00
	Jan.	24.69	49.38	74.07	98.76	197.52	493.80	987.60	9,876.00
1969	Dec.	24.69	49.38	74.07	98.76	197.52	493.80	987.60	9,876.00
	Oct. thru Nov.	24.63	49.26	73.89	98.52	197.04	492.60	985.20	9,852.00
	June thru Sep.	25.77	51.54	77.31	103.08	206.16	515.40	1,030.80	10,308.00
	Feb. thru May	24.66	49.32	73.98	98.64	197.28	493.20	986.40	9,864.00
	Jan.	25.41	50.82	76.23	101.04	203.28	508.20	1,016.40	10,164.00
1968	Dec.	25.41	50.82	76.23	101.64	203.28	508.20	1,016.40	10,164.00
	Aug. thru Nov.	25.21	50.42	75.63	100.84	201.68	504.20	1,088.40	10,084.00
	June thru July	26.81	53.62	80.43	107.24	214.48	536.20	1,072.40	10,724.00
	Feb. thru May	26.56	53.12	79.68	106.24	212.48	531.20	1,062.40	10,624.00
	Jan.	27.36	54.72	82.08	109.44	218.88	547.20	1,094.40	10,944.00
1967	Dec.	27.36	54.72	82.08	109.44	218.88	547.20	1,094.40	10,944.00
	Aug. thru Nov.	27.09	54.18	81.27	188.36	216.72	541.80	1,083.60	10,836.00
	June thru July	27.90	55.80	83.70	111.60	223.20	558.00	1,116.00	11,160.00
	Feb. thru May	27.66	55.32	82.98	110.64	221.28	553.20	1,106.40	11,064.00
	Jan.	28.49	56.98	85.47	113.96	227.92	569.80	1,139.60	11,396.00
1966	Dec.	28.49	56.98	85.47	113.96	227.92	569.80	1,139.60	11,396.00
	Aug. thru Nov.	28.26	56.52	84.78	113.04	226.08	585.20	1,130.40	11,304.00
	June thru July	29.10	58.20	87.30	116.40	232.80	582.00	1,164.00	11,640.00
	Feb. thru May	28.87	57.74	86.61	115.43	230.95	577.40	1,154.80	11,548.00
	Jan.	29.75	59.50	89.25	119.00	238.00	595.00	1,190.00	11,900.00
1965	Dec.	29.75	59.50	89.25	119.00	238.00	595.00	1,190.00	11,900.00
	Nov.	28.78	57.56	86.34	115.12	230.24	575.60	1,151.20	11,512.00
	Sep. thru Oct	29.65	59.30	88.95	118.60	237.20	593.00	1,186.00	11,860.00
	June thru Aug.	29.57	59.14	88.71	118.28	236.56	591.40	1,182.80	11,828.00
	May	29.40	58.80	88.20	117.60	235.20	588.00	1,176.00	11,760.00
	Mar. thru Apr.	30.28	60.56	90.84	121.12	242.24	605.60	1,211.20	12,112.00
	Jan. thru Feb.	30.21	60.42	90.63	120.84	241.68	604.20	1,208.40	12,084.00
1964	Dec.	30.21	60.42	90.63	120.84	241.68	604.20	1,208.40	12,084.00
	Nov.	30.03	60.06	90.09	120.12	240.24	600.60	1,201.20	12,012.00
	Sep. thru Oct.	30.92	61.84	92.76	123.68	247.38	618.40	1,236.80	12,368.00
	June thru Aug.	30.85	61.70	92.55	123.40	246.80	617.00	1,234.00	12,340.00
	May	30.65	61.30	91.95	122.60	245.20	613.00	1,226.00	12,260.00
	Mar. thru Apr.	31.57	63.14		126.28	252.56	631.40	1,262.80	12,628.00
	Jan. thru Feb.	31.49	62.98		125.96	251.92	629.80	1,259.60	12,596.00

prospectus. The open funds have several methods of participation:

(1) Lump sum purchase.
(2) Accumulation plan: after an initial deposit of a specified amount, the investor may make payments periodically or at his discretion.
(3) Contractual plan: the purchaser agrees to make regular payments over a period of years, usually 10.

Most mutual funds have a surcharge of 6 to 9 percent, which is referred to as a "loading charge." Funds that have no surcharge are called "no load" funds. If a load fund has a surcharge of 8%, your investment of $1,000 would get you only $920 of net asset value; the $80 goes to the company for fees and commissions. A similar investment in a "no load" fund would get you $1,000 of net asset value. Net asset value is the market value of the fund portfolio at a given time. Financial reports similar to the one in Fig. 7-3 are published in daily papers.

The following quotations, supplied by the National Association of Securities Dealers, Inc., are the prices at which these securities could have been sold (net asset value) or bought (value plus sales charge) Monday.

	Sell	Buy		Sell	Buy		Sell	Buy
AllAm Fd	.39	....	BLC Grth	9.27	10.14	EDIE Spl	17.36	N.L.
Allstate	9.35	10.05	Babson	9.42	N.L.	Egret Fd	9.93	10.79
Alpha	9.78	N.L.	Bayrk Fd	5.27		Elfun Tr	12.99	....
Am Birth	10.32	11.34	Bost Fdn	8.58	9.38	Reserve	1.00	N.L.
			Brwn Fd	3.03	3.12	Revere	4.64	5.07
			Calvin Bullock:			Safec Eqt	7.38	8.07
			Comp Fd	7.45	8.10			
			Concord	8.60	N.L.			
			Cons Inv	9.00	9.50			
			Drex Bur	8.72	N.L.			
			Dreyfus Grp:					
			Dreyf	10.34	11.33			
			Equit	3.88	4.15			

Fig. 7-3

(1) The left-hand column indicates the name of the fund. If a management company has more than one fund, the names are indented under the title of the management company.
(2) The column headings at the top, under "sell," indicate the selling price for one share at that time; under "buy" column, the purchase price for one share at that time.
(3) A "no load" fund has the same sell and buy price. Read down to Alpha and note the sell price, $9.78; under "buy," read "n.1.," which indicates a no-load fund. The price is the same: $9.78.

EXAMPLE 21

Michael Sears, a computer programmer, aged 25, has two young children, for whom he wants to provide money for a college education. Al Williams, a coworker, suggested that he invest in mutual funds. Yesterday, Michael purchased 500 shares of Allstate mutual fund. (a) How much did this transaction cost him? (b) If he redeemed them at the quoted price, how much did he receive?

(a) See Fig. 7-3. Read down the column to Allstate, then under the column heading "buy"; find $10.05. Multiply the cost per share by the number of shares purchased. $10.05 × 500 = $5,025 purchase price.

(b) Read down under the column heading "sell," find $9.35. Multiply the price per share by the number of shares. $9.35 × 500 = $4,675 amount received.

EXAMPLE 22

Bob Phillips, a local real estate salesman, periodically invests his savings in mutual funds. Yesterday he received a commission of $1,000, for the sale of a piece of property, which he invested in the Concord Fund. (a) How many shares did he obtain? (b) How much commission did he pay?

(a) See Fig. 7-3.   Read down to Concord and over to $8.60 under the "sell" column; n.l. under "buy."   Both are the same in a "no load" fund.   Divide the amount invested by the price per share to obtain the number of shares purchased. $1,000 ÷ $8.60 = 116.279 shares purchased.   (Shares are carried to three decimal places.)

(b) Note that buy and sell are the same: you pay no commission.

Solved Problems

7.1   Ms. Williams, a legal secretary, rents an apartment from the Jones Realty Company, which realizes a $12\frac{1}{2}$% profit on all rental payments received.   A smaller profit would not be considered sufficient due to the inherent risk involved in rental properties.   Ms. Williams' apartment costs the realty company $245 a month to own and maintain.   (a) How much rent must she pay for the company to realize their $12\frac{1}{2}$% profit?   (b) If the company owns 64 apartments, how much annual profit do they realize?

(a) Divide the monthly apartment cost by (100% − $12\frac{1}{2}$%) $87\frac{1}{2}$%, which represents that portion of the total rent desired. $P = B \times R$. $P = $245 (apartment costs); $B = 100\%$ (amount of rent); $R = (100\% - 12\frac{1}{2}\%)$ $87\frac{1}{2}\%$.

$$\$245 = B \times 0.875 \qquad B = \$245 \div 0.875 = \$280 \text{ rental charge required to make } 12\tfrac{1}{2}\% \text{ profit}$$

(b) Determine annual profit per apartment and multiply by the number of apartments.

$$\$280 \text{ (rent)} - \$245 \text{ (cost)} = \$35 \text{ profit per month}$$

$$\$35 \times 12 = \$420 \text{ annual profit per apartment}$$

$$\$420 \text{ (annual profit)} \times 64 \text{ (number owned)} = \$26,880 \text{ annual profit}$$

7.2   Paul Lowe bought an apartment house as an investment for $98,500, with a down payment of $18,500 and a $7\frac{1}{2}$% mortgage on the balance.   His annual expenses are: insurance, $520; maintenance, $1,250; real estate taxes, $2,498; and mortgage interest.   The apartment house rents for $1,040 a month.   (a) Find the net return, and   (b) the percent return on Lowe's investment.

(1) Obtain the total income.   (2) Obtain the total expenses.   (3) From total income, subtract total expenses, to obtain the net return.   (4) From the value of the property subtract the mortgage debt, to obtain the amount of investment.   (5) Divide the net return by the amount invested to obtain the percent of return on the investment.

(a) Annual rent (12 × $1,040) $12,480

    Total expenses:
      Interest on mortgage ($7\frac{1}{2}$% of $80,000) $6,000
      Insurance   520
      Maintenance   1,250
      Real estate tax   2,498   10,268
                                                                  Net return = $ 2,212

    Value of property $98,500
    Mortgage on property   80,000
    Investment $18,500

(b) To obtain the rate of return, use the formula: $P = B \times R$, or R = percentage ÷ base, where $R = \$2,212 \div \$18,500 = 0.1195$, or 12% rate of return.   (See Example 2.)

7.3   Last year, Susan Fisher, an economics instructor at a state college, who invests her money in real estate, received a net return of $7,500 on one of her pieces of property. Her rate of return was $12\frac{1}{2}\%$. What was the amount of her investment?

> Use formula $P = B \times R$. $B = ?$ investment; $P = \$7,500$; $R = 12\frac{1}{2}\%$. $B = \$7,500 \div 0.125 = \$60,000$. (See Example 3.)

7.4   Drew Classen, a pilot for American Airlines, purchased 200 shares of his company's common stock yesterday at the low price for the day. What was the cost to him? (Disregard commission.)

> Use Fig. 7-1. Read down to American Airlines (AM Airlines), then across to "Low" and read $7\frac{7}{8}$; $\$7.875$. Multiply the cost per share by the number of shares. $\$7.875 \times 200 = \$1,575$ total cost.
>
> *Note*: Whenever possible, convert fractions, such as $\frac{7}{8}$, to the equivalent decimal fraction; in this case, 0.875. (See Example 4.)

7.5   If Bertram Hall bought 100 shares of Kellogg at its closing price yesterday, would he have paid more or less than if he bought them at the closing price of the previous day? By how much?

> Use Fig. 7-1. Kellogg closed at 19 yesterday. Read down to Kellogg, then across under column heading "Close." Under "Change" ("Chg") column, read $-\frac{1}{4}$ ($-\$.25$). They closed at $19\frac{1}{4}$ the previous day. Hall paid \$25 ($\$.25 \times 100$) more by buying them on the previous day. (See Example 5.)

7.6   Harold Klein bought 100 shares of Joy Manufacturing (Joy Mfg) common stock at their low yesterday. His sister Andrea bought 100 shares of Joy at their high. (*a*) How much more did Andrea pay than Harold? (*b*) What percent saving did Harold realize based on the cost to Andrea? (Disregard commission.)

> (*a*) See Fig. 7-1. Joy Mfg—low $74\frac{3}{4} = \$74.75$; $100 \times \$74.75 = \$7,475$. Joy Mfg—high $79\frac{3}{4} = \$79.75$; $100 \times \$79.75 = \$7,975$. $\$7,975 - \$7,475 = \$500$, the amount more paid by Andrea.
>
> (*b*) Divide Harold's savings by Andrea's total cost to obtain percent of saving. $\$500 \div \$7,975 = 0.0626$, or 6.3% saving. (See Example 6.)

7.7   Ms. Helen Gordon bought 225 shares of Levitz Furniture at $6\frac{3}{8}$ several months ago with some money she had inherited from one of her aunts. Yesterday, Helen sold these shares at the high for the day in order to finance a vacation trip to Europe. (*a*) How much did she gain or lose on this transaction? (*b*) What was her percent of gain or loss? (Disregard commission and fees.)

> (*a*) See Fig. 7-1. Levitz Furn—high $5\frac{5}{8}$; $\$5.625$ per share. 225 (shares) $\times$ $\$5.625$ (selling price per share) $= \$1,265.63$ selling price. Purchase price: $225 \times \$6.375$ ($6\frac{3}{8}$) $= \$1,434.38$. Subtract the selling price from the purchase price to obtain her loss.
>
> $$\$1,434.38 \text{ (purchase price)} - \$1,265.63 \text{ (selling price)} = \$168.75 \text{ loss}$$
>
> (*b*) Percent of loss; divide the amount of the loss by the purchase price.
>
> $$\$168.75 \text{ (loss)} \div \$1,434.38 \text{ (purchase price)} = 0.1176, \text{ or } 11.8\% \text{ loss}$$

(See Example 7.)

7.8   James Connors owns 800 shares of Atlas Mfg. Co. common stock which is paying an annual dividend of $1.80 per share, and 500 shares of Giant Corporation common stock which is paying an annual dividend of $1.20 per share. What is his quarterly income from these stocks?

Divide the annual dividend by four to obtain the quarterly dividend. Multiply the quarterly return by the number of shares owned, to obtain the quarterly return. Atlas Mfg—$1.80 (annual dividend) ÷ 4 = $.45   quarterly   dividend;   800 × $.45 = $360   quarterly   return.   Giant Corp.—$1.20 ÷ 4 = $.30 quarterly dividend; 500 × $.30 = $150 quarterly return. $360 (Atlas dividend) + $150 (Giant dividend) = $510, the quarterly income from these stocks. (See Example 8.)

7.9   If stock bought at a cost of $22.50 per share including commission pays a quarterly dividend of 40 cents per share, what is its annual rate of return?

Obtain the annual dividend by multiplying the quarterly dividend by four. Divide the annual dividend by the cost per share to obtain the rate of return. $.40 × 4 = $1.60, the annual dividend per share. Annual rate of return:

$$\$1.60 \text{ (annual dividend)} \div \$22.50 \text{ (cost per share)} = 0.071, \text{ or } 7.1\%$$

(See Example 9.)

7.10   Ronald Kline inherited 800 shares of common stock from his grandfather. The stock pays a quarterly dividend of $37\frac{1}{2}$ cents a share. The price per share, including commission, was $7\frac{1}{4}$ at the time Ronald inherited the stock. Now 5 years later, the cost per share is $23\frac{7}{8}$. What was the rate of yield on the price at the time Ronald received the stock?

Obtain the annual dividend by multiplying the quarterly dividend by four. $.375 × 4 = $1.50, the annual dividend. Divide the annual dividend by the price at the time he inherited the stock to obtain the rate of yield.

$$\$1.50 \div \$7.25 = 0.2068, \text{ or } 20.7\%$$

(See Example 10.)

7.11   Elsie Cook, a microbiologist for the state Environmental Control and Anti-Pollution Agency, was advised to buy some Dredging Inc. common stock. In anticipation of future growth, Elsie purchased 300 shares at $24\frac{3}{8}$ per share. How much commission did she pay?

Obtain the total purchase price. 300 (shares) × $24.375 (price per share) = $7,312.50, the purchase price.   From Table 1, read under "Multiple Round Lot Orders;" $5,000–$19,999; 1.1178% + $28.324. Multiply the purchase price by the percent of commission; add this result to the additional charge. $7,312.50 × 0.011178 = $81.739; $81.739 + $28.324 = $110.063. Read under "Plus, for Orders $5,000 or More," first through tenth round lots, $7.452 per round lot. 300 shares = 3 round lots; 3 × $7.452 = $22.356. Total the two amounts. Commission paid:

$$\$110.063 + \$22.356 = \$132.419, \text{ or } \$132.42$$

(See Example 11.)

7.12 Ms. Rose Russo, a beautician, was interested in buying some stock in a cosmetic manufacturing firm.   She invested her money in 300 shares of Iptey common stock, a good growth potential and income-producing stock, in preparation for her retirement years.   Rose bought the stock for $6.00 per share through her broker.   (*a*) How much commission did she pay?   (*b*) To what percent of the purchase price did the commission amount?

   (*a*) See Table 1.   Representative charges; read down under column "Price" to 6, then across under the column heading 300 shares.   Find $64.44, commission fee.

   (*b*) Divide the commission by the total purchase price to obtain the percent of commission.

$$\$64.44 \div \$1,800 \,(300 \times \$6) = 0.0358, \text{or } 3.6\%$$

(See Example 12.)

7.13 Isaac Roth, proprietor of a convenience store, who needed money to expand his frozen food section, decided to sell 300 shares of Aztec common stock.   His broker sold the stock at $9\frac{3}{8}$.   The New York State tax and S.E.C. fee amounted to $6.88.   How much did he receive from this transaction?

   See Table 1.   Compute the total selling price.   Figure the commission.   Add the commission to all other charges.   Subtract this result from the total selling price to obtain the proceeds.

   Selling price: $300 \times \$9.375 = \$2,812.50$.   *Commission*: Read under multiple round lot orders; $2,500–$4,999.   Find $1.0692\% + \$27.136$; $\$2,812.50 \times 0.010692 = \$30.071$; $\$30.071 + \$27.136 = \$57.207$.   *Plus*: for orders less than $5,000, first through tenth round lot, $7.128 per lot.   300 shares = 3 round lots; $3 \times \$7.128 = \$21.384$.   Commission: $\$57.207 + \$21.384 = \$78.591$.

$$\$78.59 \,(\text{commission}) + \$6.88 \,(\text{other charges}) = \$85.47 \text{ total charges}$$

Subtract total charges from the selling price to obtain the proceeds.

$$\$2,812.50 - \$85.47 = \$2,727.03$$

(See Example 13.)

7.14 Martha Halleck, a college junior, was given 375 shares of Inland Oil Corporation $6\frac{3}{4}\%$ preferred stock.   Martha was given this stock by her father so she would receive quarterly income for her personal needs rather than a monthly allowance.   The stock is currently selling for $108\frac{3}{8}$ with a par value of $100.   (*a*) How much will Martha receive in quarterly dividends?   (*b*) What is the current rate of return?

   (*a*) Multiply the dividend rate by the par value to obtain the annual dividend per share.   Divide the annual dividend by four to obtain the quarterly dividend.   Multiply this result by the number of shares owned to obtain her quarterly return. $6\frac{3}{4}\% = 0.0675$, $\times \$100$ (par value) $= \$6.75$, the annual dividend per share. $\$6.75 \div 4 = \$1.6875$, the quarterly dividend per share.   Quarterly dividends:

$$\$1.6875 \times 375 \,(\text{number of shares}) = \$632.81$$

   (*b*) Divide the amount of the annual dividend per share by the current price to obtain the current rate of return.

$$\$6.75 \div \$108.375 \,(\text{current price}) = 0.0622 = 6.22\%$$

(See Example 14.)

7.15 Mark Cross, a railroad engineer about ready to retire, decided to cash in a 30-payment life insurance policy and purchase bonds with the proceeds, for additional income. He received enough money to purchase 8 AT&T $6\frac{1}{2}$s 79 bonds. How much did he pay for them at yesterday's closing price?

Use Fig. 7-2. *Note*: AT&T has many bond issues. Read down to AT&T $6\frac{1}{2}$s 79, then to the right under last. Read $94\frac{1}{2}$. This means Cross paid $94\frac{1}{2}$% of $1,000 per bond. $0.945 \times \$1,000 = \$945$ per bond. The total cost:

$$8\,(\text{bonds}) \times \$945 = \$7,560$$

(See Example 15.)

7.16 Roger Wilcox was seeking a high rate of interest on his bond investments. He was willing to pay a premium on high grade bonds as he was concerned with income. Yesterday, Roger purchased 10 Alcoa 9.45s 20 bonds at its high for the day. (*a*) What was the market price per bond? (*b*) To how much did the bond premium amount?

(*a*) Use Table 3. Read down to Alcoa 9.45s 20, then across under "High." Find $103\frac{1}{4}$. (*Note*: The interest rate is expressed in decimal form.) $103\frac{1}{4}\% \times \$1,000 = 1.0325 \times \$1,000 = \$1,032.50$, the price per bond.

(*b*) $\$1,032.50 - \$1,000 = \$32.50$, the bond premium which is the amount above par value of $1,000. (See Example 16.)

7.17 Milton Martin wanted to buy some bonds but didn't understand about the payment of interest, if they were purchased after the interest dates. Milton purchased 5 Alpha 7s 88 bonds at $92\frac{1}{4}$, on August 30. The interest dates on the bonds were January 1 and July 1. (*a*) How much accrued interest will he pay? (*b*) How much will this transaction cost him? (Disregard commission and taxes.)

(*a*) Determine the amount of accrued interest from July 1 to August 30 on one bond. Multiply the accrued interest on one bond by the number purchased. Use the formula, $I = P \times R \times T$. $P = \$1,000$; $R = 7\%$; $T = 60$ days (July 1 to August 30); $I =$

$$\$1,000 \times 0.07 \times \frac{\overset{1}{\cancel{60}}}{\underset{6}{\cancel{360}}} = \frac{\$70}{6} = \$11.666, \text{ accrued interest per bond. Total accrued interest:}$$

$$\$11.666 \times 5 = \$58.33$$

(*b*) Determine the cost of the bonds. Priced at $92\frac{1}{4} = 92.25\% = 0.9225 = \$1,000 = \$922.50$ per bond. $5 \times \$922.50 = \$4,612.50$, the cost of the bonds. Total cost of transaction:

$$\$4,612.50\,(\text{cost}) + \$58.33\,(\text{accrued interest}) = \$4,670.83$$

(See Example 17.)

7.18 Elliot Vance, a statistician at a local manufacturing plant, has been purchasing bonds for years. Elliot prefers to purchase bonds at a discount because the rate of yield on investment is then higher than the stated interest rate. He purchased 10 Union Electric Corporation $4\frac{3}{4}\%$ bonds at $78\frac{1}{4}$. What rate of return will Elliot receive?

Find the interest on one bond. $I = P \times R \times T$. $P = \$1,000$; $R = 4\frac{3}{4}\%$, or 0.0475; $T = 1$ year; $I = \$1,000 \times 0.0475 \times 1 = \$47.50$, the annual interest. Divide the annual interest by the cost of the bond. Rate = interest ÷ cost. Interest = $47.50; cost $= 78\frac{1}{4}\%$ or $0.7825 \times \$1,000$, which $= \$782.50$. The rate fraction:

$$\$47.50 \div \$782.50 = 0.0607, \text{ or } 6.1\%$$

(See Example 18.)

7.19   Tippi James had received Series E Bonds as gifts from members of her family over the past ten years. In order to buy a new fall wardrobe for school, Tippi redeemed a $500 Series E bond in July 1975. The bond had been given to her in December 1965. (*a*) How much money did she receive? (*b*) How much interest did she receive?

   (*a*) See Table 3. Read down to 1965, December, then to the right under $500. Find $595, the amount received.

   (*b*) This Series E appreciation bond originally cost $375. The redemption value less the purchase price equals interest earned. Interest received:

$$\$595 \text{ (redemption value)} - \$375 \text{ (purchase price)} = \$220$$

(See Example 19.)

7.20   Chet Young, a supervisor at a local automobile assembly plant, bought 4 $500 Series E bonds in July of 1964, when he was discharged from military service. Chet redeemed them in July 1975 to make a down payment on the house which he had just purchased. (*a*) How much did Chet receive? (*b*) What was the rate of interest?

   (*a*) See Table 3. Read down to 1964, June through August, then under $500. Find $617 redemption value. Total received:

$$4 \text{ (bonds)} \times \$617 \text{ (value)} = \$2,468$$

   (*b*) A $500 Series E Bond cost $375. Subtract the cost price from the redemption value to obtain the amount of interest. $617 (redemption value) − $375 (cost) = $242 interest Use the formula $I = P \times R \times T$, where $R = I \div PT$, or $R = I/PT$. $I = \$242$; $P = \$375$; $T = 11$ years (1964–1975). Rate of return:

$$R = \$242 \div \$4125 \ (\$375 \times 11) = 0.05866, \text{ or } 5.87\%$$

7.21   In order to receive steady, risk-free interest, Hiram Slocum, a local butcher, converted his bank savings into 5 Series H $5,000 bonds and 8 Series H $1,000 bonds. If the current interest rate is 5.8%, how much interest will Hiram receive semiannually?

   Compute the interest on the total value as they both receive the same interest rate. 5 × $5,000 = $25,000; 8 × $1,000 = $8,000. $25,000 + $8,000 = $33,000, total value. Use formula $I = P \times R \times T$; $P = \$33,000$; $R = 5.8\%$; $T = 6$ months.

$$I = \$33,000 \times 0.058 \times \frac{\overset{1}{\cancel{6}}}{\underset{2}{\cancel{12}}} = \$957 \text{ received semiannually}$$

(See Example 20.)

7.22   Charles Layton, who has an account with a local brokerage firm, received a recommendation from his broker to purchase shares in the Egret Mutual Fund. Charles purchased 500 shares yesterday. Also Charles learned yesterday that his sister sold 500 shares of the Egret Fund to pay for a new car she had purchased. (*a*) How much did Charles pay for his shares? (*b*) How much did his sister receive?

   (*a*) See Fig. 7-3. Egret Fund: Read down to the Egret Fd., then read under the column heading "Buy" to find $10.79. Multiply the cost per share by the number of shares purchased to get the total purchase price.

$$\$10.79 \times 500 = \$5,395$$

(b) Read the "sell" price to find $9.93. The selling price:

$$\$9.93 \times 500 = \$4,965$$

(See Example 21.)

7.23 Jane Aspen, the assistant treasurer of a shoe manufacturing company, is developing a diversified investment portfolio for her later years. She realized that she had never invested in mutual funds. After careful deliberation, Jane invested $3,500 in the Revere Fund at yesterday's quoted price. (a) How many shares did she obtain? (b) What was the rate of surcharge?

(a) See Fig. 7-3. Read down to Revere, then to the right under "buy." Find $5.07 (price per share). Divide the amount invested by the cost per share to obtain the number of shares purchased.

$$\$3,500 \div \$5.07 = 690.335$$

(b) To find the rate of surcharge, subtract the sell price from the buy price. Divide the remainder by the buy price. $5.07 (buy) − $4.64 (sell) = $.43 remainder. The rate of surcharge:

$$\$.43 \div \$5.07 = 0.0848, \text{ or } 8.48$$

(See Example 22.)

Supplementary Problems

7.24 Sue and Hank Snyder rent an apartment from the Sunny Acres Realty Company, which makes a 12% net profit on all apartment rental payments. Each of the 16 rental apartments costs $264 a month. (a) How much monthly rent must Sunny Acres charge the Snyders to realize a 12% net profit? (b) What is the annual net profit on the 16 apartments? *Ans.* (a) $300, (b) $6,912. (See Problem 7.1.)

7.25 Helen Burke and her business associate, Beth Evans, invested their savings in growth common stock. They hope to retire at a relatively early age so they can travel extensively. Each bought 100 shares of American Hospital (Am Hosp) yesterday. Beth bought at the high price for the day; Helen bought at the low. (a) How much more did Beth pay than Helen? (b) Based on the cost to Beth, by what percent did Helen pay less for her stock than did Beth? *Ans.* (a) $137.50, (b) 4.38%. (See Problem 7.6.)

7.26 Horace Hand, who has been a very successful investor, buys low-priced common stock and sells them when he can receive capital gains in excess of 18% of his purchase price. Last week, Horace sold 300 shares of common stock through his broker at $8\frac{1}{8}$. The New York State tax and the S.E.C. fee amounted to $3.94. What were his net proceeds? *Ans.* $2,359.28. (See Problem 7.13.)

7.27 Mildred Horner participated in the bond savings program at her office. Members of the office force purchased government Series E bonds to accumulate savings. Mildred, needing cash for her annual vacation, redeemed in July 1975 a $1,000 Series E bond, which she had purchased in August of 1968. (a) How much money did Mildred receive for her bond? (b) How much of this amount was interest? *Ans.* (a) $1,008.40, (b) $258.40. (See Problem 7.20.)

7.28 Emanuel Parvis invested in mutual funds to provide an educational fund for his two sons. He planned to invest periodically and to reinvest his dividends and capital gains. Emanuel purchased 750 shares of the Dreyfus Fund at yesterday's quote. (a) How much did he pay for them? A member of his car pool, Al Johnson, redeemed 750 shares of the same fund yesterday, to purchase a motor home. (b) How much did Al receive? (c) What was the percent surcharge on Emanuel's purchase? *Ans.* (a) $8,497.50, (b) $7,755.00, (c) 8.73%. (See Problem 7.22.)

7.29 Yul Binger sold 175 shares of Pfizer at their high yesterday. He had purchased them at $22\frac{7}{8}$ two years ago. (a) How much did he gain or lose on this transaction? (b) What percent of gain or loss did he realize on the original cost? *Ans.* (a) $984.37 gain, (b) 24.59%. (See Problem 7.7.)

7.30 William DePree owns 225 shares of Highland Steel $5\frac{3}{4}$% preferred stock. The stock which has a par value of $100 is currently selling at $94\frac{3}{8}$. (a) How much will he receive in quarterly dividends? (b) What is the current rate of return? *Ans.* (a) $323.44, (b) 6.1%. (See Problem 7.14.)

7.31 Andrea Lusko purchased Series E bonds at regular intervals over a number of years. In July of 1975, she redeemed 3 Series E $500 bonds which she had purchased in January of 1965, in order to take a trip to Australia. (a) How much did Andrea receive? (b) What was the rate of interest? *Ans.* (a) $1,812.60, (b) 5.82%.

7.32 Virginia Murphy invests in mutual funds which have for their goal growth and moderate income. Yesterday, Virginia sold common stock that she held and invested $7,800 of the proceeds in the Babson Mutual Fund. (a) How many shares did she receive? Her husband Al redeemed 10, $1,000 bonds yesterday and invested the money in the Brown Mutual Fund. He hoped to out-perform Virginia. (b) How many shares did Al receive? (c) What rate of surcharge did he pay? *Ans.* (a) 828.025, (b) 3,205.128, (c) 2.88%.

7.33 Marcus Lenahan, a merchant, in anticipation of an early retirement, invests in stocks that promise security of principal and reasonable income. Marcus owns 300 shares of Beta Mining stock which is paying an annual dividend of $1.20 per share, and 150 shares of Opec Oil which is paying an annual dividend of $4.00 per share. What is Marcus' quarterly income from these stocks? *Ans.* $240.

7.34 Rod Fesler, a merchant seaman, invests his savings in bonds so that he will have a fixed income with which to supplement his earnings. Upon returning from a long voyage, Rod invested the bonus that he received in 5 American Airlines 11s 88 bonds at yesterday's closing price. (a) How much did he pay for them? (b) What is Rod's rate of return? *Ans.* (a) $4,962.50, (b) 11.08%. (See Problem 7.15.)

7.35 Frank and Alice Betts have purchased U.S. Government Series H bonds over the years to provide them with a fixed income upon retirement, in addition to their Social Security benefits. At age 65, they own 6 Series H, $5,000 bonds and 8 Series H, $1,000 bonds which pay a current interest rate of 5.85%. How much interest will they receive semiannually? *Ans.* $1,111.50. (See Problem 7.21.)

7.36 Edwin Brantley, a machine designer at a local tool and die company, bought a $72,500 apartment house. He sought safety of principal and a fair rate of return on his money. He made a down-payment of $22,500 and received an 8% mortgage loan on the balance. Edwin's annual apartment house expenses are: insurance, $475; maintenance, $990; real estate taxes, 4.85%; and mortgage interest. The monthly rental income from the apartment house is $950. Find (a) the net return the first year, and (b) the percent return on Edwin's investment. *Ans.* (a) $2,418.75, (b) 10.75%. (See Problem 7.2.)

7.37 Clyde Gaston, interested in current income, purchases stock paying a high rate of return. Clyde bought a stock at $18\frac{3}{4}$ per share which pays a quarterly dividend of $37\frac{1}{2}$ cents per share. What is his annual rate of return on this issue? *Ans.* 8%. (See Problem 7.9.)

7.38   Jacob Robards was advised by his broker to purchase, Crane Co. 7s 94 bonds, because of the bonds high rating and good return. Jacob purchased 100 bonds at yesterday's low. (*a*) What was the market price of each bond? (*b*) How much was the bond discount? (*c*) What is the rate of interest?   *Ans.*   (*a*) $752.50, (*b*) $247.50, (*c*) 9.3%. (See Problem 7.16.)

7.39   Richard Coulson, who owns your apartment building, received a net return of $5,000 on his investment in the house last year. This was a net return of 8% on his investment. What is the amount of his investment?   *Ans.* $62,500. (See Problem 7.3.)

7.40   Your fiance inherited 600 shares of common stock which is paying a quarterly dividend of $62\frac{1}{2}$ cents a share. The original cost per share of this stock was $15\frac{1}{8}$. The present cost is $33\frac{3}{8}$. (*a*) What is the rate of yield on the original purchase price? (*b*) What is the rate of return on the current price?   *Ans.*   (*a*) 16.52%, (*b*) 7.49%. (See Problem 7.10.)

7.41   Chester Ralston, an efficiency expert at the Greene Manufacturing Company, received an $8,000 bonus from the company by devising a plan which would save them $25,000 a year in the use of energy. Chester invested this money for his daughter's education by purchasing 8 Beta Corp. $7\frac{1}{4}$s 95 bonds which sold for $93\frac{7}{8}$ on July 30. The bond interest dates are April 1, and October 1. (*a*) How much accrued interest did Chester pay? (*b*) How much did this transaction cost?   *Ans.*   (*a*) $193.33, (*b*) $7,703.33. (See Problem 7.17.)

7.42   John Gaston, who has a well-diversified portfolio, decided to buy a growth stock and an income-producing stock. Yesterday, John purchased 150 shares of Polaroid common at their high for the day and 50 shares of Pepsi Cola common at their low. What was the market value of this transaction?   *Ans.* $8,943.75. (See Problem 7.4.)

7.43   Dick Randall, a stockbroker, sold 200 shares of common stock to Joe Rose, one of his clients, yesterday. How much commission did Dick receive if the stock sold for $27\frac{1}{8}$ per share?   *Ans.* $103.87. (See Problem 7.11.)

7.44   Margaret Baker purchased 25 bonds on the advice of her broker. These bonds were selling at a discount of $318.50, with a $4\frac{7}{8}$% interest rate, which should give her a fair yield at relatively little risk. What rate of return will Margaret receive?   *Ans.*   7.15%. (See Problem 7.18.)

7.45   Linda Noonan wanted to invest some of her earnings in the stock market. She was interested not only in income but also in safety of principal. A business teacher associate advised her to buy some Safeway common stock. Linda checked yesterday's prices of Safeway common stock to determine how much more or less it would have cost her, had she bought 100 shares at yesterday's closing price rather than the previous day's closing price. (*a*) Would yesterday's closing price be more or less? (*b*) By how much?   *Ans.*   (*a*) More, (*b*) $125. (See Problem 7.5.)

7.46   Randall Jamison, your supervisor in the accounting department, mentioned that he had purchased 500 shares of common stock at $4.00 a share through his broker. Randall, a bachelor, purchases low priced stock in anticipation of growth and appreciation to build a large nest egg. (*a*) How much commission did Randall pay on this transaction? (*b*) To what percent of the purchase price did this amount?   *Ans.*   (*a*) $81.78, (*b*) 4.1%. (See Problem 7.12.)

Chapter 8

Using the Metric System

America is going metric. Many American companies and products now carry both customary and metric units. Because of the projected change-over, consumers are gradually becoming familiar with metrication, thinking in terms of centimeters, meters, kilometers, grams, liters, kilograms, etc., instead of inches, feet, yards, miles, ounces, pounds, quarts, gallons, and so forth.

The basic units in the metric system are the meter as a measure of length, the liter as a measure of volume, and the gram as a measure of weight. The metric system is based upon the decimal (base-10) system and is designed so that each unit is 10 times greater than the next smaller unit.

Conversion factors appear in Tables 1 and 2.

8.1 UNITS OF LENGTH

The principal unit of linear measurement is the meter. As noted in the tables, it is approximately 1.1 yards. A meter is 100 centimeters, and each centimeter is approximately 0.4 inches.

EXAMPLE 1

Tom Blaney needs to buy enough lumber to put a base board around his family room, which is 10 feet by 15 feet. Approximately how many linear meters should he buy?

The perimeter of the room is 50 feet. $50 \div 3 = 16\frac{2}{3}$ yd. 1 yd = 0.9 m.

$$16.67 \times 0.9 = \text{approximately 15 m}$$

EXAMPLE 2

On their last vacation, Bob and his family traveled approximately 4,200 kilometers in 12 days. Determine how many miles they traveled and how many miles they averaged daily.

$$4{,}200 \times 0.6 = 2{,}520 \text{ total miles} \qquad 2{,}520 \div 12 = 210 \text{ average daily miles}$$

8.2 AREA

This measurement is determined by multiplying the length times the width. The unit is then referred to as square meters, square kilometers, and so on. The symbol is then m^2, km^2, etc.

EXAMPLE 3

To determine how many square yards of carpeting are required for a room 4 meters by 5 meters:

$$4 \times 5 = 20 \text{ m}^2 \qquad 1.2 \times 20 \text{ m}^2 = 24 \text{ yd}^2$$

Table 1. Conversion Factors from U.S. Customary System to Metric System

	Symbol	When You Know	Multiply by	To Find	Symbol
Length	in.	inches	*2.5	centimeters	cm
	ft	feet	30	centimeters	cm
	yd	yards	0.9	meters	m
	mi	miles	1.6	kilometers	km
Area	in^2	square inches	6.5	square centimeters	cm^2
	ft^2	square feet	0.09	square meters	m^2
	yd^2	square yards	0.8	square meters	m^2
	mi^2	square miles	2.6	square kilometers	km^2
		acres	0.4	hectares	ha
Weight	oz	ounces	28	grams	g
	lb	pounds	0.45	kilograms	kg
		short tons (2000 lb)	0.9	tonnes	t
Volume	tsp	teaspoons	5	milliliters	ml
	Tbsp	tablespoons	15	milliliters	ml
	fl oz	fluid ounces	30	milliliters	ml
	c	cups	0.24	liters	l
	pt	pints	0.47	liters	l
	qt	quarts	0.95	liters	l
	gal	gallons	3.8	liters	l
	ft^3	cubic feet	0.03	cubic meters	m^3
	yd^3	cubic yards	0.76	cubic meters	m^3
Temperature (exact)	°F	Fahrenheit temperature	$\frac{5}{9}$ (after subtracting 32)	Celsius temperature	°C

*Rounded.

Table 2. Conversion Factors from Metric System to U.S. Customary System

	Symbol	When You Know	Multiply by	To Find	Symbol
Length	mm	millimeters	0.04	inches	in.
	cm	centimeters	0.4	inches	in.
	m	meters	3.3	feet	ft
	m	meters	1.1	yards	yd
	km	kilometers	0.6	miles	mi
Area	cm^2	square centimeters	0.16	square inches	in^2
	m^2	square meters	1.2	square yards	yd^2
	km^2	square kilometers	0.4	square miles	mi^2
	ha	hectares (10,000 m^2)	2.5	acres	
Weight	g	grams	0.035	ounces	oz
	kg	kilograms	2.2	pounds	lb
	t	tonnes (1000 kg)	1.1	short tons	
Volume	ml	milliliters	0.03	fluid ounces	fl oz
	l	liters	2.1	pints	pt
	l	liters	1.06	quarts	qt
	l	liters	0.26	gallons	gal
	m^3	cubic meters	35	cubic feet	ft^3
	m^3	cubic meters	1.3	cubic yards	yd^3
Temperature (exact)	°C	Celsius temperature	$\frac{9}{5}$ (then add 32)	Fahrenheit temperature	°F

EXAMPLE 4

Mabel Bicker wishes to make a set of drapes for her living room window. Measurements are 6 feet by 12 feet. If the material costs $11.95 a square meter, how much would the material cost her?

$6 \times 12 = 72$ ft². 72×0.09 m $= 6.48$ m, or approximately 6.5 m. Cost:

$$\$11.95 \times 6.5 = \$77.68$$

8.3 MEASURES OF VOLUME

Volume or *capacity* is the amount of space within a container expressed in liters and cubic meters or portions thereof.

EXAMPLE 5

Alice Hogan is planning a party at which she will need approximately 45 cups of coffee. Will an 8-liter coffee urn be large enough to make this many cups?

No.

$$45 \times 0.24 \text{ liters} = 10.8 \text{ liters}$$

EXAMPLE 6

The Gornto's wish to pour a cement floor for a patio. The dimensions are 20 feet by 18 feet by $\frac{1}{2}$ foot thick. Ready-mix cement costs $15 a cubic meter. Approximately how much will the cement floor cost them?

$20 \times 18 \times \frac{1}{2} = 180$ ft³. 180×0.03 m³ $= 5.4$ m³. Approximate cost:

$$\$15 \times 5.4 = \$81$$

EXAMPLE 7

It will take 5 gallons of paint to paint your house. House paint is selling for $2.15 a liter. How much will it cost you for the paint?

$$5 \times 3.8 \text{ liters} = 19 \text{ liters} \qquad 19 \times \$2.15 = \$40.85$$

8.4 GRAMS—UNITS OF WEIGHT

EXAMPLE 8

There are 20 calories in a $\frac{1}{2}$ ounce cake of yeast. You would like to know how many calories there are in 100 grams of yeast.

$100 \times 0.035 = 3.5$ oz. $3.5 \div \frac{1}{2} = 7$ cakes of yeast. Calories:

$$7 \times 20 = 140$$

EXAMPLE 9

Rachel Chanel plans to serve hamburgers at a cookout. If she buys 7 kilograms of ground beef, how much will she pay for the beef at $1.08 a pound?

7×2.2 lb $= 15.4$ pounds of beef. Cost of beef:

$$15.4 \times \$1.08 = \$16.63$$

8.5 PREFIXES

Common prefixes used with basic units are milli, centi, deci, deka, hecto, and kilo.

Linear measure: basic unit is the meter (measurements are for units of length).

1 millimeter	mm	=	0.001	of a meter
1 centimeter	cm		0.01	of a meter
1 decimeter	dm		0.1	of a meter
1 dekameter	dkm		10	meters
1 hectometer	hm		100	meters
1 kilometer	km		1000	meters

Liquid and solid measure: basic unit is the liter (measurements are for units of liquid capacity).

1 milliliter	ml	=	0.001	of a liter
1 centiliter	cl		0.01	of a liter
1 deciliter	dl		0.1	of a liter
1 dekaliter	dkl		10	liters
1 hectoliter	hl		100	liters
1 kiloliter	kl		1000	liters

Weight measure: basic unit is the kilogram.*

1 milligram	mg	=	0.001	of a gram
1 centigram	cg		0.01	of a gram
1 decigram	dg		0.1	of a gram
1 dekagram	dkg		10	grams
1 hectogram	hg		100	grams
1 kilogram	kg		1000	grams
1000 kilograms	kg		1	metric ton (t)

*Because the gram is too small a unit for practical measurement, the kilogram is the basic unit of weight measurement. It is the only basic unit in the SI system to have a numerical prefix.

Square measure: basic unit is the square meter (measurements are for units of surface or area).

100 square millimeters	mm^2	=	1 square centimeter	cm^2
100 square centimeters	cm^2		1 square decimeter	dm^2
100 square decimeters	dm^2		1 square meter	m^2
100 square meters	m^2		1 square dekameter	dkm^2
100 square dekameters	dkm^2		1 square hectometer	hm^2
100 square hectometers	hm^2		1 square kilometer	km^2

Cubic measure: basic unit is the cubic meter (measurements are for cubic units of length).

1000 cubic millimeters	mm^3	=	1 cubic centimeter	cm^3
1000 cubic centimeters	cm^3		1 cubic decimeter	dm^3
1000 cubic decimeters	dm^3		1 cubic meter	m^3
1000 cubic meters	m^3		1 cubic dekameter	dkm^3
1000 cubic dekameters	dkm^3		1 cubic hectometer	hm^3
1000 cubic hectometers	hm^3		1 cubic kilometer	km^3

EXAMPLE 10

On a recent weekend trip, Al Benson drove 358 miles. Al's car gets 7.4 kilometers to the liter of gasoline. How many liters did he use?

358×1.6 km $= 572.8$ km.

$$572.8 \div 7.4 = 77.405, \text{ or } 77.41 \text{ liters of gas}$$

EXAMPLE 11

Jim Sutton, a college track team member, runs 1,500 meters in the morning and 1,760 yards in the afternoon. How many meters and how many yards does Jim run each day?

$1,500 \times 1.1 = 1,650$ yd. $1,760 \times 0.9 = 1,584$ m.   Adding:

$$1,500 + 1,584 = 3,084 \text{ m daily} \qquad 1,650 + 1,760 = 3,410 \text{ yd daily}$$

EXAMPLE 12

The Ponsi family took a trip to the beach over the weekend to enjoy the salt water and do some surfing. Upon their return home, the odometer on their car indicated that they had traveled 389 miles. How many meters had they gone?

$$389 \times 1.6 = 622.4 \text{ km} \times 1,000 = 622,400 \text{ m}$$

EXAMPLE 13

During a chemistry laboratory problem, Jean Wellmer put 352 milliliters of a solution into a tub. Then she added 648 centiliters of another solution, and decided to add 5 dekaliters of a third solution. How many liters of liquid solution are now in the tub?

$$
\begin{array}{rll}
352 \text{ ml} & = & 0.352 \text{ liters} \\
648 \text{ cl} & = & 6.48 \quad ” \\
5 \text{ dkl} & = & \underline{50.00} \quad ” \\
\text{Total} & = & 56.832 \text{ liters of liquid}
\end{array}
$$

EXAMPLE 14

Fran's goldfish pond lost water through evaporation. She added the following amounts during a recent week: on Monday, 2 dekaliters; on Wednesday, $1\frac{1}{2}$ hectoliters; and on Saturday, 1 kiloliter and 4 dekaliters. How many gallons of water did she add?

$$
\begin{array}{rll}
2 \text{ dal} & = & 20 \text{ liters} \\
1\frac{1}{2} \text{ hl} & = & 150 \quad ” \\
1 \text{ kl} & = & 1,000 \quad ” \\
4 \text{ dkl} & = & \underline{40} \quad ” \\
\text{Total} & = & 1,210 \text{ liters}
\end{array}
$$

$$1,210 \times 0.26 \text{ gal} = 314.6 \text{ gal}$$

EXAMPLE 15

Martha Wright bought a bottle containing 375 pills from the pharmacy. Each pill weighed 4 grams and 3 decigrams. The bottle weighed 7.5 dekagrams. How much did the full bottle weigh in grams? In ounces?

375×4.3 g $= 1,612.5$ gm.

$$
\begin{aligned}
1,612.5 \text{ g} + 7.5 \text{ dkg} &\,(\text{or } 75 \text{ gm: } 7.5 \text{ dkg} \times 10) \\
&= 1,612.5 \text{ g} + 75 \text{ g} = 1,687.5 \text{ g}
\end{aligned}
$$

$$1,687.5 \text{ gm} \times 0.035 = 59.06 \text{ oz}$$

EXAMPLE 16

The Longo's living room is 6 meters long and 3.5 meters wide. Carpeting costs $12.50 a square yard. How much would it cost to buy carpeting for this living room?

6 m × 3.5 m = 21 m². 21 m² × 1.2 = 25.2 yd².

$$\$12.50 \times 25.2 = \$315 \text{ cost of carpeting}$$

EXAMPLE 17

Roger Ashley bought some farmland that is 8.6 kilometers by 7.7 kilometers. How many square miles does he own?

$$8.6 \text{ km} \times 7.7 \text{ km} = 66.22 \text{ km}^2 \qquad 66.22 \times 0.4 = 26.49 \text{ mi}^2$$

EXAMPLE 18

Bob's swimming pool is 40 feet long, 15 feet wide, and has an average depth of 4 feet. How many cubic meters does it contain?

$$40 \times 15 \times 4 = 2,400 \text{ ft}^3 \qquad 2,400 \text{ ft}^3 \times 0.03 = 72 \text{ m}^3$$

EXAMPLE 19

Margie Calkin bought a container 12 decimeters long, 8 decimeters wide, and 7.5 centimeters deep. How many cubic meters does it contain?

Convert decimeters to centimeters. Multiply the three dimensions to obtain the number of cubic centimeters. 1 dm = 10 cm. 12 dm × 10 = 120 cm. 8 dm × 10 = 80 cm. 120 cm (length) × 80 cm (width) × 7.5 cm (depth) = 72,000 cm³. There are 1,000,000 cubic centimeters (cm³) in a cubic meter (m³). Divide the number of cm³ by 1,000,000 to obtain the number of m³.

$$72,000 \text{ cm}^3 \div 1,000,000 \text{ cm}^3 = 0.072 \text{ m}^3$$

8.6 TEMPERATURE

Degrees of temperature are measured by the Celsius thermometer. To convert Fahrenheit to Celsius, the conversion formula is: $C = \frac{5}{9}(F - 32°)$. Find the Celsius temperature reading if the Fahrenheit temperature reading is 86°.

$$C = \tfrac{5}{9}(86° - 32°) = \tfrac{5}{9}(54°) = 30°$$

To convert Celsius to Fahrenheit, the conversion formula is: $F = \frac{9}{5}C + 32°$. Find the Fahrenheit temperature reading if the Celsius temperature reading is 10°.

$$F = \tfrac{9}{5}(10°) + 32° = 18° + 32° = 50°$$

A typical conversion scale is presented in Fig. 8-1.

TEMPERATURE

degrees Celsius are used

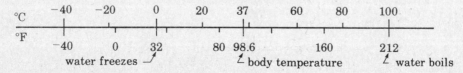

Fig. 8-1

EXAMPLE 20

Mrs. Quinn cooks her roast beef at a Fahrenheit temperature of 375°, which she claims is the optimum temperature for cooking good beef. What would her required temperature reading be on a Celsius thermometer?

Formula = $C = \frac{5}{9}(F - 32°)$.

$$C = \frac{5}{9}(375° - 32°) = \frac{5}{9}(343°) = \frac{1,715°}{9} = 190.5°$$

EXAMPLE 21

Percy Wilton uses a Celsius thermometer for his temperature readings. He said the temperature was $-10°$ Celsius at his house this morning. Mike Bond, his friend, uses a Fahrenheit thermometer. What would be the temperature reading on Mike's thermometer?

To convert Celsius readings to Fahrenheit, use the formula: $F = \frac{9}{5}C + 32°$. (*Note*: On the Celsius thermometer, water freezes at 0°. On the Fahrenheit thermometer, water freezes at 32°.)

$$F = \frac{9}{5}(-10°) + 32° = \frac{-90°}{5} + 32° = -18° + 32° = 14°$$

8.7 USING METRIC EQUIVALENTS

The unit amounts of many products are now measured in the Metric System as well as in the currently used English System. The National Bureau of Standards has approved conversion cards and slide rules to allow for quick, easy conversions. Tables 3, 4 and 5 show some typical conversions.

To convert to milliliters or liters in Table 5, *divide* the appropriate multiplying factor into the number of fluid ounces, pints, etc.

Table 3. Weight Conversions

Ounces to Grams		Grams to Ounces		Pounds to Kilograms		Kilograms to Pounds	
1	28.35	1	0.0353	1	0.4536	1	2.205
2	56.70	2	0.0705	2	0.9072	2	4.409
3	85.05	3	0.1058	3	1.361	3	6.614
4	113.4	4	0.1411	4	1.814	4	8.818
5	141.8	5	0.1764	5	2.268	5	11.02
10	283.5	10	0.3527	10	4.536	10	22.05
20	567.0	20	0.7054	20	9.072	20	44.09
30	850.5	30	1.058	30	13.61	30	66.14
40	1,134	40	1.411	40	18.14	40	88.18
50	1,418	50	1.764	50	22.68	50	110.2
100	2,835	100	3.527	100	45.36	100	220.5
200	5,670	200	7.054	200	90.72	200	440.9
500	14,175	500	17.64	500	226.8	500	1102
1,000	28,350	1,000	35.27	1,000	453.6	1,000	2205

Above values are carried to 4 places.

Table 4. Liquid Volume Conversions

U.S. Quarts	to	Liters	Liters	to	U.S. Quarts
1		0.9463	1		1.057
2		1.893	2		2.113
3		2.839	3		3.170
4		3.785	4		4.227
5		4.732	5		5.284
10		9.463	10		10.57
20		18.93	20		21.13
50		47.32	50		52.84
100		94.63	100		105.7

Above values are carried to 4 places.

Table 5. Volume Conversions

When You Know	Multiply by	To Find
milliliters	0.03	fluid ounces
liters.	2.1	pints
liters	1.06	quarts
liters	0.26	gallons

EXAMPLE 22

6 pt is equal to how many liters?

$$6 \text{ pt} \div 2.1 \text{ liters} = 2.857 \text{ liters}$$

EXAMPLE 23

A jar of instant tea contains 4 oz. How many grams does it contain (rounding off to the nearest whole gram)? Refer to Table 3. 4 oz = 113.4 gm, or 114 gm. Or solve as follows:

$$1 \text{ oz} = 28.35 \text{ gm} \qquad 4 \times 28.35 \text{ gm} = 113.4 \text{ gm, or } 114 \text{ gm}$$

EXAMPLE 24

A can of imported tea contains 400 gm. How many ounces are there in the can?

$$\text{(See Table 3.)} \quad 28.35 \text{ gm} = 1 \text{ oz} \qquad \text{Divide 400 by 28.35: 14.1 oz}$$

EXAMPLE 25

A 25-lb bag of dog food contains 11.34 kg. There are 0.4536 kg in 1 lb (see Table 3). $(25 \times 0.4536 = 11.34 \text{ kg.})$

EXAMPLE 26

An imported bag of fertilizer contains 45 kg. How many pounds are there in the bag (rounding to 1 decimal place)?

$$1 \text{ kg} = 2.205 \text{ lb} \quad \text{(See Table 3.)} \qquad 45 \times 2.205 = 99.225 \text{ lb or } 99.2 \text{ lb}$$

EXAMPLE 27

A bottle of laundry detergent contains 6 U.S. qt. How many liters does it contain (to 2 decimal places)?

$$0.9463 \text{ liters} = 1 \text{ qt} \quad \text{(See Table 4.)} \qquad 6 \times 0.9463 = 5.677, \text{ or } 5.68 \text{ liters}$$

EXAMPLE 28

While traveling in a foreign country, you filled your tank with gas and had to pay for 62 liters. How many gallons did you receive?

$$0.26 \text{ liters} = 1 \text{ gal}   \text{(See Table 4.)}   62 \text{ liters} \times 0.26 = 16.12 \text{ gal}$$

EXAMPLE 29

A jar of imported olive oil contains 15 fl oz. To find how many milliliters it contains convert ounces to milliliters and divide by 0.03 (See Table 5).

$$15 \div 0.03 = 500 \text{ ml}$$

Solved Problems

8.1   Walter and Amy Long are planning to enclose a play area in the yard for their two young children. They have measured off a rectangular area with the following dimensions: 6.4 meters long and 5.1 meters wide. How many linear feet of fencing will be required?

$$6.4 + 6.4 + 5.1 + 5.1 = 23 \text{ linear meters.}$$

$$23 \times 3.3 \text{ (ft to m)} = 75.9 \text{ linear ft}$$

(See Example 1.)

8.2   The Barrons have just purchased a new organ for their living room, which is 1.1 meters wide. The distance between the door frames is exactly 3 feet 6 inches. Can they get the organ through the doorway?

1.1 (m) × 3.3 (ft to m) = 3.63 ft. The doorway is 3 ft 6 in, or 3.5 feet. They can't get it through. (See Table 1.)

8.3   Ruth Drew has a jewelry box that is 18 centimeters and 5 millimeters long by 12 centimeters and 9 millimeters wide. What is the perimeter?

18 cm × 2 and 5 mm × 2 = 36 cm and 10 mm.   12 cm × 2 and 9 mm × 2 = 24 cm and 18 mm.

Perimeter = 60 cm (36 cm + 24 cm) and 28 mm (10 mm + 18 mm), or 62 cm 8 mm

(*Note*: 10 mm = 1 cm. 28 mm = 2 cm and 8 mm. 60 cm + 2 cm = 62 cm.)

8.4   The Morgan family keeps a record of their travel distance on all trips. Last year on their vacation trip to Canada, the odometer read 47,252 miles when they departed and 48,579 miles when they returned. How many kilometers did they travel on this trip?

48,579 − 47,252 = 1,327 miles.

1,327 × 1.6 (conversion factor of mi to km) = 2,123.2 km

(See Example 2.)

8.5   On a tour of a foreign country, Harry and Sue Dupont traveled an average of 198 kilometers a day.   How many miles did they average a day?   How many miles did they travel if they were gone 15 days?

$198 \times 15 = 2{,}970$ km.

$$2{,}970 \times 0.6 = 1{,}782 \text{ miles traveled}$$
$$1{,}782 \div 15 = 118.8 \text{ miles per day average}$$

8.6   A football field is 100 yards long and 40 yards wide.   How many square meters does it contain?

$100 \times 40 = 4{,}000$ sq yd.

$$4{,}000 \times 0.8 = 3{,}200 \text{ m}^2$$

(See Example 3.)

8.7   Maude Gilbert purchased a tapestry for her den, which was 16 inches by 11.5 inches, at a cost of $6.98.   Maude's husband, who is learning to use the metric system, wanted to know how much the tapestry cost per square centimeter.   What was the cost?

16 in $\times$ 11.5 in = 184 sq in.   184 sq in $\times$ 6.5 (conversion factor) = 1,196 cm^2.

$$\$6.98 \div 1{,}196 = \$.0058 \text{ per cm}^2$$

(See Example 4.)

8.8   Ruth Gorman wanted to buy material for a new dress.   She bought 2.5 square meters at $8.95.   Her friend Agnes Cook, wanted to know how much Ruth paid per square yard in order to compare the cost of Ruth's material with the material she had bought.

2.5 (m^2) $\times$ \$8.95 = \$22.38.   2.5 (m^2) $\times$ 1.2 (conversion factor) = 3 yd^2.

$$\$22.38 \div 3 = \$7.46 \text{ per sq yd}$$

8.9   Karen Wunderfeld made 6 liters of punch for her daughter's birthday party.   She also served 3 quarts of soda.   How many cups of drinks did she serve?

3 qt $\times$ 0.95 = 2.85 liters.   6 liters + 2.85 liters = 8.85 liters.

$$8.85 \text{ liters} \div 0.24 = 36.8, \text{ or } 37 \text{ cups of drinks}$$

(See Example 5.)

8.10   Zeke's garden plot is 12 feet long and 26 feet wide.   He wishes to cover it with top soil 6 inches deep.   Top soil costs $18 a cubic meter.   How much will Zeke pay for the top soil?

$12' \times 26' \times 0.5' = 156$ ft^3. $156 \times 0.03 = 4.68$ m^3.

$$\$18 \times 4.68 \text{ (m}^3) = \$84.24$$

(See Example 6.)

8.11 Alex Falstaff wants to buy sufficient paint to cover his house, which contains 2,200 square feet. One gallon of paint will cover 400 square feet. How much will Alex pay for the paint, which sells for $1.98 per liter?

2,200 ÷ 400 = 5.5 gal.   5.5 gal × 3.8 (conversion factor) = 20.9 liters.

$$20.9 × \$1.98 = \$41.38$$

(See Example 7.)

8.12 Eric Barbery's cows produce 850 quarts of milk a day. (a) How many liters do they produce daily? (b) At $.37 a liter, what is Eric's income?

(a) 850 × 0.95 = 807.5 liters.

(b) 807.5 liters × $.37 = $298.78 income.

8.13 Marge Beam, a member of Weight Watchers, counts her calories very carefully. Before purchasing most food items, Marge figures the calories per ounce. She picked up a loaf of bread weighing 600 grams and containing 273 calories. How many calories are there per ounce in this loaf of bread?

600 × 0.035 = 21 oz.

$$273 ÷ 21 = 13 \text{ cal per oz}$$

(See Example 8.)

8.14 Ron Overstreet is going to act as the chef at his family cookout. Ron is planning to serve 60 $\frac{1}{4}$-pound hamburgers at the cookout. How many kilograms of ground beef must he buy?

60 × $\frac{1}{4}$ = 15 lb.

$$15 \text{ lb} × 0.45 = 6.75 \text{ kg}$$

(See Example 9.)

8.15 Albie Royster, a real estate salesman, drove his car 450 miles last week taking clients around to see the various properties he had listed. Albie's car travels 15 miles on a gallon of gasoline. How many liters of gasoline did he consume?

450 ÷ 15 = 30 gal.

$$30 × 3.8 = 114 \text{ liters}$$

(See Example 10.)

8.16 John Saxby's car consumes one gallon of gasoline every 18 miles. His friend Jake gets 5 miles on a liter of gasoline. Which one gets the better mileage?

3.8 liters = 1 gal. 3.8 × 5 = 19 m. Jake gets better mileage by 1 mile per gallon. (See Example 10.)

8.17 Your son runs four 1,000-meter laps a day at track practice. (a) How many yards does he run? (b) How many kilometers is that?

(a) 4 × 1,000 = 4,000.   4,000 × 1.1 = 4,400 yd.

(b) 4,000 ÷ 1,000 = 4 km.   (See Example 11.)

8.18 The Adams family took a trip to Canada last vacation. They traveled 203 miles on the first day and 49 miles on the last day in the United States. While in Canada, they traveled 389 kilometers on one day and 285 kilometers on the second day. (a) How many miles did they travel? (b) The total miles traveled were equal to how many kilometers?

Miles: 203 + 49 = 252.   Kilometers: 389 + 285 = 674.   252 mi × 1.6 = 403.2 km.   674 km × 0.6 = 404.4 mi.

(a) 252 mi + 404.4 mi = 656.4 mi.

(b) 674 km + 403.2 km = 1,077.2 km.   (See Example 12.)

8.19 During a chemistry laboratory experiment, Joan Fonda prepared a solution which required 295 milliliters of one liquid, 840 centiliters of another, 0.3 deciliters of a third, and 4.2 dekaliters of a fourth. How many liters did she prepare?

$$
\begin{array}{rcl}
295.0 \text{ ml} &=& 0.295 \text{ liters} \\
840.0 \text{ cl} &=& 8.40 \quad '' \\
0.3 \text{ dl} &=& 0.03 \quad '' \\
4.2 \text{ dkl} &=& 42.00 \quad '' \\
\hline
\text{Total} &=& 50.725 \text{ liters}
\end{array}
$$

(See Example 13.)

8.20 Due to evaporation and splashing out, Moe Roth added the following amount of water to his swimming pool on successive days: 1.3 hectoliters; 8 dekaliters; 6.7 dekaliters; and $\frac{1}{2}$ kiloliter. How many gallons did he add?

$$
\begin{array}{rcl}
1.3 \text{ hl} &=& 130 \text{ liters} \\
8.0 \text{ dkl} &=& 80 \quad '' \\
6.7 \text{ dkl} &=& 67 \quad '' \\
0.5 \text{ kl} &=& 500 \quad '' \\
\hline
\text{Total} &=& 777 \text{ liters}
\end{array}
$$

777 × 0.26 = 202.02 gal.   (See Example 14.)

8.21 Annie Yost bought a bag of peanuts which weighed 100 grams and 80 decigrams. The bag cost $.49. What was the price per ounce?

1 decigram = 0.1 gram.   100 g + 80 dg (8g) = 108 g.   108 × 0.035 = 3.78 oz.

$.49 ÷ 3.78 = $.129, or $.13 per ounce

(See Example 15.)

8.22 Bonnie Clode was given a prescription by her doctor, which she had filled at a local pharmacy. She received a container of pills which weighed 13 ounces. If the container weighed 6 ounces, how many dekagrams did the pills weigh?

13 − 6 = 7, the weight of the pills in ounces.   1 dkg = 10 gm.   1 oz = 28 gm.   1 oz = 28 ÷ 10 = 2.8 dkg.   Therefore

$$7 \times 2.8 = 19.6 \text{ dkg}$$

8.23 Mark Hadden wishes to put asbestos tile on his playroom floor. The floor is 16 feet long and 12 feet wide. If the tile costs $3.00 a square meter, how much did Mark pay for the tile? (Round to a full square meter.)

16 ft × 12 ft = 192 sq ft. 192 × 0.09 = 17.28 m^2, or 18 m^2. Cost:

$$18 \times \$3 = \$54$$

(See Example 16.)

8.24 Clyde Nelson has a rectangular piece of farm land, 3.4 miles × 2.7 miles. How many square kilometers of land does he own?

3.4 mi × 2.7 mi = 9.18 sq mi.

$$9.18 \times 2.6 \text{ km}^2 = 23.87 \text{ km}^2$$

(See Example 17.)

8.25 The Andersons had a swimming pool constructed for their three young children so they could learn to swim and have an enjoyable time at home. The pool is 10 meters long, 4 meters wide, and has an average depth of 1 meter. How many cubic yards does it contain?

10 m × 4 m × 1 m = 40 m^3.

$$40 \text{ m}^3 \times 1.3 = 52 \text{ yd}^3$$

(See Example 18.)

8.26 Mrs. Oliphant bought a plastic container to keep her fudge and candy in. Her young-sters were always bringing their friends in after school for a few goodies. The container is 8 decimeters long, 60 centimeters wide, and 90 millimeters deep. How many cubic decimeters does it contain?

Convert all dimensions to centimeters. 8 dm = 80 cm. (10 cm = 1 dm. 8 dm × 10 = 80 cm.) 90 mm = 9 cm. (10 mm = 1 cm. 90 ÷ 10 = 9 cm.) 80 cm × 60 cm × 9 cm = 43,200 cm^3.

$$43,200 \text{ cm} \div 1,000 \text{ (conversion factor)} = 43.2 \text{ dm}^3$$

(See Example 19.)

8.27 The Bostrums, while vacationing at the beach, noticed that the temperature reached 95 °F during the day. What temperature reading would be recorded on a Celsius thermometer?

To convert temperature from Fahrenheit to Celsius, use the formula: $C = \frac{5}{9}(F - 32°)$. If Fahrenheit reading is 95°,

$$C = \tfrac{5}{9}(95° - 32°) = \tfrac{5}{9}(63°) = 35 °\text{Celsius}$$

(See Example 20.)

8.28 Billie Jensen is ill and has a temperature of 40 °Celsius. The local hospital uses the Celsius thermometer. Mrs. Jensen wants to know what Billie's temperature is on a Fahrenheit thermometer. What is the corresponding Fahrenheit reading?

Use the formula for conversion: $F = \frac{9}{5}C + 32°$. Celsius is 40°.

$$F = \tfrac{9}{5}(40°) + 32° = 72° + 32° = 104°$$

(See Example 21.)

8.29 The local TV weather newscaster gave the temperature in Alaska as 10 °Celsius and the temperature in Montana as 48 °Fahrenheit. Which state has the colder temperature?

Use the formula: $F = \frac{9}{5}C + 32°$. $F = \frac{9}{5}(10°) + 32° = 18° + 32° = 50°$ in Alaska. It is 50 °F in Alaska and 48 °F in Montana. Therefore, Montana is 2 °F colder.

8.30 Ms. Blakemore sets her apartment thermostat at 68 °F in order to maintain a steady temperature throughout the day. Her friend Barbara wants to know to what she should set her Celsius thermostat in order to have the equivalent temperature.

Use the formula: $C = \frac{5}{9}(F - 32°)$.

$$C = \frac{5}{9}(68° - 32°) = \frac{5}{9}(36°) = 20°$$

(See Problem 10.20.)

8.31 A bottle of pills contains 6 oz. How many grams are there in the bottle?

$$1 \text{ oz} = 28.35 \text{ gm} \text{ (See Table 3.)} 28.35 \times 6 = 170.1 \text{ gm}$$

8.32 A package contains 6 kg. How many pounds are in the package?

$$1 \text{ kg} = 2.205 \text{ lb} \text{ (See Table 3.)} 6 \times 2.205 = 13.230, \text{ or } 13.23 \text{ lb}$$

8.33 A bottle of mouthwash contains $1\frac{1}{2}$ qt. How many liters does it contain?

$$1 \text{ qt} = 0.9463 \text{ liters} \text{ (See Table 4.)} 1.5 \text{ qt} \times 0.9463 = 1.419 \text{ or } 1.42 \text{ liters}$$

8.34 You wanted to buy approximately $2\frac{1}{2}$ gallons of distilled water. How many liters would $2\frac{1}{2}$ gallons of water be equivalent to?

$$1 \text{ liter} = 0.26 \text{ gal}$$

(See Table 5.)   Dividing $2\frac{1}{2}$ gallons by 0.26 you get 9.6 liters

8.35 Mrs. Pappas was visiting Greece and wished to prepare a special meal that required 18 lb of lamb. How many kilograms should she ask for?

$$1 \text{ lb} = 0.4536 \text{ kg} \text{ (See Table 3.)} 18 \times 0.4536 = 8.1648 \text{ or } 8.2 \text{ kg}$$

8.36 Mrs. Ganz has a special recipe for a cake that requires 227 gm of butter. How many ounces does she need?

$$227 \div 28.35 = 8 \text{ oz} \text{ (See Table 3.)}$$

8.37 While traveling in a foreign country during vacation, Bob Smoak drove into a service station that advertised gasoline for 16¢ a liter. Upon filling the tank, the attendant stated that he put 16 gal into Bob's tank. How much did Bob pay for the gasoline?

$$16 \div 0.26 = 61.538, \text{ or } 61.54 \text{ liters} \text{ (See Table 5.)}$$

$$61.54 \times \$.16 = \$9.846, \text{ or } \$9.85 \text{ for the gasoline}$$

8.38   While shopping in a foreign country, a man bought 2.5 kg of chicken for which he paid
$2.69.   How much did he pay per pound?

$$2.5 \div 0.4536 = 5.51 \text{ lb}   \text{(See Table 3.)}   \$2.69 \div 5.51 = \$.488, \text{or } \$.49 \text{ per pound}$$

8.39   Mrs. Higgins received a 1-lb can of tea from a friend who was traveling in the
Orient.   She noticed the price of $3.98 stamped on the can.   When she buys oriental
imported tea at her local delicatessen, it is priced by the gram.   She wanted to know the
cost per gram of this tea.   How much was it?

$$16(\text{oz}) \times 28.35 = 453.6 \text{ gm.}   \$3.98 \div 453.6 = \$.0087, \text{or } 9\text{¢ per gram}$$

8.40   The Carlsons received a letter from their daughter in Australia.   She mentioned that
milk was rather high because she paid $.48 a liter.   How much would that be per gallon?

$$1 \text{ qt} = 0.9463 \text{ liters}   4(\text{qt or 1 gal}) \times 0.9463 = 3.785 \text{ liters}   \text{(See Table 4.)}$$

$$3.785 \times \$.48 = \$1.816, \text{ or } \$1.82 \text{ per gallon}$$

Supplementary Problems

8.41   Sonny Bolles received a dog for his birthday.   He asked his father to enclose an area 60 feet long
by 40 feet wide for the dog.   Fencing material is on sale at a local building supply store, where
they sell it by the meter.   How many linear meters of fencing will be required?   *Ans.*   60
linear.   (See Problem 8.1.)

8.42   Joyce and Cleo, local schoolteachers, went on a travel tour in Mexico last summer.   They traveled
an average of 143 kilometers a day during their 13-day tour.   How many miles did they
travel?   *Ans.*   1,115.4 mi.   (See Problem 8.5.)

8.43   The Ladies' Auxiliary of a local church served 8 quarts of soda and 15 liters of punch at their last
club outing.   How many cups of liquid refreshments did they serve?   *Ans.*   94 cups.   (See
Problem 8.9.)

8.44   Frank Jessup's cows produce 1,200 liters of milk daily.   How many gallons do they produce
daily?   At $1.12 a gallon, what is his daily income?   *Ans:*   312 gal; $349.44.   (See Problem
8.12.)

8.45   You walk back and forth to work and also for your lunch daily.   It is approximately 1,230 meters
from home to work.   How many kilometers do you walk?   How many miles would that be?
Ans.   2.95 mi; 4.92 km.   (See Problem 8.17.)

8.46   Susan Blythe has an outdoor fish pond for her tropical fish.   The pond is losing water daily due to
a leak or seepage.   On successive days, Susan added 1.1 hectoliters, 6.9 dekaliters, 8.7 dekaliters,
and 0.25 kiloliters.   How many gallons did she add?   *Ans:*   134.16 gal.   (See Problem 8.20.)

8.47   Jerry Sloan was remodeling his basement into a living area and decided to make a den 12 feet long
by $10\frac{1}{2}$ feet wide.   He wants to cover the ceiling with acoustic tile which sells for $5.98 a square
meter.   How much will the tile cost?   *Ans.* $67.81.   (See Problem 8.23.)

8.48 Rosie Jeffrey bought a garment which came in a container with the following dimensions: 6.8 decimeters long, 83 centimeters wide, and 98 millimeters deep. She wants to keep it to put articles in. How many cubic decimeters does it contain?   *Ans.*   55.31 dm^3. (See Problem 8.26.)

8.49 The TV weather man stated that it was 30 °Celsius in Tampa, Florida, and 85 °Fahrenheit in Dallas, Texas. Which city had the higher temperature?   *Ans.*   86 °F in Tampa. (See Problem 8.29.)

8.50 Your new boat is 3.2 meters wide; your carport is 10 feet wide between its posts. Will the boat fit into the carport?   *Ans.*   Width of boat is 10.56 ft.   No.   (See Problem 8.2.)

8.51 Eric and Stacey Waldron built a new patio onto the side of their house, to provide additional recreational space. How many square meters of floor space does it contain if it is 18 feet long and 13$\frac{1}{2}$ feet wide?   *Ans.*   21.87 m^2. (See Problem 8.6.)

8.52 The Clearys have measured off an area which is 80 feet long and 60 feet wide for their new lawn. They plan to cover this area with 2 inches of peat. If peat costs $9.50 a cubic meter, how much will they pay for the peat?   *Ans.* $228. (See Problem 8.10.)

8.53 Ma Bryant bakes a delicious loaf of spice cake which weighs 500 grams and contains 312 calories. How many calories are there in a serving which weighs 2 ounces?   *Ans.*   35.6 cal per 2-oz piece. (See Problem 8.13.)

8.54 You decided to take a 6-day bicycle trip. You covered the following distances each day. First day, 58 km; second day, 73 km; third day, 69 km; fourth day, 32 mi; fifth day, 47 mi; and sixth day, 33 mi. (*a*) How many miles did you cover on your trip? (*b*) How many kilometers is this equivalent to?   *Ans.*   (*a*) 232 mi;   (*b*) 379.2 km. (See Problem 8.18.)

8.55 Millie French wanted some pecans for the holiday season. She saw a bag of shelled pecans, which weighed 350 grams and 35 decigrams, selling for $1.79. She wanted to know the price per ounce. What is it?   *Ans.*   14.5 cents per ounce. (See Problem 8.21.)

8.56 Stan and Martha Lukes wanted to purchase some farmland so they could raise beef cattle and have a little truck garden. They decided to purchase a piece of land that measured 2.75 miles by 1.84 miles. How many square kilometers of land did they purchase?   *Ans.*   13.16 km^2. (See Problem 8.24.)

8.57 The Ridenours have their air conditioner thermostat set to go on when the temperature reaches 77 °F. If their thermometer records Celsius temperature, at what temperature on the Celsius thermometer will the air conditioner go on?   *Ans.*   25 °C. (See Problem 8.30.)

8.58 Anne Bilbo wants to place a gold band around a gift package which is 75 centimeters and 8 millimeters long and 37 centimeters and 9 millimeters wide. What is the perimeter of the gift package?   *Ans.*   227 cm 4 mm. (See Problem 8.3.)

8.59 George Manfried has a driveway which is 100 feet long and 10 feet wide. He has decided to cover it with 3 inches of limerock, which should make a good, strong surface to drive on. Limerock is selling for $18.00 a cubic meter. How much will he pay for enough limerock to cover the driveway?   *Ans.* $135. (See Problem 8.10.)

8.60 Ray Thomas obtains 6 hamburger patties from 1 pound of ground beef. He wants to serve 120 hamburgers at his son's party. How many kilograms of ground beef must he buy?   *Ans.*   9 kg. (See Problem 8.14.)

8.61   Angie and Gus were mixing various solutions in the chemistry lab. They poured into the container 749 centiliters of one solution, 487 milliliters of another, 7.9 deciliters of another, and 0.258 dekaliters of another. How many liters of liquid solution did they have? *Ans.*   11.35 liters.   (See Problem 8.19.)

8.62   Allen Baker purchased a bottle of perfume for his girlfriend as a birthday gift.   The bottle and its contents weighed $7\frac{3}{4}$ ounces. If the bottle weighed 5 ounces, how many dekagrams did the perfume weigh?   *Ans.*   7.7 dkm.   (See Problem 8.22.)

8.63   Our neighbors have a swimming pool which is 40 feet long by 18 feet wide, with an average depth of 2 feet. How many cubic meters of water does it contain? *Ans.*   43.2 m³. (See Problem 8.25.)

8.64   Your recipe calls for an oven temperature of 150 °Celsius.   What would the Fahrenheit temperature read?   *Ans.*   302 °F.   (See Problem 8.28.)

8.65   The Kaufmans rented an automobile while they were in Germany on their vacation.   The odometer reading was 50,112 kilometers when they rented the car; upon returning the car, the odometer reading was 52,098 kilometers.   How many miles did the Kaufmans travel in the rented car?   *Ans.*   1,191.6 mi. (See Problem 8.4.)

8.66   Hillary Jameson's house has not been painted since 1970. The house has 2,600 square feet of painting surface. If 1 gallon will cover 400 square feet, how much will Jameson pay for the paint, if it costs $2.15 a liter?   *Ans.* $53.11. (See Problem 8.11.)

8.67   Your car gets 23 miles per gallon of gasoline.   If gasoline costs $.19 per liter, how much did it cost you for gasoline last month, if you traveled 1,248 miles?   *Ans.* $39.18.   (See Problem 8.16.)

8.68   Mrs. Stout purchased a package of imported sugar which contained $2\frac{1}{2}$ kg and cost $2.60.   (*a*) How many pounds did the package weigh? (*b*) What was the unit cost per pound? *Ans.*   (*a*) 5.5 lb,   (*b*) $.47 per pound. (See Problem 8.32.)

8.69   Ron Blake, a chemistry major, bought a $1\frac{1}{2}$-oz bottle of perfume for $7.50 for his girlfriend for a special occasion. His lab partner wanted to know its cost per milliliter. How much did it cost per millimeter?   *Ans.*   1.5¢ per millimeter. (See Table 5.)

8.70   Mrs. Roundtree planned to serve shrimp at a dinner party.   She visited a local fish market which was selling shrimp for $3.39 a kilogram.   She wished to pay for her 8-lb purchase by check.   For what amount must the check be made out?   *Ans.* $12.31.

8.71   You stopped at a service station and asked the attendant to fill your tank with gasoline and to add needed oil.   He put in 60 liters of gasoline and $1\frac{1}{2}$ liters of oil.   How much did you pay, if gas costs $.64 a gallon and oil costs $1.10 a quart?   *Ans.* $11.92. (See Problem 8.37.)

8.72   While visiting Niagara Falls, Jodie and Bill Taylor bought 16.5 gallons of gasoline for $9.98.   (*a*) If they purchased this gasoline on the Canadian side of the Falls, how many liters did they receive? (*b*) What was the price per liter?   *Ans.*   (*a*) 62.45 liters,   (*b*) 16¢. (See Problem 8.34.)

8.73   Susie Williams wanted to buy some goldfish food.   The local pet store had the food on sale for $.98 for a 56.7-gm package.   Susie wanted to know how many ounces she bought and the unit price per ounce. (*a*) How many ounces were in the package? (*b*) What was the price per ounce? *Ans.*   (*a*) 2 oz,   (*b*) $.49 per ounce. (See Problem 8.36.)

8.74 You wanted to paint the rooms in your house and so purchased 5 gal of paint. (*a*) The 5 gal would
be equivalent to how many liters? (*b*) If the paint costs $9.90 per gallon, what is the unit price
per liter? (Use volume conversion chart.)   *Ans.*   (*a*) 19.2 liters, (*b*) $2.58 per liter (due to
rounding off, answer will be approximate).

8.75 Mrs. Gianini bought a package of egg noodles which contained 800 gm for $1.05. She wanted to
compare the price of these noodles with her regular brand. What is the unit price per pound of
these noodles?   *Ans.*   800 gm = 28 oz (rounded), or 1 lb 12 oz. 60¢ per pound. (See Problem 8.39.)

Examination II

Chapters 1-8

1. Joel Burton works on a commission basis at Burstein's Men's Shop as follows:

    3% on all sales
    additional $\frac{1}{2}$% on all sales between $20,000 and $30,000
    additional 1% on all sales above $30,000

    During the month of March, Burton's sales amounted to $37,600. How much commission did he earn?

2. Your fiance earns a $3\frac{1}{2}$% commission on all the automobiles he sells at the Ace Used Car Agency. During the month of July he sold the following cars at these prices. #1, $1,850; #2, $1,680; #3, $2,795; #4, $875; #5, $1,295; #6, $1,990; #7, $2,275; #8, $3,150; and #9, $2,850. What was his commission for the month of July?

3. As a single person with a weekly salary of $280, determine your take-home pay after income tax withholding, with two exemptions; plus Social Security withholding; and payroll deductions of $5.00 for union dues and $6.25 for savings bonds.

4. Linda Haskins, the assistant personnel director at the local hosiery factory, has $64.35 a month withheld from her pay for Social Security tax. What is her gross monthly pay?

5. Ralph and Maria Casper plan to purchase a house using the guidance rule of paying not more than three times their annual income. (a) How much should their annual income be if they desire to purchase a house priced at $42,900? (b) Using the 1% rule of thumb for monthly housing costs, they should not exceed how much per month?

6. With take-home pay of $1,480 a month, you plan to budget 28% for food, 30% for housing, 16% for transportation, 11% for clothing, 8% for recreation, and 5% for church. (a) How much money will you allocate to each item? (b) How much money will be left for miscellaneous expenditures and savings?

7. Mrs. Harold Stark bought various items for her new home on the installment plan. She agreed to make $75 monthly installment payments on her purchases. (a) What percent of her budget do the installment payments represent if the family take-home pay is $980? (b) If the total take-home pay is $1,480?

8. A $4\frac{1}{2}$-oz can of tuna fish costs $.39 and a 12-oz can costs $.98. (a) Which can is the more economical purchase? (b) What is the cost per ounce per can?

9. Mrs. Lila Ross recently redecorated and refurnished her home. She wanted the children to play in the family room so she bought a new color TV set for the room. The TV set was priced at $698. Mrs. Ross purchased it at a cash price of $649. What percent of discount did she receive by paying cash?

10. On a vacation trip to France, you rented a car on terms that required that you pay for all gasoline that you used. If you bought 68 liters of gasoline at 17.5 cents a liter, (*a*) how many gallons did you buy? (*b*) What was the price per gallon?

11. A 12-oz bottle of detergent costs $.69, an 18-oz bottle of the same brand costs $.99, and a 22-oz bottle of the same brand costs $1.19. (*a*) What is the unit price per bottle? (*b*) Which size is the best buy?

12. An upright freezer may be purchased for $399 cash or on the installment plan by paying $49 down and $18 a month for 24 months. Find the installment carrying charge and the actual rate of interest.

13. Andy Tyler decided to borrow the money from the bank to pay for his new boat rather than to purchase the boat on the installment plan. He would save money by doing it this way. The loan was for $1,450 for one year and the bank interest was $8\frac{3}{4}\%$. How much interest did Andy pay?

14. A small loan company granted Joseph Carr a 3-month loan, by discounting his $800 note. They gave Carr $760 after deducting interest for the 3-month period. What was the true interest rate that the loan company charged Carr?

15. Edgar Gaston, a teacher at the local high school, borrowed $3,250 for thirty months from his credit union for the payment of his new car. Edgar's monthly payments are $125.94. (*a*) How much interest did Edgar pay? (*b*) What was the annual rate of interest?

16. Helen Grant's bank statement shows a balance of $193.85 on March 31. Her checkstub balance is $87.40 on March 31. Checks #65 for $48.27, #67 for $19.38, and #68 for $39.65 are not enclosed with her statement. The bank has deducted a service charge of $.85. She asks you to reconcile her bank statement.

17. Ms. Anne Johnson wanted to pay her dentist upon the completion of her dental work. She borrowed $365, the amount of the dental bill, from her bank for 80 days at $8\frac{3}{4}\%$ interest. How much would Anne repay the bank?

18. Tony Salino borrowed $1,500 from his bank to assist his son with some of his college expenses. Tony repaid the bank $1,530 at the end of 72 days. What was the rate of interest?

19. Roger Lamont, a service man, deposited $3,000 of his reenlistment bonus several years ago in his bank at $5\frac{1}{2}\%$ interest, compounded annually. The original deposit has grown to $6,697.50. For how many years has Roger's money been invested? (See Compound Interest table.)

20. Nancy Giles purchased a new car. After all charges and the trade-in allowance, there was an unpaid balance of $3,500 due on the car. Nancy arranged a loan at her bank at $7\frac{1}{2}\%$ interest for the $3,500, to be paid back in three years. (*a*) How much are her monthly payments? (*b*) How much will she pay back? (*c*) What rate of interest is Nancy actually paying?

21. The Klingers wanted to figure out how much they should budget each month for transportation. They drive a two-year-old car which is paid for and which gets 17.5 miles per gallon. They drove 16,500 miles last year and paid an average of 67.9 cents per gallon for gasoline. Their other transportation expenses are: insurance, $295; maintenance and repairs, $185; registration and licenses, $38. In addition, they want to set aside $30 a month toward a new car. (*a*) How much should they budget per month for transportation? (*b*) How much does it cost the Klingers per mile for operating expenses?

22. Debbie Hunt, single, age 18, drives her family car, which is used for farm use only. The car is garaged in Territory 08 and the family had no accidents last year. How much will the premium amount to for the following coverage; bodily injury liability, 50 and 100; property damage $10,000, medical payments of $1,000? Debbie has had driver training.

23. The Alden family, consisting of four persons, lives in a rented three-bedroom house. Last year, they spent the following amounts for housing costs: rent, $1,800; electricity, $980; water, sewage, and garbage disposal, $275; heating oil, $198; installment payments for appliances, $375; maintenance and repair, $72; and yard care, $88. (a) What was their average monthly housing costs? (b) If this amount is 26% of their annual budget, what is the total annual budget?

24. Mark Crane is buying a house appraised at $42,700, with an F.H.A. approved loan. (a) How much is the required down payment? (b) To how much will the loan amount? (See Table 1, page 95.)

25. Allen Graham owned a house for 12 years at a monthly maintenance cost of $375. He sold it at a profit of $9,200. His itemized deductions over the 12 years for taxes and interest allowed him an income tax savings of $3,750. What were his actual monthly housing costs?

26. Rose Kestner owns a house valued at $37,600, which she insured for $25,000. She bought a homeowner's policy (HO-2) with an 80% coinsurance clause, under Group 7, with full coverage. (a) How much is her three-year premium? (b) A fire caused damage in the amount of $9,500. How much did she receive from the insurance company?

27. Roscoe Appleby, age 30, who works with Jake Trumble in the shipping room of the local electrical plant, bought an $8,000 whole life insurance policy and a $15,000 five-year term policy, to provide protection for his wife and two children. He purchased an additional $12,000 five-year term life policy for his wife, age 28, to provide financial aid in the event of her death. (a) How much are Roscoe's annual premium payments? (b) His wife's? (c) The insurance premium payments require what percent of their annual budget of $16,000?

28. Matthew Hill retired at age 65 with full coverage for Social Security benefits. His wife was 62 years of age. Mr. Hill had average yearly earnings of $6,000. (a) To how much did their monthly Social Security benefits amount? (b) If he died three years later, to how much would Mrs. Hill's monthly benefits amount?

29. Jackson Whipple is accumulating an estate for his wife and family of three children by investing his money in stocks and other securities. Yesterday, Jackson purchased 300 shares of RCA common stock at their closing price. (a) What was the market price of the stock? (b) What was the commission fee? (See stock quotations on page 134.)

30. Pearl Steck, a business education major friend of yours, inherited 300 shares of preferred stock paying a quarterly dividend of 62.5 cents per share. She also owns 20 ABC $7\frac{1}{2}$% bonds, which she received as a birthday gift from her grandfather. (a) How much does Pearl receive annually from the stock? (b) From the bonds? (c) What is her total income from these investments?

31. Clint Eastlake is building up a retirement fund to supplement his company's retirement plan. Clint recently invested $8,000 in the Allstate Mutual Fund. (a) How many shares did he receive? (b) What was the rate of surcharge?

32. Alice waters her lawn and garden every other day and uses approximately 1,250 gallons of water each time.   Water costs $.82 per thousand gallons.   During a typical 150-day season, (*a*) how many gallons of water does she use? (*b*) How much does it cost?

33. Last summer, while on vacation in Italy, you traveled 308 km a day by car.   The car traveled 7 km on a liter of gasoline.   The gasoline was sold at 21 cents a liter.   (*a*) How many miles did you travel during your 10-day tour?   (*b*) How many gallons of gasoline did you use?   (*c*) How much did it cost?

34. Mrs. Pottelby, a member of Weight Watchers, has a new recipe for a loaf of cake that weighs 900 gm and contains 750 calories.   (*a*) How many calories are in an ounce?   (*b*) In a pound?

35. The Director of Social Activities is instructed by the Board of Trustees of a community center to buy carpeting for the recreation room, which is 92 ft by 48 ft.   The carpeting costs $9.48 per square meter.   (*a*) How many square meters will he need?   (*b*) How much will it cost?

36. You bought 15 gallons of gasoline.   (*a*) How many liters are 15 gallons of gasoline equal to?   (*b*) If gasoline is selling at 17.5¢ a liter, how much did you pay?   (*c*) What is the cost per gallon?   (See Conversion Tables on page 161.)

Solutions to Examination II

1.
$$3\% \times \$37,600 \qquad \$1,128 \text{ on all sales}$$
$$\tfrac{1}{2}\% \times \$10,000 \qquad\quad 50 \text{ between } \$20,000 \text{ and } \$30,000$$
$$1\% \times \$7,600 \qquad\quad\ \ 76 \text{ above } \$30,000$$
$$\text{Total commission} = \$1,254$$

2. $1,850 + $1,680 + $2,795 + $875 + $1,295 + $1,990 + $2,275 + $3,150 + $2,850 = $18,760 gross sales. $18,760 (gross sales) × 0.035 (commission rate) = $656.60 income.

3. Income tax withholding: single, 2 exemptions, $280 (weekly salary) = $50.80. Social Security withholding: on $280, $16.38. $50.80 (I.T.W.) + $16.38 (S.S.) + $5.00 (union) + $6.25 (bond) = $78.43 total withholding. $280 (salary) − $78.43 (withholding) = $201.57 take-home pay.

4. $64.35 (S.S. tax) ÷ 0.0585 (rate) = $1,100 gross pay.

5. (*a*) $42,900 ÷ 3 = $14,300 annual income.
    (*b*) $42,900 × 0.01 = $429 maximum monthly housing costs.

6.
Food, 28% × $1,480	$ 414.40
Housing, 30% × $1,480	444.00
Transportation, 16% × $1,480	236.80
Clothing, 11% × $1,480	162.80
Recreation, 8% × $1,480	118.40
Church, 5% × $1,480	74.00
98% budgeted =	$1,450.40

$1,480 (total take-home pay) − $1,450.40 (budgeted) = $29.60 remaining.

7. (a) $75 ÷ $980 = 0.0765 = 7.7\%$ of take-home pay.
(b) $75 ÷ $1,480 = 0.0506 = 5.1\%$ of take-home pay.

8. (a) The 12-oz can is a more economical purchase.
(b) $.39 ÷ 4.5 = $.0866$, the cost per ounce; $.98 ÷ 12 = $.0816$, the cost per ounce.

9. $698 − $649 = 49 discount; $49 ÷ $698 = 0.0702$, or 7% discount.

10. (a) 68 (liters) × 0.26 = 17.68 gallons.
(b) $68 × $.175 = 11.90, the cost of 68 liters, or 17.68 gallons. $11.90 ÷ 17.68$ (gallons) = $.673$, or 67.3¢, price per gallon.

11. (a) $.69 ÷ 12 = $.0575 = 5.75$¢ per ounce. $.99 ÷ 18 = $.055$, or 5.5¢ per ounce. $1.19 ÷ 22 = $.05409$, or 5.41¢ per ounce.
(b) The 22-oz bottle is the best buy.

12.

Down payment	$ 49	
Monthly payments (24 × $18)	432	$481
Cash price		399
Carrying charge =		$ 82

$$R = \frac{24 × C}{P × (n × 1)} = \frac{24 × \$82}{\$350 × (24 + 1)} = \frac{\$1,968}{\$8,750}. \qquad R = 0.2249, \text{or } 22.5\%.$$

13. $I = P × R × T: I = \$1,450 × 0.0875 × 1 = \$126.88.$

14. $D = P × R × T: \$40 = \$760 × R × \frac{3}{12}. \qquad \$40 = \$190R. \qquad R = 21\%.$

15. (a) $125.94 × 30 = $3,778.20.$ $3,778.20 − $3,250 = 528.20 interest.
(b) $R = \dfrac{24 × C}{P × (n + 1)} = \dfrac{24 × \$528.20}{\$3,250 × 31} = \dfrac{\$12,676.80}{\$100,750} = 0.1258,$ or 12.6%.

16.

Bank balance March 31,	$193.85	Checkbook balance	$87.40
Less outstanding checks		Less:	
#65 $48.27		Service charge	0.85
#67 19.38			
#68 39.65	107.30		
Adjusted bank balance	$ 86.55	Adjusted checkbook balance	$86.55

17. $I = P × R × T:$ $I = \$365 × 0.0875 × \dfrac{80}{360}.$ $I = \$7.097,$ or $7.10.$ $365 + $7.10 = \mathbf{\$372.10}$ repayment.

18. $I = P × R × T: R = \dfrac{I}{P × T}.$ $R = \dfrac{\$30}{\$1,500 × \dfrac{72}{360}}.$ $R = \dfrac{\$30}{\$300} = 10\%.$

19. $6,697.50 ÷ $3,000 = 2.2325.$ Check with compound interest table at $5\frac{1}{2}\%$; read down, then across to left; find 15 years.   (See Chapter 3 for Compound Interest table.)

20. (a) $3,500 at $7\frac{1}{2}\%$, 3 years, $108.87 monthly payments.
(b) $108.87 × 36 = $3,919.92$, the total amount to be paid back.
(c) $419.92 ÷ $3,500 = 0.1199$, or 12% actual interest.

21. (a) 16,500 (miles) ÷ 17.5 (miles per gallon) = 942.85 gallons, rounded to 943. $.679 × 943 = $640.30, the cost of gasoline. $640.30 (gas) + $295 (insurance) + $185 (repairs) + $38 (license) + $360 (set aside) = $1,518.30, the total to be budgeted per year. $1,518.30 ÷ 12 = $126.53 budgeted per month.

(b) $1,518.30 − $360 = $1,158.30, the annual cost. $1,158.30 ÷ 16,500 = 0.0702, or 7.02 cents per mile.

22.

Bodily injury liability, 50 and 100, Territory 08	$ 90
Property damage, $10,000	49
Medical payments, $1,000	9
Total base premium =	$148

$148 (base premium) × 1.20 (factor) = $177.60, the total premium.

23. (a) $1,800 + $980 + $275 + $198 + $375 + $72 + $88 = $3,788, the total annual housing costs. $3,788 ÷ 12 = $315.67, monthly housing costs.

(b) $P = B × R$: $3,788 = B × 0.26. $B = $3,788 ÷ 0.26 = $14,569.23, the total annual budget.

24. (a)

Up to $25,000 = 3%; 3% × $25,000	$ 750
$25,000 − $35,000 = 10%; 10% × $10,000	1,000
$35,000 − $45,000 = 20%; 20% × $7,700	1,540
Total down payment =	$3,290

(b) $42,700 − $3,290 = $39,410, the amount of the loan.

25. $9,200 (profit) + $3,750 (savings) = $12,950 total return. $12,950 ÷ 144 (months) = $89.93 monthly return. $375 − $89.93 = $285.07 actual monthly cost.

26. (a) $297 premium.

(b) $37,600 × 80% = $30,080; $30,000, full coverage. $\dfrac{\$25,000}{\$30,000} × \$9,500 = \$7,916.67$ received from company.

27. (a) Male, age 30 = $8,000 whole life, $20.26 per $1,000. $8 × $20.26 = $162.08. Male, age 30 = 5-year term, $3.52 per $1,000; 15 × $3.52 = $52.80. $162.08 + $52.80 = $214.88 for his premium.

(b) Female, age 28 = $3.40 per $1,000; 12 × $3.40 = $40.80, wife's premium.

(c) $214.88 × $40.80 = $255.68, total premiums. $255.68 ÷ $16,000 = 0.0159, or 1.6%, of budget.

28. (a) Matthew Hill, age 65, $6,000 average earnings = $323.40, monthly benefits. Mrs. Hill, age 62 = $121.30 (monthly benefits); $323.40 + $121.30 = $444.70, total monthly benefits.

(b) $323.40.

29. (a) 300 RCA × 18¾; 300 × $18.75 = $5,625, the market price.

(b) $5,625 × 1.1178% + 28.324; $5,625 × 0.011178 = $62.876, + $28.324 = $91.20; $91.20 + 3(7.452) = $91.20 + $22.356 = $113.56 commission.

30. (a) 300 × 0.625 = $187.50 quarterly, × 4 = $750.00 annually.

(b) 20 × $75.00 = $1,500 bond interest annually.

(c) $750 + $1,500 = $2,250 annual return.

31. (a) $8,000 ÷ $10.05 = 796.020 shares;

(b) $10.05 − $9.35 = $.70 charge; $.70 ÷ $10.05 = 0.06965, or 6.97%.

32.   150 ÷ 2 = 75 times.
(*a*) 1,250 × 75 = 93,750 gallons consumed.
(*b*) 93.75 × $.82 = $76.88, the cost of the water.

33.   (*a*) 308 × 10 = 3,080 kilometers; 3,080 × 0.6 = 1,848 miles traveled.
(*b*) 3,080 ÷ 7 = 440 liters of gasoline; 440 × 0.26 = 114.4 gallons, rounded to 115.
(*c*) 440 × $.21 = $92.40.

34.   (*a*) 900 × 0.035 = 31.5 oz.
(*b*) 750 ÷ 31.5 = 23.8 calories per ounce.
(*c*) 23.8 × 16 = 380.8 calories per pound.

35.   (*a*) 92 × 48 = 4,416 sq ft; 4,416 × 0.09 = 397.44 m^2, rounded to 398.
(*b*) 398 × $9.48 = $3,773.04, the cost of the carpeting.

36.   (*a*) 15 gallons ÷ 0.26 = 57.7 liters.
(*b*) 57.7 × $.175 = $10.10 cost.
(*c*) $10.10 ÷ 15 = 67.3¢ per gallon.

Appendix 1

Social Security Employee Tax Table

5.85 percent employee tax deductions

Wages		Tax to be withheld	Wages		Tax to be withheld	Wages		Tax to be withheld	Wages		Tax to be withheld
At least	But less than		At least	But less than		At least	But less than		At least	But less than	
$44.36	$44.53	$2.60	$55.48	$55.65	$3.25	$66.59	$66.76	$3.90	$77.70	$77.87	$4.55
44.53	44.71	2.61	55.65	55.82	3.26	66.76	66.93	3.91	77.87	78.04	4.56
44.71	44.88	2.62	55.82	55.99	3.27	66.93	67.10	3.92	78.04	78.21	4.57
44.88	45.05	2.63	55.99	56.16	3.28	67.10	67.27	3.93	78.21	78.38	4.58
45.05	45.22	2.64	56.16	56.33	3.29	67.27	67.44	3.94	78.38	78.55	4.59
45.22	45.39	2.65	56.33	56.50	3.30	67.44	67.61	3.95	78.55	78.72	4.60
45.39	45.56	2.66	56.50	56.67	3.31	67.61	67.78	3.96	78.72	78.89	4.61
45.56	45.73	2.67	56.67	56.84	3.32	67.78	67.95	3.97	78.89	79.06	4.62
45.73	45.90	2.68	56.84	57.01	3.33	67.95	68.12	3.98	79.06	79.24	4.63
45.90	46.07	2.69	57.01	57.18	3.34	68.12	68.30	3.99	79.24	79.41	4.64
46.07	46.24	2.70	57.18	57.36	3.35	68.30	68.47	4.00	79.41	79.58	4.65
46.24	46.42	2.71	57.36	57.53	3.36	68.47	68.64	4.01	79.58	79.75	4.66
46.42	46.59	2.72	57.53	57.70	3.37	68.64	68.81	4.02	79.75	79.92	4.67
46.59	46.76	2.73	57.70	57.87	3.38	68.81	68.98	4.03	79.92	80.09	4.68
46.76	46.93	2.74	57.87	58.04	3.39	68.98	69.15	4.04	80.09	80.26	4.69
46.93	47.10	2.75	58.04	58.21	3.40	69.15	69.32	4.05	80.26	80.43	4.70
47.10	47.27	2.76	58.21	58.38	3.41	69.32	69.49	4.06	80.43	80.60	4.71
47.27	47.44	2.77	58.38	58.55	3.42	69.49	69.66	4.07	80.60	80.77	4.72
47.44	47.61	2.78	58.55	58.72	3.43	69.66	69.83	4.08	80.77	80.95	4.73
47.61	47.78	2.79	58.72	58.89	3.44	69.83	70.00	4.09	80.95	81.12	4.74
47.78	47.95	2.80	58.89	59.06	3.45	70.00	70.18	4.10	81.12	81.29	4.75
47.95	48.12	2.81	59.06	59.24	3.46	70.18	70.35	4.11	81.29	81.46	4.76
48.12	48.30	2.82	59.24	59.41	3.47	70.35	70.52	4.12	81.46	81.63	4.77
48.30	48.47	2.83	59.41	59.58	3.48	70.52	70.69	4.13	81.63	81.80	4.78
48.47	48.64	2.84	59.58	59.75	3.49	70.69	70.86	4.14	81.80	81.97	4.79
48.64	48.81	2.85	59.75	59.92	3.50	70.86	71.03	4.15	81.97	82.14	4.80
48.81	48.98	2.86	59.92	60.09	3.51	71.03	71.20	4.16	82.14	82.31	4.81
48.98	49.15	2.87	60.09	60.26	3.52	71.20	71.37	4.17	82.31	82.48	4.82
49.15	49.32	2.88	60.26	60.43	3.53	71.37	71.54	4.18	82.48	82.65	4.83
49.32	49.49	2.89	60.43	60.60	3.54	71.54	71.71	4.19	82.65	82.83	4.84
49.49	49.66	2.90	60.60	60.77	3.55	71.71	71.89	4.20	82.83	83.00	4.85
49.66	49.83	2.91	60.77	60.95	3.56	71.89	72.06	4.21	83.00	83.17	4.86
49.83	50.00	2.92	60.95	61.12	3.57	72.06	72.23	4.22	83.17	83.34	4.87
50.00	50.18	2.93	61.12	61.29	3.58	72.23	72.40	4.23	83.34	83.51	4.88
50.18	50.35	2.94	61.29	61.46	3.59	72.40	72.57	4.24	83.51	83.68	4.89
50.35	50.52	2.95	61.46	61.63	3.60	72.57	72.74	4.25	83.68	83.85	4.90
50.52	50.69	2.96	61.63	61.80	3.61	72.74	72.91	4.26	83.85	84.02	4.91
50.69	50.86	2.97	61.80	61.97	3.62	72.91	73.08	4.27	84.02	84.19	4.92
50.86	51.03	2.98	61.97	62.14	3.63	73.08	73.25	4.28	84.19	84.36	4.93
51.03	51.20	2.99	62.14	62.31	3.64	73.25	73.42	4.29	84.36	84.53	4.94
51.20	51.37	3.00	62.31	62.48	3.65	73.42	73.59	4.30	84.53	84.71	4.95
51.37	51.54	3.01	62.48	62.65	3.66	73.59	73.77	4.31	84.71	84.88	4.96
51.54	51.71	3.02	62.65	62.83	3.67	73.77	73.94	4.32	84.88	85.05	4.97
51.71	51.89	3.03	62.83	63.00	3.68	73.94	74.11	4.33	85.05	85.22	4.98
51.89	52.06	3.04	63.00	63.17	3.69	74.11	74.28	4.34	85.22	85.39	4.99
52.06	52.23	3.05	63.17	63.34	3.70	74.28	74.45	4.35	85.39	85.56	5.00
52.23	52.40	3.06	63.34	63.51	3.71	74.45	74.62	4.36	85.56	85.73	5.01
52.40	52.57	3.07	63.51	63.68	3.72	74.62	74.79	4.37	85.73	85.90	5.02
52.57	52.74	3.08	63.68	63.85	3.73	74.79	74.96	4.38	85.90	86.07	5.03
52.74	52.91	3.09	63.85	64.02	3.74	74.96	75.13	4.39	86.07	86.24	5.04
52.91	53.08	3.10	64.02	64.19	3.75	75.13	75.30	4.40	86.24	86.42	5.05
53.08	53.25	3.11	64.19	64.36	3.76	75.30	75.48	4.41	86.42	86.59	5.06
53.25	53.42	3.12	64.36	64.53	3.77	75.48	75.65	4.42	86.59	86.76	5.07
53.42	53.59	3.13	64.53	64.71	3.78	75.65	75.82	4.43	86.76	86.93	5.08
53.59	53.77	3.14	64.71	64.88	3.79	75.82	75.99	4.44	86.93	87.10	5.09
53.77	53.94	3.15	64.88	65.05	3.80	75.99	76.16	4.45	87.10	87.27	5.10
53.94	54.11	3.16	65.05	65.22	3.81	76.16	76.33	4.46	87.27	87.44	5.11
54.11	54.28	3.17	65.22	65.39	3.82	76.33	76.50	4.47	87.44	87.61	5.12
54.28	54.45	3.18	65.39	65.56	3.83	76.50	76.67	4.48	87.61	87.78	5.13
54.45	54.62	3.19	65.56	65.73	3.84	76.67	76.84	4.49	87.78	87.95	5.14
54.62	54.79	3.20	65.73	65.90	3.85	76.84	77.01	4.50	87.95	88.12	5.15
54.79	54.96	3.21	65.90	66.07	3.86	77.01	77.18	4.51	88.12	88.30	5.16
54.96	55.13	3.22	66.07	66.24	3.87	77.18	77.36	4.52	88.30	88.47	5.17
55.13	55.30	3.23	66.24	66.42	3.88	77.36	77.53	4.53	88.47	88.64	5.18
55.30	55.48	3.24	66.42	66.59	3.89	77.53	77.70	4.54	88.64	88.81	5.19

Wages		Tax to be withheld	Wages		Tax to be withheld	Wages		Tax to be withheld	Wages		Tax to be withheld
At least	But less than		At least	But less than		At least	But less than		At least	But less than	
$88.81	$88.98	$5.20	$99.92	$100.09	$5.85	$111.03	$111.20	$6.50	$122.14	$122.31	$7.15
88.98	89.15	5.21	100.09	100.26	5.86	111.20	111.37	6.51	122.31	122.48	7.16
89.15	89.32	5.22	100.26	100.43	5.87	111.37	111.54	6.52	122.48	122.65	7.17
89.32	89.49	5.23	100.43	100.60	5.88	111.54	111.71	6.53	122.65	122.83	7.18
89.49	89.66	5.24	100.60	100.77	5.89	111.71	111.89	6.54	122.83	123.00	7.19
89.66	89.83	5.25	100.77	100.95	5.90	111.89	112.06	6.55	123.00	123.17	7.20
89.83	90.00	5.26	100.95	101.12	5.91	112.06	112.23	6.56	123.17	123.34	7.21
90.00	90.18	5.27	101.12	101.29	5.92	112.23	112.40	6.57	123.34	123.51	7.22
90.18	90.35	5.28	101.29	101.46	5.93	112.40	112.57	6.58	123.51	123.68	7.23
90.35	90.52	5.29	101.46	101.63	5.94	112.57	112.74	6.59	123.68	123.85	7.24
90.52	90.69	5.30	101.63	101.80	5.95	112.74	112.91	6.60	123.85	124.02	7.25
90.69	90.86	5.31	101.80	101.97	5.96	112.91	113.08	6.61	124.02	124.19	7.26
90.86	91.03	5.32	101.97	102.14	5.97	113.08	113.25	6.62	124.19	124.36	7.27
91.03	91.20	5.33	102.14	102.31	5.98	113.25	113.42	6.63	124.36	124.53	7.28
91.20	91.37	5.34	102.31	102.48	5.99	113.42	113.59	6.64	124.53	124.71	7.29
91.37	91.54	5.35	102.48	102.65	6.00	113.59	113.77	6.65	124.71	124.88	7.30
91.54	91.71	5.36	102.65	102.83	6.01	113.77	113.94	6.66	124.88	125.05	7.31
91.71	91.89	5.37	102.83	103.00	6.02	113.94	114.11	6.67	125.05	125.22	7.32
91.89	92.06	5.38	103.00	103.17	6.03	114.11	114.28	6.68	125.22	125.39	7.33
92.06	92.23	5.39	103.17	103.34	6.04	114.28	114.45	6.69	125.39	125.56	7.34
92.23	92.40	5.40	103.34	103.51	6.05	114.45	114.62	6.70	125.56	125.73	7.35
92.40	92.57	5.41	103.51	103.68	6.06	114.62	114.79	6.71	125.73	125.90	7.36
92.57	92.74	5.42	103.68	103.85	6.07	114.79	114.96	6.72	125.90	126.07	7.37
92.74	92.91	5.43	103.85	104.02	6.08	114.96	115.13	6.73	126.07	126.24	7.38
92.91	93.08	5.44	104.02	104.19	6.09	115.13	115.30	6.74	126.24	126.42	7.39
93.08	93.25	5.45	104.19	104.36	6.10	115.30	115.48	6.75	126.42	126.59	7.40
93.25	93.42	5.46	104.36	104.53	6.11	115.48	115.65	6.76	126.59	126.76	7.41
93.42	93.59	5.47	104.53	104.71	6.12	115.65	115.82	6.77	126.76	126.93	7.42
93.59	93.77	5.48	104.71	104.88	6.13	115.82	115.99	6.78	126.93	127.10	7.43
93.77	93.94	5.49	104.88	105.05	6.14	115.99	116.16	6.79	127.10	127.27	7.44
93.94	94.11	5.50	105.05	105.22	6.15	116.16	116.33	6.80	127.27	127.44	7.45
94.11	94.28	5.51	105.22	105.39	6.16	116.33	116.50	6.81	127.44	127.61	7.46
94.28	94.45	5.52	105.39	105.56	6.17	116.50	116.67	6.82	127.61	127.78	7.47
94.45	94.62	5.53	105.56	105.73	6.18	116.67	116.84	6.83	127.78	127.95	7.48
94.62	94.79	5.54	105.73	105.90	6.19	116.84	117.01	6.84	127.95	128.12	7.49
94.79	94.96	5.55	105.90	106.07	6.20	117.01	117.18	6.85	128.12	128.30	7.50
94.96	95.13	5.56	106.07	106.24	6.21	117.18	117.36	6.86	128.30	128.47	7.51
95.13	95.30	5.57	106.24	106.42	6.22	117.36	117.53	6.87	128.47	128.64	7.52
95.30	95.48	5.58	106.42	106.59	6.23	117.53	117.70	6.88	128.64	128.81	7.53
95.48	95.65	5.59	106.59	106.76	6.24	117.70	117.87	6.89	128.81	128.98	7.54
95.65	95.82	5.60	106.76	106.93	6.25	117.87	118.04	6.90	128.98	129.15	7.55
95.82	95.99	5.61	106.93	107.10	6.26	118.04	118.21	6.91	129.15	129.32	7.56
95.99	96.16	5.62	107.10	107.27	6.27	118.21	118.38	6.92	129.32	129.49	7.57
96.16	96.33	5.63	107.27	107.44	6.28	118.38	118.55	6.93	129.49	129.66	7.58
96.33	96.50	5.64	107.44	107.61	6.29	118.55	118.72	6.94	129.66	129.83	7.59
96.50	96.67	5.65	107.61	107.78	6.30	118.72	118.89	6.95	129.83	130.00	7.60
96.67	96.84	5.66	107.78	107.95	6.31	118.89	119.06	6.96	130.00	130.18	7.61
96.84	97.01	5.67	107.95	108.12	6.32	119.06	119.24	6.97	130.18	130.35	7.62
97.01	97.18	5.68	108.12	108.30	6.33	119.24	119.41	6.98	130.35	130.52	7.63
97.18	97.36	5.69	108.30	108.47	6.34	119.41	119.58	6.99	130.52	130.69	7.64
97.36	97.53	5.70	108.47	108.64	6.35	119.58	119.75	7.00	130.69	130.86	7.65
97.53	97.70	5.71	108.64	108.81	6.36	119.75	119.92	7.01	130.86	131.03	7.66
97.70	97.87	5.72	108.81	108.98	6.37	119.92	120.09	7.02	131.03	131.20	7.67
97.87	98.04	5.73	108.98	109.15	6.38	120.09	120.26	7.03	131.20	131.37	7.68
98.04	98.21	5.74	109.15	109.32	6.39	120.26	120.43	7.04	131.37	131.54	7.69
98.21	98.38	5.75	109.32	109.49	6.40	120.43	120.60	7.05	131.54	131.71	7.70
98.38	98.55	5.76	109.49	109.66	6.41	120.60	120.77	7.06	131.71	131.89	7.71
98.55	98.72	5.77	109.66	109.83	6.42	120.77	120.95	7.07	131.89	132.06	7.72
98.72	98.89	5.78	109.83	110.00	6.43	120.95	121.12	7.08	132.06	132.23	7.73
98.89	99.06	5.79	110.00	110.18	6.44	121.12	121.29	7.09	132.23	132.40	7.74
99.06	99.24	5.80	110.18	110.35	6.45	121.29	121.46	7.10	132.40	132.57	7.75
99.24	99.41	5.81	110.35	110.52	6.46	121.46	121.63	7.11	132.57	132.74	7.76
99.41	99.58	5.82	110.52	110.69	6.47	121.63	121.80	7.12	132.74	132.91	7.77
99.58	99.75	5.83	110.69	110.86	6.48	121.80	121.97	7.13	132.91	133.08	7.78
99.75	99.92	5.84	110.86	111.03	6.49	121.97	122.14	7.14	133.08	133.25	7.79

Wages		Tax to be withheld	Wages		Tax to be withheld	Wages		Tax to be withheld	Wages		Tax to be withheld
At least	But less than		At least	But less than		At least	But less than		At least	But less than	
$133.25	$133.42	$7.80	$144.36	$144.53	$8.45	$155.48	$155.65	$9.10	$166.59	$166.76	$9.75
133.42	133.59	7.81	144.53	144.71	8.46	155.65	155.82	9.11	166.76	166.93	9.76
133.59	133.77	7.82	144.71	144.88	8.47	155.82	155.99	9.12	166.93	167.10	9.77
133.77	133.94	7.83	144.88	145.05	8.48	155.99	156.16	9.13	167.10	167.27	9.78
133.94	134.11	7.84	145.05	145.22	8.49	156.16	156.33	9.14	167.27	167.44	9.79
134.11	134.28	7.85	145.22	145.39	8.50	156.33	156.50	9.15	167.44	167.61	9.80
134.28	134.45	7.86	145.39	145.56	8.51	156.50	156.67	9.16	167.61	167.78	9.81
134.45	134.62	7.87	145.56	145.73	8.52	156.67	156.84	9.17	167.78	167.95	9.82
134.62	134.79	7.88	145.73	145.90	8.53	156.84	157.01	9.18	167.95	168.12	9.83
134.79	134.96	7.89	145.90	146.07	8.54	157.01	157.18	9.19	168.12	168.30	9.84
134.96	135.13	7.90	146.07	146.24	8.55	157.18	157.36	9.20	168.30	168.47	9.85
135.13	135.30	7.91	146.24	146.42	8.56	157.36	157.53	9.21	168.47	168.64	9.86
135.30	135.48	7.92	146.42	146.59	8.57	157.53	157.70	9.22	168.64	168.81	9.87
135.48	135.65	7.93	146.59	146.76	8.58	157.70	157.87	9.23	168.81	168.98	9.88
135.65	135.82	7.94	146.76	146.93	8.59	157.87	158.04	9.24	168.98	169.15	9.89
135.82	135.99	7.95	146.93	147.10	8.60	158.04	158.21	9.25	169.15	169.32	9.90
135.99	136.16	7.96	147.10	147.27	8.61	158.21	158.38	9.26	169.32	169.49	9.91
136.16	136.33	7.97	147.27	147.44	8.62	158.38	158.55	9.27	169.49	169.66	9.92
136.33	136.50	7.98	147.44	147.61	8.63	158.55	158.72	9.28	169.66	169.83	9.93
136.50	136.67	7.99	147.61	147.78	8.64	158.72	158.89	9.29	169.83	170.00	9.94
136.67	136.84	8.00	147.78	147.95	8.65	158.89	159.06	9.30	170.00	170.18	9.95
136.84	137.01	8.01	147.95	148.12	8.66	159.06	159.24	9.31	170.18	170.35	9.96
137.01	137.18	8.02	148.12	148.30	8.67	159.24	159.41	9.32	170.35	170.52	9.97
137.18	137.36	8.03	148.30	148.47	8.68	159.41	159.58	9.33	170.52	170.69	9.98
137.36	137.53	8.04	148.47	148.64	8.69	159.58	159.75	9.34	170.69	170.86	9.99
137.53	137.70	8.05	148.64	148.81	8.70	159.75	159.92	9.35	170.86	171.03	10.00
137.70	137.87	8.06	148.81	148.98	8.71	159.92	160.09	9.36	171.03	171.20	10.01
137.87	138.04	8.07	148.98	149.15	8.72	160.09	160.26	9.37	171.20	171.37	10.02
138.04	138.21	8.08	149.15	149.32	8.73	160.26	160.43	9.38	171.37	171.54	10.03
138.21	138.38	8.09	149.32	149.49	8.74	160.43	160.60	9.39	171.54	171.71	10.04
138.38	138.55	8.10	149.49	149.66	8.75	160.60	160.77	9.40	171.71	171.89	10.05
138.55	138.72	8.11	149.66	149.83	8.76	160.77	160.95	9.41	171.89	172.06	10.06
138.72	138.89	8.12	149.83	150.00	8.77	160.95	161.12	9.42	172.06	172.23	10.07
138.89	139.06	8.13	150.00	150.18	8.78	161.12	161.29	9.43	172.23	172.40	10.08
139.06	139.24	8.14	150.18	150.35	8.79	161.29	161.46	9.44	172.40	172.57	10.09
139.24	139.41	8.15	150.35	150.52	8.80	161.46	161.63	9.45	172.57	172.74	10.10
139.41	139.58	8.16	150.52	150.69	8.81	161.63	161.80	9.46	172.74	172.91	10.11
139.58	139.75	8.17	150.69	150.86	8.82	161.80	161.97	9.47	172.91	173.08	10.12
139.75	139.92	8.18	150.86	151.03	8.83	161.97	162.14	9.48	173.08	173.25	10.13
139.92	140.09	8.19	151.03	151.20	8.84	162.14	162.31	9.49	173.25	173.42	10.14
140.09	140.26	8.20	151.20	151.37	8.85	162.31	162.48	9.50	173.42	173.59	10.15
140.26	140.43	8.21	151.37	151.54	8.86	162.48	162.65	9.51	173.59	173.77	10.16
140.43	140.60	8.22	151.54	151.71	8.87	162.65	162.83	9.52	173.77	173.94	10.17
140.60	140.77	8.23	151.71	151.89	8.88	162.83	163.00	9.53	173.94	174.11	10.18
140.77	140.95	8.24	151.89	152.06	8.89	163.00	163.17	9.54	174.11	174.28	10.19
140.95	141.12	8.25	152.06	152.23	8.90	163.17	163.34	9.55	174.28	174.45	10.20
141.12	141.29	8.26	152.23	152.40	8.91	163.34	163.51	9.56	174.45	174.62	10.21
141.29	141.46	8.27	152.40	152.57	8.92	163.51	163.68	9.57	174.62	174.79	10.22
141.46	141.63	8.28	152.57	152.74	8.93	163.68	163.85	9.58	174.79	174.96	10.23
141.63	141.80	8.29	152.74	152.91	8.94	163.85	164.02	9.59	174.96	175.13	10.24
141.80	141.97	8.30	152.91	153.08	8.95	164.02	164.19	9.60	175.13	175.30	10.25
141.97	142.14	8.31	153.08	153.25	8.96	164.19	164.36	9.61	175.30	175.48	10.26
142.14	142.31	8.32	153.25	153.42	8.97	164.36	164.53	9.62	175.48	175.65	10.27
142.31	142.48	8.33	153.42	153.59	8.98	164.53	164.71	9.63	175.65	175.82	10.28
142.48	142.65	8.34	153.59	153.77	8.99	164.71	164.88	9.64	175.82	175.99	10.29
142.65	142.83	8.35	153.77	153.94	9.00	164.88	165.05	9.65	175.99	176.16	10.30
142.83	143.00	8.36	153.94	154.11	9.01	165.05	165.22	9.66	176.16	176.33	10.31
143.00	143.17	8.37	154.11	154.28	9.02	165.22	165.39	9.67	176.33	176.50	10.32
143.17	143.34	8.38	154.28	154.45	9.03	165.39	165.56	9.68	176.50	176.67	10.33
143.34	143.51	8.39	154.45	154.62	9.04	165.56	165.73	9.69	176.67	176.84	10.34
143.51	143.68	8.40	154.62	154.79	9.05	165.73	165.90	9.70	176.84	177.01	10.35
143.68	143.85	8.41	154.79	154.96	9.06	165.90	166.07	9.71	177.01	177.18	10.36
143.85	144.02	8.42	154.96	155.13	9.07	166.07	166.24	9.72	177.18	177.36	10.37
144.02	144.19	8.43	155.13	155.30	9.08	166.24	166.42	9.73	177.36	177.53	10.38
144.19	144.36	8.44	155.30	155.48	9.09	166.42	166.59	9.74	177.53	177.70	10.39

Wages		Tax to be withheld	Wages		Tax to be withheld	Wages		Tax to be withheld	Wages		Tax to be withheld
At least	But less than		At least	But less than		At least	But less than		At least	But less than	
$177.70	$177.87	$10.40	$188.81	$188.98	$11.05	$199.92	$200.09	$11.70	$211.03	$211.20	$12.35
177.87	178.04	10.41	188.98	189.15	11.06	200.09	200.26	11.71	211.20	211.37	12.36
178.04	178.21	10.42	189.15	189.32	11.07	200.26	200.43	11.72	211.37	211.54	12.37
178.21	178.38	10.43	189.32	189.49	11.08	200.43	200.60	11.73	211.54	211.71	12.38
178.38	178.55	10.44	189.49	189.66	11.09	200.60	200.77	11.74	211.71	211.89	12.39
178.55	178.72	10.45	189.66	189.83	11.10	200.77	200.95	11.75	211.89	212.06	12.40
178.72	178.89	10.46	189.83	190.00	11.11	200.95	201.12	11.76	212.06	212.23	12.41
178.89	179.06	10.47	190.00	190.18	11.12	201.12	201.29	11.77	212.23	212.40	12.42
179.06	179.24	10.48	190.18	190.35	11.13	201.29	201.46	11.78	212.40	212.57	12.43
179.24	179.41	10.49	190.35	190.52	11.14	201.46	201.63	11.79	212.57	212.74	12.44
179.41	179.58	10.50	190.52	190.69	11.15	201.63	201.80	11.80	212.74	212.91	12.45
179.58	179.75	10.51	190.69	190.86	11.16	201.80	201.97	11.81	212.91	213.08	12.46
179.75	179.92	10.52	190.86	191.03	11.17	201.97	202.14	11.82	213.08	213.25	12.47
179.92	180.09	10.53	191.03	191.20	11.18	202.14	202.31	11.83	213.25	213.42	12.48
180.09	180.26	10.54	191.20	191.37	11.19	202.31	202.48	11.84	213.42	213.59	12.49
180.26	180.43	10.55	191.37	191.54	11.20	202.48	202.65	11.85	213.59	213.77	12.50
180.43	180.60	10.56	191.54	191.71	11.21	202.65	202.83	11.86	213.77	213.94	12.51
180.60	180.77	10.57	191.71	191.89	11.22	202.83	203.00	11.87	213.94	214.11	12.52
180.77	180.95	10.58	191.89	192.06	11.23	203.00	203.17	11.88	214.11	214.28	12.53
180.95	181.12	10.59	192.06	192.23	11.24	203.17	203.34	11.89	214.28	214.45	12.54
181.12	181.29	10.60	192.23	192.40	11.25	203.34	203.51	11.90	214.45	214.62	12.55
181.29	181.46	10.61	192.40	192.57	11.26	203.51	203.68	11.91	214.62	214.79	12.56
181.46	181.63	10.62	192.57	192.74	11.27	203.68	203.85	11.92	214.79	214.96	12.57
181.63	181.80	10.63	192.74	192.91	11.28	203.85	204.02	11.93	214.96	215.13	12.58
181.80	181.97	10.64	192.91	193.08	11.29	204.02	204.19	11.94	215.13	215.30	12.59
181.97	182.14	10.65	193.08	193.25	11.30	204.19	204.36	11.95	215.30	215.48	12.60
182.14	182.31	10.66	193.25	193.42	11.31	204.36	204.53	11.96	215.48	215.65	12.61
182.31	182.48	10.67	193.42	193.59	11.32	204.53	204.71	11.97	215.65	215.82	12.62
182.48	182.65	10.68	193.59	193.77	11.33	204.71	204.88	11.98	215.82	215.99	12.63
182.65	182.83	10.69	193.77	193.94	11.34	204.88	205.05	11.99	215.99	216.16	12.64
182.83	183.00	10.70	193.94	194.11	11.35	205.05	205.22	12.00	216.16	216.33	12.65
183.00	183.17	10.71	194.11	194.28	11.36	205.22	205.39	12.01	216.33	216.50	12.66
183.17	183.34	10.72	194.28	194.45	11.37	205.39	205.56	12.02	216.50	216.67	12.67
183.34	183.51	10.73	194.45	194.62	11.38	205.56	205.73	12.03	216.67	216.84	12.68
183.51	183.68	10.74	194.62	194.79	11.39	205.73	205.90	12.04	216.84	217.01	12.69
183.68	183.85	10.75	194.79	194.96	11.40	205.90	206.07	12.05	217.01	217.18	12.70
183.85	184.02	10.76	194.96	195.13	11.41	206.07	206.24	12.06	217.18	217.36	12.71
184.02	184.19	10.77	195.13	195.30	11.42	206.24	206.42	12.07	217.36	217.53	12.72
184.19	184.36	10.78	195.30	195.48	11.43	206.42	206.59	12.08	217.53	217.70	12.73
184.36	184.53	10.79	195.48	195.65	11.44	206.59	206.76	12.09	217.70	217.87	12.74
184.53	184.71	10.80	195.65	195.82	11.45	206.76	206.93	12.10	217.87	218.04	12.75
184.71	184.88	10.81	195.82	195.99	11.46	206.93	207.10	12.11	218.04	218.21	12.76
184.88	185.05	10.82	195.99	196.16	11.47	207.10	207.27	12.12	218.21	218.38	12.77
185.05	185.22	10.83	196.16	196.33	11.48	207.27	207.44	12.13	218.38	218.55	12.78
185.22	185.39	10.84	196.33	196.50	11.49	207.44	207.61	12.14	218.55	218.72	12.79
185.39	185.56	10.85	196.50	196.67	11.50	207.61	207.78	12.15	218.72	218.89	12.80
185.56	185.73	10.86	196.67	196.84	11.51	207.78	207.95	12.16	218.89	219.06	12.81
185.73	185.90	10.87	196.84	197.01	11.52	207.95	208.12	12.17	219.06	219.24	12.82
185.90	186.07	10.88	197.01	197.18	11.53	208.12	208.30	12.18	219.24	219.41	12.83
186.07	186.24	10.89	197.18	197.36	11.54	208.30	208.47	12.19	219.41	219.58	12.84
186.24	186.42	10.90	197.36	197.53	11.55	208.47	208.64	12.20	219.58	219.75	12.85
186.42	186.59	10.91	197.53	197.70	11.56	208.64	208.81	12.21	219.75	219.92	12.86
186.59	186.76	10.92	197.70	197.87	11.57	208.81	208.98	12.22	219.92	220.09	12.87
186.76	186.93	10.93	197.87	198.04	11.58	208.98	209.15	12.23	220.09	220.26	12.88
186.93	187.10	10.94	198.04	198.21	11.59	209.15	209.32	12.24	220.26	220.43	12.89
187.10	187.27	10.95	198.21	198.38	11.60	209.32	209.49	12.25	220.43	220.60	12.90
187.27	187.44	10.96	198.38	198.55	11.61	209.49	209.66	12.26	220.60	220.77	12.91
187.44	187.61	10.97	198.55	198.72	11.62	209.66	209.83	12.27	220.77	220.95	12.92
187.61	187.78	10.98	198.72	198.89	11.63	209.83	210.00	12.28	220.95	221.12	12.93
187.78	187.95	10.99	198.89	199.06	11.64	210.00	210.18	12.29	221.12	221.29	12.94
187.95	188.12	11.00	199.06	199.24	11.65	210.18	210.35	12.30	221.29	221.46	12.95
188.12	188.30	11.01	199.24	199.41	11.66	210.35	210.52	12.31	221.46	221.63	12.96
188.30	188.47	11.02	199.41	199.58	11.67	210.52	210.69	12.32	221.63	221.80	12.97
188.47	188.64	11.03	199.58	199.75	11.68	210.69	210.86	12.33	221.80	221.97	12.98
188.64	188.81	11.04	199.75	199.92	11.69	210.86	211.03	12.34	221.97	222.14	12.99

Wages		Tax to be withheld	Wages		Tax to be withheld	Wages		Tax to be withheld	Wages		Tax to be withheld
At least	But less than		At least	But less than		At least	But less than		At least	But less than	
$222.14	$222.31	$13.00	$233.25	$233.42	$13.65	$244.36	$244.53	$14.30	$255.48	$255.65	$14.95
222.31	222.48	13.01	233.42	233.59	13.66	244.53	244.71	14.31	255.65	255.82	14.96
222.48	222.65	13.02	233.59	233.77	13.67	244.71	244.88	14.32	255.82	255.99	14.97
222.65	222.83	13.03	233.77	233.94	13.68	244.88	245.05	14.33	255.99	256.16	14.98
222.83	223.00	13.04	233.94	234.11	13.69	245.05	245.22	14.34	256.16	256.33	14.99
223.00	223.17	13.05	234.11	234.28	13.70	245.22	245.39	14.35	256.33	256.50	15.00
223.17	223.34	13.06	234.28	234.45	13.71	245.39	245.56	14.36	256.50	256.67	15.01
223.34	223.51	13.07	234.45	234.62	13.72	245.56	245.73	14.37	256.67	256.84	15.02
223.51	223.68	13.08	234.62	234.79	13.73	245.73	245.90	14.38	256.84	257.01	15.03
223.68	223.85	13.09	234.79	234.96	13.74	245.90	246.07	14.39	257.01	257.18	15.04
223.85	224.02	13.10	234.96	235.13	13.75	246.07	246.24	14.40	257.18	257.36	15.05
224.02	224.19	13.11	235.13	235.30	13.76	246.24	246.42	14.41	257.36	257.53	15.06
224.19	224.36	13.12	235.30	235.48	13.77	246.42	246.59	14.42	257.53	257.70	15.07
224.36	224.53	13.13	235.48	235.65	13.78	246.59	246.76	14.43	257.70	257.87	15.08
224.53	224.71	13.14	235.65	235.82	13.79	246.76	246.93	14.44	257.87	258.04	15.09
224.71	224.88	13.15	235.82	235.99	13.80	246.93	247.10	14.45	258.04	258.21	15.10
224.88	225.05	13.16	235.99	236.16	13.81	247.10	247.27	14.46	258.21	258.38	15.11
225.05	225.22	13.17	236.16	236.33	13.82	247.27	247.44	14.47	258.38	258.55	15.12
225.22	225.39	13.18	236.33	236.50	13.83	247.44	247.61	14.48	258.55	258.72	15.13
225.39	225.56	13.19	236.50	236.67	13.84	247.61	247.78	14.49	258.72	258.89	15.14
225.56	225.73	13.20	236.67	236.84	13.85	247.78	247.95	14.50	258.89	259.06	15.15
225.73	225.90	13.21	236.84	237.01	13.86	247.95	248.12	14.51	259.06	259.24	15.16
225.90	226.07	13.22	237.01	237.18	13.87	248.12	248.30	14.52	259.24	259.41	15.17
226.07	226.24	13.23	237.18	237.36	13.88	248.30	248.47	14.53	259.41	259.58	15.18
226.24	226.42	13.24	237.36	237.53	13.89	248.47	248.64	14.54	259.58	259.75	15.19
226.42	226.59	13.25	237.53	237.70	13.90	248.64	248.81	14.55	259.75	259.92	15.20
226.59	226.76	13.26	237.70	237.87	13.91	248.81	248.98	14.56	259.92	260.09	15.21
226.76	226.93	13.27	237.87	238.04	13.92	248.98	249.15	14.57	260.09	260.26	15.22
226.93	227.10	13.28	238.04	238.21	13.93	249.15	249.32	14.58	260.26	260.43	15.23
227.10	227.27	13.29	238.21	238.38	13.94	249.32	249.49	14.59	260.43	260.60	15.24
227.27	227.44	13.30	238.38	238.55	13.95	249.49	249.66	14.60	260.60	260.77	15.25
227.44	227.61	13.31	238.55	238.72	13.96	249.66	249.83	14.61	260.77	260.95	15.26
227.61	227.78	13.32	238.72	238.89	13.97	249.83	250.00	14.62	260.95	261.12	15.27
227.78	227.95	13.33	238.89	239.06	13.98	250.00	250.18	14.63	261.12	261.29	15.28
227.95	228.12	13.34	239.06	239.24	13.99	250.18	250.35	14.64	261.29	261.46	15.29
228.12	228.30	13.35	239.24	239.41	14.00	250.35	250.52	14.65	261.46	261.63	15.30
228.30	228.47	13.36	239.41	239.58	14.01	250.52	250.69	14.66	261.63	261.80	15.31
228.47	228.64	13.37	239.58	239.75	14.02	250.69	250.86	14.67	261.80	261.97	15.32
228.64	228.81	13.38	239.75	239.92	14.03	250.86	251.03	14.68	261.97	262.14	15.33
228.81	228.98	13.39	239.92	240.09	14.04	251.03	251.20	14.69	262.14	262.31	15.34
228.98	229.15	13.40	240.09	240.26	14.05	251.20	251.37	14.70	262.31	262.48	15.35
229.15	229.32	13.41	240.26	240.43	14.06	251.37	251.54	14.71	262.48	262.65	15.36
229.32	229.49	13.42	240.43	240.60	14.07	251.54	251.71	14.72	262.65	262.83	15.37
229.49	229.66	13.43	240.60	240.77	14.08	251.71	251.89	14.73	262.83	263.00	15.38
229.66	229.83	13.44	240.77	240.95	14.09	251.89	252.06	14.74	263.00	263.17	15.39
229.83	230.00	13.45	240.95	241.12	14.10	252.06	252.23	14.75	263.17	263.34	15.40
230.00	230.18	13.46	241.12	241.29	14.11	252.23	252.40	14.76	263.34	263.51	15.41
230.18	230.35	13.47	241.29	241.46	14.12	252.40	252.57	14.77	263.51	263.68	15.42
230.35	230.52	13.48	241.46	241.63	14.13	252.57	252.74	14.78	263.68	263.85	15.43
230.52	230.69	13.49	241.63	241.80	14.14	252.74	252.91	14.79	263.85	264.02	15.44
230.69	230.86	13.50	241.80	241.97	14.15	252.91	253.08	14.80	264.02	264.19	15.45
230.86	231.03	13.51	241.97	242.14	14.16	253.08	253.25	14.81	264.19	264.36	15.46
231.03	231.20	13.52	242.14	242.31	14.17	253.25	253.42	14.82	264.36	264.53	15.47
231.20	231.37	13.53	242.31	242.48	14.18	253.42	253.59	14.83	264.53	264.71	15.48
231.37	231.54	13.54	242.48	242.65	14.19	253.59	253.77	14.84	264.71	264.88	15.49
231.54	231.71	13.55	242.65	242.83	14.20	253.77	253.94	14.85	264.88	265.05	15.50
231.71	231.89	13.56	242.83	243.00	14.21	253.94	254.11	14.86	265.05	265.22	15.51
231.89	232.06	13.57	243.00	243.17	14.22	254.11	254.28	14.87	265.22	265.39	15.52
232.06	232.23	13.58	243.17	243.34	14.23	254.28	254.45	14.88	265.39	265.56	15.53
232.23	232.40	13.59	243.34	243.51	14.24	254.45	254.62	14.89	265.56	265.73	15.54
232.40	232.57	13.60	243.51	243.68	14.25	254.62	254.79	14.90	265.73	265.90	15.55
232.57	232.74	13.61	243.68	243.85	14.26	254.79	254.96	14.91	265.90	266.07	15.56
232.74	232.91	13.62	243.85	244.02	14.27	254.96	255.13	14.92	266.07	266.24	15.57
232.91	233.08	13.63	244.02	244.19	14.28	255.13	255.30	14.93	266.24	266.42	15.58
233.08	233.25	13.64	244.19	244.36	14.29	255.30	255.48	14.94	266.42	266.59	15.59

Wages		Tax to be withheld	Wages		Tax to be withheld	Wages		Tax to be withheld	Wages		Tax to be withheld
At least	But less than		At least	But less than		At least	But less than		At least	But less than	
$266.59	$266.76	$15.60	$277.70	$277.87	$16.25	$288.81	$288.98	$16.90	$299.92	$300.09	$17.55
266.76	266.93	15.61	277.87	278.04	16.26	288.98	289.15	16.91	300.09	300.26	17.56
266.93	267.10	15.62	278.04	278.21	16.27	289.15	289.32	16.92	300.26	300.43	17.57
267.10	267.27	15.63	278.21	278.38	16.28	289.32	289.49	16.93	300.43	300.60	17.58
267.27	267.44	15.64	278.38	278.55	16.29	289.49	289.66	16.94	300.60	300.77	17.59
267.44	267.61	15.65	278.55	278.72	16.30	289.66	289.83	16.95	300.77	300.95	17.60
267.61	267.78	15.66	278.72	278.89	16.31	289.83	290.00	16.96	300.95	301.12	17.61
267.78	267.95	15.67	278.89	279.06	16.32	290.00	290.18	16.97	301.12	301.29	17.62
267.95	268.12	15.68	279.06	279.24	16.33	290.18	290.35	16.98	301.29	301.46	17.63
268.12	268.30	15.69	279.24	279.41	16.34	290.35	290.52	16.99	301.46	301.63	17.64
268.30	268.47	15.70	279.41	279.58	16.35	290.52	290.69	17.00	301.63	301.80	17.65
268.47	268.64	15.71	279.58	279.75	16.36	290.69	290.86	17.01	301.80	301.97	17.66
268.64	268.81	15.72	279.75	279.92	16.37	290.86	291.03	17.02	301.97	302.14	17.67
268.81	268.98	15.73	279.92	280.09	16.38	291.03	291.20	17.03	302.14	302.31	17.68
268.98	269.15	15.74	280.09	280.26	16.39	291.20	291.37	17.04	302.31	302.48	17.69
269.15	269.32	15.75	280.26	280.43	16.40	291.37	291.54	17.05	302.48	302.65	17.70
269.32	269.49	15.76	280.43	280.60	16.41	291.54	291.71	17.06	302.65	302.83	17.71
269.49	269.66	15.77	280.60	280.77	16.42	291.71	291.89	17.07	302.83	303.00	17.72
269.66	269.83	15.78	280.77	280.95	16.43	291.89	292.06	17.08	303.00	303.17	17.73
269.83	270.00	15.79	280.95	281.12	16.44	292.06	292.23	17.09	303.17	303.34	17.74
270.00	270.18	15.80	281.12	281.29	16.45	292.23	292.40	17.10	303.34	303.51	17.75
270.18	270.35	15.81	281.29	281.46	16.46	292.40	292.57	17.11	303.51	303.68	17.76
270.35	270.52	15.82	281.46	281.63	16.47	292.57	292.74	17.12	303.68	303.85	17.77
270.52	270.69	15.83	281.63	281.80	16.48	292.74	292.91	17.13	303.85	304.02	17.78
270.69	270.86	15.84	281.80	281.97	16.49	292.91	293.08	17.14	304.02	304.19	17.79
270.86	271.03	15.85	281.97	282.14	16.50	293.08	293.25	17.15	304.19	304.36	17.80
271.03	271.20	15.86	282.14	282.31	16.51	293.25	293.42	17.16	304.36	304.53	17.81
271.20	271.37	15.87	282.31	282.48	16.52	293.42	293.59	17.17	304.53	304.71	17.82
271.37	271.54	15.88	282.48	282.65	16.53	293.59	293.77	17.18	304.71	304.88	17.83
271.54	271.71	15.89	282.65	282.83	16.54	293.77	293.94	17.19	304.88	305.05	17.84
271.71	271.89	15.90	282.83	283.00	16.55	293.94	294.11	17.20	305.05	305.22	17.85
271.89	272.06	15.91	283.00	283.17	16.56	294.11	294.28	17.21	305.22	305.39	17.86
272.06	272.23	15.92	283.17	283.34	16.57	294.28	294.45	17.22	305.39	305.56	17.87
272.23	272.40	15.93	283.34	283.51	16.58	294.45	294.62	17.23	305.56	305.73	17.88
272.40	272.57	15.94	283.51	283.68	16.59	294.62	294.79	17.24	305.73	305.90	17.89
272.57	272.74	15.95	283.68	283.85	16.60	294.79	294.96	17.25	305.90	306.07	17.90
272.74	272.91	15.96	283.85	284.02	16.61	294.96	295.13	17.26	306.07	306.24	17.91
272.91	273.08	15.97	284.02	284.19	16.62	295.13	295.30	17.27	306.24	306.42	17.92
273.08	273.25	15.98	284.19	284.36	16.63	295.30	295.48	17.28	306.42	306.59	17.93
273.25	273.42	15.99	284.36	284.53	16.64	295.48	295.65	17.29	306.59	306.76	17.94
273.42	273.59	16.00	284.53	284.71	16.65	295.65	295.82	17.30	306.76	306.93	17.95
273.59	273.77	16.01	284.71	284.88	16.66	295.82	295.99	17.31	306.93	307.10	17.96
273.77	273.94	16.02	284.88	285.05	16.67	295.99	296.16	17.32	307.10	307.27	17.97
273.94	274.11	16.03	285.05	285.22	16.68	296.16	296.33	17.33	307.27	307.44	17.98
274.11	274.28	16.04	285.22	285.39	16.69	296.33	296.50	17.34	307.44	307.61	17.99
274.28	274.45	16.05	285.39	285.56	16.70	296.50	296.67	17.35	307.61	307.78	18.00
274.45	274.62	16.06	285.56	285.73	16.71	296.67	296.84	17.36	307.78	307.95	18.01
274.62	274.79	16.07	285.73	285.90	16.72	296.84	297.01	17.37	307.95	308.12	18.02
274.79	274.96	16.08	285.90	286.07	16.73	297.01	297.18	17.38	308.12	308.30	18.03
274.96	275.13	16.09	286.07	286.24	16.74	297.18	297.36	17.39	308.30	308.47	18.04
275.13	275.30	16.10	286.24	286.42	16.75	297.36	297.53	17.40	308.47	308.64	18.05
275.30	275.48	16.11	286.42	286.59	16.76	297.53	297.70	17.41	308.64	308.81	18.06
275.48	275.65	16.12	286.59	286.76	16.77	297.70	297.87	17.42	308.81	308.98	18.07
275.65	275.82	16.13	286.76	286.93	16.78	297.87	298.04	17.43	308.98	309.15	18.08
275.82	275.99	16.14	286.93	287.10	16.79	298.04	298.21	17.44	309.15	309.32	18.09
275.99	276.16	16.15	287.10	287.27	16.80	298.21	298.38	17.45	309.32	309.49	18.10
276.16	276.33	16.16	287.27	287.44	16.81	298.38	298.55	17.46	309.49	309.66	18.11
276.33	276.50	16.17	287.44	287.61	16.82	298.55	298.72	17.47	309.66	309.83	18.12
276.50	276.67	16.18	287.61	287.78	16.83	298.72	298.89	17.48	309.83	310.00	18.13
276.67	276.84	16.19	287.78	287.95	16.84	298.89	299.06	17.49	310.00	310.18	18.14
276.84	277.01	16.20	287.95	288.12	16.85	299.06	299.24	17.50	310.18	310.35	18.15
277.01	277.18	16.21	288.12	288.30	16.86	299.24	299.41	17.51	310.35	310.52	18.16
277.18	277.36	16.22	288.30	288.47	16.87	299.41	299.58	17.52	310.52	310.69	18.17
277.36	277.53	16.23	288.47	288.64	16.88	299.58	299.75	17.53	310.69	310.86	18.18
277.53	277.70	16.24	288.64	288.81	16.89	299.75	299.92	17.54	310.86	311.03	18.19

Wages At least	Wages But less than	Tax to be withheld	Wages At least	Wages But less than	Tax to be withheld	Wages At least	Wages But less than	Tax to be withheld	Wages At least	Wages But less than	Tax to be withheld
$311.03	$311.20	$18.20	$322.14	$322.31	$18.85	$333.25	$333.42	$19.50	$344.36	$344.53	$20.15
311.20	311.37	18.21	322.31	322.48	18.86	333.42	333.59	19.51	344.53	344.71	20.16
311.37	311.54	18.22	322.48	322.65	18.87	333.59	333.77	19.52	344.71	344.88	20.17
311.54	311.71	18.23	322.65	322.83	18.88	333.77	333.94	19.53	344.88	345.05	20.18
311.71	311.89	18.24	322.83	323.00	18.89	333.94	334.11	19.54	345.05	345.22	20.19
311.89	312.06	18.25	323.00	323.17	18.90	334.11	334.28	19.55	345.22	345.39	20.20
312.06	312.23	18.26	323.17	323.34	18.91	334.28	334.45	19.56	345.39	345.56	20.21
312.23	312.40	18.27	323.34	323.51	18.92	334.45	334.62	19.57	345.56	345.73	20.22
312.40	312.57	18.28	323.51	323.68	18.93	334.62	334.79	19.58	345.73	345.90	20.23
312.57	312.74	18.29	323.68	323.85	18.94	334.79	334.96	19.59	345.90	346.07	20.24
312.74	312.91	18.30	323.85	324.02	18.95	334.96	335.13	19.60	346.07	346.24	20.25
312.91	313.08	18.31	324.02	324.19	18.96	335.13	335.30	19.61	346.24	346.42	20.26
313.08	313.25	18.32	324.19	324.36	18.97	335.30	335.48	19.62	346.42	346.59	20.27
313.25	313.42	18.33	324.36	324.53	18.98	335.48	335.65	19.63	346.59	346.76	20.28
313.42	313.59	18.34	324.53	324.71	18.99	335.65	335.82	19.64	346.76	346.93	20.29
313.59	313.77	18.35	324.71	324.88	19.00	335.82	335.99	19.65	346.93	347.10	20.30
313.77	313.94	18.36	324.88	325.05	19.01	335.99	336.16	19.66	347.10	347.27	20.31
313.94	314.11	18.37	325.05	325.22	19.02	336.16	336.33	19.67	347.27	347.44	20.32
314.11	314.28	18.38	325.22	325.39	19.03	336.33	336.50	19.68	347.44	347.61	20.33
314.28	314.45	18.39	325.39	325.56	19.04	336.50	336.67	19.69	347.61	347.78	20.34
314.45	314.62	18.40	325.56	325.73	19.05	336.67	336.84	19.70	347.78	347.95	20.35
314.62	314.79	18.41	325.73	325.90	19.06	336.84	337.01	19.71	347.95	348.12	20.36
314.79	314.96	18.42	325.90	326.07	19.07	337.01	337.18	19.72	348.12	348.30	20.37
314.96	315.13	18.43	326.07	326.24	19.08	337.18	337.36	19.73	348.30	348.47	20.38
315.13	315.30	18.44	326.24	326.42	19.09	337.36	337.53	19.74	348.47	348.64	20.39
315.30	315.48	18.45	326.42	326.59	19.10	337.53	337.70	19.75	348.64	348.81	20.40
315.48	315.65	18.46	326.59	326.76	19.11	337.70	337.87	19.76	348.81	348.98	20.41
315.65	315.82	18.47	326.76	326.93	19.12	337.87	338.04	19.77	348.98	349.15	20.42
315.82	315.99	18.48	326.93	327.10	19.13	338.04	338.21	19.78	349.15	349.32	20.43
315.99	316.16	18.49	327.10	327.27	19.14	338.21	338.38	19.79	349.32	349.49	20.44
316.16	316.33	18.50	327.27	327.44	19.15	338.38	338.55	19.80	349.49	349.66	20.45
316.33	316.50	18.51	327.44	327.61	19.16	338.55	338.72	19.81	349.66	349.83	20.46
316.50	316.67	18.52	327.61	327.78	19.17	338.72	338.89	19.82	349.83	350.00	20.47
316.67	316.84	18.53	327.78	327.95	19.18	338.89	339.06	19.83	350.00	350.18	20.48
316.84	317.01	18.54	327.95	328.12	19.19	339.06	339.24	19.84	350.18	350.35	20.49
317.01	317.18	18.55	328.12	328.30	19.20	339.24	339.41	19.85	350.35	350.52	20.50
317.18	317.36	18.56	328.30	328.47	19.21	339.41	339.58	19.86	350.52	350.69	20.51
317.36	317.53	18.57	328.47	328.64	19.22	339.58	339.75	19.87	350.69	350.86	20.52
317.53	317.70	18.58	328.64	328.81	19.23	339.75	339.92	19.88	350.86	351.03	20.53
317.70	317.87	18.59	328.81	328.98	19.24	339.92	340.09	19.89	351.03	351.20	20.54
317.87	318.04	18.60	328.98	329.15	19.25	340.09	340.26	19.90	351.20	351.37	20.55
318.04	318.21	18.61	329.15	329.32	19.26	340.26	340.43	19.91	351.37	351.54	20.56
318.21	318.38	18.62	329.32	329.49	19.27	340.43	340.60	19.92	351.54	351.71	20.57
318.38	318.55	18.63	329.49	329.66	19.28	340.60	340.77	19.93	351.71	351.89	20.58
318.55	318.72	18.64	329.66	329.83	19.29	340.77	340.95	19.94	351.89	352.06	20.59
318.72	318.89	18.65	329.83	330.00	19.30	340.95	341.12	19.95	352.06	352.23	20.60
318.89	319.06	18.66	330.00	330.18	19.31	341.12	341.29	19.96	352.23	352.40	20.61
319.06	319.24	18.67	330.18	330.35	19.32	341.29	341.46	19.97	352.40	352.57	20.62
319.24	319.41	18.68	330.35	330.52	19.33	341.46	341.63	19.98	352.57	352.74	20.63
319.41	319.58	18.69	330.52	330.69	19.34	341.63	341.80	19.99	352.74	352.91	20.64
319.58	319.75	18.70	330.69	330.86	19.35	341.80	341.97	20.00	352.91	353.08	20.65
319.75	319.92	18.71	330.86	331.03	19.36	341.97	342.14	20.01	353.08	353.25	20.66
319.92	320.09	18.72	331.03	331.20	19.37	342.14	342.31	20.02	353.25	353.42	20.67
320.09	320.26	18.73	331.20	331.37	19.38	342.31	342.48	20.03	353.42	353.59	20.68
320.26	320.43	18.74	331.37	331.54	19.39	342.48	342.65	20.04	353.59	353.77	20.69
320.43	320.60	18.75	331.54	331.71	19.40	342.65	342.83	20.05	353.77	353.94	20.70
320.60	320.77	18.76	331.71	331.89	19.41	342.83	343.00	20.06	353.94	354.11	20.71
320.77	320.95	18.77	331.89	332.06	19.42	343.00	343.17	20.07	354.11	354.28	20.72
320.95	321.12	18.78	332.06	332.23	19.43	343.17	343.34	20.08	354.28	354.45	20.73
321.12	321.29	18.79	332.23	332.40	19.44	343.34	343.51	20.09	354.45	354.62	20.74
321.29	321.46	18.80	332.40	332.57	19.45	343.51	343.68	20.10	354.62	354.79	20.75
321.46	321.63	18.81	332.57	332.74	19.46	343.68	343.85	20.11	354.79	354.96	20.76
321.63	321.80	18.82	332.74	332.91	19.47	343.85	344.02	20.12	354.96	355.13	20.77
321.80	321.97	18.83	332.91	333.08	19.48	344.02	344.19	20.13	355.13	355.30	20.78
321.97	322.14	18.84	333.08	333.25	19.49	344.19	344.36	20.14	355.30	355.48	20.79

Wages At least	Wages But less than	Tax to be withheld	Wages At least	Wages But less than	Tax to be withheld	Wages At least	Wages But less than	Tax to be withheld	Wages At least	Wages But less than	Tax to be withheld
$355.48	$355.65	$20.80	$366.59	$366.76	$21.45	$377.70	$377.87	$22.10	$388.81	$388.98	$22.75
355.65	355.82	20.81	366.76	366.93	21.46	377.87	378.04	22.11	388.98	389.15	22.76
355.82	355.99	20.82	366.93	367.10	21.47	378.04	378.21	22.12	389.15	389.32	22.77
355.99	356.16	20.83	367.10	367.27	21.48	378.21	378.38	22.13	389.32	389.49	22.78
356.16	356.33	20.84	367.27	367.44	21.49	378.38	378.55	22.14	389.49	389.66	22.79
356.33	356.50	20.85	367.44	367.61	21.50	378.55	378.72	22.15	389.66	389.83	22.80
356.50	356.67	20.86	367.61	367.78	21.51	378.72	378.89	22.16	389.83	390.00	22.81
356.67	356.84	20.87	367.78	367.95	21.52	378.89	379.06	22.17	390.00	390.18	22.82
356.84	357.01	20.88	367.95	368.12	21.53	379.06	379.24	22.18	390.18	390.35	22.83
357.01	357.18	20.89	368.12	368.30	21.54	379.24	379.41	22.19	390.35	390.52	22.84
357.18	357.36	20.90	368.30	368.47	21.55	379.41	379.58	22.20	390.52	390.69	22.85
357.36	357.53	20.91	368.47	368.64	21.56	379.58	379.75	22.21	390.69	390.86	22.86
357.53	357.70	20.92	368.64	368.81	21.57	379.75	379.92	22.22	390.86	391.03	22.87
357.70	357.87	20.93	368.81	368.98	21.58	379.92	380.09	22.23	391.03	391.20	22.88
357.87	358.04	20.94	368.98	369.15	21.59	380.09	380.26	22.24	391.20	391.37	22.89
358.04	358.21	20.95	369.15	369.32	21.60	380.26	380.43	22.25	391.37	391.54	22.90
358.21	358.38	20.96	369.32	369.49	21.61	380.43	380.60	22.26	391.54	391.71	22.91
358.38	358.55	20.97	369.49	369.66	21.62	380.60	380.77	22.27	391.71	391.89	22.92
358.55	358.72	20.98	369.66	369.83	21.63	380.77	380.95	22.28	391.89	392.06	22.93
358.72	358.89	20.99	369.83	370.00	21.64	380.95	381.12	22.29	392.06	392.23	22.94
358.89	359.06	21.00	370.00	370.18	21.65	381.12	381.29	22.30	392.23	392.40	22.95
359.06	359.24	21.01	370.18	370.35	21.66	381.29	381.46	22.31	392.40	392.57	22.96
359.24	359.41	21.02	370.35	370.52	21.67	381.46	381.63	22.32	392.57	392.74	22.97
359.41	359.58	21.03	370.52	370.69	21.68	381.63	381.80	22.33	392.74	392.91	22.98
359.58	359.75	21.04	370.69	370.86	21.69	381.80	381.97	22.34	392.91	393.08	22.99
359.75	359.92	21.05	370.86	371.03	21.70	381.97	382.14	22.35	393.08	393.25	23.00
359.92	360.09	21.06	371.03	371.20	21.71	382.14	382.31	22.36	393.25	393.42	23.01
360.09	360.26	21.07	371.20	371.37	21.72	382.31	382.48	22.37	393.42	393.59	23.02
360.26	360.43	21.08	371.37	371.54	21.73	382.48	382.65	22.38	393.59	393.77	23.03
360.43	360.60	21.09	371.54	371.71	21.74	382.65	382.83	22.39	393.77	393.94	23.04
360.60	360.77	21.10	371.71	371.89	21.75	382.83	383.00	22.40	393.94	394.11	23.05
360.77	360.95	21.11	371.89	372.06	21.76	383.00	383.17	22.41	394.11	394.28	23.06
360.95	361.12	21.12	372.06	372.23	21.77	383.17	383.34	22.42	394.28	394.45	23.07
361.12	361.29	21.13	372.23	372.40	21.78	383.34	383.51	22.43	394.45	394.62	23.08
361.29	361.46	21.14	372.40	372.57	21.79	383.51	383.68	22.44	394.62	394.79	23.09
361.46	361.63	21.15	372.57	372.74	21.80	383.68	383.85	22.45	394.79	394.96	23.10
361.63	361.80	21.16	372.74	372.91	21.81	383.85	384.02	22.46	394.96	395.13	23.11
361.80	361.97	21.17	372.91	373.08	21.82	384.02	384.19	22.47	395.13	395.30	23.12
361.97	362.14	21.18	373.08	373.25	21.83	384.19	384.36	22.48	395.30	395.48	23.13
362.14	362.31	21.19	373.25	373.42	21.84	384.36	384.53	22.49	395.48	395.65	23.14
362.31	362.48	21.20	373.42	373.59	21.85	384.53	384.71	22.50	395.65	395.82	23.15
362.48	362.65	21.21	373.59	373.77	21.86	384.71	384.88	22.51	395.82	395.99	23.16
362.65	362.83	21.22	373.77	373.94	21.87	384.88	385.05	22.52	395.99	396.16	23.17
362.83	363.00	21.23	373.94	374.11	21.88	385.05	385.22	22.53	396.16	396.33	23.18
363.00	363.17	21.24	374.11	374.28	21.89	385.22	385.39	22.54	396.33	396.50	23.19
363.17	363.34	21.25	374.28	374.45	21.90	385.39	385.56	22.55	396.50	396.67	23.20
363.34	363.51	21.26	374.45	374.62	21.91	385.56	385.73	22.56	396.67	396.84	23.21
363.51	363.68	21.27	374.62	374.79	21.92	385.73	385.90	22.57	396.84	397.01	23.22
363.68	363.85	21.28	374.79	374.96	21.93	385.90	386.07	22.58	397.01	397.18	23.23
363.85	364.02	21.29	374.96	375.13	21.94	386.07	386.24	22.59	397.18	397.36	23.24
364.02	364.19	21.30	375.13	375.30	21.95	386.24	386.42	22.60	397.36	397.53	23.25
364.19	364.36	21.31	375.30	375.48	21.96	386.42	386.59	22.61	397.53	397.70	23.26
364.36	364.53	21.32	375.48	375.65	21.97	386.59	386.76	22.62	397.70	397.87	23.27
364.53	364.71	21.33	375.65	375.82	21.98	386.76	386.93	22.63	397.87	398.04	23.28
364.71	364.88	21.34	375.82	375.99	21.99	386.93	387.10	22.64	398.04	398.21	23.29
364.88	365.05	21.35	375.99	376.16	22.00	387.10	387.27	22.65	398.21	398.38	23.30
365.05	365.22	21.36	376.16	376.33	22.01	387.27	387.44	22.66	398.38	398.55	23.31
365.22	365.39	21.37	376.33	376.50	22.02	387.44	387.61	22.67	398.55	398.72	23.32
365.39	365.56	21.38	376.50	376.67	22.03	387.61	387.78	22.68	398.72	398.89	23.33
365.56	365.73	21.39	376.67	376.84	22.04	387.78	387.95	22.69	398.89	399.06	23.34
365.73	365.90	21.40	376.84	377.01	22.05	387.95	388.12	22.70	399.06 and over		
365.90	366.07	21.41	377.01	377.18	22.06	388.12	388.30	22.71	5.85% of wages		
366.07	366.24	21.42	377.18	377.36	22.07	388.30	388.47	22.72			
366.24	366.42	21.43	377.36	377.53	22.08	388.47	388.64	22.73			
366.42	366.59	21.44	377.53	377.70	22.09	388.64	388.81	22.74			

Federal Income Tax Tables

SINGLE Persons—WEEKLY Payroll Period

And the wages are—		And the number of withholding allowances claimed is—									
At least	But less than	0	1	2	3	4	5	6	7	8	9	10 or more
		The amount of income tax to be withheld shall be—										
$80	$82	$12.00	$9.10	$6.50	$3.90	$1.80	$0	$0	$0	$0	$0	$0
82	84	12.40	9.50	6.90	4.30	2.10	0	0	0	0	0	0
84	86	12.80	9.80	7.20	4.60	2.30	.30	0	0	0	0	0
86	88	13.20	10.20	7.60	5.00	2.60	.60	0	0	0	0	0
88	90	13.60	10.60	8.00	5.40	2.90	.90	0	0	0	0	0
90	92	14.10	11.00	8.30	5.70	3.20	1.20	0	0	0	0	0
92	94	14.50	11.40	8.70	6.10	3.50	1.40	0	0	0	0	0
94	96	14.90	11.90	9.00	6.40	3.90	1.70	0	0	0	0	0
96	98	15.30	12.30	9.40	6.80	4.20	2.00	0	0	0	0	0
98	100	15.70	12.70	9.80	7.20	4.60	2.30	.30	0	0	0	0
100	105	16.50	13.40	10.40	7.80	5.20	2.80	.80	0	0	0	0
105	110	17.50	14.50	11.50	8.70	6.10	3.50	1.50	0	0	0	0
110	115	18.60	15.50	12.50	9.60	7.00	4.40	2.20	.10	0	0	0
115	120	19.60	16.60	13.60	10.50	7.90	5.30	2.90	.80	0	0	0
120	125	20.70	17.60	14.60	11.60	8.80	6.20	3.60	1.50	0	0	0
125	130	21.70	18.70	15.70	12.60	9.70	7.10	4.50	2.20	.20	0	0
130	135	22.80	19.70	16.70	13.70	10.70	8.00	5.40	2.90	.90	0	0
135	140	23.80	20.80	17.80	14.70	11.70	8.90	6.30	3.70	1.60	0	0
140	145	24.90	21.80	18.80	15.80	12.80	9.80	7.20	4.60	2.30	.30	0
145	150	25.90	22.90	19.90	16.80	13.80	10.80	8.10	5.50	3.00	1.00	0
150	160	27.50	24.50	21.40	18.40	15.40	12.30	9.50	6.90	4.30	2.00	0
160	170	29.60	26.60	23.50	20.50	17.50	14.40	11.40	8.70	6.10	3.50	1.40
170	180	31.70	28.70	25.60	22.60	19.60	16.50	13.50	10.50	7.90	5.30	2.80
180	190	33.80	30.80	27.70	24.70	21.70	18.60	15.60	12.60	9.70	7.10	4.50
190	200	35.90	32.90	29.80	26.80	23.80	20.70	17.70	14.70	11.70	8.90	6.30
200	210	38.10	35.00	31.90	28.90	25.90	22.80	19.80	16.80	13.80	10.70	8.10
210	220	40.40	37.10	34.00	31.00	28.00	24.90	21.90	18.90	15.90	12.80	9.90
220	230	42.70	39.30	36.10	33.10	30.10	27.00	24.00	21.00	18.00	14.90	11.90
230	240	45.10	41.60	38.30	35.20	32.20	29.10	26.10	23.10	20.10	17.00	14.00
240	250	47.80	43.90	40.60	37.30	34.30	31.20	28.20	25.20	22.20	19.10	16.10
250	260	50.50	46.60	42.90	39.60	36.40	33.30	30.30	27.30	24.30	21.20	18.20
260	270	53.20	49.30	45.40	41.90	38.60	35.40	32.40	29.40	26.40	23.30	20.30
270	280	56.20	52.00	48.10	44.20	40.90	37.60	34.50	31.50	28.50	25.40	22.40
280	290	59.30	54.80	50.80	46.90	43.20	39.90	36.60	33.60	30.60	27.50	24.50
290	300	62.40	57.90	53.50	49.60	45.70	42.20	38.90	35.70	32.70	29.60	26.60
300	310	65.50	61.00	56.50	52.30	48.40	44.60	41.20	37.80	34.80	31.70	28.70
310	320	68.60	64.10	59.60	55.10	51.10	47.30	43.50	40.10	36.90	33.80	30.80
320	330	71.70	67.20	62.70	58.20	53.80	50.00	46.10	42.40	39.10	35.90	32.90
330	340	74.80	70.30	65.80	61.30	56.90	52.70	48.80	44.90	41.40	38.10	35.00
340	350	78.30	73.40	68.90	64.40	60.00	55.50	51.50	47.60	43.70	40.40	37.10
350	360	81.80	76.80	72.00	67.50	63.10	58.60	54.20	50.30	46.40	42.70	39.40
360	370	85.30	80.30	75.30	70.60	66.20	61.70	57.20	53.00	49.10	45.20	41.70
370	380	88.80	83.80	78.80	73.70	69.30	64.80	60.30	55.90	51.80	47.90	44.00
380	390	92.30	87.30	82.30	77.20	72.40	67.90	63.40	59.00	54.50	50.60	46.70
390	400	95.80	90.80	85.80	80.70	75.70	71.00	66.50	62.10	57.60	53.30	49.40
400	410	99.30	94.30	89.30	84.20	79.20	74.10	69.60	65.20	60.70	56.20	52.10
410	420	102.80	97.80	92.80	87.70	82.70	77.60	72.70	68.30	63.80	59.30	54.80
420	430	106.30	101.30	96.30	91.20	86.20	81.10	76.10	71.40	66.90	62.40	57.90
430	440	109.80	104.80	99.80	94.70	89.70	84.60	79.60	74.50	70.00	65.50	61.00
440	450	113.30	108.30	103.30	98.20	93.20	88.10	83.10	78.00	73.10	68.60	64.10
450	460	116.80	111.80	106.80	101.70	96.70	91.60	86.60	81.50	76.50	71.70	67.20
460	470	120.30	115.30	110.30	105.20	100.20	95.10	90.10	85.00	80.00	74.90	70.30
470	480	123.80	118.80	113.80	108.70	103.70	98.60	93.60	88.50	83.50	78.40	73.40
480	490	127.30	122.30	117.30	112.20	107.20	102.10	97.10	92.00	87.00	81.90	76.90
		35 percent of the excess over $490 plus—										
$490 and over		129.10	124.00	119.00	114.00	108.90	103.90	98.80	93.80	88.70	83.70	78.60

MARRIED Persons—WEEKLY Payroll Period

And the wages are—		And the number of withholding allowances claimed is—										
At least	But less than	0	1	2	3	4	5	6	7	8	9	10 or more
		The amount of income tax to be withheld shall be—										
$0	$11	$0	$0	$0	$0	$0	$0	$0	$0	$0	$0	$0
11	12	.10	0	0	0	0	0	0	0	0	0	0
12	13	.30	0	0	0	0	0	0	0	0	0	0
13	14	.40	0	0	0	0	0	0	0	0	0	0
14	15	.50	0	0	0	0	0	0	0	0	0	0
15	16	.70	0	0	0	0	0	0	0	0	0	0
16	17	.80	0	0	0	0	0	0	0	0	0	0
17	18	1.00	0	0	0	0	0	0	0	0	0	0
18	19	1.10	0	0	0	0	0	0	0	0	0	0
19	20	1.20	0	0	0	0	0	0	0	0	0	0
20	21	1.40	0	0	0	0	0	0	0	0	0	0
21	22	1.50	0	0	0	0	0	0	0	0	0	0
22	23	1.70	0	0	0	0	0	0	0	0	0	0
23	24	1.80	0	0	0	0	0	0	0	0	0	0
24	25	1.90	0	0	0	0	0	0	0	0	0	0
25	26	2.10	.10	0	0	0	0	0	0	0	0	0
26	27	2.20	.20	0	0	0	0	0	0	0	0	0
27	28	2.40	.40	0	0	0	0	0	0	0	0	0
28	29	2.50	.50	0	0	0	0	0	0	0	0	0
29	30	2.60	.60	0	0	0	0	0	0	0	0	0
30	31	2.80	.80	0	0	0	0	0	0	0	0	0
31	32	2.90	.90	0	0	0	0	0	0	0	0	0
32	33	3.10	1.10	0	0	0	0	0	0	0	0	0
33	34	3.20	1.20	0	0	0	0	0	0	0	0	0
34	35	3.30	1.30	0	0	0	0	0	0	0	0	0
35	36	3.50	1.50	0	0	0	0	0	0	0	0	0
36	37	3.60	1.60	0	0	0	0	0	0	0	0	0
37	38	3.80	1.80	0	0	0	0	0	0	0	0	0
38	39	3.90	1.90	0	0	0	0	0	0	0	0	0
39	40	4.10	2.00	0	0	0	0	0	0	0	0	0
40	41	4.20	2.20	.20	0	0	0	0	0	0	0	0
41	42	4.40	2.30	.30	0	0	0	0	0	0	0	0
42	43	4.50	2.50	.40	0	0	0	0	0	0	0	0
43	44	4.70	2.60	.60	0	0	0	0	0	0	0	0
44	45	4.90	2.70	.70	0	0	0	0	0	0	0	0
45	46	5.00	2.90	.90	0	0	0	0	0	0	0	0
46	47	5.20	3.00	1.00	0	0	0	0	0	0	0	0
47	48	5.30	3.20	1.10	0	0	0	0	0	0	0	0
48	49	5.50	3.30	1.30	0	0	0	0	0	0	0	0
49	50	5.70	3.40	1.40	0	0	0	0	0	0	0	0
50	51	5.80	3.60	1.60	0	0	0	0	0	0	0	0
51	52	6.00	3.70	1.70	0	0	0	0	0	0	0	0
52	53	6.10	3.90	1.80	0	0	0	0	0	0	0	0
53	54	6.30	4.00	2.00	0	0	0	0	0	0	0	0
54	55	6.50	4.10	2.10	.10	0	0	0	0	0	0	0
55	56	6.60	4.30	2.30	.20	0	0	0	0	0	0	0
56	57	6.80	4.50	2.40	.40	0	0	0	0	0	0	0
57	58	6.90	4.60	2.50	.50	0	0	0	0	0	0	0
58	59	7.10	4.80	2.70	.70	0	0	0	0	0	0	0
59	60	7.30	4.90	2.80	.80	0	0	0	0	0	0	0
60	62	7.50	5.20	3.00	1.00	0	0	0	0	0	0	0
62	64	7.80	5.50	3.30	1.30	0	0	0	0	0	0	0
64	66	8.10	5.80	3.60	1.60	0	0	0	0	0	0	0
66	68	8.50	6.10	3.90	1.80	0	0	0	0	0	0	0
68	70	8.80	6.50	4.20	2.10	.10	0	0	0	0	0	0
70	72	9.10	6.80	4.50	2.40	.40	0	0	0	0	0	0
72	74	9.40	7.10	4.80	2.70	.70	0	0	0	0	0	0
74	76	9.70	7.40	5.10	3.00	.90	0	0	0	0	0	0
76	78	10.10	7.70	5.40	3.20	1.20	0	0	0	0	0	0
78	80	10.40	8.10	5.80	3.50	1.50	0	0	0	0	0	0
80	82	10.70	8.40	6.10	3.80	1.80	0	0	0	0	0	0
82	84	11.00	8.70	6.40	4.10	2.10	0	0	0	0	0	0
84	86	11.30	9.00	6.70	4.40	2.30	.30	0	0	0	0	0
86	88	11.70	9.30	7.00	4.70	2.60	.60	0	0	0	0	0
88	90	12.00	9.70	7.40	5.00	2.90	.90	0	0	0	0	0
90	92	12.30	10.00	7.70	5.40	3.20	1.20	0	0	0	0	0
92	94	12.60	10.30	8.00	5.70	3.50	1.40	0	0	0	0	0
94	96	12.90	10.60	8.30	6.00	3.70	1.70	0	0	0	0	0
96	98	13.30	10.90	8.60	6.30	4.00	2.00	0	0	0	0	0
98	100	13.60	11.30	9.00	6.60	4.30	2.30	.30	0	0	0	0

(Continued on next page)

MARRIED Persons—WEEKLY Payroll Period

And the wages are—		And the number of withholding allowances claimed is—										
At least	But less than	0	1	2	3	4	5	6	7	8	9	10 or more
		The amount of income tax to be withheld shall be—										
$100	$105	$14.10	$11.80	$9.50	$7.20	$4.90	$2.80	$.80	$0	$0	$0	$0
105	110	14.90	12.60	10.30	8.00	5.70	3.50	1.50	0	0	0	0
110	115	15.70	13.40	11.10	8.80	6.50	4.20	2.20	.10	0	0	0
115	120	16.50	14.20	11.90	9.60	7.30	5.00	2.90	.80	0	0	0
120	125	17.30	15.00	12.70	10.40	8.10	5.80	3.60	1.50	0	0	0
125	130	18.10	15.80	13.50	11.20	8.90	6.60	4.30	2.20	.20	0	0
130	135	18.90	16.60	14.30	12.00	9.70	7.40	5.10	2.90	.90	0	0
135	140	19.70	17.40	15.10	12.80	10.50	8.20	5.90	3.60	1.60	0	0
140	145	20.50	18.20	15.90	13.60	11.30	9.00	6.70	4.40	2.30	.30	0
145	150	21.30	19.00	16.70	14.40	12.10	9.80	7.50	5.20	3.00	1.00	0
150	160	22.50	20.20	17.90	15.60	13.30	11.00	8.70	6.40	4.10	2.00	0
160	170	24.10	21.80	19.50	17.20	14.90	12.60	10.30	8.00	5.70	3.40	1.40
170	180	26.00	23.40	21.10	18.80	16.50	14.20	11.90	9.60	7.30	5.00	2.80
180	190	28.00	25.20	22.70	20.40	18.10	15.80	13.50	11.20	8.90	6.60	4.30
190	200	30.00	27.20	24.30	22.00	19.70	17.40	15.10	12.80	10.50	8.20	5.90
200	210	32.00	29.20	26.30	23.60	21.30	19.00	16.70	14.40	12.10	9.80	7.50
210	220	34.40	31.20	28.30	25.40	22.90	20.60	18.30	16.00	13.70	11.40	9.10
220	230	36.80	33.30	30.30	27.40	24.50	22.20	19.90	17.60	15.30	13.00	10.70
230	240	39.20	35.70	32.30	29.40	26.50	23.80	21.50	19.20	16.90	14.60	12.30
240	250	41.60	38.10	34.60	31.40	28.50	25.60	23.10	20.80	18.50	16.20	13.90
250	260	44.00	40.50	37.00	33.60	30.50	27.60	24.70	22.40	20.10	17.80	15.50
260	270	46.40	42.90	39.40	36.00	32.50	29.60	26.70	24.00	21.70	19.40	17.10
270	280	48.80	45.30	41.80	38.40	34.90	31.60	28.70	25.80	23.30	21.00	18.70
280	290	51.20	47.70	44.20	40.80	37.30	33.90	30.70	27.80	25.00	22.60	20.30
290	300	53.60	50.10	46.60	43.20	39.70	36.30	32.80	29.80	27.00	24.20	21.90
300	310	56.00	52.50	49.00	45.60	42.10	38.70	35.20	31.80	29.00	26.10	23.50
310	320	58.40	54.90	51.40	48.00	44.50	41.10	37.60	34.10	31.00	28.10	25.20
320	330	60.80	57.30	53.80	50.40	46.90	43.50	40.00	36.50	33.10	30.10	27.20
330	340	63.60	59.70	56.20	52.80	49.30	45.90	42.40	38.90	35.50	32.10	29.20
340	350	66.40	62.40	58.60	55.20	51.70	48.30	44.80	41.30	37.90	34.40	31.20
350	360	69.20	65.20	61.10	57.60	54.10	50.70	47.20	43.70	40.30	36.80	33.40
360	370	72.00	68.00	63.90	60.00	56.50	53.10	49.60	46.10	42.70	39.20	35.80
370	380	74.80	70.80	66.70	62.70	58.90	55.50	52.00	48.50	45.10	41.60	38.20
380	390	77.60	73.60	69.50	65.50	61.50	57.90	54.40	50.90	47.50	44.00	40.60
390	400	80.40	76.40	72.30	68.30	64.30	60.30	56.80	53.30	49.90	46.40	43.00
400	410	83.20	79.20	75.10	71.10	67.10	63.00	59.20	55.70	52.30	48.80	45.40
410	420	86.30	82.00	77.90	73.90	69.90	65.80	61.80	58.10	54.70	51.20	47.80
420	430	89.50	84.80	80.70	76.70	72.70	68.60	64.60	60.50	57.10	53.60	50.20
430	440	92.70	88.00	83.50	79.50	75.50	71.40	67.40	63.30	59.50	56.00	52.60
440	450	95.90	91.20	86.60	82.30	78.30	74.20	70.20	66.10	62.10	58.40	55.00
450	460	99.10	94.40	89.80	85.20	81.10	77.00	73.00	68.90	64.90	60.90	57.40
460	470	102.30	97.60	93.00	88.40	83.90	79.80	75.80	71.70	67.70	63.70	59.80
470	480	105.50	100.80	96.20	91.60	87.00	82.60	78.60	74.50	70.50	66.50	62.40
480	490	108.70	104.00	99.40	94.80	90.20	85.60	81.40	77.30	73.30	69.30	65.20
490	500	112.20	107.20	102.60	98.00	93.40	88.80	84.20	80.10	76.10	72.10	68.00
500	510	115.80	110.60	105.80	101.20	96.60	92.00	87.40	82.90	78.90	74.90	70.80
510	520	119.40	114.20	109.10	104.40	99.80	95.20	90.60	86.00	81.70	77.70	73.60
520	530	123.00	117.80	112.70	107.60	103.00	98.40	93.80	89.20	84.50	80.50	76.40
530	540	126.60	121.40	116.30	111.10	106.20	101.60	97.00	92.40	87.70	83.30	79.20
540	550	130.20	125.00	119.90	114.70	109.50	104.80	100.20	95.60	90.90	86.30	82.00
550	560	133.80	128.60	123.50	118.30	113.10	108.00	103.40	98.80	94.10	89.50	84.90
560	570	137.40	132.20	127.10	121.90	116.70	111.50	106.60	102.00	97.30	92.70	88.10
570	580	141.00	135.80	130.70	125.50	120.30	115.10	109.90	105.20	100.50	95.90	91.30
580	590	144.60	139.40	134.30	129.10	123.90	118.70	113.50	108.40	103.70	99.10	94.50
590	600	148.20	143.00	137.90	132.70	127.50	122.30	117.10	111.90	106.90	102.30	97.70
600	610	151.80	146.60	141.50	136.30	131.10	125.90	120.70	115.50	110.30	105.50	100.90
610	620	155.40	150.20	145.10	139.90	134.70	129.50	124.30	119.10	113.90	108.70	104.10
620	630	159.00	153.80	148.70	143.50	138.30	133.10	127.90	122.70	117.50	112.30	107.30
630	640	162.60	157.40	152.30	147.10	141.90	136.70	131.50	126.30	121.10	115.90	110.70
		36 percent of the excess over $640 plus—										
$640 and over		164.40	159.20	154.10	148.90	143.70	138.50	133.30	128.10	122.90	117.70	112.50

MARRIED Persons—BIWEEKLY Payroll Period

And the wages are—		And the number of withholding allowances claimed is—										
At least	But less than	0	1	2	3	4	5	6	7	8	9	10 or more
		The amount of income tax to be withheld shall be—										
$200	$210	$28.30	$23.60	$19.00	$14.40	$9.80	$5.50	$1.50	$0	$0	$0	$0
210	220	29.90	25.20	20.60	16.00	11.40	6.90	2.90	0	0	0	0
220	230	31.50	26.80	22.20	17.60	13.00	8.40	4.30	.30	0	0	0
230	240	33.10	28.40	23.80	19.20	14.60	10.00	5.70	1.70	0	0	0
240	250	34.70	30.00	25.40	20.80	16.20	11.60	7.10	3.10	0	0	0
250	260	36.30	31.60	27.00	22.40	17.80	13.20	8.60	4.50	.40	0	0
260	270	37.90	33.20	28.60	24.00	19.40	14.80	10.20	5.90	1.80	0	0
270	280	39.50	34.80	30.20	25.60	21.00	16.40	11.80	7.30	3.20	0	0
280	290	41.10	36.40	31.80	27.20	22.60	18.00	13.40	8.80	4.60	.60	0
290	300	42.70	38.00	33.40	28.80	24.20	19.60	15.00	10.40	6.00	2.00	0
300	320	45.10	40.40	35.80	31.20	26.60	22.00	17.40	12.80	8.10	4.10	.10
320	340	48.30	43.60	39.00	34.40	29.80	25.20	20.60	16.00	11.30	6.90	2.90
340	360	52.10	46.80	42.20	37.60	33.00	28.40	23.80	19.20	14.50	9.90	5.70
360	380	56.10	50.30	45.40	40.80	36.20	31.60	27.00	22.40	17.70	13.10	8.50
380	400	60.10	54.30	48.60	44.00	39.40	34.80	30.20	25.60	20.90	16.30	11.70
400	420	64.10	58.30	52.50	47.20	42.60	38.00	33.40	28.80	24.10	19.50	14.90
420	440	68.70	62.30	56.50	50.80	45.80	41.20	36.60	32.00	27.30	22.70	18.10
440	460	73.50	66.60	60.50	54.80	49.00	44.40	39.80	35.20	30.50	25.90	21.30
460	480	78.30	71.40	64.50	58.80	53.00	47.60	43.00	38.40	33.70	29.10	24.50
480	500	83.10	76.20	69.30	62.80	57.00	51.20	46.20	41.60	36.90	32.30	27.70
500	520	87.90	81.00	74.10	67.20	61.00	55.20	49.50	44.80	40.10	35.50	30.90
520	540	92.70	85.80	78.90	72.00	65.00	59.20	53.50	48.00	43.30	38.70	34.10
540	560	97.50	90.60	83.70	76.80	69.80	63.20	57.50	51.70	46.50	41.90	37.30
560	580	102.30	95.40	88.50	81.60	74.60	67.70	61.50	55.70	49.90	45.10	40.50
580	600	107.10	100.20	93.30	86.40	79.40	72.50	65.60	59.70	53.90	48.30	43.70
600	620	111.90	105.00	98.10	91.20	84.20	77.30	70.40	63.70	57.90	52.20	46.90
620	640	116.70	109.80	102.90	96.00	89.00	82.10	75.20	68.30	61.90	56.20	50.40
640	660	121.60	114.60	107.70	100.80	93.80	86.90	80.00	73.10	66.20	60.20	54.40
660	680	127.20	119.40	112.50	105.60	98.60	91.70	84.80	77.90	71.00	64.20	58.40
680	700	132.80	124.70	117.30	110.40	103.40	96.50	89.60	82.70	75.80	68.80	62.40
700	720	138.40	130.30	122.30	115.20	108.20	101.30	94.40	87.50	80.60	73.60	66.70
720	740	144.00	135.90	127.90	120.00	113.00	106.10	99.20	92.30	85.40	78.40	71.50
740	760	149.60	141.50	133.50	125.40	117.80	110.90	104.00	97.10	90.20	83.20	76.30
760	780	155.20	147.10	139.10	131.00	122.90	115.70	108.80	101.90	95.00	88.00	81.10
780	800	160.80	152.70	144.70	136.60	128.50	120.50	113.60	106.70	99.80	92.80	85.90
800	820	166.40	158.30	150.30	142.20	134.10	126.00	118.40	111.50	104.60	97.60	90.70
820	840	172.50	163.90	155.90	147.80	139.70	131.60	123.60	116.30	109.40	102.40	95.50
840	860	178.90	169.70	161.50	153.40	145.30	137.20	129.20	121.10	114.20	107.20	100.30
860	880	185.30	176.10	167.10	159.00	150.90	142.80	134.80	126.70	119.00	112.00	105.10
880	900	191.70	182.50	173.30	164.60	156.50	148.40	140.40	132.30	124.20	116.80	109.90
900	920	198.10	188.90	179.70	170.40	162.10	154.00	146.00	137.90	129.80	121.70	114.70
920	940	204.50	195.30	186.10	176.80	167.70	159.60	151.60	143.50	135.40	127.30	119.50
940	960	210.90	201.70	192.50	183.20	174.00	165.20	157.20	149.10	141.00	132.90	124.80
960	980	217.30	208.10	198.90	189.60	180.40	171.20	162.80	154.70	146.60	138.50	130.40
980	1,000	224.50	214.50	205.30	196.00	186.80	177.60	168.40	160.30	152.20	144.10	136.00
1,000	1,020	231.70	221.30	211.70	202.40	193.20	184.00	174.70	165.90	157.80	149.70	141.60
1,020	1,040	238.90	228.50	218.10	208.80	199.60	190.40	181.10	171.90	163.40	155.30	147.20
1,040	1,060	246.10	235.70	225.30	215.20	206.00	196.80	187.50	178.30	169.10	160.90	152.80
1,060	1,080	253.30	242.90	232.50	222.10	212.40	203.20	193.90	184.70	175.50	166.50	158.40
1,080	1,100	260.50	250.10	239.70	229.30	218.90	209.60	200.30	191.10	181.90	172.60	164.00
1,100	1,120	267.70	257.30	246.90	236.50	226.10	216.00	206.70	197.50	188.30	179.00	169.80
1,120	1,140	274.90	264.50	254.10	243.70	233.30	223.00	213.10	203.90	194.70	185.40	176.20
1,140	1,160	282.10	271.70	261.30	250.90	240.50	230.20	219.80	210.30	201.10	191.80	182.60
1,160	1,180	289.30	278.90	268.50	258.10	247.70	237.40	227.00	216.70	207.50	198.20	189.00
1,180	1,200	296.50	286.10	275.70	265.30	254.90	244.60	234.20	223.80	213.90	204.60	195.40
1,200	1,220	303.70	293.30	282.90	272.50	262.10	251.80	241.40	231.00	220.60	211.00	201.80
1,220	1,240	310.90	300.50	290.10	279.70	269.30	259.00	248.60	238.20	227.80	217.40	208.20
1,240	1,260	318.10	307.70	297.30	286.90	276.50	266.20	255.80	245.40	235.00	224.60	214.60
1,260	1,280	325.30	314.90	304.50	294.10	283.70	273.40	263.00	252.60	242.20	231.80	221.40
		36 percent of the excess over $1,280 plus—										
$1,280 and over		328.90	318.50	308.10	297.70	287.30	277.00	266.60	256.20	245.80	235.40	225.00

SINGLE Persons—SEMIMONTHLY Payroll Period

And the wages are—		And the number of withholding allowances claimed is—										
At least	But less than	0	1	2	3	4	5	6	7	8	9	10 or more
		The amount of income tax to be withheld shall be—										
$0	$24	$0	$0	$0	$0	$0	$0	$0	$0	$0	$0	$0
24	26	.30	0	0	0	0	0	0	0	0	0	0
26	28	.60	0	0	0	0	0	0	0	0	0	0
28	30	.90	0	0	0	0	0	0	0	0	0	0
30	32	1.10	0	0	0	0	0	0	0	0	0	0
32	34	1.40	0	0	0	0	0	0	0	0	0	0
34	36	1.70	0	0	0	0	0	0	0	0	0	0
36	38	2.00	0	0	0	0	0	0	0	0	0	0
38	40	2.30	0	0	0	0	0	0	0	0	0	0
40	42	2.50	0	0	0	0	0	0	0	0	0	0
42	44	2.80	0	0	0	0	0	0	0	0	0	0
44	46	3.10	0	0	0	0	0	0	0	0	0	0
46	48	3.40	0	0	0	0	0	0	0	0	0	0
48	50	3.70	0	0	0	0	0	0	0	0	0	0
50	52	3.90	0	0	0	0	0	0	0	0	0	0
52	54	4.20	0	0	0	0	0	0	0	0	0	0
54	56	4.50	.10	0	0	0	0	0	0	0	0	0
56	58	4.80	.40	0	0	0	0	0	0	0	0	0
58	60	5.10	.70	0	0	0	0	0	0	0	0	0
60	62	5.30	1.00	0	0	0	0	0	0	0	0	0
62	64	5.60	1.20	0	0	0	0	0	0	0	0	0
64	66	5.90	1.50	0	0	0	0	0	0	0	0	0
66	68	6.20	1.80	0	0	0	0	0	0	0	0	0
68	70	6.50	2.10	0	0	0	0	0	0	0	0	0
70	72	6.70	2.40	0	0	0	0	0	0	0	0	0
72	74	7.00	2.60	0	0	0	0	0	0	0	0	0
74	76	7.30	2.90	0	0	0	0	0	0	0	0	0
76	78	7.70	3.20	0	0	0	0	0	0	0	0	0
78	80	8.00	3.50	0	0	0	0	0	0	0	0	0
80	82	8.40	3.80	0	0	0	0	0	0	0	0	0
82	84	8.70	4.00	0	0	0	0	0	0	0	0	0
84	86	9.10	4.30	0	0	0	0	0	0	0	0	0
86	88	9.50	4.60	.20	0	0	0	0	0	0	0	0
88	90	9.80	4.90	.50	0	0	0	0	0	0	0	0
90	92	10.20	5.20	.80	0	0	0	0	0	0	0	0
92	94	10.50	5.40	1.10	0	0	0	0	0	0	0	0
94	96	10.90	5.70	1.30	0	0	0	0	0	0	0	0
96	98	11.30	6.00	1.60	0	0	0	0	0	0	0	0
98	100	11.60	6.30	1.90	0	0	0	0	0	0	0	0
100	102	12.00	6.60	2.20	0	0	0	0	0	0	0	0
102	104	12.30	6.80	2.50	0	0	0	0	0	0	0	0
104	106	12.70	7.10	2.70	0	0	0	0	0	0	0	0
106	108	13.10	7.40	3.00	0	0	0	0	0	0	0	0
108	110	13.40	7.80	3.30	0	0	0	0	0	0	0	0
110	112	13.80	8.10	3.60	0	0	0	0	0	0	0	0
112	114	14.10	8.50	3.90	0	0	0	0	0	0	0	0
114	116	14.50	8.90	4.10	0	0	0	0	0	0	0	0
116	118	14.90	9.20	4.40	0	0	0	0	0	0	0	0
118	120	15.20	9.60	4.70	.30	0	0	0	0	0	0	0
120	124	15.80	10.10	5.10	.70	0	0	0	0	0	0	0
124	128	16.50	10.80	5.70	1.30	0	0	0	0	0	0	0
128	132	17.20	11.60	6.20	1.90	0	0	0	0	0	0	0
132	136	17.90	12.30	6.80	2.40	0	0	0	0	0	0	0
136	140	18.60	13.00	7.40	3.00	0	0	0	0	0	0	0
140	144	19.40	13.70	8.10	3.50	0	0	0	0	0	0	0
144	148	20.10	14.40	8.80	4.10	0	0	0	0	0	0	0
148	152	20.80	15.20	9.50	4.70	.30	0	0	0	0	0	0
152	156	21.50	15.90	10.30	5.20	.90	0	0	0	0	0	0
156	160	22.20	16.60	11.00	5.80	1.40	0	0	0	0	0	0
160	164	23.10	17.30	11.70	6.30	2.00	0	0	0	0	0	0
164	168	23.90	18.00	12.40	6.90	2.50	0	0	0	0	0	0
168	172	24.70	18.80	13.10	7.50	3.10	0	0	0	0	0	0
172	176	25.60	19.50	13.90	8.20	3.70	0	0	0	0	0	0
176	180	26.40	20.20	14.60	9.00	4.20	0	0	0	0	0	0
180	184	27.30	20.90	15.30	9.70	4.80	.40	0	0	0	0	0

(Continued on next page)

SINGLE Persons—SEMIMONTHLY Payroll Period

And the wages are—		And the number of withholding allowances claimed is—										
At least	But less than	0	1	2	3	4	5	6	7	8	9	10 or more
		The amount of income tax to be withheld shall be—										
$184	$188	$28.10	$21.60	$16.00	$10.40	$5.30	$1.00	$0	$0	$0	$0	$0
188	192	28.90	22.40	16.70	11.10	5.90	1.50	0	0	0	0	0
192	196	29.80	23.20	17.50	11.80	6.50	2.10	0	0	0	0	0
196	200	30.60	24.10	18.20	12.60	7.00	2.60	0	0	0	0	0
200	210	32.10	25.50	19.40	13.80	8.20	3.60	0	0	0	0	0
210	220	34.20	27.60	21.20	15.60	10.00	5.00	.60	0	0	0	0
220	230	36.30	29.70	23.20	17.40	11.80	6.40	2.00	0	0	0	0
230	240	38.40	31.80	25.30	19.20	13.60	8.00	3.40	0	0	0	0
240	250	40.50	33.90	27.40	21.00	15.40	9.80	4.80	.50	0	0	0
250	260	42.60	36.00	29.50	22.90	17.20	11.60	6.20	1.90	0	0	0
260	270	44.70	38.10	31.60	25.00	19.00	13.40	7.70	3.30	0	0	0
270	280	46.80	40.20	33.70	27.10	20.80	15.20	9.50	4.70	.30	0	0
280	290	48.90	42.30	35.80	29.20	22.60	17.00	11.30	6.10	1.70	0	0
290	300	51.00	44.40	37.90	31.30	24.70	18.80	13.10	7.50	3.10	0	0
300	320	54.10	47.60	41.00	34.50	27.90	21.50	15.80	10.20	5.20	.80	0
320	340	58.30	51.80	45.20	38.70	32.10	25.50	19.40	13.80	8.20	3.60	0
340	360	62.50	56.00	49.40	42.90	36.30	29.70	23.20	17.40	11.80	6.40	2.00
360	380	66.70	60.20	53.60	47.10	40.50	33.90	27.40	21.00	15.40	9.80	4.80
380	400	70.90	64.40	57.80	51.30	44.70	38.10	31.60	25.00	19.00	13.40	7.70
400	420	75.10	68.60	62.00	55.50	48.90	42.30	35.80	29.20	22.60	17.00	11.30
420	440	79.30	72.80	66.20	59.70	53.10	46.50	40.00	33.40	26.80	20.60	14.90
440	460	83.80	77.00	70.40	63.90	57.30	50.70	44.20	37.60	31.00	24.50	18.50
460	480	88.40	81.20	74.60	68.10	61.50	54.90	48.40	41.80	35.20	28.70	22.10
480	500	93.00	85.80	78.80	72.30	65.70	59.10	52.60	46.00	39.40	32.90	26.30
500	520	98.00	90.40	83.20	76.50	69.90	63.30	56.80	50.20	43.60	37.10	30.50
520	540	103.40	95.00	87.80	80.70	74.10	67.50	61.00	54.40	47.80	41.30	34.70
540	560	108.80	100.40	92.40	85.20	78.30	71.70	65.20	58.60	52.00	45.50	38.90
560	580	114.20	105.80	97.30	89.80	82.60	75.90	69.40	62.80	56.20	49.70	43.10
580	600	119.90	111.20	102.70	94.40	87.20	80.10	73.60	67.00	60.40	53.90	47.30
600	620	126.10	116.60	108.10	99.70	91.80	84.70	77.80	71.20	64.60	58.10	51.50
620	640	132.30	122.60	113.50	105.10	96.60	89.30	82.10	75.40	68.80	62.30	55.70
640	660	138.50	128.80	119.10	110.50	102.00	93.90	86.70	79.60	73.00	66.50	59.90
660	680	144.70	135.00	125.30	115.90	107.40	99.00	91.30	84.10	77.20	70.70	64.10
680	700	150.90	141.20	131.50	121.80	112.80	104.40	96.00	88.70	81.50	74.90	68.30
700	720	157.10	147.40	137.70	128.00	118.30	109.80	101.40	93.30	86.10	79.10	72.50
720	740	163.60	153.60	143.90	134.20	124.50	115.20	106.80	98.30	90.70	83.50	76.70
740	760	170.60	159.80	150.10	140.40	130.70	121.00	112.20	103.70	95.30	88.10	80.90
760	780	177.60	166.70	156.30	146.60	136.90	127.20	117.60	109.10	100.70	92.70	85.50
780	800	184.60	173.70	162.80	152.80	143.10	133.40	123.70	114.50	106.10	97.70	90.10
800	820	191.60	180.70	169.80	159.00	149.30	139.60	129.90	120.20	111.50	103.10	94.70
820	840	198.60	187.70	176.80	165.80	155.50	145.80	136.10	126.40	116.90	108.50	100.00
840	860	205.60	194.70	183.80	172.80	161.90	152.00	142.30	132.60	123.00	113.90	105.40
860	880	212.60	201.70	190.80	179.80	168.90	158.20	148.50	138.80	129.20	119.50	110.80
880	900	219.60	208.70	197.80	186.80	175.90	164.90	154.70	145.00	135.40	125.70	116.20
900	920	226.60	215.70	204.80	193.80	182.90	171.90	161.00	151.20	141.60	131.90	122.20
920	940	233.60	222.70	211.80	200.80	189.90	178.90	168.00	157.40	147.80	138.10	128.40
940	960	240.60	229.70	218.80	207.80	196.90	185.90	175.00	164.10	154.00	144.30	134.60
960	980	247.60	236.70	225.80	214.80	203.90	192.90	182.00	171.10	160.20	150.50	140.80
980	1,000	254.60	243.70	232.80	221.80	210.90	199.90	189.00	178.10	167.10	156.70	147.00
1,000	1,020	261.60	250.70	239.80	228.80	217.90	206.90	196.00	185.10	174.10	163.20	153.20
1,020	1,040	268.60	257.70	246.80	235.80	224.90	213.90	203.00	192.10	181.10	170.20	159.40
1,040	1,060	275.60	264.70	253.80	242.80	231.90	220.90	210.00	199.10	188.10	177.20	166.30
35 percent of the excess over $1,060 plus—												
$1,060 and over		279.10	268.20	257.30	246.30	235.40	224.40	213.50	202.60	191.60	180.70	169.80

MARRIED Persons—SEMIMONTHLY Payroll Period

And the wages are—		And the number of withholding allowances claimed is—										
At least	But less than	0	1	2	3	4	5	6	7	8	9	10 or more
		The amount of income tax to be withheld shall be—										
$0	$24	$0	$0	$0	$0	$0	$0	$0	$0	$0	$0	$0
24	26	.30	0	0	0	0	0	0	0	0	0	0
26	28	.60	0	0	0	0	0	0	0	0	0	0
28	30	.90	0	0	0	0	0	0	0	0	0	0
30	32	1.10	0	0	0	0	0	0	0	0	0	0
32	34	1.40	0	0	0	0	0	0	0	0	0	0
34	36	1.70	0	0	0	0	0	0	0	0	0	0
36	38	2.00	0	0	0	0	0	0	0	0	0	0
38	40	2.30	0	0	0	0	0	0	0	0	0	0
40	42	2.50	0	0	0	0	0	0	0	0	0	0
42	44	2.80	0	0	0	0	0	0	0	0	0	0
44	46	3.10	0	0	0	0	0	0	0	0	0	0
46	48	3.40	0	0	0	0	0	0	0	0	0	0
48	50	3.70	0	0	0	0	0	0	0	0	0	0
50	52	3.90	0	0	0	0	0	0	0	0	0	0
52	54	4.20	0	0	0	0	0	0	0	0	0	0
54	56	4.50	.10	0	0	0	0	0	0	0	0	0
56	58	4.80	.40	0	0	0	0	0	0	0	0	0
58	60	5.10	.70	0	0	0	0	0	0	0	0	0
60	62	5.30	1.00	0	0	0	0	0	0	0	0	0
62	64	5.60	1.20	0	0	0	0	0	0	0	0	0
64	66	5.90	1.50	0	0	0	0	0	0	0	0	0
66	68	6.20	1.80	0	0	0	0	0	0	0	0	0
68	70	6.50	2.10	0	0	0	0	0	0	0	0	0
70	72	6.70	2.40	0	0	0	0	0	0	0	0	0
72	74	7.00	2.60	0	0	0	0	0	0	0	0	0
74	76	7.30	2.90	0	0	0	0	0	0	0	0	0
76	78	7.60	3.20	0	0	0	0	0	0	0	0	0
78	80	7.90	3.50	0	0	0	0	0	0	0	0	0
80	82	8.10	3.80	0	0	0	0	0	0	0	0	0
82	84	8.40	4.00	0	0	0	0	0	0	0	0	0
84	86	8.70	4.30	0	0	0	0	0	0	0	0	0
86	88	9.00	4.60	.20	0	0	0	0	0	0	0	0
88	90	9.30	4.90	.50	0	0	0	0	0	0	0	0
90	92	9.60	5.20	.80	0	0	0	0	0	0	0	0
92	94	10.00	5.40	1.10	0	0	0	0	0	0	0	0
94	96	10.30	5.70	1.30	0	0	0	0	0	0	0	0
96	98	10.60	6.00	1.60	0	0	0	0	0	0	0	0
98	100	10.90	6.30	1.90	0	0	0	0	0	0	0	0
100	102	11.20	6.60	2.20	0	0	0	0	0	0	0	0
102	104	11.60	6.80	2.50	0	0	0	0	0	0	0	0
104	106	11.90	7.10	2.70	0	0	0	0	0	0	0	0
106	108	12.20	7.40	3.00	0	0	0	0	0	0	0	0
108	110	12.50	7.70	3.30	0	0	0	0	0	0	0	0
110	112	12.80	8.00	3.60	0	0	0	0	0	0	0	0
112	114	13.20	8.20	3.90	0	0	0	0	0	0	0	0
114	116	13.50	8.50	4.10	0	0	0	0	0	0	0	0
116	118	13.80	8.80	4.40	0	0	0	0	0	0	0	0
118	120	14.10	9.10	4.70	.30	0	0	0	0	0	0	0
120	124	14.60	9.60	5.10	.70	0	0	0	0	0	0	0
124	128	15.20	10.20	5.70	1.30	0	0	0	0	0	0	0
128	132	15.90	10.90	6.20	1.90	0	0	0	0	0	0	0
132	136	16.50	11.50	6.80	2.40	0	0	0	0	0	0	0
136	140	17.20	12.20	7.40	3.00	0	0	0	0	0	0	0
140	144	17.80	12.80	7.90	3.50	0	0	0	0	0	0	0
144	148	18.40	13.40	8.50	4.10	0	0	0	0	0	0	0
148	152	19.10	14.10	9.10	4.70	.30	0	0	0	0	0	0
152	156	19.70	14.70	9.70	5.20	.90	0	0	0	0	0	0
156	160	20.40	15.40	10.40	5.80	1.40	0	0	0	0	0	0
160	164	21.00	16.00	11.00	6.30	2.00	0	0	0	0	0	0
164	168	21.60	16.60	11.60	6.90	2.50	0	0	0	0	0	0
168	172	22.30	17.30	12.30	7.50	3.10	0	0	0	0	0	0
172	176	22.90	17.90	12.90	8.00	3.70	0	0	0	0	0	0
176	180	23.60	18.60	13.60	8.60	4.20	0	0	0	0	0	0
180	184	24.20	19.20	14.20	9.20	4.80	.40	0	0	0	0	0
184	188	24.80	19.80	14.80	9.80	5.30	1.00	0	0	0	0	0
188	192	25.50	20.50	15.50	10.50	5.90	1.50	0	0	0	0	0
192	196	26.10	21.10	16.10	11.10	6.50	2.10	0	0	0	0	0
196	200	26.80	21.80	16.80	11.80	7.00	2.60	0	0	0	0	0
200	210	27.90	22.90	17.90	12.90	8.00	3.60	0	0	0	0	0

SINGLE Persons—MONTHLY Payroll Period

And the wages are—		And the number of withholding allowances claimed is—										
At least	But less than	0	1	2	3	4	5	6	7	8	9	10 or more
		The amount of income tax to be withheld shall be—										
$368	$376	$56.20	$43.30	$32.00	$20.80	$10.70	$1.90	$0	$0	$0	$0	$0
376	384	57.90	44.80	33.50	22.20	11.80	3.00	0	0	0	0	0
384	392	59.60	46.40	34.90	23.70	12.90	4.20	0	0	0	0	0
392	400	61.20	48.10	36.40	25.10	14.00	5.30	0	0	0	0	0
400	420	64.20	51.10	38.90	27.60	16.40	7.20	0	0	0	0	0
420	440	68.40	55.30	42.50	31.20	20.00	10.00	1.30	0	0	0	0
440	460	72.60	59.50	46.30	34.80	23.60	12.80	4.10	0	0	0	0
460	480	76.80	63.70	50.50	38.40	27.20	15.90	6.90	0	0	0	0
480	500	81.00	67.90	54.70	42.00	30.80	19.50	9.70	.90	0	0	0
500	520	85.20	72.10	58.90	45.80	34.40	23.10	12.50	3.70	0	0	0
520	540	89.40	76.30	63.10	50.00	38.00	26.70	15.50	6.50	0	0	0
540	560	93.60	80.50	67.30	54.20	41.60	30.30	19.10	9.30	.60	0	0
560	580	97.80	84.70	71.50	58.40	45.30	33.90	22.70	12.10	3.40	0	0
580	600	102.00	88.90	75.70	62.60	49.50	37.50	26.30	15.00	6.20	0	0
600	640	108.30	95.20	82.00	68.90	55.80	42.90	31.70	20.40	10.40	1.60	0
640	680	116.70	103.60	90.40	77.30	64.20	51.10	38.90	27.60	16.40	7.20	0
680	720	125.10	112.00	98.80	85.70	72.60	59.50	46.30	34.80	23.60	12.80	4.10
720	760	133.50	120.40	107.20	94.10	81.00	67.90	54.70	42.00	30.80	19.50	9.70
760	800	141.90	128.80	115.60	102.50	89.40	76.30	63.10	50.00	38.00	26.70	15.50
800	840	150.30	137.20	124.00	110.90	97.80	84.70	71.50	58.40	45.30	33.90	22.70
840	880	158.70	145.60	132.40	119.30	106.20	93.10	79.90	66.80	53.70	41.10	29.90
880	920	167.60	154.00	140.80	127.70	114.60	101.50	88.30	75.20	62.10	49.00	37.10
920	960	176.80	162.40	149.20	136.10	123.00	109.90	96.70	83.60	70.50	57.40	44.30
960	1,000	186.00	171.60	157.60	144.50	131.40	118.30	105.10	92.00	78.90	65.80	52.60
1,000	1,040	196.00	180.80	166.40	152.90	139.80	126.70	113.50	100.40	87.30	74.20	61.00
1,040	1,080	206.80	190.00	175.60	161.30	148.20	135.10	121.90	108.80	95.70	82.60	69.40
1,080	1,120	217.60	200.70	184.80	170.50	156.60	143.50	130.30	117.20	104.10	91.00	77.80
1,120	1,160	228.40	211.50	194.60	179.70	165.30	151.90	138.70	125.60	112.50	99.40	86.20
1,160	1,200	239.70	222.30	205.40	188.90	174.50	160.30	147.10	134.00	120.90	107.80	94.60
1,200	1,240	252.10	233.10	216.20	199.40	183.70	169.30	155.50	142.40	129.30	116.20	103.00
1,240	1,280	264.50	245.10	227.00	210.20	193.30	178.50	164.10	150.80	137.70	124.60	111.40
1,280	1,320	276.90	257.50	238.20	221.00	204.10	187.70	173.30	159.20	146.10	133.00	119.80
1,320	1,360	289.30	269.90	250.60	231.80	214.90	198.00	182.50	168.20	154.50	141.40	128.20
1,360	1,400	301.70	282.30	263.00	243.60	225.70	208.80	191.90	177.40	163.00	149.80	136.60
1,400	1,440	314.10	294.70	275.40	256.00	236.60	219.60	202.70	186.60	172.20	158.20	145.00
1,440	1,480	327.30	307.10	287.80	268.40	249.00	230.40	213.50	196.70	181.40	167.00	153.40
1,480	1,520	341.30	319.50	300.20	280.80	261.40	242.00	224.30	207.50	190.60	176.20	161.80
1,520	1,560	355.30	333.40	312.60	293.20	273.80	254.40	235.10	218.30	201.40	185.40	171.00
1,560	1,600	369.30	347.40	325.50	305.60	286.20	266.80	247.50	229.10	212.20	195.30	180.20
1,600	1,640	383.30	361.40	339.50	318.00	298.60	279.20	259.90	240.50	223.00	206.10	189.40
1,640	1,680	397.30	375.40	353.50	331.60	311.00	291.60	272.30	252.90	233.80	216.90	200.00
1,680	1,720	411.30	389.40	367.50	345.60	323.80	304.00	284.70	265.30	245.90	227.70	210.80
1,720	1,760	425.30	403.40	381.50	359.60	337.80	316.40	297.10	277.70	258.30	238.90	221.60
1,760	1,800	439.30	417.40	395.50	373.60	351.80	329.90	309.50	290.10	270.70	251.30	232.40
1,800	1,840	453.30	431.40	409.50	387.60	365.80	343.90	322.00	302.50	283.10	263.70	244.40
1,840	1,880	467.30	445.40	423.50	401.60	379.80	357.90	336.00	314.90	295.50	276.10	256.80
1,880	1,920	481.30	459.40	437.50	415.60	393.80	371.90	350.00	328.10	307.90	288.50	269.20
1,920	1,960	495.30	473.40	451.50	429.60	407.80	385.90	364.00	342.10	320.30	300.90	281.60
1,960	2,000	509.30	487.40	465.50	443.60	421.80	399.90	378.00	356.10	334.30	313.30	294.00
2,000	2,040	523.30	501.40	479.50	457.60	435.80	413.90	392.00	370.10	348.30	326.40	306.40
2,040	2,080	537.30	515.40	493.50	471.60	449.80	427.90	406.00	384.10	362.30	340.40	318.80
2,080	2,120	551.30	529.40	507.50	485.60	463.80	441.90	420.00	398.10	376.30	354.40	332.50
		35 percent of the excess over $2,120 plus—										
$2,120 and over		558.30	536.40	514.50	492.60	470.80	448.90	427.00	405.10	383.30	361.40	339.50

MARRIED Persons—MONTHLY Payroll Period

And the wages are—		And the number of withholding allowances claimed is—										
At least	But less than	0	1	2	3	4	5	6	7	8	9	10 or more
		The amount of income tax to be withheld shall be—										
$0	$48	$0	$0	$0	$0	$0	$0	$0	$0	$0	$0	$0
48	52	.60	0	0	0	0	0	0	0	0	0	0
52	56	1.10	0	0	0	0	0	0	0	0	0	0
56	60	1.70	0	0	0	0	0	0	0	0	0	0
60	64	2.30	0	0	0	0	0	0	0	0	0	0
64	68	2.80	0	0	0	0	0	0	0	0	0	0
68	72	3.40	0	0	0	0	0	0	0	0	0	0
72	76	3.90	0	0	0	0	0	0	0	0	0	0
76	80	4.50	0	0	0	0	0	0	0	0	0	0
80	84	5.10	0	0	0	0	0	0	0	0	0	0
84	88	5.60	0	0	0	0	0	0	0	0	0	0
88	92	6.20	0	0	0	0	0	0	0	0	0	0
92	96	6.70	0	0	0	0	0	0	0	0	0	0
96	100	7.30	0	0	0	0	0	0	0	0	0	0
100	104	7.90	0	0	0	0	0	0	0	0	0	0
104	108	8.40	0	0	0	0	0	0	0	0	0	0
108	112	9.00	.20	0	0	0	0	0	0	0	0	0
112	116	9.50	.80	0	0	0	0	0	0	0	0	0
116	120	10.10	1.40	0	0	0	0	0	0	0	0	0
120	124	10.70	1.90	0	0	0	0	0	0	0	0	0
124	128	11.20	2.50	0	0	0	0	0	0	0	0	0
128	132	11.80	3.00	0	0	0	0	0	0	0	0	0
132	136	12.30	3.60	0	0	0	0	0	0	0	0	0
136	140	12.90	4.20	0	0	0	0	0	0	0	0	0
140	144	13.50	4.70	0	0	0	0	0	0	0	0	0
144	148	14.00	5.30	0	0	0	0	0	0	0	0	0
148	152	14.60	5.80	0	0	0	0	0	0	0	0	0
152	156	15.10	6.40	0	0	0	0	0	0	0	0	0
156	160	15.70	7.00	0	0	0	0	0	0	0	0	0
160	164	16.30	7.50	0	0	0	0	0	0	0	0	0
164	168	16.80	8.10	0	0	0	0	0	0	0	0	0
168	172	17.40	8.60	0	0	0	0	0	0	0	0	0
172	176	18.00	9.20	.40	0	0	0	0	0	0	0	0
176	180	18.60	9.80	1.00	0	0	0	0	0	0	0	0
180	184	19.30	10.30	1.60	0	0	0	0	0	0	0	0
184	188	19.90	10.90	2.10	0	0	0	0	0	0	0	0
188	192	20.60	11.40	2.70	0	0	0	0	0	0	0	0
192	196	21.20	12.00	3.20	0	0	0	0	0	0	0	0
196	200	21.80	12.60	3.80	0	0	0	0	0	0	0	0
200	204	22.50	13.10	4.40	0	0	0	0	0	0	0	0
204	208	23.10	13.70	4.90	0	0	0	0	0	0	0	0
208	212	23.80	14.20	5.50	0	0	0	0	0	0	0	0
212	216	24.40	14.80	6.00	0	0	0	0	0	0	0	0
216	220	25.00	15.40	6.60	0	0	0	0	0	0	0	0
220	224	25.70	15.90	7.20	0	0	0	0	0	0	0	0
224	228	26.30	16.50	7.70	0	0	0	0	0	0	0	0
228	232	27.00	17.00	8.30	0	0	0	0	0	0	0	0
232	236	27.60	17.60	8.80	.10	0	0	0	0	0	0	0
236	240	28.20	18.20	9.40	.70	0	0	0	0	0	0	0
240	248	29.20	19.20	10.20	1.50	0	0	0	0	0	0	0
248	256	30.50	20.50	11.40	2.60	0	0	0	0	0	0	0
256	264	31.80	21.80	12.50	3.70	0	0	0	0	0	0	0
264	272	33.00	23.00	13.60	4.90	0	0	0	0	0	0	0
272	280	34.30	24.30	14.70	6.00	0	0	0	0	0	0	0
280	288	35.60	25.60	15.80	7.10	0	0	0	0	0	0	0
288	296	36.90	26.90	17.00	8.20	0	0	0	0	0	0	0
296	304	38.20	28.20	18.20	9.30	.60	0	0	0	0	0	0
304	312	39.40	29.40	19.40	10.50	1.70	0	0	0	0	0	0
312	320	40.70	30.70	20.70	11.60	2.80	0	0	0	0	0	0
320	328	42.00	32.00	22.00	12.70	3.90	0	0	0	0	0	0
328	336	43.30	33.30	23.30	13.80	5.10	0	0	0	0	0	0
336	344	44.60	34.60	24.60	14.90	6.20	0	0	0	0	0	0
344	352	45.80	35.80	25.80	16.10	7.30	0	0	0	0	0	0
352	360	47.10	37.10	27.10	17.20	8.40	0	0	0	0	0	0
360	368	48.40	38.40	28.40	18.40	9.50	.80	0	0	0	0	0
368	376	49.70	39.70	29.70	19.70	10.70	1.90	0	0	0	0	0
376	384	51.00	41.00	31.00	21.00	11.80	3.00	0	0	0	0	0
384	392	52.20	42.20	32.20	22.20	12.90	4.20	0	0	0	0	0
392	400	53.50	43.50	33.50	23.50	14.00	5.30	0	0	0	0	0
400	420	55.80	45.80	35.80	25.80	16.00	7.20	0	0	0	0	0

(Continued on next page)

MARRIED Persons—MONTHLY Payroll Period

And the wages are—		And the number of withholding allowances claimed is—										
At least	But less than	0	1	2	3	4	5	6	7	8	9	10 or more
		The amount of income tax to be withheld shall be—										
$420	$440	$59.00	$49.00	$39.00	$29.00	$19.00	$10.00	$1.30	$0	$0	$0	$0
440	460	62.20	52.20	42.20	32.20	22.20	12.80	4.10	0	0	0	0
460	480	65.40	55.40	45.40	35.40	25.40	15.60	6.90	0	0	0	0
480	500	68.60	58.60	48.60	38.60	28.60	18.60	9.70	.90	0	0	0
500	520	71.80	61.80	51.80	41.80	31.80	21.80	12.50	3.70	0	0	0
520	540	75.00	65.00	55.00	45.00	35.00	25.00	15.30	6.50	0	0	0
540	560	78.20	68.20	58.20	48.20	38.20	28.20	18.20	9.30	.60	0	0
560	580	81.40	71.40	61.40	51.40	41.40	31.40	21.40	12.10	3.40	0	0
580	600	84.60	74.60	64.60	54.60	44.60	34.60	24.60	14.90	6.20	0	0
600	640	89.40	79.40	69.40	59.40	49.40	39.40	29.40	19.40	10.40	1.60	0
640	680	95.80	85.80	75.80	65.80	55.80	45.80	35.80	25.80	16.00	7.20	0
680	720	102.20	92.20	82.20	72.20	62.20	52.20	42.20	32.20	22.20	12.80	4.10
720	760	109.20	98.60	88.60	78.60	68.60	58.60	48.60	38.60	28.60	18.60	9.70
760	800	117.20	105.00	95.00	85.00	75.00	65.00	55.00	45.00	35.00	25.00	15.30
800	840	125.20	112.70	101.40	91.40	81.40	71.40	61.40	51.40	41.40	31.40	21.40
840	880	133.20	120.70	108.20	97.80	87.80	77.80	67.80	57.80	47.80	37.80	27.80
880	920	141.30	128.70	116.20	104.20	94.20	84.20	74.20	64.20	54.20	44.20	34.20
920	960	150.90	136.70	124.20	111.70	100.60	90.60	80.60	70.60	60.60	50.60	40.60
960	1,000	160.50	145.50	132.20	119.70	107.20	97.00	87.00	77.00	67.00	57.00	47.00
1,000	1,040	170.10	155.10	140.20	127.70	115.20	103.40	93.40	83.40	73.40	63.40	53.40
1,040	1,080	179.70	164.70	149.70	135.70	123.20	110.70	99.80	89.80	79.80	69.80	59.80
1,080	1,120	189.30	174.30	159.30	144.30	131.20	118.70	106.20	96.20	86.20	76.20	66.20
1,120	1,160	198.90	183.90	168.90	153.90	139.20	126.70	114.20	102.60	92.60	82.60	72.60
1,160	1,200	208.50	193.50	178.50	163.50	148.50	134.70	122.20	109.70	99.00	89.00	79.00
1,200	1,240	218.10	203.10	188.10	173.10	158.10	143.10	130.20	117.70	105.40	95.40	85.40
1,240	1,280	227.70	212.70	197.70	182.70	167.70	152.70	138.20	125.70	113.20	101.80	91.80
1,280	1,320	237.30	222.30	207.30	192.30	177.30	162.30	147.30	133.70	121.20	108.70	98.20
1,320	1,360	246.90	231.90	216.90	201.90	186.90	171.90	156.90	141.90	129.20	116.70	104.60
1,360	1,400	256.50	241.50	226.50	211.50	196.50	181.50	166.50	151.50	137.20	124.70	112.20
1,400	1,440	266.80	251.10	236.10	221.10	206.10	191.10	176.10	161.10	146.10	132.70	120.20
1,440	1,480	278.00	260.70	245.70	230.70	215.70	200.70	185.70	170.70	155.70	140.70	128.20
1,480	1,520	289.20	271.70	255.30	240.30	225.30	210.30	195.30	180.30	165.30	150.30	136.20
1,520	1,560	300.40	282.90	265.40	249.90	234.90	219.90	204.90	189.90	174.90	159.90	144.90
1,560	1,600	311.60	294.10	276.60	259.50	244.50	229.50	214.50	199.50	184.50	169.50	154.50
1,600	1,640	322.80	305.30	287.80	270.30	254.10	239.10	224.10	209.10	194.10	179.10	164.10
1,640	1,680	334.00	316.50	299.00	281.50	264.00	248.70	233.70	218.70	203.70	188.70	173.70
1,680	1,720	345.20	327.70	310.20	292.70	275.20	258.30	243.30	228.30	213.30	198.30	183.30
1,720	1,760	356.40	338.90	321.40	303.90	286.40	268.90	252.90	237.90	222.90	207.90	192.90
1,760	1,800	367.90	350.10	332.60	315.10	297.60	280.10	262.60	247.50	232.50	217.50	202.50
1,800	1,840	380.70	361.30	343.80	326.30	308.80	291.30	273.80	257.10	242.10	227.10	212.10
1,840	1,880	393.50	373.50	355.00	337.50	320.00	302.50	285.00	267.50	251.70	236.70	221.70
1,880	1,920	406.30	386.30	366.30	348.70	331.20	313.70	296.20	278.70	261.30	246.30	231.30
1,920	1,960	419.10	399.10	379.10	359.90	342.40	324.90	307.40	289.90	272.40	255.90	240.90
1,960	2,000	431.90	411.90	391.90	371.90	353.60	336.10	318.60	301.10	283.60	266.10	250.50
2,000	2,040	444.70	424.70	404.70	384.70	364.80	347.30	329.80	312.30	294.80	277.30	260.10
2,040	2,080	457.50	437.50	417.50	397.50	377.50	358.50	341.00	323.50	306.00	288.50	271.00
2,080	2,120	470.30	450.30	430.30	410.30	390.30	370.30	352.20	334.70	317.20	299.70	282.20
2,120	2,160	484.60	463.10	443.10	423.10	403.10	383.10	363.40	345.90	328.40	310.90	293.40
2,160	2,200	499.00	476.50	455.90	435.90	415.90	395.90	375.90	357.10	339.60	322.10	304.60
2,200	2,240	513.40	490.90	468.70	448.70	428.70	408.70	388.70	368.70	350.80	333.30	315.80
2,240	2,280	527.80	505.30	482.80	461.50	441.50	421.50	401.50	381.50	362.00	344.50	327.00
2,280	2,320	542.20	519.70	497.20	474.70	454.30	434.30	414.30	394.30	374.30	355.70	338.20
2,320	2,360	556.60	534.10	511.60	489.10	467.10	447.10	427.10	407.10	387.10	367.10	349.40
2,360	2,400	571.00	548.50	526.00	503.50	481.00	459.90	439.90	419.90	399.90	379.90	360.60
2,400	2,440	585.40	562.90	540.40	517.90	495.40	472.90	452.70	432.70	412.70	392.70	372.70
2,440	2,480	599.80	577.30	554.80	532.30	509.80	487.30	465.50	445.50	425.50	405.50	385.50
2,480	2,520	614.20	591.70	569.20	546.70	524.20	501.70	479.20	458.30	438.30	418.30	398.30
2,520	2,560	628.60	606.10	583.60	561.10	538.60	516.10	493.60	471.10	451.10	431.10	411.10
2,560	2,600	643.00	620.50	598.00	575.50	553.00	530.50	508.00	485.50	463.90	443.90	423.90
2,600	2,640	657.40	634.90	612.40	589.90	567.40	544.90	522.40	499.90	477.40	456.70	436.70
2,640	2,680	671.80	649.30	626.80	604.30	581.80	559.30	536.80	514.30	491.80	469.50	449.50
2,680	2,720	686.20	663.70	641.20	618.70	596.20	573.70	551.20	528.70	506.20	483.70	462.30
2,720	2,760	700.60	678.10	655.60	633.10	610.60	588.10	565.60	543.10	520.60	498.10	475.60
		36 percent of the excess over $2,760 plus—										
$2,760 and over		707.80	685.30	662.80	640.30	617.80	595.30	572.80	550.30	527.80	505.30	482.80

INDEX

Catalog

If you are interested in a list of SCHAUM'S
OUTLINE SERIES in Science, Mathematics,
Engineering and other subjects, send your name
and address, requesting your free catalog, to:

SCHAUM'S OUTLINE SERIES, Dept. C
McGRAW-HILL BOOK COMPANY
1221 Avenue of Americas
New York, N.Y. 10020